DATE DUE

JA 7 '94			
JE 17 '94			
DE 2 '94			

EUROQUAKE

Europe's Explosive Economic Challenge Will Change the World

Daniel Burstein

A TOUCHSTONE BOOK
Published by Simon & Schuster

New York / London / Toronto / Sydney / Tokyo / Singapore

TOUCHSTONE
Simon & Schuster Building
Rockefeller Center
1230 Avenue of the Americas
New York, New York 10020

1   2   3   4   5   6   7   8   9   10
    2   3   4   5   6   7   8   9   10 (pbk)

Library of Congress Cataloging-in-Publication Data

Burstein, Daniel.
    Euroquake: Europe's explosive economic challenge will
change the world / Daniel Burstein.
      p.   cm.
    Includes bibliographical references and index.
    1. Europe 1992. 2. Europe—Economic integration.
3. Europe—Foreign economic relations. 4. European
Economic Community.   5. International economic
integration. I. Title.
HC241.2.B764   1991
337—dc20   90-28273
                                 CIP

ISBN: 0-671-69033-7
        75675-3 (pbk)

Dedication

For Julie, a twentieth-anniversary present in celebration of all we have shared in Europe . . . from the Hôtel de Médicis to the Hôtel du Cap; from our first steps together in the hills behind Pedregalejos to David's first steps in London, Brussels, and Bonn.

Contents

2   *Contents*

PART II   THE EMERGING EUROPEAN SUPRASTATE

PART III STORMING THE FORTRESS: AMERICANS AND JAPANESE IN EUROPE

EUROQUAKE

Preface to the Touchstone Edition

It often appears as if we live in an era in which change is so rapid, total, and unprecedented, that the most useful generalization one can make about the future is to "expect the unexpected."

Like farm animals sensing something strange just before an earthquake, most of us have developed an inchoate sense that the particular historic dividing line we are approaching—the turn of the century and the arrival of the new millennium—signifies fundamental changes in the way we live and in the world as we know it. Yet we lack certitude about such basic issues as whether the future will be brighter or darker than the present, whether we will be richer or poorer, whether we will be more likely to find ourselves at war or at peace, or which among today's great powers has the best chance of making the transition to global leadership in the twenty-first century.

Given that context, it is not surprising that the "New Europe," which is the chief protagonist of this story, has ridden a roller coaster of outward change in the short interval since this book was first published. So too have the other characters which occupy much of the discussion between these covers—the United States and Japan, the Soviet Union, Eastern Europe, and the New Germany.

The Gulf War has come and gone. The hardline coup of August, 1991, in Moscow failed—and the Soviet empire has begun to break up in earnest as a result. The U.S. economy has begun to raise its head above the recessionary waters only to encounter new difficulties. Japan has been mired in ever-widening financial scandals. Germany has discovered just how costly and long-term the proposition of renovating its East will be. A bitter, violent civil war in Yugoslavia has reminded everyone of the enormous dangers that accompany the opportunities of the new era. And 1992—the actual year in which the European Community's single market program will take effect—is upon us.

Carried along by this swift torrent of events, a number of the predictions in the last chapter of this book have come true much earlier than I forecasted: Berlin, for example, has already been named the capital of Germany, the Baltic republics have broken away from Moscow, Yugoslavia has broken up as predicted, and Gorbachev has already been overthrown *and* made his comeback *and* has been shunted aside again. (When I made the latter forecast, I assumed the fall and return of Gorbachev was a scenario that would take place over several years, not the mere seventy-two hours of the August coup!)

The dramatic events of the last twelve months appear scattered, patternless, and unpredictable. That is certainly the message one gets from our news media. They are extremely good at giving us information and extremely poor at making an analysis or tying together the disparate headlines and sound bites of our times.

As I have argued in *Euroquake,* we often lack the new intellectual "software" to process the tumultuous and conflicting information we receive. I am not sure, however, that current events are so random or that the future is so unknowable. Certainly, in a world of flux and volatility, the outward surface of the news represents a constant stream of surprises. But I believe such surprises are created and driven by deeper political, economic, and social forces. And those forces *are* knowable, at least to a large degree. They *are* exhibiting themselves with a certain pattern and consistency. They *do* tell us some meaningful things about the future. And we would do well to listen.

Let us take the Gulf War. A year ago, when we were all spellbound by the moment-to-moment news coming out of the Mideast, the Gulf War appeared to some people as a refutation of this book's central themes. I have argued throughout this book that *economic* competition will be the chief form of international rivalry in the future, although I have also recognized throughout that military conflicts will continue to develop from time to time. But stressing the primacy of economic issues was hardly a popular position to hold when half a million American troops and a coalition of nations from around the world were engaged in the biggest single military operation since World War II.

A year later, however, the Gulf War is on the verge of being forgotten. Even with the direct participation of half a million Americans, intense media coverage, popular war heroes like General Schwarzkopf, a hateful enemy like Saddam Hussein, and the national thrill of a certifiable American victory, this brief war did not turn out to be the watershed that Vietnam had been in another era, let alone the world wars of the first half of the twentieth century. No longer blinded by the Patriot missiles' red glare, thoughtful Americans are again willing to examine the premise that the future will be dominated by more or less "peaceful" economic competition. The Gulf War, which I have argued in this book *was* principally an economic conflict focused on the price and supply of oil, was nonetheless an aberration in this new era in that it became such a huge military undertaking.

The triumphant American military machine that seemed so important and so integral to discussions about the world's future a year ago, now seems decidedly less so, especially in light of the growing impetus for joint U.S.–Soviet arms reductions on a massive scale. Conversely, the domestic American problems that existed before the war are slowly but steadily returning to center stage: debt and deficits, the lack of savings and investment in America, short-term time horizons of business, an eroding manufacturing base, crises in the educational system, health care's escalating consumption of GNP, and a host of other issues summed up by the society's general loss of "competitiveness" vis-à-vis others in East Asia and Europe.

The notion of an American-led "unipolar" world proffered by some pundits in the days shortly after the Gulf War ended is now far less credible. Yes, the United States demonstrated what it can do as a nation when it mobilizes its resources. And yes, the Gulf War made clear that no other nation has the political and military leadership skills the United States possesses. But George Bush has *not* been able to translate his wartime victory into anything even vaguely akin to the kind of peacetime economic leadership that was demonstrated by Truman and Eisenhower after World War II. This is not necessarily Bush's fault. Rather, it is the product of a reality that was knowable before the shooting started: The

United States holds a dominant share of world military power, but a minority—and declining—share of world economic power.

The European Community (E.C.) may well have shown itself to be "an economic giant, but a political dwarf and a military worm," as Luxembourg's witty foreign minister observed at the height of the build-up leading to the war. (He might have said the same thing about Japan, for that matter.) But now that the war is over, we must ask ourselves how significant is it that Europe—or Japan—is indeed only a "worm" when it comes to military matters, or only a "dwarf" on political matters? And let us weigh that judgment against the significance of the fact that these, our competitors in the world, *are* now full-fledged "economic giants."

This is not to say the Gulf War was an uninfluential event, or that it changed nothing. In Europe, it was the catalyst that destroyed the last vestiges of the "Europhoria" that prevailed from the time the EC's 1992 program entered the public consciousness in 1987–88 to the fall of the Berlin Wall at the end of 1989. Perceiving Europe as weak and directionless in the Gulf conflict, many Europeans began to wonder if the EC could rise to the challenges before it: the completion of the 1992 program in a time of slower economic growth triggered by the Gulf War, Germany's increasingly expensive digestion of the east, the broadening immigration crisis, and looming instability throughout Eastern Europe and the Soviet Union.

Europe's economic growth in the next year or two will no doubt be far less dazzling than it was in 1989–90, and probably weaker than I originally forecast in this book. Although Europe is unlikely to creep back under the sheets of early 1980s-style "Europessimism," today's "Euro-realism" is downbeat enough to foreclose the possibility of a renewed runaway boom there in the immediate future.

A somewhat similar process can be seen unfolding in Japan, where Japanese, frustrated by their government's political paralysis on the Gulf as well as many other matters, and shocked by the competence, technical prowess, and political-military excellence shown by the United States in Iraq, began to question the staying power of earlier ideas about Japan-as-superpower. This introspection was heightened by the onset of the financial scandals that followed quickly on the heels of the war.

Thus, the European economy and even the Japanese economy have lost some of their appeal as straight-line success stories. But the short-term problems besetting America's competitors should not be mistaken for a fundamental shift in the long-term trends. Those who know Japan best know that underneath the muck of financial scandal and the frustrations of weak political leadership, Japanese businesses are still bringing on-line their most awe-inspiring competitive products and new technologies. They are pushing toward a time in the first decade of the next century when their economy, with only half the population of the United States, may surpass America's in total output.

The wheels of history have not stopped spinning in Europe, either. To be sure, they are spinning slower and less visibly than a year or two ago when the notion of a new European superpower got its proverbial fifteen minutes in the American limelight. But the key processes are all continuing: unifying a dynamic Germany, integrating the economies of the EC's twelve member states, dismantling physical frontiers within Continental Europe, building newly competitive pan-European corporations, creating newly competitive industries in Europe, evolving a common European currency, expanding American investment, opening Europe to massive new Japanese investment, and establishing market economies, however fragile, in Eastern Europe.

It is important to dwell on Germany, at least for a moment, since Germany is a country which figures prominently in the text of this book. In the United States it has become commonplace to view German reunification as an economic disaster. Some see it as a bottomless pit of costs and subsidies tying Germany down for a very long time and preventing it from ever becoming the superpowerful force outside its borders which I forecast in this book.

On a recent trip to Germany, however, I discovered that even critics of the government's policy had little question but that Germany would succeed in the end. Many of them believed that the economy in the East had already touched bottom and was beginning to rebound.

Perhaps even these skeptical-minded Germans are overly optimistic. But I rather think that it is the American perspective that is off-base. We look at East Germany less than two years after the world-historic amalgamation of a communist economy with a capitalist one, and freely dub it a "disaster" because it hasn't yet produced a miracle and is still running on borrowed money. I remain convinced that we will think differently a decade hence.

Something similar could be said about the European Community as a whole, and the 1992 program in particular. Two years ago, Americans were focused on the opportunities and challenges presented by the new

European market. But today, the focus of discussion is on how real political union still eludes the Europeans, on how new problems are overtaking the efforts of the Eurocrats in Brussels to deal with the old ones still on the table, and how the 1992 plan itself remains so far from completion.

All these points have merit. But to me, they reflect short-term observations rather than long-term trends. If one looks back to the realities of just five years ago, then even today's partial successes at developing and implementing the EC's single market program are nothing short of astounding. Tomorrow's will be more so.

Many surprises await us as the rest of this decade unfolds and as the next century rises up to greet us. But this book bets that through it all Europe will become a bigger economy and a more important political force than it is today, that a unified Germany will embody an increasingly successful economic model capable even of managing the integration of the backward east; that Japan will continue to be a super-competitor and the home to the world's most advanced commercial manufacturing systems and technologies, that the United States will be haunted by a crisis of eroding global economic competitiveness until some hard choices are made, and that trade, technology, investment, and other economic issues will be more critical to the shape of the world than military warfare or political ideologies.

The Cold War is over. It is being superseded by the "battle of capitalisms," which is outlined in some detail in this book. Governments in Europe, Japan, and the United States, as well as large corporations and business leaders in each part of the world, all have their own ideas, approaches, and policies toward meeting the challenges of the twenty-first century. If one is looking for certainties about the future, perhaps the most overarching one is that the various interests represented by these government and business forces will compete intensely with each other in the years ahead. The process of this competition—and its outcome—will define the world order of the next era.

Daniel Burstein
West Redding, Connecticut
December 1991

Introduction—Five Hundred Years After Columbus: The Old World as New Frontier

> The European challenge is to restore the Europe of 1914, when Europe was the biggest economic power in the world and had the best educated population, one that [will have] twice the population of the United States and four times the population of Japan.
>
> HANS-JÖRG RUDLOFF, *Chairman, Crédit Suisse–First Boston*[1]

EUROPE SHIFTS THE GLOBAL POWER BALANCE

A seismic shift is occurring in the composition of global wealth. It is convulsing the structure of international power relationships and changing the rules of international business competition. It is the Euroquake.

Europe has become the most important theater of contemporary world events. Its importance does not yet derive from being able to wield the combined power of its many nations through any one central voice or vehicle, although that may eventually come. For now, the mere potential energy of what *may* happen in Europe, and the scramble by Americans, Japanese, Russians, and others to position themselves for these upcoming events, is enough to influence the balance of every type of power in the world—financial, technological, industrial, corporate, political, military, governmental, cultural, and ideological.

Will the twenty-first century open with a global economic boom or with debilitating trade wars?

Will American business use the explosion of new opportunity in Europe to regain its competitive edge? Or will the United States decline more rapidly under the pressure of what now looms as a Japanese-European competitive pincer?

Will international relations make a successful transition to true multipolarity and a borderless economy? Or will they be plunged backward into rival nationalisms, chaos, and fragmentation?

Will German reunification yield a new citadel of peace and prosperity or a new threat to global stability?

Will the Soviets and the formerly communist nations of Eastern Europe find a way out of their misery or fall back on the hard-line tactics they know so well?

Will the United States and Europe succeed in slowing the relentless conquest of world markets by the Japanese? Or will Japan find new advantages in Europe that make it more powerful still?

Will there be nuclear disarmament and a substantial peace dividend? Or will armies and defense industries succeed in convincing governments that the world's new security dangers require the same massive weapons programs and budget outlays that characterized the Cold War?

Will the world develop a successful collective security system that can minimize what is currently an unbearable burden on the United States for defending international order? Or will fiscal and other constraints on American (and Soviet) power, coupled with a lack of military will on the part of Europe and Japan, leave the world of the twenty-first century increasingly hostage to blackmail and aggression by rogue regimes?

What is happening at this very moment in Europe—and the course of events that will continue to unfold during the 1990s—holds many of the clues needed to answer these crucial questions about the shape of tomorrow's world. This book examines how such a change in Europe's role occurred, what might happen next, and what it means for all of us—especially those of us who aren't Europeans.

THE GUNS OF AUGUST 1990

The process of change in the global balance of power described in this book was more easily discernible and better understood in the late 1980s than today. Beginning with the launch of the European Community's "Project 1992," and continuing through the fall of the Berlin Wall, the end of the Cold War, and the historic drama of German reunification, events in Europe gained a consistently expanding "share of mind" among thinking people everywhere. Until August 2, 1990, that is. On that day, as Iraqi tanks blitzed across the desert to seize oil-rich Kuwait, the fragmentary images the world had been accumulating about the new global order—and Europe's role within it—seemed suddenly invalidated.

The proposition that economic power would supersede military power seemed dubious in light of the huge wartime buildup in the Persian Gulf. Similarly, the assumption that America was a nation in a state of generalized decline relative to new "economic superpowers" (Germany and Japan) seemed contradicted by events. As Washington deployed hundreds of thousands of troops and hundreds of billions of dollars' worth of weapons to the Gulf, there was audible relief around the world that America was able and willing to lead these efforts. Germany and Japan, on the other hand, faced international criticism for doing too little too late to participate in the defense of the very oil fields and shipping lanes on which they themselves depended.

As news from the Gulf crisis pushed most other world issues out of the spotlight, pundits (mostly American, a few British) seized the opportunity to declare that the new age of Europe was over before it had begun— just as Henry Kissinger's much-touted "Year of Europe" had been aborted by the Yom Kippur War and the ensuing oil shock nearly two decades earlier. These same pundits tended to view the cratering of Tokyo financial markets in 1990 as proof that the sun was setting on the Japanese economic miracle. Thus, they argued, the bipolar world of the last forty years was not becoming "multipolar" but "unipolar"—i.e., more American-led and -influenced than before.

Such a view, however, represents only the newest self-deception, the latest avoidance mechanism to keep Americans from addressing the country's loss of economic competitiveness and the near-total inability of its political system to provide leadership for change. By focusing attention on the one area where the United States is irrefutably preeminent (military power), the Gulf crisis insidiously cut short debate about the U.S. trade and budget deficits, the S&L fiasco, the high cost of American capital, and other critical issues that, in the summer of 1990, were finally beginning to trigger the wide public concern they deserved after a decade under Ronald Reagan's hypnotic spell.

Much has changed since August 2, 1990, in perceptions about the shape of the new global order. It is now obvious that even in the absence of a Soviet threat, the world will continue to face grave threats to its security and stability. In that context, it is fair to say that American military leadership is today seen as more valuable and more important than it was a year ago. By the same token, the weaknesses of the Japanese and Germans as world leaders have been vividly highlighted.

But for all that has changed since August 2, 1990, it is also important to bear in mind what has *not* changed. Beneath the image of strength suggested by the display of U.S. military power in the Gulf was the open secret that Washington could not afford this engagement. Even before a single shot was fired, the Bush administration had to seek unprecedented financial support from Europeans, Japanese, and Arabs—and accept weighty constraints on political and military options in the bargain. Beneath the image of weakness on the part of Europe and Japan, however, were unmistakable signs of strength. It was the first military crisis in modern times in which the U.S. dollar plummeted while the Japanese yen and the German mark rose. The currency markets anticipated what Washington refused to acknowledge: An already weak U.S. economy would be pushed into recession by the costs of the Gulf conflict, while Europe and Japan, highly vulnerable to oil shocks in the past, would be less adversely affected this time because of their new financial resources and competitive strengths.

Eventually the desert dust will settle on the Persian Gulf crisis of 1990–91. When it does, certain long-term trends will once more stand out in sharp relief. Japan and Germany, having effectively insulated themselves from the Gulf conflict, will be visibly ascendant once again. A declining America, having continued to ignore its domestic crisis and the erosion of its economic competitiveness, will be headed toward more precipitous decline.

The new world order will have been scarred at birth with the reminder that military power is still important and that the world is still a dangerous place. But perceptions will shift back to the understanding that the business of the world is now business as never before. Economic power *will be* the moving force defining the new world ahead.

The Iraq crisis itself may eventually come to be understood principally as an economic event, despite its nightmarish military aspects. It originated, after all, not with the large political/ideological themes that characterized most twentieth-century warfare, but rather with elemental economic issues—notably, Saddam Hussein's desire to control the price and supply of oil and the unwillingness of the United States and others to allow him to do so. Another elemental economic concern permeated all discussion of military strategy: cost. Never before was so much attention paid to fiscal constraints *before* the shooting started. The ''doves'' of this crisis scarcely bothered to invoke traditional concerns about loss of life. Instead, they disclosed estimates that it would cost the U.S. *a billion dollars per day* to fight a full-scale war in the Middle East and explained the devastating impact such an expenditure could have on an already debt-swollen U.S. economy.

Never in recent times has a great power been so overtly compelled toward military options by mistaken domestic *economic policy*. The United States, with the capacity to be energy self-sufficient, had *chosen* to become ever more reliant on imported oil despite the bitter experiences of two prior oil shocks and numerous Mideast wars, revolutions, and hostage-taking dramas. By refusing to tax gasoline as Europeans and Japanese do, by failing to encourage alternative energy sources, by avoiding a national program to make industry more energy-efficient, and by allowing market forces to destroy indigenous oil production, an energy-rich America perversely became *more* vulnerable to the vicissitudes of Mideast politics than Germany and Japan, which have almost no oil resources of their own. The ''American way of life'' George Bush said he was defending with the deployment of U.S. troops to the Arabian peninsula had precious little to do with ideals such as ''democracy'' or ''freedom.'' Sadly, the ''American way of life'' had become characterized by the desire to drive gas-guzzling cars, to fill them with cheap gasoline, and to sustain a political culture which favored such kinds of short-term consumption at the expense of long-term national interest.

America's obsession with Iraq contrasted sharply with the responses of Germany and Japan. As Washington sought to construct an international coalition against Iraq in the latter months of 1990, Tokyo steadfastly resisted American pressure to contribute even symbolic forces. A tepid proposal to send a token detachment of noncombat troops was resoundingly rejected. Meanwhile, Japan spurned appeals for generous ''checkbook diplomacy'' and kept its initial financial commitment to a very modest $4 billion, although the eventual total reached $13 billion. Germany was even less forthcoming. Like the Japanese, Germans argued that their constitution precluded responsibility for military burden-sharing. Their contribution was hardly commensurate with their financial resources or their stake in defending the free flow of oil. Germans found no embarrassment in pleading a lack of funds to support the U.S. operation in the Gulf at a moment when they were spending lavishly to turn the former East Germany into a new economic miracle and a major new market. Indeed, Germans were so absorbed in their national reunification process that the *Frankfurter Allgemeine Zeitung* was perhaps alone among the world's elite newspapers in headlining domestic news over the story of Iraq's invasion of Kuwait during most of the first week's fighting.

The different responses by the U.S., Japan, and Germany—the world's three wealthiest nations—to the seminal events in the Gulf reflect their varied national characters, international commitments, and histories. But they also illustrate the degree to which the United States, Japan, and Germany have different beliefs about how to generate national wealth and how best to foster a global environment maximizing that pursuit. As history proceeds through the 1990s, the new world order is far more likely to be shaped and defined by the interplay of those differences than by any other factor—including the legacy of current military events in the Gulf.

THE BATTLE OF THE CAPITALISMS

Central to this book is the premise that the end of the Cold War marks the beginning of *the battle of the capitalisms:* capitalism*s*—plural—because while communism is in global collapse and capitalism seems everywhere triumphant, it is not one single form of capitalism which is winning the day. In fact, there are at least *three* forms of capitalism now thriving in the world. These could be loosely termed the American, Japanese, and German varieties. More specifically, they can be identified as follows:

- The Anglo-American model has its cultural roots in Adam Smith and the experience of the Industrial Revolution. Very broadly speaking, this type of capitalism prevails in the United States, the United Kingdom, Canada, Australia, and elsewhere in the English-speaking world. It emphasizes maximum personal freedom, minimum government intervention in the private sector, free trade, free markets, and high risks as well as high rewards for the individual entrepreneur. The Anglo-American model rejects the idea of national economic planning or a broad industrial strategy on the part of government. These are considered anticompetitive and contrary to personal and marketplace freedom. Although the U.S. added many kinds of protectionism to its economy in the 1980s, one need look no further than its enormous trade deficit to see that it remains the most open market in the world.

- The Japanese/East Asian model has cultural roots in Confucianism, feudalism, the Meiji Revolution, and the New Deal American industrialism imposed on Japan after World War II. It predominates in Japan, Korea, and Taiwan, and is admired among all the New Industrial Economies (NIEs) of Asia. It emphasizes long-term national strategies for economic development, exported-led mercantilist trade (accurately characterized by some experts as "adversarial trade"), and a benevolent political-economic despotism which promotes the interests of collective units—corporations or the nation itself—even at the expense of individual liberty, consumer interests, and marketplace freedom.

- The German/European model is increasingly prevalent throughout continental Europe. Its "social market" philosophy has cultural roots in the history of German social democracy and in the postwar centralized direction of economic reconstruction. This type of capitalism occupies a middle ground between the American and Japanese forms. While offering a high degree of personal freedom and a free and liberal marketplace in many areas, the German model also insists on heavy doses of macroeconomic management and governmental intervention, based on nationally determined strategies for long-term development. Much less collectivist than the Japanese model, it nonetheless values its collective units more highly than the American model, and provides broad social insurance and insulation from risk to both individuals and companies.

All three capitalisms are now engaged in extensive internal debates about how to adapt to the challenges of not only a new century but also a new economic era.

Unique historical circumstances (notably the forty-five-year-long nuclear balance of terror) constrained the normal development of intracapitalist competition in the old era. Now, two new things are happening.

First, the collective fears that caused European and Japanese capitalists to huddle at all costs under the American nuclear umbrella are dissipating, as is America's sense of strategic responsibility for Europe and Japan. Thus, the search for competitive economic advantage will no longer be restrained by the fear of the mushroom cloud. Second, new markets are opening up as communism's appeal declines. With the threat of force removed, people all over the world are following their natural attraction to freedom and the capitalist marketplace.

But because capitalism itself thrives on competition, the competition among various capitalist power centers—governments, economic blocs, private-sector corporations, and even individuals—is likely to intensify as new markets open up. With the great powers now tacitly agreeing to confine their rivalry to the economic arena, a society's "competitiveness" will become the means by which it expresses its national beliefs and tests the mettle of others. In the absence of military conflict, economic warfare will become the mechanism of last resort for distributing global wealth and power to those societies whose competitiveness is sharpening and away from those experiencing economic decline.

In the battle of the capitalisms, corporations will function as the new armies. CEOs and managers will be more important in some instances than presidents and prime ministers. Espionage will focus less on Soviet tank designs and more on the competition's new civilian technology. The educational level and skills of individual employees—as well as their degree of loyalty and belief in their corporation's mission—will be as important as good troop training was in traditional military conflicts.

To most American businesspeople, the idea of a world order in which corporate power predominates has an attractive sound to it. But they would do well to bear in mind some essential facts about how the future is shaping up. One is that capital resources are to future economic competition what oil and steel were to armies in World War II. On this front, Americans are poorly positioned; many of the best-capitalized companies in the world are now Japanese, and European corporations are entering what may prove to be a sustained period of revolution that is sure to liberate the enormous asset potential in their capital markets.

Furthermore, while economics may well obtain primacy over politics in the new global order, government will continue to set its society's agenda, provide major elements of a nation's overall competitiveness, and determine the conditions of its playing field. In this regard, Japanese and European systems that intelligently practice a blended political economy will have a crucial advantage. This is especially true now that Europeans are moving away from political direction of their economies and are allowing business and marketplace forces to play a greater role. The American system, meanwhile, continues to drive a destructive wedge between politics and the marketplace. Washington claims the moral high ground by insisting that government stay out of economic decision-making. Yet the political system then turns around and adopts policies which end up influencing the marketplace anyway—often to the detriment of U.S. competitiveness.

In another era, the American separation of government and business was both a glorious ideal and a workable system. Unfortunately, the excellence of that arrangement rested on the presumption of American hegemony in a world where the nations that *did* use their governments to promote competitiveness were too weak to matter. Clinging to that outdated vision today has become naive and nostalgic at best, downright suicidal at worst.

AMERICA: ODD MAN OUT IN THE TRIAD

In the 1980s, the global economy was the scene of a giant battle between American and Japanese capitalisms—in which the Japanese side appeared to be steadily gaining ground. But as the 1990s dawned, German-led European capitalism burst into the arena, not only making the competition three-sided, but also fundamentally altering its rules, its nature, and perhaps its outcome.

As capitalist societies, the United States, Japan, and Europe have a great deal in common. But it is their decidedly different values, emphases, operational practices, assets, and liabilities which will be put to the test in the years to come. All three forms of capitalism represented by these societies are enormously complex, dynamic systems. For every generalization about them, a thousand exceptions can be cited. Yet certain realities come to the fore over and over again.

American capitalism has a stunning historical record. It provided more material wealth, innovation, and opportunity over a longer period of time to more people across a wider social spectrum than any previous system. Yet just as obvious to anyone willing to take even a cursory look at today's global marketplace is the fact that American competitiveness is rapidly eroding.

Although Japanese and European capitalism are quite different from each other, the structural challenges they pose to the American system are remarkably similar. Neither Japan nor Europe, for example, accepts Washington's laissez-faire attitudes about foreign trade and foreign investment. Both Japan and Europe believe that government must help set the agenda for the development of new industries, technologies, and world-leading export products. Both Japan and Europe (especially Germany) practice fiscal policies which create low-cost capital, encourage savings and investment over consumption, and allow businesses to plan with bold vision for the long term. Sad to say, this is not the case in the United States. Both Japan and Europe (again, especially Germany) have institutionalized systems of government-business-labor partnerships, an idea which remains anathema in America. And so on, down a long line of other systemic similarities between Japan and Europe which are increasingly making the U.S. the odd man out in the three-cornered capitalist world.

It would be an overstatement to suggest that the contest among the capitalisms will inevitably reach levels of animosity comparable to the violence of the great military conflicts of the twentieth century. Some of the skirmishing will be little more than friendly competition, perhaps producing "win-win" results. None of the capitalisms will function as a monolith. Corporations will not only invest heavily across their borders, but will ally themselves with partners indigenous to the other capitalisms.

Yet the battle will be intense and highly visible. The stakes will include national and regional living standards, the success or failure of major corporations, access to the fruits of new technological developments, the quality of the environment, and insulation from security risks, both old and new. Life and death for large numbers of people may not hang in the balance in this battle, but the quality of life and even the extent of human freedom will be in question. At times, of course, those issues can prove even more emotionally gripping (and are always more complex) than the simple question of life and death in war.

The constant search for new markets is the primal quest of capitalism. Many large, intriguing potential markets of the distant future call out to adventurous capitalists to conquer them. But the focal point of current corporate competition generally lies in the already developed and accessible markets of the so-called Triad consisting of North America, Japan/East Asia, and Europe. The Triad is the proving ground in modern capitalism's fight for the survival of the fittest. Recent events in Europe, however, have suddenly caused the Triad to change shape and add new muscle. This, in turn, will make the Darwinian struggle all the more fierce. Exactly 500 years after Columbus, Europe suddenly beckons with New World–style excitement and optimism. The Old World has become the new frontier.

THE FOUR PLOTS DRIVING THE EUROPEAN DRAMA OF THE 1990s

As in the plot of a good Russian novel, at least four major stories are unfolding simultaneously as one moves from West to East across the map of the New Europe. Each mirrors and interacts with the others, but it is the thickening plot they represent together which is altering the shape of the Triad:

- Farthest to the west, in Brussels, the European Community (EC) is moving full speed ahead with its plan to put in place by December 31, 1992, a single market stretching across the borders of its twelve member countries. (The current EC roster includes Belgium, Denmark, France, Germany, Greece, Ireland, Italy, Luxembourg, the Netherlands, Portugal, Spain, and the United Kingdom.) The "EC-92" plan, discussed at length throughout this volume, represents a radical new ingredient in the world economy. It seeks to create a working supranational entity, which, because of its ability to speak collectively, will gain a new and perhaps disproportionate influence in trade matters, cross-border investment, patents and intellectual property, and the world financial system.

  The 1992 program is already responsible for stimulating European growth rates and stock market prices to levels unimaginable a few short years ago. It has triggered an unprecedented wave of cross-border investments, alliances, and mergers and acquisitions. Economists trying to quantify the effects of 1992's relaxation of national barriers estimate that the EC's gross product could jump by 5 percent or more—that's $250 billion annually—simply as a result of increased efficiencies. These estimates don't take into account the compounding effect of robust new investment, Europe's new psychological confidence, and the EC's growing integration with Eastern Europe and the countries of the European Free Trade Association (EFTA)—Austria, Finland, Iceland, Norway, Sweden, and Switzerland.

If European economic integration is carried to its fullest extent, and if growth in Western and Eastern Europe follows even a modestly optimistic pattern, the greater Europe of the year 2000 will have a gross product of $9 trillion. To put that figure in some perspective, it means that Europe will have grown a *new market* about equal in size to the *entire U.S. economy today*.

· Just a few hundred kilometers east of Brussels, the new German superpower is being born. It is Germany that is the EC's locomotive of financial, technological, and industrial strength. A profoundly creative and talented society, with enormously competitive features built into its business system, Germany now has the wide expanse of all Europe as a home market. Although in the postwar era Germany has usually felt a need to move quietly and act gently, recent events are changing that. Its leaders have been encouraged, even *compelled,* by history to begin to assert the nation's true power. Neither global politics nor the corporate competition will ever be the same.

Germany is expanding—not just through its absorption of East Germany, but through the extension of elements of the West German *Wirtschaftswunder* ("economic miracle") to all its neighbors. *Mitteleuropa* (Central Europe) is becoming a meaningful designation once again. For intellectuals in Eastern Europe—and for a growing number in the West as well—the long-sought "third road" between socialism and capitalism is no longer a mere theoretical construct. It already exists and is working fairly well in the form of the German social market.

· A few kilometers deeper into the Continent, the whole question of the future of Eastern Europe opens up. Tumultuously, and with enormous problems, 100 million new consumers are being welcomed into the Triad. Hungary, Czechoslovakia, Poland, Romania, Bulgaria, and Yugoslavia are relatively poor and backward today. Forty years of communist rule have made a polluted shambles of their business infrastructure. But they have also left them with an educated population, a disciplined low-cost work force trained in basic manufacturing skills, some outstanding scientific and technological personnel, and most of all, a thirst for new opportunities and possibilities. These countries are industrialized, albeit badly industrialized. They are accessible from Western Europe in just a few hours' travel time. Their history has been twisted and corrupted, but at bottom, they share European values which will make possible the development of business and trading systems Western partners can understand.

"They need *everything* in Eastern Europe," says AT&T's CEO, Robert Allen. "The process of providing it to them will exert a stimulus on Western business far larger than you could calculate just by looking at the population numbers." Thus, the cocktail lounge in the Warsaw Marriott has come to resemble the famous intergalactic space bar from *Star Wars*. Here, entrepreneurs from all corners of the Triad gather to pick up information and leads about whether to prospect in this latter-day gold rush—which some already disgruntled foreign capitalists would call a rush for fool's gold. In the general scheme of the world's 5 billion population, 100 million-plus Eastern Europeans are not terribly significant. But the important fact in the eyes of global corporations is that they are *Europeans*. Never before has so much virgin Triad territory been opened up.

A last jump to the east and one arrives at the "European" part of the Soviet Union, generally considered to be the territory west of the Ural mountains. Mikhail Gorbachev's effort to implement his vision of *perestroika*—what with the pushing and shoving of the left, the right, and the nationalities who want to break free altogether—was already the most complex political drama of our time and has become all the more so since the failed coup of August, 1991 and the declarations of independence by the many republics.

Almost regardless of the outcome, however, events in the Soviet Union will continue to expand the total extent of the Triad. True, the USSR is an economic nightmare today. But it is also one of the world's largest economies, with many assets. When one looks at people in the streets of Moscow and other places in the European parts of the Soviet Union, they are clearly not impoverished people. These are European consumers, albeit without much hard cash. And when one looks at the hardware-manufacturing side of the Soviet military and space programs, one cannot deny the brilliance in the work of some of the world's best scientists and engineers.

The opening of the Soviet market will be a long, involved story with many pendulum swings and cycles. But as McDonald's popular Moscow franchise and PepsiCo's planned multibillion-dollar swap of soda pop for vodka demonstrate, future-minded corporations aren't waiting. They are already staking their claims to what is potentially the largest new piece of the Triad.

FOLLOW THE MONEY

The intertwining of the four stories above—particularly the first two, but to some degree the latter two as well—has turned the corporate map of Europe into a chessboard of frenzied mergers-and-acquisitions (M&A) deals by the biggest names in European, American, and Japanese business. Total M&A activity in Europe during 1989, for example, was up an astounding 2,900 percent over 1985 levels. "Follow the money," as Deep Throat once said, and you understand the story better.

New pan-European empires are being built by Europe's indigenous companies. The banking, insurance, media, and food-retailing industries are being aggressively consolidated and restructured through M&A deals that would have shocked a staid Old World Europe just a few years ago. When Italian financier Carlo De Benedetti attempted a raid on the Brussels-based Société Générale in 1988, his move was characterized, with only moderate hyperbole, as an attempt to "buy Belgium," since Générale accounted for such a high percentage of that country's financial and real estate holdings. De Benedetti was rebuffed, but a tidal wave of giant cross-border deals has followed since.

German electronics giant Siemens reaches over to England to snap up Plessey . . . Frankfurt's Deutsche Bank buys the venerable Morgan Grenfell investment bank in the City of London . . . French food leader BSN goes on a $3 billion food-company shopping spree across Europe . . . Dutch consumer-electronics king Philips buys into Danish upscale audio leader Bang & Olufsen and acquires Island Records in England too . . . Sweden's Volvo and France's Renault forge a strategic cross-ownership link . . . French-based LVMH, the world's ultimate luxury-goods company, cobbled together from a merger of luggage maker Louis Vuitton, champagne maker Moët, and cognac maker Hennessy, reaches out to Guinness, the famed U.K. distiller, in a novel (and at times soap operatic) scheme of corporate cross-shareholdings designed to thwart a bid by some of LVMH's biggest French shareholders for power. . . . Meanwhile, from Volkswagen to Fiat, from Alcatel to Elf, leading Western European companies are building facilities and creating joint ventures across Eastern Europe and the Soviet Union.

Americans were somewhat slow to take the New Europe seriously. A poll taken as recently as 1988 indicated that only one in five U.S. CEOs had even heard of the EC's 1992 plans. When they did begin to hear of

1992, it was in the context of a menacing "fortress Europe." All that has now changed. Today, *every* CEO of a major American corporation has heard of 1992. It has even become a visible force in domestic U.S. deal-making.

"Only strong American companies will survive after the formation of a unified European market in 1992," said Warner Communications chairman Steven J. Ross when he announced his company's merger with Time Inc. in 1989. To his way of thinking, this merger of American behemoths was a creative response to 1992 and to powerful foreign competition in the media business.[2]

The American corporate community's response to the New Europe is analyzed at length in chapter 7. Here it can simply be noted that there is no longer a single important U.S. company which hasn't commissioned internal studies and hired consultants and lobbyists in Brussels or investment bankers in New York, London, and Paris to advise them on how best to approach the single market. The majority have chosen to see 1992 as an opportunity, although none ignore the element of threat. But they are investing heavily in the upside potential. Americans actually expended greater sums buying European companies in 1989 than the Germans, the French, or the British—over $15 billion.[3]

A sampling of what U.S. firms have acquired recently in Europe suggests the extent of American interest: Ford bought Jaguar for $2.5 billion. General Motors invested $600 million for a 50 percent stake in Saab. AT&T bought 20 percent of the Italian phone company, Italtel, for $135 million. International Paper shelled out $300 million for French paper-maker Aussedat Rey. Emerson Electric picked up Leroy-Somer, a French electric-components firm, for $460 million. Du Pont bought a British printing-plate maker; Businessland, a West German computer retailer, and Sara Lee acquired the upscale French hosiery leader, Dim. Philip Morris made the biggest deal to date with its purchase of 80 percent of Swiss chocolate-maker Jacobs Suchard for $3.8 billion. Canadian-based companies have also been active opportunity seekers in Europe—witness Northern Telecom's $2.6 billion offer for the three-quarters it didn't already own of British telecommunications leader STC.

Aside from making acquisitions, American companies are expanding their indigenous European organizations, building new plants and buying new real estate. Intel, for example, is building a $400 million chip-making plant in Ireland, and Texas Instruments is erecting a billion-dollar facility in Italy. Analysts who follow Disney believe that its Euro Disneyland project, now under construction outside Paris, could become the best-attended theme park in the world.

Perhaps the most telling indicator of Europe's new centrality to corporate planning is the fact that profits earned by leading U.S. firms in Europe such as Ford, GM, Compaq, and IBM have been greater than domestic U.S. profits in recent quarters.

IBM provides a particularly good illustration of the Euro-shift taking place in the strategic thinking of American companies. In West Germany, for example, IBM's revenues jumped 14 percent in 1989, compared with domestic U.S. revenue growth of just 3 percent. While 35,000 jobs were being eliminated in IBM's U.S. operations, 300 were being added in West Germany. That was before the current slowdown in the European computer market. But it was also before the opening of East Germany, which IBM forecasts will develop into a $20 billion market for computer equipment by the year 2000.[4]

"Europe is now critically important to the world's most significant computer manufacturer," observes the *Financial Times,* noting that IBM's European management style, market growth, and new opportunities are the talk of the boardroom back home in Armonk, New York. "Europe is providing a model for IBM's efforts to strip away bureaucracy, decentralize its decision-making and align itself more exactly with its customers. What it can achieve in Europe, the argument goes, it can also achieve in the U.S.—if it learns the right lessons."[5]

SYMBOLIC ALLIANCES: IBM/SIEMENS AND MITSUBISHI/DAIMLER-BENZ

Anyone disinclined to believe that the battle of the capitalisms has distinct national, geographic, and cultural roots might want to consider another critical element of IBM's strategy—its announcement in 1990 of a strategic alliance to develop next-generation computer memory chips with Siemens, the German-based giant. The two firms have agreed to share technology, costs, and risks in bringing 64-megabit D-RAM chips to market. Although IBM and Siemens are two of the biggest, best-capitalized electronics companies in the world, both see the project as too costly to undertake alone. And both are afraid of losing more control of the chip-making business to the Japanese. Indeed, the fundamental point of the alliance is to catch up to Japanese competitors such as Hitachi,

which appears to be far ahead in the race. Even a diplomatic IBM spokesman made that clear in announcing the alliance: "This is part of the
strategy to improve the balance in a global sense. The Japanese are
systems makers whom we compete against. We are trying to strengthen
the other two legs of the triangle."[6]

Six weeks after the IBM/Siemens alliance was made public—almost as
a direct counterweight to it—another wide-ranging cross-border alliance
was announced. One party to the deal was Daimler-Benz, Germany's
biggest industrial company, best known in the United States for its Mercedes automobiles—although it is a diversified conglomerate that recently
acquired Germany's leading aircraft maker, MBB. The other was Mitsubishi, the largest industrial group in Japan. The alliance covers "nothing less than the future of the world auto, aerospace and electronics
industries."[7]

The Mitsubishi/Daimler-Benz pact came dripping with irony, as it
brought together the parent companies of two firms that had built the most
legendary enemy combat aircraft of World War II, the Mitsubishi Zero
and the Messerschmitt Bf 109. But aside from providing chilling echoes
of Axis history, the deal also sent a clear-cut message to Boeing and other
American aircraft and automotive manufacturers: A German-Japanese
alliance made up of two of the world's biggest and most outstanding
industrial companies was on the (economic) warpath—and was headed
for their markets.

THE JAPANESE: MOVING TO EUROPE

All of which brings us last, but most assuredly not least, to the Japanese.
If one measures rate of investment growth rather than total investment,
then the Japanese, starting from a low investment base, are certainly the
biggest enthusiasts of the New Europe's prospects. The role of Japanese
business is analyzed in chapter 8. Despite a strong shift of world attention
to Europe in the 1990s—and, indeed, to a certain extent because of
it—Japan may end up the world's number-one power in the twenty-first
century.

It is common knowledge in Tokyo that the 1992 plan first won support within the EC because it was imagined as a way of keeping the
Japanese out of Europe. But this did not deter them. Thriving on adversity, the Japanese chose to see 1992 as a good reason to rush into

European investments and establish beachheads before it was too late. Europe became a magnet. Japanese direct investment, which had been running at $2–3 billion a year in Europe during 1985–86, suddenly exploded to nearly $7 billion in 1987, $9 billion in 1988, and over $14 billion in 1989. As Sony founder Akio Morita said of the years remaining before 1992, "Japanese are not fools. Japanese managers know what they should do. Japanese industry will move technology to Europe."[8]

They have begun to do just that. In the course of a single week in January 1989, three giant Japanese companies—Toyota, Fujitsu, and Toshiba—all announced plans to build major assembly facilities at various EC locations before the end of 1992. Since then, Japanese companies have become active participants in European M&A. Honda, for example, bought 20 percent of British Rover. Mitsubishi Electric acquired the hardware division of Britain's Apricot Computer. Japanese fashion houses have purchased majority shares of leading names in European fashion, such as Germany's Hugo Boss, France's Jean-Louis Scherrer, and Britain's Aquascutum and Laura Ashley groups. In one of the most significant deals, Japan's Fujitsu bought ICL, Britain's biggest computer maker, for $1.3 billion. The deal will not only give Fujitsu an important new channel into the European market, but will also allow it to leapfrog over the U.S.-based DEC to become the world's second-largest computer company. No less significant is the stake taken in German steel-maker Klöckner-Werke by the giant Japanese trading house C. Itoh & Co. Although it amounts to only 6 percent of the equity in Klöckner, C. Itoh's acquisition represents the first time a Japanese firm has penetrated the politically sacred steel industry in the heart of Europe. The two companies are extending their alliance still further by building a joint venture plant in Bremen to make galvanized steel for the European automobile industry.

Japanese interest in Europe is so great that it is beginning to cause a noticeable shift in Japanese asset-allocation patterns away from the United States. When Japanese real estate investment in the United States dipped for the first time in several years during 1989, the reason was obvious to Jack Rodman, the dean of Japanese real estate investment watchers: "This investment cooling was not unexpected. Japan's large institutional investors are examining Western European markets as the 1992 deadline for economic unification looms."[9] In other words, the one-sided Japanese infatuation with the American market is coming to an end.

A *DEUS EX MACHINA* FOR AMERICA

The rise of the New Europe may prove to be very good news for the United States in the short run. Despite numerous structural problems afflicting American capitalism at the moment, the U.S. business community is well positioned to capitalize on Europe's new dynamism. This view is explained in detail in chapter 7.

The "peace dividend" from reductions in U.S. military spending in Europe—even if it is less than it ought to be and even if it is not being used to creative long-term advantage—has the potential to be a *deus ex machina* rescuing the United States from the enormity of its budget deficit. It offers a glimmer of hope that the cost of American capital may go down, that Washington may become less reliant on Japanese financial support, and that government resources will be available for badly needed initiatives to boost domestic competitiveness.

The United States, moreover, remains the most global power. Its relationships with both Japan and Europe, for example, are (at least for now) much deeper and more substantial than Japanese-European bilateral relations. As far as Eastern Europe and the Soviet Union go, the United States has enormous political capital and much to offer in the marketplace.

America's two biggest economic competitors, Japan and Germany, are suddenly preoccupied with difficult challenges. Germany will be successful in its effort to renovate the East over the long term, but it will take up the better part of the nation's attention (and the lion's share of its surplus capital) for several years to come. The rest of the European business community will also be preoccupied by the completion of the 1992 process.

Japan, meanwhile, has been forced to adjust to a new international order in which increased global consciousness about the advantages of economic power prevents it from pursuing its overtly mercantilist and adversarial trade policies as aggressively as before. The Japanese have realized the importance of Europe and have begun to invest actively there, but they have yet to adjust fully to the three-cornered competition. Japanese businesses that had witnessed the steady collapse of their American competition must now contend with forceful new rivals from Germany and elsewhere in Europe. This is especially true in industries such as machine-tool and automotive manufacturing, in which Japanese qual-

ity, productivity, and advanced manufacturing systems long ago surpassed those of the American competition. The Tokyo Stock Exchange
crash of 1990 was an indicator that the Japanese are not as supremely
confident about the battle of the capitalisms as they were when they were
facing off against American business only.

Since America's competitors are largely preoccupied with their own
troubles—and because the United States still possesses a vast supply of
assets and remains an important global leader—the early part of the 1990s
could prove favorable for American interests. Within a few short years,
though, the Japanese are very likely to have turned their present difficulties around and successfully adapted their system to the new global climate. Europeans will have constructed the biggest, richest market in the
world and will be far more competitive as a result.

If the next few years are not used wisely to elaborate a new vision and
to initiate the process of adapting the American system to the new realities, then the rest of the 1990s will be an extremely difficult time for the
United States. The twentieth century, at one time referred to as the
"American century," will end with American companies floundering and
failing as the "competitiveness gap" between them and their European
and Japanese counterparts grows ever wider. The twenty-first century,
which once held thrilling prospects for Americans, could even witness the
loss of the country's greatest assets: its world leadership in technological
innovation and its ability to be a land of opportunity for the vast majority
of its people.

THE WORRIED NIGHTS OF THE AMERICAN CEO

Right now, American leadership is complacent in the extreme about the
need to change. Short-term economic difficulties are becoming increasingly obvious, but no imminent catastrophe is forcing the Bush administration to make the tough choices or embark on the rebuilding work so
badly needed. Despite all the high-profile shenanigans of Washington's
"budget summit" in October 1990, the U.S. deficit continues to spin out
of control toward new record totals. Despite the rapid spread of the
default cancer from the S&Ls to the banking system to insurance companies, government is doing little that is constructive to rebuild the U.S.
financial system. And in the face of what many experts now believe could
be a long-lasting recession, the Bush administration has failed to offer a

single creative proposal on how to inject new vigor into the economy—let alone on how the United States might regain its lost competitive edge in key industries.

Ordinary Americans are angry about what they sense is a Japan that has already passed America by and a Europe that might do the same. The man in the street feels there is little he can do about this predicament. Corporate executives who've seen the problem at first hand are making some successful efforts to revolutionize their own domains and hone their companies' abilities to compete. They will surely be rewarded. Even if the worst happens, there will still be a strong body of sleek, supercompetitive American firms in the future.

But talk to the wisest among these corporate leaders and the discussion quickly turns to their fears. These enterprises may call themselves "global corporations," and they may even earn large revenues abroad, but they remain largely reliant for their position in the world on the vitality and competitive advantages of their home market. Since nation-states haven't yet disappeared—they are, in point of fact, only beginning to show the first signs of waning—American business still needs a national home that can educate its future work force properly; advance the nexus of skills, capital, and suppliers to perform the most sophisticated engineering and manufacturing processes; maintain the requisite fiscal policies to keep corporate borrowing costs low and U.S. dollars strong abroad; and judiciously exercise its political clout to ensure that U.S. companies making high-quality products are able to compete in foreign markets.

What keeps the most thoughtful CEOs awake at night is the growing perception that their America is unable to fulfill those functions adequately. Meanwhile, their chief global competitors enjoy a much more hospitable climate in Japan and Europe.

In the last two years, corporate America has responded intelligently to the rise of a New Europe by identifying opportunities and moving appropriate resources there. Similarly, the Bush administration has done a reasonably competent, although sorely uninspired, job of navigating treacherous European political waters. These are steps in the right direction, but they are far from sufficient. Ultimately, new initiatives at home will be the most important response to the changes in the global situation.

On that score, the United States is failing. Without a change of direction, America stands to become the biggest casualty in the twenty-first-century battle of the capitalisms.

PART I

The Dawn
of a Post-Postwar World

1

Scene: An Abbey Outside of Paris; Enter: The New Europe

A day will come when you, France; you, Russia; you, Italy; you, Britain; and you, Germany—all of you, all nations of the Continent will merge tightly, without losing your identities and your remarkable originality, into some higher society and form a European fraternity. . . . A day will come when markets, open to trade, and minds, open to ideas, will become the sole battlefields.

VICTOR HUGO[1]

SURVIVAL OR DECLINE?

It is sometimes difficult to recall how unimportant and even irrelevant Europe seemed in the early 1980s, when it was suffering the twin ills of "Eurosclerosis" (economic stagnation) and "Europessimism" (the loss of political will to stem the tide of decline). Europe—the cradle of Western civilization, the birthplace of capitalism, the founding theater of the

35

nation-state, the battleground of history's biggest conflagrations, the home for half a millennium to the world's greatest empires—was moving rapidly to the margins of international influence.

It was against that backdrop that Jacques Delors, the incoming president of the European Community's executive commission, summoned his fellow commissioners to a contemplative retreat at Royaumont Abbey outside of Paris in December 1984.

"Europe's choice is between survival and decline," he told them. If Europe failed to seize this historic moment, it could anticipate a twenty-first century in which it would be little more than a "museum to be visited by American and Japanese tourists who like our cuisine and culture." If, however, the EC was willing to undertake a "solemn commitment" to what Delors believed was its most viable survival plan, then Europe not only could survive but was likely to emerge "as a great power in the world again," able to compete fully in the global economic race with the United States and Japan.

Later, Delors would become famous for offhand comments that cut through the EC's courtly diplomacy. He reportedly once accused a British representative of being "a lackey of the Labour Party," a Greek of being "not smart enough to run a taverna," and West German Chancellor Helmut Kohl (a powerful Delors supporter) of being "fat-assed."[2] In one of the milder barbs he would direct at British Prime Minister Margaret Thatcher, his chief antagonist in community politics until her resignation in 1990, he likened her behavior to that of a character in the *Texas Chainsaw Massacre*.

But at Royaumont Abbey, Delors did not attack individuals. Rather, he confined his brutal frankness to the crisis of Europe and the failed dream of European unity. The EC's member nations had never recovered from the stagflation of the oil-shocked 1970s, and their fastest-growing new "product" was unemployment. In 1982–83, two million additional workers joined the already swollen ranks of Western Europe's unemployed. Economic growth averaged a dismal 1.5 percent, and new investment was completely static.[3]

The plain truth was that no one was investing in Europe because future prospects appeared uninviting. By many broad measures of economic competitiveness, Europe was falling further and faster behind both the United States and Japan. It was running "the risk of losing contact with the other two corners of the Triad," as Olivetti's Carlo De Benedetti put it.[4]

The views of European governments had ceased to matter in the great geopolitical game. Europe was now merely the chessboard over which American and Soviet masters made their strategic moves. This fact of life had been reluctantly accepted long ago by European leaders. What was new in the early 1980s was that political collapse was being joined by economic collapse as well. An emerging U.S.-Japanese economic order was beginning to dominate the globe just as the bipolar U.S.-Soviet political order had done for four decades.

A few optimistic leaders wanted to believe that Europe was suffering only a cyclic downturn. No, said Delors. It was time to face facts. Europe was suffering a *structural* crisis. To escape its predicament, it would have to remake its basic structures.

Everything about Western Europe's situation seemed wrong. Its workers were too highly paid and its social welfare states too generous, making it impossible for Western European corporations to compete globally on cost. Its home markets were too small to afford the economies of scale necessary to spawn global-size companies. Even the biggest, most economically successful European country—West Germany—had a market only half as big as Japan's and a quarter the size of America's. And although West Germany was the envy of the rest of Europe, it too had a large unemployment problem and a low growth rate.

Generations of European political intervention in the marketplace—led by socialists from the left as well as nationalists from the right—had rendered much of Europe's private sector too protected, anticompetitive, and inefficient to encourage the innovation necessary to compete with the Americans and Japanese. Mrs. Thatcher, it had to be admitted, was having some success in stirring Great Britain from its long downward economic spiral. Her methods of dismantling the welfare state were too extreme, however, and her truculent ideological beliefs too alien to be acceptable to most Europeans. But Jacques Delors, an iconoclastic Socialist, believed there were lessons to be learned from Thatcher—as well as from Ronald Reagan—on the issue of removing government barriers. The question was how to have the competitive stimulus of a free market without the excesses of Thatcher and Reagan—and especially without the laissez-faire policies that had spawned a Japanese invasion of both the U.S. and the U.K. That was a matter for considerable thought. It would be hard enough just to convince European governments to drop the hundreds of protections, overt and insidious, that doomed most European business to inward-looking inefficiency.

Delors had spent the second half of 1984 visiting each of the EC capitals and holding extensive discussions with political leaders. All sensed the need to "do something"—to launch an ambitious, grand gesture aimed at revitalizing Europe. The EC, despite many problems, was the logical vehicle for any master plan relating to pan-European change.

After World War II, various cross-border associations, such as the European Coal and Steel Community, were established to facilitate the economic recovery of the Continent and to encourage collaboration among its nations. The 1957 Treaty of Rome gathered these organizations together into the Common Market, which gradually evolved into a more comprehensive economic alliance including most of Western Europe. That coalition—now alternately known as the European Economic Community, the European Community, the Community, the Twelve, or, for simplicity's sake, the EC—had always been regarded as the most likely means of solving Europe's many economic and political problems.

The trouble was that it hadn't worked. Over the years, national politics continued to wreak havoc with the EC dream. No matter how small and geographically proximate European countries were, they had large political and economic differences. A drawn-out fight had taken place over admission of the U.K. in the early 1970s. After joining in 1973, the British spent much of the decade threatening to leave. Norway had been accepted as a member, only to have its people, in a bitterly contested referendum, reject the offer. Showdowns over its own budget and the extremely sensitive issue of agricultural policy had further polarized the EC along strictly national lines.

Like the Europe it reflected, the Community as an institution appeared moribund. Its twenty-fifth anniversary in 1982 was commemorated on the cover of *The Economist* with a tombstone. In 1983, the leaders of Europe's most important foreign-policy think tanks—Karl Kaiser, Cesare Merlini, Thierry de Montbrial, Edmund Wellenstein, and William Wallace—issued an unprecedented joint report in which they declared, in part:

> The existence of the European Community is under threat. The position of Western Europe seems to be challenged from all sides. If nothing is done, we are faced with the disintegration of the most important European achievement since World War II. Failure to resolve the Community's internal contradictions will only make Western Europe more marginal to the central issues of global security and global economic management. Failure

to draw the conclusions for common action which follow from our common predicament is itself a sort of choice, by default, for disintegration and decline.[5]

By 1984, however, Delors saw a critical ray of hope. After a protracted brouhaha involving French President François Mitterrand, Britain's Margaret Thatcher, and Germany's Helmut Kohl, the Community was headed toward settlement of the inordinately divisive and immensely political system of price supports and subsidies to farmers known as the Common Agricultural Policy. A formula had been found to quiet Mrs. Thatcher's incessant complaints about Britain putting too much into the EC's coffers and receiving too little in return.

"The big family quarrel was settled, so the opportunity now arose to propose a new scheme in 1984, a new frontier for Europe," says Delors in retrospect. Indeed, it may have been his recognition of that new frontier which permitted him to accept the presidency of the Brussels-based European Commission—a post some observers had reason to see as a demotion to a backwater for the brilliant Monsieur Delors from Paris.

Delors, after all, had been one of the most powerful men in France. He had been minister of finance in a country whose tradition of influential finance ministers reached back three centuries to Colbert, the father of mercantilism. By all accounts, Delors had acquitted himself exceptionally well in the service of Mitterrand. First, he warned his Socialist Party colleagues against their plan to nationalize the banks and launch big new public-spending programs after the "pink revolution" that brought Mitterrand to power in 1981. Overruled, he carried out the Socialist game plan anyway. But when it became obvious that the French economy was headed for disaster, Mitterrand turned to Delors to stop the hemorrhage. When allowed at last to pursue his own approach, Delors did a highly respectable salvage job, administering austerity measures and hitching the historically undisciplined French economy to the strictly disciplined German system. The effort was so successful that Delors was rumored to be next in line for the post of prime minister.

For a variety of political reasons, however, Delors, at fifty-nine, was passed over when Mitterrand named a new—and younger—prime minister in 1984. What to do with the intellect, the managerial talents, and the European political passions of Jacques Delors? Mitterrand had an idea, an idea that was encouraged by his unlikely friend in Bonn, the conservative Helmut Kohl. Perhaps Delors would be a good next president for that rather strange and amorphous institutional animal in Brussels known as the European Commission—the body that functions as the executive branch of the equally strange and amorphous European Community. Mitterrand, the classic French man of ideas, and Kohl, who would ultimately prove to be one of modern Europe's shrewdest politicians, both believed the world was changing. Their Europe, which over the last century had managed to change its axis from Franco-German enmity to Franco-German amity, might now be able to solve its structural crisis and play a new role on the world stage. Perhaps, they thought, the time was right to do something with this European Community after all.

Delors agreed. Being president of the European Commission would be a demotion only if he failed to revitalize it. If he succeeded, he would become the "man who made the New Europe."

THE TRUMP CARD OF JACQUES DELORS: A SINGLE EUROPEAN HOME

Delors took four proposals with him to his meetings with European leaders in the summer of 1984. The first called for "institutional reform" of the EC's own institutions. These included the European Commission in Brussels, the all-but-powerless European Parliament, and the Council of Ministers, which is the highest decision-making body of the EC. (The latter is made up of the ministers of the various governments meeting to make decisions relevant to their portfolios, i.e., finance ministers having final say over issues relating to European finance, etc.) Institutional reform was badly needed, to be sure. In fact, the EC has now declared it a priority for the 1990s. But back in 1984 it was an issue only bureaucrats could love. It lacked appeal as a popular rallying cry. It offered heads of state scant glory and much headache.

The second proposal was to rebuild the EC around a common European defense policy and security system. This had strong nationalist political appeal, especially at a time when many governments disagreed profoundly with what they believed was the Reagan administration's exaggerated assessment of the Soviet threat. What's more, it offered a *dirigiste*'s dream of economic pump-priming to soak up European unemployment. If Europe were to take responsibility for its own defense, it would logically rely on its own companies for even more of its defense contracting than it already did. Yet, although that very idea may triumph in the 1990s, it didn't seriously tempt anyone in 1984. It was immediately understood to be far too ambitious politically. It would rock too many boats with both the United States and the Soviet Union, and would lead to greater military spending and bigger European budget deficits.

Delors's third suggestion was "monetary union." This meant building on the successful foundation of the European Monetary System (EMS), which was then working surprisingly well in setting exchange rates for most EC currencies. The EMS would be moved more consciously and purposefully toward the creation of a unified European currency, a shared central bank, and a merged fiscal policy. At the Madrid summit in 1989, the EC would adopt the "Delors Report," which set the Community on exactly that course. But it was far too controversial in 1984. Mrs. Thatcher wouldn't even begin to entertain the idea. The German Bundesbank, which would inevitably be the center of any European monetary union, wasn't yet interested either.

"I kept the fourth proposal, my last card, until the end," recalls Delors. He waited for the right moment to present his trump card to each leader, one by one. And one by one, they saw the logic in it, not just because Delors made a convincing argument, but because it was obviously the right idea for the time. It was this fourth proposal that Delors would ask the commissioners to approve in December at Royaumont Abbey.

The essence of this last plan was to turn Europe into a single unified internal market—a giant "home market" to all European businesses. With more than 320 million consumers, the EC would become the biggest single market in the world.

Revolutionary as this vision was, it was elegant in its simplicity. The goal of a unified market, as well as the means for achieving it, had already been established by the Treaty of Rome, which ensured—in principle, at least—its signatories' commitment to the free movement of goods, services, capital, and people throughout the Community. If these freedoms could actually be achieved, then European businesses would be able to benefit from the innovation, competition, and economies of scale that would result from having all of Europe as a "home market."

The plan called for eliminating physical borders within the European Community. The EC would work to harmonize the complex array of national distinctions on matters of tax and accounting law, consumer safety and the environment, government procurement, investments, insurance, banking, trucking, and all the other procedural differences that created invisible frontiers between Community members. Not only would business be borderless, but individual citizens would be free to move where the market for their talents best rewarded them. A Spanish architect could set up shop in Germany, a British doctor in France, and a Danish engineer in England—without needing any certification other than what he had earned in his home country.

To further promote the goal of a single Europe, the EC would also upgrade its campaign to back new technologies on a Europe-wide basis. There would be collaborative research on space, satellites, and superconductivity, as well as EC-wide initiatives to develop new computer chips and High-Definition Television. The Community would substantially increase its "structural funds" program, through which capital from wealthy northern European countries is channeled to less developed areas to improve roads, ports, canals, and other elements of infrastructure. These projects not only would help unify Europe economically, but would make remote parts of the Continent more accessible and the single market more of a physical reality.

Once the single market was in place, the EC would reach for grander elements of the plan, such as a common currency and a common defense policy. For these goals, the Treaty of Rome would need amending. But as far as the basic elements of the single market were concerned, the existing treaty provided a solid basis on which to proceed.

A landmark 1979 legal battle had given the treaty new teeth, in fact. At issue was the case of a West German importer prohibited from selling French Cassis de Dijon because the Bonn government held that the liqueur did not conform to German national standards. The European Court of Justice, in Luxembourg, ruled that the Treaty of Rome was on the side of the Cassis. Germany had a right to set national standards, but not to use those standards as a way of closing the market to legitimate competition from across its European borders. Since there was nothing particularly unhealthy about the French cassis and nothing that contravened tax or consumer-protection laws, Germany could not prevent the sale of the liqueur. The point was affirmed: Signatories to the treaty had an obligation to open their markets to competition from all EC companies.

Yet, more than a quarter of a century after the Treaty of Rome, and five years after the Cassis de Dijon ruling, goods, capital, services, and people still did not circulate freely through the EC. As a matter of fact, their movement was impeded at virtually every turn, if not by tariffs, then by those nettlesome invisible barriers of national regulations and local business practices.

So many barriers remained, in fact, that they led to a number of absurd inefficiencies. One often-cited example was the case of the hapless truck driver who needed dozens of separate documents—weighing two pounds by some estimates—to satisfy all the different frontier authorities as he hauled his cargo across the EC's many borders. Or the TV-set manufacturer who needed a team of seventy engineers and a budget of $20 million annually to do nothing but adapt the same basic product to the special technical and safety standards required by each European government. Or the pitiable businessman starting a trip through Europe with $1,000 in his pocket: Changing money into each currency as he crossed every EC border, he would, without spending a cent, end up with just over $500 at the end of his travels. The other half of his money would be lost to exchange transaction costs.

"Because of national political considerations, Europe now has fourteen rail-locomotive manufacturers, when post-1992, assuming an efficient market, the number may contract to only half that many," observes Iain Stitt, the managing partner of the Brussels office of Arthur Andersen & Co. "We have eighteen companies making electrical turbine generators in Europe, when the American market, with greater power consumption, sustains only two. The phenomenon we saw within the EC over the last decade was an absurd race by governments to compete with each other in protecting domestic industries—simply because they were 'theirs'—and to foolishly subsidize the expansion of capacity in sunset industries with declining demand."

Such egregious inefficiencies were choking European economic growth. It was not that the EC hadn't attempted to solve these problems, or that European leaders didn't know that the net effect was to keep their market more *uncommon* than common. The problem was that vested interests usually doomed the process of trying to harmonize specific rules and regulations. At best, it involved interminable efforts to resolve the smallest points. "EC members argued for 10 years, including at the ministerial level, over setting standards for fork-lift trucks before coming to a decision—the main point of contention being the most appropriate pedal system."[6]

To invoke a metaphor Delors would often employ in the years ahead, the reality of the European market was comparable to a United States in which each state had its own currency (not to mention its own language), radically different laws to govern business, and systematic methods to deny market access to "imports" from neighboring states.

"I have no miracle to offer you," Delors told those gathered at Royaumont Abbey. "But if you turn Europe into a big, single market of 320 million consumers—if you abolish all the economic barriers separating European countries—then I am certain Europe will have the potential to fight and win fairly in the economic competition with any power, including the United States and Japan."

The meeting at Royaumont Abbey was a turning point. In Delors, the commission at last had the forceful figure necessary to cut through fog, muddle, and inertia, and to ignite the "relaunch of Europe." The EC could finally dare to challenge the petty nationalisms that had stifled its work for so long.

Although no one could know then just how successful Delors and his commission would be, accounts of the Royaumont Abbey meeting carried by the French press hinted that something new was afoot. *Le Matin* spoke of Delors's desire to "get rid of the old habits" in the commission's inner workings. *Le Monde* reported that he was in favor of a "fresh start," beginning by assigning portfolios based on competence rather than nationality. Both newspapers alluded to the possibility of grand new projects for monetary union, high technology, and "the realization of a true single market."

With the activist tone set at Royaumont, the commission would soon win the single most important ingredient necessary to turn the new interest in European unity into a practical force: a system of majority rule. After three decades of trying to win unanimous support for every decision, the EC was at last ready to allocate a representative weight to each country's vote and allow the majority to rule on key issues. With that critical shift, pious words about unity could at last be turned into real-world political deals. The EC would no longer be a glorified European debating society, but the forerunner of a genuine European government.

"The outside world may have thought what happened at Royaumont banal," reflects Peter Sutherland, the Irishman who was then the commissioner dealing with competition policy. "But those of us who were there recognized that it was a powerful reaffirmation of the direction originally charted in the Treaty of Rome—to create a political union of Europe with real power."

Actually, most Americans heard nothing of the Royaumont Abbey meeting. Nor did they hear much about the flurry of pivotal EC summits and decisions that followed in 1985–86. Passage of the Single European Act (which had the effect of amending the Treaty of Rome to make the 1992 program law) made no headlines in the U.S.; neither did the momentous "White Paper" developed by Lord Cockfield, the commissioner for the internal market. This detailed some 300 directives (later consolidated to 279) on specific issues from broadcasting to banking that would need to be addressed in order to put a unified market in place. One correspondent for a leading American daily tells of actually being rebuked by his editors for taking too much interest in the future of the EC. Ignore the twaddle in Brussels about unity, he was advised—there was no news story there.

By early 1988, however, the European unity drive was beginning to snowball. The U.S. business community, along with a coterie of Capitol Hill "trade hawks," experienced a sudden traumatic realization about what was happening. Not only were the Europeans succeeding in unifying their market, it looked as if they might be creating a protectionist "fortress Europe" that would seek to exclude imports and businesses from outside the Community.

No less a global business guru than Peter Drucker examined the trends in Europe and declared, "The central problem for American trade policy for the next few years is not going to be Japan; it will be the European Community. We must prevent it from becoming a 'fortress Europe.' Yet that is precisely what many European politicians and businessmen have in mind. They see in European economic unification the road to General de Gaulle's old objective of a Europe without Americans."[7]

The panic engendered by the protectionist elements of the EC's plan would subsequently be defused in both the United States and Japan. But European unity was no longer a banal subject. Europe was suddenly *the* hot issue in boardrooms from Detroit to Osaka.

1992: THE MAGIC NUMBER

"If the European Community had hired the world's top headhunter to search for the one executive who could make the single market work, the headhunter would eventually have come to Delors," says Pascal Lamy, Delors's cabinet secretary (and a man whose own brutal efficiency has earned him the nickname "the Exocet"). Delors combines just the right mix of many ingredients. He is a typical French intellectual, yet he maintains a healthy contempt for the traditional Parisian elite, having grown up in a working-class community and studied not at one of the *grandes écoles* but at night school. He was a teenager in Nazi-occupied France, yet he is an admirer of the present-day German economic miracle and harbors no discernible ill will toward Germany. He is a passionate Socialist and a devout Catholic but is coolly nonideological when it comes to economic and fiscal matters. His political self-description is apt: "I am to the extreme right of the left and to the extreme left of the right." Like Jean Monnet, the father of the European Community and the pioneer who first proposed a "United States of Europe" after World War II, Delors can sway a meeting with his powerful vision and sense of purpose. Yet, also like Monnet, Delors generally shuns "big-picture" debates, preferring instead to focus on the nitty-gritty—the details of creating the structures that will bind Europeans together so tightly that ultimately the option of going their separate ways will be impossible.

One of Delors's greatest strengths is his intuitive flair for marketing. And just after the Royaumont meeting, he revealed his boldest marketing stroke. While working to prepare his first major address as president of the European Commission, he had been rereading the works of Jean Monnet and had been struck by the importance Monnet attached to setting specific deadlines for grand projects. "It is the way to show people you are serious," Delors told Lamy and the rest of his cabinet. "I think when we announce this program, it should have a specific date."

Everyone liked the idea, but the debate over what date to set quickly bogged down. The favorites were suggested principally because they were easy-to-remember round numbers: 1990, 1995, 2000. A second meeting to discuss the proposed date had to be called. At that meeting, Jacques Delors said the magic words: "1992," he told his colleagues. "I think we can accomplish this plan by the end of 1992."

Before long, "1992" would emerge as goal, symbol, and beacon. *Quatre-vingt-douze* . . . *zweiundneunzig* . . . *el horizonte noventa y dos* . . . *novantadue* . . . In every European language, "1992" quickly became a code word expressing a volume of ideas about the future. These ideas were often at odds with one another. But 1992 offered something to look forward to for everyone. It was a positive vision of the future for an otherwise exhausted and despondent Europe. With the launch of the 1992 project, Europe gathered up its self-confidence and announced to the world that it was back in the global game.

Even in Eastern Europe and the Soviet Union, 1992 became a date charged with meaning. The promise of a borderless Western Europe after 1992 encouraged people across the Soviet bloc to wish that a few more borders would fall so that they could join the real Europe again. ''We knew we were already so far behind Western Europe, we didn't want 1992 to leave us further behind,'' says Dénes Baracs, the Brussels bureau chief of Hungary's official news agency, MTI. ''Suddenly we had an incentive to remember that we too were Europeans.''

Mikhail Gorbachev was among those most enchanted with the concept of 1992. As far back as Lenin's day, Soviet leaders had always opposed the attempt to unify Europe. Lenin himself had called it an imperialist plot to suppress the cause of socialism on the Continent. But Gorbachev had no trouble dispensing with that anachronistic view. For him, 1992 was such a brilliant idea, he wanted to be part of it. He praised the EC's plan and urged its leaders to extend their vision to what he termed a ''common European house''—a borderless region that would include not just Western Europe but Eastern Europe and the Soviet Union as well.

Legends later sprang up about how the 1992 date was chosen. One rumor had Delors consulting an astrologer; according to another, a secret market research group used an esoteric computer program to calculate the optimum date. The truth, according to Delors, was more prosaic. It seemed to him that eight years (which meant two four-year terms of the EC presidency) was about the necessary amount of time.

Delors never suffered any illusion that all the necessary work would be completed by December 31, 1992. But the deadline provided what was needed most—a sense of urgency. It was distant enough to prevent the project from being dismissed as impossible, but soon enough to discourage any lethargy about getting down to work. ''Nineteen ninety-two is right up there with the greatest private-sector marketing campaigns of all time, like Coca-Cola and Levi's,'' says Andrew Napier, head of the 1992 task force for Ford of Europe. ''Delors knew what he was doing when he picked that date.''

''THE CLOCK IS AT FIVE TO TWELVE''

Delors and his Brussels ''Eurocrats'' were also under considerable pressure from the business community. Wisse Dekker, the outspoken chairman of Netherlands-based Philips, had already developed his own plan for unifying European product standards, harmonizing tax policies, facilitating cross-border transportation and trade, and opening up the government procurement business to pan-European competition. He was mobilizing a consensus on these matters among the CEOs of some of Europe's biggest, most prestigious companies.

Dekker had lived in Japan for six years, where he had watched the Japanese develop their strategy for devouring the U.S. consumer-electronics industry, once a world leader. The same thing had taken place in Britain and was beginning to happen in continental Europe. His conclusion: "We must build a European home market of sufficient scale to compete with the Japanese—recognizing that their home market has now become Japan plus the United States."

As the leader of a company with solid technological credentials (Philips was the first to develop the Compact Disc and had been a pioneer of the VCR and hundreds of other audio and video products), Dekker knew what he was talking about. Others throughout the European business community shared his concerns about Japanese competition.

At a conference in Brussels just a few weeks after the Royaumont Abbey meeting, Dekker formally proposed his own agenda for action. He presented specific plans for how the EC could fully implement the Treaty of Rome and its goal of a truly common market. For European business, he warned, time was running out. "The clock is at five to twelve," he cautioned, and suggested a target date of 1990 for developing a single European market.

Over the next few months, Dekker appeared at a number of public meetings with Lord Cockfield. The two men enjoyed a friendly running argument about the date for the completion of the internal market. Dekker, the businessman, kept pushing for faster action and a timetable ending in 1990. Cockfield, the politician, needed time to surmount the political problems that lay ahead. He was keenly aware of one problem in particular: Margaret Thatcher, the prime minister who had dispatched him to Brussels, was looking on the very program he was helping to create with increasing suspicion. In sparring with Dekker, Cockfield would defend the 1992 deadline, certain that the political wrangling would take at least that long.

Dekker doesn't mind that he eventually lost the argument and that the date was fixed at 1992. "The important fact was that the EC got the message from the business world and was ready to act," he says. Indeed, the business community's support for 1992 is indispensable. As Sir Roy Denman, the EC's recently retired ambassador to Washington, puts it,

"The reason 1992 will work when every other European integration scheme has gone aground is that this time the business community is driving the process. The business community is at least one step ahead of Brussels. They do not need to be exhorted into building a single market—they are already doing it."

THE EC'S EIGHT GREAT SYNCHRONICITIES WITH HISTORY

Although the endorsement of the business world is essential, that factor alone does not explain the steady ground swell of public enthusiasm for 1992 which eventually transformed "Europessimism" into "Europhoria." While Europe found itself seriously divided at the beginning of the 1980s, by the latter part of the decade, the 1992 issue had won near-unanimous backing from normally fractious interest groups. By 1988, *The New York Times* noted, it had become "rare for a Western European leader to deliver a policy statement without dedicating a significant passage to 1992. When Prime Minister Ciriaco De Mita of Italy presented his new government's program in April, he mentioned 1992 some 16 times. In the spring presidential campaign in France, the leading candidates vied to show their ardor for a unified Europe. . . . Giovanni Goria, the former Italian Prime Minister, remarked that the 1992 rendezvous sometimes seemed like 'one with a very beautiful, mysterious lover, or a utopia, or the promise of a great marvelous future. Maybe '92 is all these things. . . .' "[8]

Today, it is not just big business that supports 1992, but the labor movement; not just Europe's big countries, but its small ones; not just Catholic Europe, but Protestant Europe as well. The global-minded industrialists of northern Europe are all for it, but so too are the new entrepreneurs in Mediterranean Europe. Spain—shunned by Europe during its half century of fascist rule—is now often cited as one of the "most European" EC members and looks forward to its potential role as the "California of the Community."

The protean ability to adapt to radically altered circumstances which the 1992 program has shown in the six years since the Royaumont Abbey meeting is rooted in its fundamental compatibility with some of the most sweeping long-term trends in global affairs. At first a by-product of global change, 1992 is now a cause of it. But either way, its synchronicity with larger historical, geopolitical, and geo-economic forces has allowed it to continue gathering momentum even as revolutions in Eastern Europe and the reunification of Germany have profoundly rocked the status quo. Below is a brief examination of eight of those larger forces:

1. The Rise and Fall of Reaganomics. The very first impetus toward 1992 owed much to European envy of the robust growth experienced by the American economy in the 1983–86 period. These were the most decisive years in the formulation of the specifics of the European plan. The fabulous Reagan-era "jobs machine" was then creating millions of new jobs annually in the U.S., while unemployment remained an insoluble problem in Europe. Renewed American economic vigor, produced by a combination of high-tech innovation and deregulation of U.S. financial services, proved the wisdom of reducing barriers to business. Even European socialists were ready to accept the idea that the cowboy-actor Reagan had understood some basic economic truths which had eluded the high-IQ European political leadership.

Yet the failures of Reaganomics were equally influential in shaping European ideas about what the Community did *not* want from 1992. Earlier and more incisively than most Americans, Europeans realized that much of the apparent success of Reaganomics was supported by an unconscionable and unsustainable debt burden, the mortgaging of long-term interests for short-term profits, and a horrific Faustian bargain with the Japanese which allowed them a free run at American business and a large ownership interest in the American economy in return for short-term financing of the U.S. deficit. Europeans did not want to repeat these mistakes. But more important, they understood that these policies were contributing to the erosion of America's power in the world. American decline meant an end to Europe's postwar junior-partner status with the United States and an opportunity—a vital need, in fact—for Europeans to assert their own interests. A more unified Europe would give them the vehicle for doing just that.

2. The Rise and Rise of Japan. Fundamental to the history of Europe's drive toward the single market was fear of Japan. As 1992 was being put on the drawing boards, European companies, already accustomed to sharp competitive pressure from the Americans, were beginning to worry that their own markets might evaporate completely in the heat of Japanese competition unless a concerted pan-European response was launched. Whereas European countries were making little headway on their own in solving bilateral trade problems with Japan, the collective force of the EC—and the attraction of its collective market—could enormously increase their bargaining power with Tokyo. From its new position of strength, the EC is becoming more confident that it can handle active Japanese participation in its economy. Learning from American and British mistakes, Brussels is endeavoring to drive a harder bargain with Japan over market access. So far it seems to be succeeding.

3. Gorbachev and the New East. European leaders were much quicker than Americans to grasp the historic change represented by Mikhail Gorbachev's ascent to power in March 1985. Already, on Gorbachev's first visits to Paris and London, Europe was more than ready to embrace him. Even Thatcher pronounced him a man with whom the West could "do business." Her choice of words was apt. As the plans for 1992 proceeded, an enlarged Western European market yielding newly vigorous private-sector companies would be in an excellent position to do plenty of business in the Soviet Union and Eastern Europe.

"Eastern Europe is Western Europe's hinterland," says John H. Forsyth, a director of the London-based Morgan Grenfell investment bank. "The drive to conquer markets in the East, to build businesses there, to supply all those hardworking Eastern Europeans with consumer goods—this drive could affect Western Europe's economic future the way settling the West stimulated the American economy in the nineteenth century." Such a prospect was all the more reason to press on with 1992 and create a European system in which Eastern countries could aspire to participate.

Gorbachev's willingness to retreat from Europe militarily and his acknowledgment of the internal crisis faced by the Soviet Union coincided perfectly with the breakup of American hegemony over Europe. *Both* superpowers were getting out of Europe, leaving Europeans free for the first time in four decades to pursue an independent vision of the future. The collapse of the communist regimes at the end of the 1980s made the EC's 1985 decision to embark on the path to unification look more farsighted still.

4. The German Question. While the suddenness with which German reunification emerged as an issue in 1989–90 came as a surprise to most Europeans, the essence of the so-called German question—the nation's growing power—was not. Even in the dismal days of Eurosclerosis, West

Germany was far stronger economically than most of the rest of Europe. By the mid-1980s, German growth so far outstripped the European norm, and its industrial companies had become so powerful throughout the Continent, that the rest of the European leadership was once again forced to ask itself "what to do about Germany."

The lesson Europe had eventually learned from the settlement of World War I was that if you try to keep the Germans down, they will only come back later with a vengeance. After World War II, Jean Monnet tried a new approach: Rather than keep Germany down, Europe would give it room to rise and grow. The EC sought to provide institutions which would channel German energies into the building of Europe, and, it hoped, prevent them from being directed into disputes with other European countries.

In the mid-1980s, European leaders saw the 1992 program as a strategic tool for updating Western Europe's not-so-subtle forty-year-old policy of friendly containment of Germany. Although the story is not yet over, it appears that Europe has won by allowing Germany to win. For a brief moment at the end of 1989, German reunification looked as if it might throw the 1992 project off track. But in choosing not to obstruct reunification, the EC has managed to give Germany what it wants. In return, the Community has gotten a stronger, more important Germany that seems to want to work more urgently than ever with its EC partners for the realization of the 1992 program and further unity initiatives beyond.

5. The Borderless Economy and the Decisiveness of Financial Power. It is generally accepted today that the world is progressing toward a borderless economy. Europe, although late to join the movement, is now at its vanguard. Nowhere else in the world are national borders being so deliberately erased. Nowhere else in the world is so much careful thought being given to the question of supranational organizations and institutions.

There is a new and special significance to *financial* power—as distinct from other kinds of economic power—in an increasingly borderless world. Money moves faster, more efficiently, and more freely than even the most freely traded goods. Thus, capital flows have dwarfed even the rapidly surging global trade flows. In 1989, for example, cross-border M&A was up by a factor of 450 percent over 1985, compared with a leap of "only" 55 percent in world trade during the same period.[9]

The cost barriers to developing new technology have escalated, making the financial assets of high-tech companies as important as, or even more important than, the brilliance of their scientists and engineers. The opening up of Eastern Europe to Western business has become largely a question of which companies and national governments are willing and able to invest how much. And world financial markets have become the single most integrated aspect of the world economy. The best illustration of the new relevance of financial power is provided by Japan. More than its manufacturing and trading excellence, what transformed Japan from super trading state into full-fledged global superpower during the 1980s was its extraordinary creation and global deployment of financial assets.

Europe now appears poised to duplicate in the 1990s at least a few elements of the Japanese experience of the 1980s. Old European companies with powerful franchises in their home country are suddenly exploding in stock market value as they follow a strategy of using their existing base to become pan-European, and their pan-European base to become global. The enormous private family wealth of Old Europe, the massive but long-slumbering state-owned sector, and even the frozen and deformed business world of Eastern Europe are all beginning to use their previously untouchable assets for aggressive trading.

One sign of the monumental upward revaluation and expansion of Europe's asset base is the vibrancy of the financial-services sector itself. According to a Bank of England study, business among European banks in the first nine months of 1989 was more than double that for the entire year of 1988.[10] In this field, 1992 has already arrived and European borders have ceased to matter. By embarking on the road to a common European currency, the EC is giving its supercharged financial industry even more muscle to become a leading force in the wider process of global financial convergence.

6. The Green Movement. Beginning with the founding of West Germany's Green Party a decade ago, the ecology-oriented ''green movement'' has gathered momentum worldwide, and environmental issues have now emerged at the forefront of the European political process. The German Green Party itself has become hopelessly splintered and even more incoherent than it was at its inception. Several of its factions are among the few voices consistently critical of 1992 on principle. But the growing influence of eco-politics across Europe is quite compatible with 1992 and has become a driving force in support of it. The main discernible theme among many trends and counter-trends in the June 1989 European Parliament elections was an EC-wide concern with "green" issues.

In Europe, where waste from a factory on the Rhine can contribute to pollution in half a dozen countries, or where the fallout from Chernobyl can damage crops in Denmark, it has always been obvious that real efforts to ensure a clean environment must be pan-European. The discovery of the extent of the environmental disaster in Eastern Europe has driven this point home more vividly still. Around the globe people are coming to agree that "borderless" efforts are needed to clean up a world where pollution knows no boundaries. But the EC, with its supranational structure and with 1992 as its linchpin, is the world's only institution in a position to implement meaningful environmental policies across national boundaries.

7. Travel and the New "European" Citizen. What do Serge July, the French intellectual who edits the leftish *Libération*, and James Robinson III, CEO of American Express, have in common? They both believe that travel and tourism are profoundly changing Europe. Robinson points to the little-known fact that tourism is already the world's largest industry—a fact that augurs well for the goal of minimizing national differences and teaching people to live together in a global economy.

As for Serge July, he maintains that the extensive demographic pattern of Europeans crisscrossing their continent (half the entire West German population passes through France annually on its way to vacations in Spain and Italy) is a key factor in the rise of a new "European" consciousness transcending traditional national limits. "Nineteen ninety-two never could have worked even a decade ago, when Europeans didn't know each other firsthand as well as they do now," says July. In World War I and even World War II, the majority of German and French soldiers had never been in one another's country during peacetime. Today, the soldier-age population in both countries is intimately familiar with the other side.

Travel is integral to European unification. Airline deregulation, high-speed train service linking European downtowns, the "Chunnel" connecting England to the Continent, the Danube Canal project, the end of customs red tape, and the abolition of physical frontiers within the EC are all bolstering the concept of the "free movement of people" enshrined first in the Treaty of Rome and now in the 1992 program. The explosion in Eastern Europe actually began with "tourism"—East German vacationers using their holidays in Czechoslovakia to escape to Hungary and from there to West Germany. A central demand of East Germany's peaceful revolution was freedom of travel, symbolically epitomized by the right to walk freely across the city of Berlin.

European youth are especially borderless in their thinking. "It is the youth who will make the New Europe happen," says Michael Johnson, editor of the London-based magazine *International Management*. Although national identities are not disappearing, Johnson believes the individual sense of being "European" as well as French or Dutch or Danish is growing. For the first time, those who think of themselves as Europeans are not just a handful of ivory-towered intellectuals, but millions of young people who "really don't care about the battles of their grandparents."

8. Integration, Disintegration, and Reintegration. When the idea of the single market first gained prominence around 1985, it seemed oddly out of step with certain other large patterns of structural and global change. In passing from the Industrial Age to the Information Age, it was widely assumed that the world was entering a period which would be chiefly characterized by decentralization and fragmentation. At least, these were the trends that had been observed in America, which was in the vanguard of this process of change. The tiny microchip had proved more economically powerful than the giant blast furnace; the entrepreneurial company, lean and mean, had become more successful than old established leaders of industry with their much-vaunted economies of scale. Small was not just beautiful, it was more practical, more efficient, faster-moving, more innovative, and ultimately more profitable than big.

In the United States during the early 1980s, the trend toward disintegration was visible everywhere. AT&T was being broken up, cable television and the VCR were smashing the standardized system of home information and entertainment, and upstart Apple Computer was successfully winning its battle with IBM. Fast and furious deregulation was tearing down Wall Street's old traditions and creating hundreds of never-before-imagined financial products and diverse new centers of financial power. Corporate raiders were buying up companies only to disassemble them and sell the pieces.

Against this backdrop, Europe's dream of larger-size institutions and greater economies of scale seemed quaint if not downright dinosaurian—

a throwback to a stage of economic development which was already passing from the scene. The savvy skeptic would argue that if Europe really wanted to achieve its stated goal of becoming more globally competitive, then unifying into a big single market was exactly the wrong way to proceed. The American experience suggested that innovation and job growth would henceforth come principally from small companies, not bigger ones. Business needed less government, not a new level of control in Brussels. The idea of a single market seemed particularly unworkable in a world where even well-integrated "single" markets such as the United States were fragmenting into segments and niches so distinct as to constitute totally different worlds.

Then something happened. Around the time of the October 1987 stock market crash, fears that the world might be spinning out of control seemed to exert some countervailing pressure. Suddenly, after having appeared irreversibly headed toward fragmentation, the world looked as if it was coming back together again. For the two years that followed the 1987 crash, "convergence" was the key word in international financial circles. Before 1987, the world's leading industrial democracies had tried to use floating exchange rates as economic weapons to slice away at the sum of world wealth and gather more of it to their side of the table. After 1987, those same countries deliberately sought to preserve the totality of world wealth by limiting exchange-rate fluctuations to circumscribed target zones.

By the end of the 1980s, the deregulated U.S. airline industry had reconsolidated into a near-monopoly structure. So too had telecommunications providers, computer hardware and software suppliers, and other businesses that earlier in the decade had looked as if they would continue breeding new companies and competition forever. The very Reagan-era officials who had first popularized the idea that small businesses were driving employment growth recanted, saying they had misinterpreted their data. The huge centralized bureaucracy of the United States government had to bail out the deregulated, disintegrating savings-and-loan industry. Another part of that same vast bureaucracy was engaged in a massive campaign to bring the most decentralized powers in the American economy to heel—the insider traders and the junk-bond kings. Mike Milken's bond machine at Drexel Burnham Lambert had created a systematic means of putting the future of every major American corporation in doubt. American business was not about to return to a new age of certainty, but with the bankruptcy of Drexel and the conviction of Milken, the ease with which raiders could take over a company and hack away at its pieces was curtailed.

The Industrial Age was still fading from the global stage, but amid the chaos and confusion, old-fashioned large-scale organizations *were* finding successful ways to reinvent themselves. The factory-studded midwestern "Rust Belt" experienced a renaissance. Certain Industrial Age principles about large markets, standardized products, and economies of scale were proving valid and applicable even to the revolutionary industries of the Information Age.

Politically, too, the world seemed to veer back from the precipice of further fragmentation. Divisions everywhere were being mended. The vicious, intractable Iran-Iraq war came to an end, as did conflicts in Afghanistan and Central America. The thirty-year-old Sino-Soviet split was patched up. Not only was Germany being reunified, but North and South Yemen were united, Koreans spoke seriously about reunification, and even the pope and the archbishop of Canterbury held a dialogue aimed at healing a schism in the church dating back to 1534. The United Nations once again played a useful role in settling global conflicts; Moscow wanted to join the General Agreement on Tariffs and Trade (GATT) and the International Monetary Fund (IMF); and Albania, the country most self-consciously split off from the world community, signaled a desire to end its isolation. By the beginning of 1990, although seething antagonisms remained in the U.S.-Japan relationship, politicians from the two nations had succeeded in preventing a trade war.

Certainly, there were countercurrents: witness Yugoslavia's descent into civil war. But even where disintegration continued as a visible trend, it was frequently less cataclysmic than expected. The Soviet Union, which appeared to be violently fracturing early in 1990, ultimately moved to a generally more peaceful process of dissolution, although the story is not yet over. A long-simmering constitutional crisis in Canada over special status for Quebec may ultimately result in the breakup of Canada as a single nation-state. But while this is a serious issue, with strong feelings on both sides, Canada seems to be taking it all in stride. Absent are the angry passions and violence associated with the Quebec separatist movement of twenty years ago.

Iraq's invasion of Kuwait offered ample evidence that a general trend toward reintegration does not necessarily mean the world is becoming one big peaceful family. But the global response to Iraq did underscore the theme of reintegration, after a fashion, in the way, as the United

States, the Soviet Union, the EC, Japan, China, and the entire UN Security Council all immediately denounced Iraq. Never before in a century marked by conflict in the Middle East had the world community reacted so quickly and unanimously to an act of aggression in that region.

Reintegration does not guarantee stability, either. Ironically, as the world economy becomes increasingly borderless, the chances of instability are growing rather than diminishing. This is true especially as the "have-not" population of the world explodes while the "have" population remains confined to the low-birthrate Triad. Even as Europe becomes more powerful and prosperous, those living on its periphery in Africa and the Middle East are becoming poorer and angrier. Iraq's invasion of Kuwait is a good example of the type of conflict the world may expect to see in this new age. It was, in a sense, the ultimate hostile takeover, and its implications immediately convulsed world financial markets.

Even ordinary, nonviolent news emanating from the "have" part of the world can destabilize the borderless economy. When a think tank in Germany forecasts that the costs of reunification will be higher than expected, it triggers a whirlwind of stability in the American and Japanese bond markets as central banks (which once thought of themselves as stable and independent) assess the likely impact of this cost overrun on their now-interdependent and volatile money supplies and interest rates.

The point is not that integration has somehow permanently triumphed over disintegration. Rather, *both* integration and disintegration are parts of the global march into the future; for the moment, integration has assumed the more powerful role, just as disintegration seemed to predominate a few years ago. As Japan has already demonstrated, and as the Europeans are now attempting to amplify with their own experience, large-scale organizations, economies of scale, big markets with common standards, and mass manufacturing techniques can actually be useful tools in creating Information Age industries. While maximizing opportunity, they help minimize the social dislocation that accompanies the transition from the old order to the new. Learning to distinguish what should be centralized from what is better decentralized—and understanding how to blend the two forms—is a crucial new skill that will be needed by managers, political leaders, and institution-builders of all kinds.

Were the EC simply trying to fulfill the old Industrial Age dream of a "United States of Europe," the project would probably fail. Instead, the plan is to keep sovereign national power alive, albeit in somewhat downgraded form, while at the same time creating a federal structure in Brussels that is influential but specifically not a massively centralized new nation-state. Thus there is room for a dialectic to operate, with the emphasis alternating between the national and the supranational. The test of long-term success for the New Europe may well be the degree to which it is able to maintain a creative tension between the centralized and the decentralized.

Italian Foreign Minister Gianni De Michelis, who has a penchant for futurology, views the situation this way: "Globalization is the dominant characteristic of our times but it inevitably creates reactions among countries and peoples which are disintegratory—protectionism, unilateral debt moratoria, racism, and phenomena of this type." Integration, in the sense of deepening interdependence, is the answer to disintegration, he maintains, *if* that integration allows sufficiently for differences of individuality and identity. The reason Europe has become the center of world attention, De Michelis believes, is that "people are becoming aware, consciously or unconsciously, that the choice is between integration and disintegration." The kind of loose, interdependent integration Europe has embarked upon appears as an attractive alternative to the chaos of further global disintegration.[11]

A DANGEROUS PASSAGE ACROSS THE MILLENNIUM

Jacques Delors is sipping a beer at the end of a long, exhausting day supervising the construction of the New Europe. We are in his office on the top floor of the Berlaymont, the Brussels building which serves as a de facto capital for the EC. On the thirteen floors below, throughout the drab, endless corridors of this architecturally horrifying modernist edifice, Eurocrats are debating in a babble of European languages. The horse-trading is growing more feverish as they attempt to hammer out the compromises that will enable them to formulate the necessary directives by the fast-approaching deadline.

I ask Delors what the Europe of the future looks like to him. He waxes eloquent on the great themes of European history. He draws analogies with ancient Greece, Rome, and Christendom. He foresees a Europe that will incorporate the best from these traditions—"Roman law, the Greek spirit, and the personalism of Christianity." He believes Europe will also invent a new kind of capitalism, striking the right balance between the

Japanese model, which is "too collectivist," and the American model, which is "too individualist."

To Delors, the single market is only the first stepping-stone across an admittedly dangerous, untamed river. On the near side of this river—the side everyone can see clearly and discuss in specific terms—the now quiescent but once ferociously warring nationalisms of Europe's traumatic past are gathered. On the far side, shrouded in the thick fog of the unknown, lies the Europe of the future. It is rich with opportunity, dense with possibilities.

The borders of this New Europe will very likely reach beyond those of the twelve current EC members. The Community has already incorporated what was once East Germany. Many others want in. It is even possible that the New Europe will someday extend all the way to those geographic limits first imagined long ago by Charles de Gaulle and recently invoked once more by Mikhail Gorbachev—that it will be a "Europe from the Atlantic to the Urals."

Whether or not it ever reaches that far, the vague, foggy outlines of the future Europe already suggest that it could well become the great force in world affairs that Delors desperately wants it to be. Europe might even become what Delors carefully stops short of predicting: the world's *greatest* power; the center of global wealth, prosperity, and learning; the influencer of events far and wide, from Asia to America—just as it was before 1914.

But 1914, of course, was a fateful year. It was then that Europe began the long process of destroying itself through world wars, bitter nationalist rivalries, power struggles, class struggles, and frightening totalitarian regimes. And there is no guarantee it will not happen again.

The river passage that Delors is organizing will last a minimum of a decade—perhaps two or even three. The Europe that gave birth to the modern nation-state must now pioneer the world beyond national borders. It must develop new political and economic forms to transcend the old fixed walls of sovereignty, and meld the countries of Europe into the world's first large, organic, supranational entity.

The institutional forms Delors and his successors invent may end up serving as models for those of us in other parts of the world, who will eventually have to join Europe in crossing the river into the third millennium. But Delors's creation could also turn out to be a catastrophic failure—a latter-day League of Nations whose glowing ideals of international peace and prosperity only briefly manage to conceal the explosive brew of conflicting interests bubbling beneath the surface.

Since no one can see clearly to the other side of the river, there are many opinions about just how deep and dangerous it is. Those ready to undertake the journey know they will encounter fierce rapids somewhere during the crossing. Just to put the first stepping-stone in place—the single market of 1992—Delors's crew already has had to navigate the quickening whirlpool of German reunification. Some experts expected the developments in Germany to throw the engineers of European unity off course. Delors argued that his scheme could withstand German reunification and even benefit from it—and so far, he appears right. But as his successors go on to lay down the rest of the stepping-stones in the 1990s—creating first a common European currency, then a common foreign policy, a common defense policy, and ultimately a political union—they may encounter worse hazards yet.

Any sixteenth-century European mapmaker, after outlining the borders of the known world, would invariably sketch a few savage sea monsters at the edges of his map, representing the dangers of that far-off *terra incognita*. Now, as the leaders of modern Europe seek to chart the unknown territory before them, they too imagine frightening possibilities lurking in the distance. An early fear which has since subsided, was that Europe might succeed for a time in digesting German reunification, only to find itself later chafing at the domination of a highly successful German superpower. Another, which was given an especially potent jolt of reality in 1991, was the fear that Gorbachev might be overthrown by hard-liners who would once again threaten Europe militarily. Still another is that a severe recession could revive intra-European conflicts over economic policy, revitalize the protectionist current in trade policy, and ultimately trigger a global trade war. And then there is what is now taking place in Yugoslavia. Bismarck's prophetic pre–World War I warning, in fact, is still apt: "If there is ever another war in Europe, it will come out of some damned silly thing in the Balkans."

Delors is guardedly optimistic, not just about the success of 1992, but also about the wider efforts to create a new structure that could someday incorporate all of Europe. "My work is much like that of an engineer," he says. "It is a process that goes step-by-step. My job is to make the *engrenage* [meshing of the gears] happen."

Slowly, surely, ineluctably, the gears are meshing. Occasionally, there have been loud grinding noises from 10 Downing Street. From time to time, Europe must lurch over some new obstacle with yet another collective leap of faith. A few setbacks have already been experienced—deadlines missed, political differences papered over with compromises so vague as to be laughable. The threats are real, but for now, at any rate, they are on the distant horizon.

Overall the process is working. The *engrenage* is happening.

2

And the Wall Came Tumbling Down

Only Today Is the War Really Over.

Sign in the crowds celebrating the opening of the Berlin Wall

THE GLOBAL EPIPHANY

In the chill night air on November 9, 1989, as the Berlin Wall opened and East Berliners began pouring through the gates to the West, a collective epiphany occurred to thinking people around the world watching these historic events on television: *The war is over*. The shadows of World War II—and the Cold War it begat—were suddenly fading from the horizon. For much of the globe, and in particular for the industrial countries, World War II and the Cold War had provided the most visceral, seminal, and self-defining experiences of the twentieth century. It was in the crucible of these two closely interconnected conflicts that modern consciousness had been born.

Until that night in Berlin, we all knew we lived in the postwar era. We knew what was meant by the postwar economic or political order. We spoke intelligently about postwar art, postwar literature, postwar education, and postwar philosophy. We denominated events in the postwar frame of reference, as in "the longest postwar economic expansion." Most of us were either parents or children of the "postwar baby boom." From television to the computer chip, from fast food to shopping malls, from the breakup of the nuclear family to the threat of nuclear war, the innovations and social changes of the postwar era surrounded us and fashioned our thinking.

We had come to take certain postwar geopolitical circumstances for granted: a bipolar world, cleaved into American- and Soviet-led blocs; American leadership of the best-functioning part of the global economy and its institutions; an aggressive Soviet Union posing a constant threat to world peace; a United States serving as guarantor of the free world's security; an Eastern Europe forever imprisoned; a Western Europe perhaps prosperous, but always politically, economically, and militarily dependent; a Germany perhaps *very* prosperous, but always a quiet shadow of its former muscular, overbearing self; a Japan that was sometimes a ferocious adversary to the U.S. on economic matters but which was always ultimately dependent on Washington for its own security.

We had begun to view all these facts as part of a permanent, immutable order rather than as the historical aberrations they were. We had come to feel as if they had been with us forever, failing to remember that they were actually quite recent. Forgotten in the late 1980s was the deliberate design work and careful negotiating that had gone on at places like Teheran, Yalta, Dumbarton Oaks, San Francisco, and Bretton Woods in the 1940s. Ignored—especially by Americans—was the fact that the postwar order which seemed so natural and right was not some God-given arrangement of the global landscape, but a man-made creation, born of a particular set of historic conditions and not necessarily valid for all time.

The American understanding of contemporary economic issues—the notion, for example, that the United States should be the consistent and absolute champion of free trade and open investment markets—was largely based on relative truths, conditioned in ways no longer visible by a trail of assumptions that worked its way back to World War II and its causes, as well as its Cold War aftermath. "Revisionists" appeared on the political-economy scene in the late 1980s to question whether America's friends and trading partners—particularly the Japanese, but to a lesser extent other Asians and Europeans as well—weren't taking unfair advantage of the American commitment to open markets. But the postwar belief system had the staying power of religion. Despite overwhelming evidence that the nature of world economic competition had changed, the revisionists had great difficulty getting a serious hearing.

The postwar world order was so brilliantly constructed that it remained workable and modern far longer than its original architects could have dared hope. In retrospect, the year 1945 became the great divide of the century. The time before had more in common with the nineteenth century; the time after was what constituted the twentieth century proper. Until the 1980s, the postwar order appeared seamless and transparent; it wholly defined the modern era.

In the mid-1980s, avant-garde artists popularized the paradox that modernism was out of date. Critics began writing extensively—and often completely inaccessibly—on the theme of "postmodernism." But it wasn't until the events of November 9, 1989, in Berlin that, willingly or unwillingly, we all became postmodernists. It was on that night the world began to realize we would need post-postwar politics, a post-postwar economics, a post-postwar security system, and much else. We had reached the end of modern times, and now we needed a postmodern way of understanding the world.

Watching Berliners drink *Sekt* and dance atop the Wall that had once divided them, there was a shared sense from Washington to Tokyo, from Paris to Moscow, that what is normally imperceptible to the human eye—the enormous force of history in the very act of changing course—had suddenly been made powerfully visible. The post-postwar era had begun. The "realities" accepted yesterday as the bedrock of the global order were no longer valid. They had been replaced with a series of question marks. Tomorrow—the 1990s and the twenty-first century—would clearly be quite different from today.

Whether the issue was cross-border alliances in the corporate world or the transatlantic alliance in the political realm, capital spending plans on Wall Street or defense spending plans in Washington, anyone who did not open his mind up to the question of how the fall of the Wall might affect his strategy was simply not a strategic thinker. And anyone who managed to get through that mental process with his old beliefs still intact was not a very good one.

THE TRIUMPH OF THE IMPOSSIBLE

Just a few weeks before the Wall fell, East German dictator Erich Honecker had appeared firmly entrenched in power. In an unintentionally ironic echo of Hitler's prediction of a "thousand-year Reich," Honecker had declared the Berlin Wall would last another hundred years. But in the days that followed November 9, Berliners chipped away at Honecker's Wall with pickaxes while newly rehumanized East German border guards looked on with approving smiles. Entrepreneurs even carted off chunks of this quintessential symbol of the postwar era to be sold on Fifth Avenue street corners, on the Champs-Elysées, and in the Ginza. The peaceful crowds in East Berlin—the intensity of their basic human emotions and the moral force of their simple demands—had rendered completely impotent the barbaric old gray men of Stalinism. Erich Honecker was jailed and charged with treason while East Berliners went shopping on West Berlin's glittering Ku'damm.

It was the ultimate arbitrage of the marketplace in the Information Age: Two societies, both German, stood face-to-face for forty years, with one succeeding and the other failing. Then, suddenly, as West Germany was preparing to make a new quantum leap in its success story via the 1992 project, East Germany was being dragged down by the god that had not only failed in Moscow, but now even admitted failure. With the news of all of this being beamed to East German living rooms daily via West German television, the old values simply could not hold. They imploded, bringing the Wall down with them.

Describing the experience of the two million East Germans who flooded into West Berlin the weekend after the Wall fell, Timothy Garton Ash, an incisive commentator on Germany with an eye for detail, wrote:

> They bought one or two small items, perhaps some fresh fruit, a Western newspaper and toys for the children. Then, clasping their shopping bags, they walked quietly back through the Wall, through the gray, deserted streets of East Berlin, home. It is very difficult to describe the quality of this experience because what they actually did was so stunningly ordinary. . . . Berliners walked the streets of Berlin. What could be more normal? And yet, what could be more fantastic?[1]

The impossible had happened. Yesterday's surreal dream was today's fact. In a world cynical about the possibilities for large-scale political change *anywhere*—let alone in East Germany, of all places—long-fixed global realities would be cut loose from their moorings, history would be stood on its head, and overwhelming change would be unleashed everywhere.

Just a few months earlier, *New York Times* foreign-affairs columnist Flora Lewis had dismissed the plausibility of German reunification, reflecting the then-prevailing wisdom of most experts. If voices in Bonn were speaking of reunification, she wrote, it was only the empty rhetoric of "traditional piety." There was "nothing doing" on this issue. "The Soviets," she said, "wouldn't dream of it."[2] When Vernon Walters, the U.S. ambassador to West Germany, answered yes in a September radio program to an interviewer's question about whether he could imagine a united Germany in the near future, senior American diplomats rushed to dismiss Walters as not knowing what he was talking about.

That same September, I conducted forty interviews with West German business and political leaders, most of whom were extremely well informed about the situation in East Germany. Many were already engaged in building the extensive network of East-West business dealings which was laying the economic groundwork for reunification as early as the mid-'80s. Yet even among this group of august German knowledgeables, not one predicted in September the events that would follow in November. Many of them thought nothing would be possible until the death of Honecker.

The most visionary was Alfred Herrhausen, the powerful speaker (chief executive) of Germany's largest bank, Deutsche Bank. His reputation for both power and vision later made him a target of West German terrorists. Herrhausen alone suggested that most people were underestimating the rapidity with which things might change in East Germany. Reunification—which he very much favored—was the only solution to East Germany's problems, in his opinion. But even he thought it would take another year or two for reunification to become a pressing political issue.

Seven weeks later, as the Wall fell, a spontaneous kind of German reunification began instantaneously. Aristocratic Mercedes-Benzes from the West mingled democratically in exuberant traffic jams with their shabby cousins, the East German Trabants. Youth from both Berlins danced in the streets wearing the same blue jeans and Batman jackets and singing the same rock songs. East Berliners waited in bank lines for their 100 deutsche marks in Western "welcome money" and the chance to be consumers for a day in the miracle economy their fellow Germans had built. Companies such as Siemens, Volkswagen, and Deutsche Bank rushed to announce their plans for new factories and offices in the East. The mayors of both Berlins shook hands at the Potsdamer Platz and reminded each other of the days when this now-desolate neighborhood adjacent to the Wall had been the epicenter of European café society and the crossroads of Europe's flourishing intellectual world.

As the weeks went on, the signs and slogans in the East German crowds grew more explicit in demanding what had so recently been unthinkable and yet was suddenly so terribly obvious: *"Ein Deutschland"*—one Germany, one Fatherland, one people, one nation.

Just a few months earlier, in the spring that preceded the Berlin fall, the NATO alliance had been caught up in a sharp and divisive debate about deploying a new generation of costly short-range nuclear missiles in West Germany to counter Soviet forces to the East. Some members of the Bush administration had openly declared that, *glasnost* and *perestroika* notwithstanding, Mikhail Gorbachev did not represent a sufficient change in Kremlin policy to warrant a substantive shift in NATO defense strategy. The Pentagon would go on spending millions of dollars a day developing new Lance missiles to better defend against the Soviet threat in Europe.

Yet, after November 9, NATO strategy and the $300 billion U.S. defense budget began to look as anachronistic as the machine-gun towers being torn down along the Wall or the ferocious East German guard dogs for whom Western animal-protection organizations now scurried to find homes. No matter how one assessed Mikhail Gorbachev's chances of success or survival, no one could credibly argue any longer that he didn't represent meaningful change. Everyone knew that the Wall would not have been opened without Gorbachev's assurances that the Berlin of 1989 would not be a repetition of Budapest '56 or Prague '68 or the threat to Warsaw in '81. This time, the Soviet tanks stayed away.

Gorbachev's acquiescence was, in effect, the strongest statement he could possibly make about the future of the "Soviet threat" to the West. If the Soviets would not fight to keep control of East Germany, their forward base for attacking the West and defending themselves from any perceived Western threat, if they would not act to prevent the fall of Berlin, the city whose fate had nearly pushed the world to nuclear war in the past, then they would not fight anywhere against the West. They might fight *inside* the Soviet Union—in Azerbaijan, in the Baltic republics, or in the streets of Moscow. No one could rule out the possibility of a Soviet version of what had occurred in China's Tiananmen Square in

June 1989. But once the Kremlin had declined to engage the West over Berlin, a future encounter became much less likely. Mikhail Gorbachev might not have been able to foresee everything that would happen after November 9, but he is too keen a thinker to have missed the big picture. He no doubt realized that once he had blinked over Berlin, the East German army and the Warsaw Pact itself would begin to collapse, along with all the rest of the military infrastructure that had enabled the Soviet Union to pose a constant conventional military threat to Western Europe.

By providing that litmus test of Moscow's new thinking, Gorbachev ended the Cold War with an act not even the most utopian "dove" could have imagined possible. He surrendered unilaterally to the West without firing a shot, and went home to deal with the mounting problems of his own country.

"THE MOST INTERESTING YEAR EVER"

History, like human psychology, is always "overdetermined"—the product of multiple factors and forces. Perhaps the first link in the chain of events leading up to the peaceful revolutions of the fall of 1989 had been forged a decade earlier when a Polish electrician named Lech Walesa and his colleagues in the Gdansk shipyards started organizing an independent trade union called Solidarity. Maybe it was the selection of a Polish pope, the enormous political impact of his views on the Soviet bloc, and his leadership in reviving religious institutions in the East as an organized force for social change. Possibly, as most political scientists will argue, the rise to power of Mikhail Gorbachev in March 1985 was the key event from which all others flowed. Or perhaps it was the brave decision of Hungary's leaders in September 1989 to risk a showdown with East Berlin by continuing to allow German refugees to pass through Hungarian territory on their flight to freedom in the West.

Yet it is possible to imagine a Solidarity-led Poland, an Eastern Europe with greater religious freedom, an East Germany permitting an outward flow of refugees, and a Mikhail Gorbachev implementing major reforms in all aspects of Soviet life—without concluding that the dam of communist control would absolutely have to burst. And had that dam not broken, the Cold War could never really have ended.

As late as October 1989, Gorbachev was still fully intent on staying the course he had chosen: reforming the Soviet system, trying to make it more productive, efficient, democratic, and peaceful, but leaving its internal and, most important, its *external* power structures intact.

It was Berlin that interrupted Gorbachev's plan and forced the final rapid wind-down of the Cold War. And it is in that sense that November 9, 1989, is the key date. Berlin was not the first link in the chain of events; rather, it was the link that broke the chain. As the Wall opened, so too did the floodgates of history, allowing long-standing verdicts to be reversed and the long-suppressed passion for human freedom to rush torrentially across Eastern Europe and much of the rest of the world.

In the days that followed November 9, Bush and Gorbachev suddenly agreed at Malta to begin the process, four decades overdue, of disarming and demobilizing American and Soviet forces in Europe. Peaceful crowds massed in Prague's Wenceslas Square day after day until the old, cynical regime exited and the oft-jailed truth-telling playwright Václav Havel assumed the presidency of Czechoslovakia. Todor Zhivkov, the Bulgarian strongman who had ruled with an iron fist for thirty-five years, quietly surrendered. Romania's brutal dictator, Nicolae Ceauşescu, chose to meet demands for reform with violence, but ended up being tried for treason and executed by firing squad. The Communist Party of the Soviet Union at last rejected one of the fundamental tenets of Leninism—the party's monopoly on power—and began laying the groundwork for political pluralism. Lithuania declared its independence from the Soviet Union, and other Soviet republics followed suit. The once-crackerjack East German army was plagued with defections and insubordination, and the combat readiness of all the Warsaw Pact forces was called into question even by Pentagon generals, who traditionally had a vested interest in overstating the Eastern Bloc's military prowess. By the end of 1990, of course, the world had changed to such a fantastic degree that Warsaw Pact generals routinely stopped in at NATO headquarters in Brussels to chat about military strategy. And the government in Bonn, with the full support of its NATO allies, actually began *paying* the salaries of the hundreds of thousands of Soviet soldiers remaining in eastern Germany as part of the price for quick, smooth reunification of the country.

Communist parties throughout Eastern Europe were changing their names or disbanding altogether. The huge statues of Lenin that had dominated town squares throughout the Soviet bloc were being unceremoniously toppled. The people of Karl-Marx-Stadt in East Germany were demanding restoration of the city's pre-1953 name, Chemnitz; and tens of thousands of streets, squares, schools, and factories named for Marx or

Lenin, or former Eastern European dictators, or the dates on which Soviet occupation forces had arrived, were being changed as well. Hungary declared its 1956 uprising no longer officially reactionary but officially revolutionary; Czechoslovakia, which for two decades had officially thanked the Soviets for invading in 1968, now officially denounced the action. The Soviet Union decided that its own invasion of Afghanistan was illegal; the Soviet Politburo, led by Gorbachev himself, eulogized the once-excoriated Andrei Sakharov as a cherished critic of Soviet society. A prolific outburst of pluralism shattered the communists' former political monopoly in Eastern Europe, as seventy parties emerged in Hungary, thirty sprang up in East Germany, and virtually hundreds loomed in the Soviet Union. The biggest of these parties not only received money, equipment, and crash courses in the electoral process from fraternal parties in Western Europe, they also imported American consultants to teach them the art of the thirty-second TV spot. . . .

No less stunning was the daily stream of bulletins chronicling the many attempts to de-communize the ossified economies of the East: General Electric buying a light bulb factory in Hungary . . . McDonald's opening a Moscow franchise . . . the Polish government hiring American economists to devise plans to save its collapsing economic system . . . Dresdner Bank, one of West Germany's biggest, reopening its ancestral home in the East German city of Dresden . . . Carl Zeiss of West Germany and Carl Zeiss Jena of East Germany, once a single company, which had been separated at the birth of the Cold War, considering a new East-West merger . . . Murdoch, Maxwell, Turner, and the other global media barons buying up the propaganda organs of communism and turning them into a lively and profitable free press . . . a magazine devoted to Hungarian castles for the international real estate set . . . mutual funds designed to encourage investment in Eastern Europe launched on Wall Street with great fanfare . . . the once-fearsome East German sports machine offering to sell its secret training manuals to the highest Western bidder . . . Japanese automakers announcing plans for new plants and sales offices in Eastern Europe . . . Soviet factory chiefs enrolling in Harvard Business School . . . Frank Zappa, the leader of the 1960s rock band Mothers of Invention, meeting with Havel[3] to discuss a business plan to catapult telephone-short Czechoslovakia into the cellular age. . . .

Historic events in other parts of the world were also influenced in profound if not always obvious ways by what happened in Berlin on

November 9. The release of the world's best-known political prisoner, Nelson Mandela, opened up the amazing possibility of majority rule in South Africa. Both Mandela and F. W. de Klerk, the white prime minister who set him free, repeatedly made the observation that if the Berlin Wall could fall and the two Germanys could bridge their differences, perhaps blacks and whites in South Africa could come together, too. In Managua, there was a similar story. While a decade of Washington-backed guerrilla warfare by the *Contras* hadn't succeeded in overthrowing the Sandinista government, that goal was accomplished in a day at the ballot box, when the people of Nicaragua elected opposition leader Violeta Chamorro as their new president. It is questionable whether Sandinista chief Daniel Ortega would have stood aside to let Doña Violeta win a free election had he not seen what had so recently happened to Erich Honecker, Nicolae Ceauşescu, and others in Eastern Europe who had tried to hold back the tide of democratic will. Even as far away as Mongolia, the expanding forces of pluralism and democracy took courage from Berlin.

Each of these events had its own dynamics, and each was a symbol of the radical change that began sweeping the world in 1989—the year that columnist George Will dubbed "the most startling, interesting, promising and consequential year *ever*."[4] Yet, owing to its unique place in history— and to the crude but powerful image of the Wall itself—what happened in Berlin was the ultimate symbol, the ultimate catharsis, and the ultimate turning point.

BISMARCK, HITLER, AND *THE SPY WHO CAME IN FROM THE COLD*

As the German newspaper *BZ* proclaimed in its headline on the morning after the Wall opened, "Berlin Is Berlin Again."[5] A city much forgotten by non-Germans in recent years, Berlin lies at the heart of modern history. Bismarck made his capital in Berlin, and it was there that he welded together a vigorous, centralized German nation-state. Many historians argue that the emergence of this new power in the heart of an Old World already jealously divided among the existing Great Powers made World War I a virtual inevitability—the product of poor solutions to what Josef Joffe, the foreign-affairs editor of *Suddeutsche Zeitung*, has recently called "the oldest problem of modern European history: how to balance

German national aspirations against the claims of European stability."[6]

It was also in Berlin, exactly fifty-one years earlier—on the night of November 9, 1938—that Hitler's shock troops had viciously vandalized the stores of Jewish merchants in the infamous Kristallnacht pogrom, giving the world a vivid foretaste of the Nazi terror that would eventually become World War II. In the very Potsdamer Platz where the throngs now celebrated the opening of the Wall, Hitler had made his final bunker. And to a very large extent, it was what had happened in that horrible war which had dictated the architecture of the ensuing peace and necessitated what most people had viewed—until November 9—as permanent, institutionalized realities: the division of the European continent, the division of the German nation, and the division of the city of Berlin itself.

Those divisions were the fault lines of the Cold War. The Berlin Wall epitomized the polarization of the world into Soviet- and American-led blocs, "communist" and "capitalist" camps, the Warsaw Pact and NATO alliances. Even when the superpower chess game was played out over Cuba in 1962—and even when blood was shed over Vietnam in the 1970s—it was always in Europe that the greatest concentration of armies and planet-threatening nuclear warheads faced each other at close range. Thus, at the height of the paranoid Cultural Revolution in China, with a million Soviet troops on China's northern border and the U.S. fighting a massive war in Indochina to the south, Mao Zedong still had the Sun Tzu–like sense of strategy to recognize that despite such goings-on in Asia, "the focus of U.S.-Soviet contention is Europe."

The United States lost more than 100,000 lives, expended what is now estimated at more than $10 trillion,[7] and laid out prodigious human and political resources over the years in keeping itself on constant guard against the Soviet threat. Experts imagined all sorts of ways in which the USSR might launch an attack, but the single most realistic scenario suggested that on some dark night, Soviet tank columns would come rolling out of East Germany, cross the Fulda Gap into the West German heartland, and threaten Frankfurt, the rest of Europe—and world peace—in no time. It was just that sort of scenario which General Sir John Hackett, a former top NATO commander, described in his best-seller, *The Third World War*—a book which military officialdom cited as offering the most graphic depiction of why NATO needed to remain armed to the teeth in Europe in the early 1980s.[8] Prior to 1989, no NATO strategist could have imagined that it would be thousands of Trabant-loads of East

German workers and shoppers, not Soviet tanks, that would soon come pouring into the West.

The Berlin Wall separated the colorful, vibrant, free world of capitalism from the austere, gray, forbidding world of communism. This was an obvious cliché, and yet it struck any tourist visiting for the first time as a stunning personal revelation. The actual physical city of Berlin may have seemed remote to most Americans at the end of the 1980s, but it remained deeply rooted in the subconscious of a range of generations: Some were old enough to have fought there or fled from there. Some were just old enough to remember John F. Kennedy's *"Ich bin ein Berliner"* speech there. And some were young enough to have just seen *The Spy Who Came In from the Cold* for the first time on late-night TV. When Richard Burton ends up hit in a hail of machine-gun fire after he and his naive communist lover have attempted to scale the Wall, the message of the imagery comes through loud and clear, even from the murk of John le Carré's morally ambivalent world: The Wall is what makes *us* different from *them*. Only on *their* side of this wall do they kill people who seek to escape. Kennedy had put it well: "Freedom has many difficulties and democracy is not perfect, but we have never had to put a wall up to keep our people in."

Perhaps Sigmund Freud, who himself had fled from Hitler's closing noose in Vienna half a century earlier, would have understood the Berlin events better than the politicians or military strategists. Revisiting and confronting the scene of the modern world's primal nightmare, Berliners were collectively beginning to heal themselves and the world after four decades of postwar schizophrenia. What took place in Berlin on November 9, 1989, was a long-delayed version of what had happened in Times Square forty-four years earlier. The war was over and the people celebrated. Berliners set about the process of making whole again that which had been so traumatically divided.

The television coverage of the night of November 9 "changed the American image of the Germans," writes Peter Schneider, the West Berlin author of the powerful novel *Wall Jumper*. "The West German 'economic miracle' brought a kind of bloodless respect, but by its very nature—*economic* news—it could never seriously overcome the black-and-white pictures of the Nazis extending their arms to greet Hitler. Perhaps November 9 was the first time since the war that the Germans encountered American—even worldwide—affection. . . . The hated Nazi German and the tedious, if possibly respected, economic-miracle

German were joined in the mind of foreigners by the warm, sympathetic German!''[9]

Perhaps Schneider overstates the case. Some Americans, as well as many Europeans, Soviets, and others, will remain distrustful of a reunified Germany and less than affectionate toward Germans for a long time to come. Nothing can erase the world's collective memory of the Nazis, and nothing should. But the television reports on Berlin did serve to take Germany from the far periphery of the American mind, put it on center stage, and make it instantly "hot." One didn't have to fall in love with this newly visible Germany to recognize its new importance.

The coming together of the two Berlins symbolized the vibrancy of German society and, more widely, of Europe as well. The human energies and talents that would be devoted to fulfilling the arduous demands of both Germany's and Europe's unification would amply demonstrate the commanding new competitive capabilities of German and European capitalism. Germany's confidence and readiness to take on the myriad challenges before it were indicative of its status as a rising superpower.

THE WALL BETWEEN TRUTH AND FALSEHOOD

Egon Krenz was a lifelong communist bureaucrat who, for a brief moment in 1989, thought he could become an East German Gorbachev. His personal record was bound up with the hated secret police, but by refusing to fire on demonstrators in Leipzig and allowing the Wall to be opened, he believed he might be able to remain in power and preside, like Gorbachev (whose blessings he had obtained), over the gradual evolution of East Germany into a reformed socialist state.

But history was already moving too fast. Reform had lost its appeal; only a total break with the past was acceptable. Krenz was swept out of power almost as soon as he had appeared—after forty-six days, to be exact. (An edition of *Time* went to bed on Friday, December 1, 1989, touting the first interview with Krenz by an American magazine.[10] By the time it hit the newsstands the next Monday, Krenz had been toppled, and demonstrators in Leipzig were ridiculing his absurdly short-lived tenure with signs that said, "Who Was Egon Krenz?")

Yet Krenz apparently learned something from the experience. In his memoir, *When Walls Fall,* he observed that it was not just the Berlin Wall which had fallen, but "the walls between the people and the leadership, and between truth and falsehood."[11] The communists had always claimed to represent the interests of 99 percent of the people. Barely five months after the Wall fell, they found themselves competing in East Germany's first freely contested electoral battle—in which they could capture no more than 16 percent of the vote.

The old falsehoods lay glaringly exposed in the brilliant lights of the Western videocameras. The new truths, however, had yet to be determined. The depth of the infrastructure of lies supporting communism in Eastern Europe became shockingly apparent. The stories began to emerge of sumptuous hunting lodges for Honecker and his cronies, of the despised Madame Honecker's regular shuttle to Paris for the sake of her coiffure, of the Stasi's secret police files containing detailed information on millions of citizens. Soon, similar tales were coming from other Eastern European capitals: the gold-plated bathrooms and X-rated videos of the Ceauşescus, the cities polluted beyond human habitation, the thousands of Romanian children infected with AIDS. For all the things that communism's critics had surmised or guessed at, there was now disgusting and horrifying proof.

"The worst thing is that we are living in a decayed moral environment. We have become morally ill, because we have become accustomed to saying one thing and thinking another." Václav Havel, the new president of Czechoslovakia, offered this assessment of his nation's malady in an address delivered on New Year's Day, 1990. It was the only speech by a leader anywhere, East or West, to attempt to set a visionary moral agenda for the new decade. Not since Abraham Lincoln's second inaugural address, declared *Newsweek,* had a head of state delivered such a searching moral statement. Havel continued:

> We have learned not to believe in anything, not to care about one another and only to look after ourselves. Notions such as love, friendship, compassion, humility and forgiveness have lost their depth and dimension, and for many of us they represent merely some kind of psychological idiosyncrasy, or appear as some kind of stray relic from times past, something rather comical in the era of computers and space rockets. . . . The previous regime . . . denigrated man into a production force and nature into a production tool. In this way it attacked the very essence of the relationship between them. It made talented people . . . into cogs in some kind of monstrous, ramshackle, smelly machine whose purpose no one can understand.[12]

A few weeks later, Havel would receive a tumultuous standing ovation as he told the U.S. Congress that all nations must "escape from the rather antiquated straitjacket of a bipolar view of the world and . . . enter at last into a period of multipolarity, that is, into an era in which all of us—large and small, former slaves and former masters—will be able to create what Abraham Lincoln called the 'family of man.' " Then he noted pointedly, "The only genuine backbone of all our actions, if they are to be moral, is responsibility. Responsibility to something higher than my family, my country, my firm, my success. . . ."

Havel had intended to draw attention to the utter lack of morality that had afflicted Czechoslovakia and the other Soviet bloc nations for so long. But no one who heard him could help but sense that he was referring to the less heinous Western moral deficiencies as well. Your own vision in the West, Havel seemed to be saying, can no longer be shaped by the simple anti-Sovietism of the Cold War. You have given your people prosperity, opportunity, and shopping malls crammed with consumer goods—"success." But even we who lack those things know it is not enough. Your societies too feel a spiritual void and a loss of meaning. You have not polluted your rivers and forests as badly as the communists, but you have polluted the earth just the same. You have not strayed as far from your ideals as the communists have from theirs, but remember, you are no Abraham Lincolns, either. You, too, need a new moral vision.

It would take time for the West to appreciate what Havel had hinted at. Even today, after gaining considerably more perspective and experiencing life in the post-postwar world for a while, we are only just beginning to understand. What happened in Berlin and in all the Eastern European revolutions that followed happened, of course, to *them*. But the impact on *us*—on our systems, our institutions, our economies, on the way we live and think—will be enormous.

POLITICS NOT AS USUAL

One visible legacy of the end of the postwar era has been the questions it has raised about traditional politics. Both the Democrats and the Republicans in the United States—as well as other leading political parties in many other countries—recognize that the "Soviet threat" and varying assessments of how to wage the Cold War have been central to election campaigns and political coalition-building for most of recent memory.

Now that substantive issues about the New Europe, the new world economy, and the new world security order are manifesting themselves daily, old political alignments are fracturing. In the United States, isolationism, although still a minority current, is gaining its first serious political following since World War I. In Japan, conversely, ideas about expanding the country's military role, although still opposed by most Japanese, are more openly discussed than at any time since World War II. In Europe, the issue of a Western European defense union is emerging as a new political touchstone.

The prospect of a post–Cold War "peace dividend" in the United States has been temporarily overwhelmed by the high and unexpected costs of the Middle East deployment. Eventually, however, the issue of defense-spending priorities will be renewed as it becomes painfully evident that the United States can ill afford to maintain current levels of military preparedness against the Soviet Union *as well as* new levels of preparedness against future Saddam Husseins.

Does the Pentagon continue devoting the lion's share of its defense spending to manpower, missile systems, and bases designed principally to prevent Soviet aggression in Europe? Should Washington push Germany and Japan to contribute more heavily to the cause of collective security? If American military deployments are to be heavily underwritten by European and Japanese money, will American soldiers end up as the Hessians of the 1990s? Should Japan take over American military responsibilities in East Asia? Should the United States look favorably on a Western European defense union? What are the consequences in Europe and Asia of encouraging Germany and Japan to increase their ability to project military power beyond their borders? What value is NATO as a pillar of American defense strategy if future conflicts are increasingly likely to be outside the Alliance's authorized zone of activity? Do politically valuable collective security commitments of money and troops from other nations end up precluding the American military machinery from operating effectively in combat? All these good questions—and many others along the same line—defy traditional partisan pigeonholing and will likely lead to a proliferation of new political alliances as they are pursued. Everyone knows the Cold War assumptions are out of date, but few even dare to suggest what the new assumptions should be.

"Every night for forty years we walked into the bedroom, opened the closet and looked under the bed to see if we could find a communist. And one day we walked in, and he was in our bed, smiling. It's very confusing," acknowledged Congressman Dante B. Fascell, a Florida Democrat. Republican Party master strategist Lee Atwater was just as mindful of the changed circumstances: "If our candidates are foolish enough to campaign as if the Cold War were still on they'll get hurt," he admitted. And William Bodie, a key fund-raiser for conservative groups that figured prominently in American politics in the 1980s, observed, "The collapse of communism also means the collapse of a lot of the glue that has connected the various strands of the conservative movement."[13]

The Cold War "imparted a clarifying logic to American foreign policy that will now be missing," writes Charles William Maynes, the editor of *Foreign Policy*. "As the Cold War ends, therefore, American foreign policy will lose more than its enemy. *It will lose the sextant by which the ship of state has been guided since 1945*." In such an environment, Maynes warns, misjudgments in shaping tomorrow's world will not merely revive "costly Cold War stability," but could lead to "even more costly interwar *instability*."[14]

John J. Mearsheimer, chairman of the political science department at the University of Chicago, suspects that such instability is inevitable: "The prospect of major crises, even wars, in Europe is likely to increase now that the Cold War is receding into history." From the Peace of Westphalia in 1648 through to the end of World War II in 1945, Europe was characterized by multipolarity, he maintains; the result was that, the "European state system was plagued by war from first to last." Multipolarity led to fifty million deaths in European wars between 1900 and 1945, whereas the bipolarity of the postwar era claimed a scant fifteen thousand lives in Europe, according to Mearsheimer's calculations. "Europe," he worries, "is returning to a state system that created powerful incentives for aggression in the past."[15]

In retrospect, it is amazing that the world somehow survived four decades teetering atop a precarious U.S.-Soviet balance of terror. The bipolar world order, with its nuclear weapons and the assumptions inherent in the doctrine of Mutually Assured Destruction (MAD), provided the fear and discipline necessary to keep the world remarkably stable—in security terms—even as it underwent wrenching, ever-accelerating political, economic, and social change in recent years.

Although the world thought it had become accustomed to rapid change in the 1980s, nothing prepared it for the events of the second half of 1989. At the end of a decade widely believed to have been apolitical, more than a decade's worth of political developments suddenly exploded in the space of a few months.

History was moving faster than even the best-trained observers believed possible. In an October 30, 1989, report from Germany, *Business Week* cautioned its readers, "Change may come to East Berlin. But its pace will be *painfully slow.*"[16] Ten days later, of course, *everything* had changed in East Berlin.

Foreign experts at first couldn't believe that East Germans, conditioned by the rhetoric as well as the reality of the socialist welfare state for most of their lives, would reject socialism completely when given the chance to vote freely. That they would reject communism was obvious. But outside observers made a logical case for why East Germans would find the kinder, gentler thinking of West Germany's Social Democratic Party more appealing than the hard-driving conservatism of Helmut Kohl and his Christian Democratic Union–Christian Social Union coalition. The operating assumption was that human beings in their millions simply don't change their minds that completely that fast. Carl Bernstein, an American journalist who, by reputation, ought to have been able to investigate the truth beneath any surface reality, reported in January 1990 that he "could hardly find any citizens who said they wanted a reunified, single Germany." According to Bernstein, East Germans "love their country—the German Democratic Republic, not the Federal Republic of the West. They believe in socialism. Still."[17]

But Bernstein and many others were wrong. A few weeks later, East Germans rejected not just the communists but the Social Democrats and all the softer leftists as well. They voted overwhelmingly for the Christian Democrats, who represented the most rapid possible path to unity with West Germany.

Even after Berlin, after Sofia, and after Prague, many in the West still refused to believe what their eyes and ears were telling them about what was happening in the world—as evidenced by the many experts who doubted similar change would occur in Bucharest. On November 25, 1989—two weeks after the fall of the Wall—*The New York Times* ran a story under the headline "In Romania, the Old Order Won't Budge." But just one month later, on Christmas day, the chief of the old order that wouldn't budge was captured and arrested. Now the *Times* dutifully proclaimed, "New Leaders Promise Fair Trial" for Ceauşescu. To most American newspaper readers, the idea of a "fair trial" connoted a long extensive process. This story, however, was all over by morning: "Army Executes Ceauşescu and Wife for Genocide Role," said the next day's banner headline.[18]

The new unpredictability of global events is related, of course, not only to the new speed at which they are unfolding but also to the new speed with which information about these events—statements and counterstatements, actions and reactions—is diffused. Yet our inability to accurately predict developments also stems from our lack of experience with the new era we have entered. We have not yet developed any post-postwar models to explain the forces now at work. And if we rely for our forecasting on the old models inherited from the earlier era, we will surely get the wrong answers.

To borrow a metaphor from the technology central to the Information Age, it is as if the world in the late 1980s began running on a much faster set of computer chips. But the software to control this new superfast hardware and take maximum advantage of the new possibilities it presents has yet to be written. "Change in the '90s will make the '80s look like a picnic—a walk in the park," predicts the man reputed to be the American business community's toughest-minded manager, John F. Welch, Jr., CEO of General Electric.[19]

Global nuclear war between the superpowers may be less likely than ever. But regional military conflicts and other kinds of power struggles threaten international stability in new ways, especially because the overarching security discipline of the postwar era is gone. This is true particularly in the Middle East, where major portions of the world economy are tethered to relatively weak and fractious governments, but it also applies to a number of other global hot spots.

Military conflict is not the only possibility threatening global stability. The lack of an agreed-upon new world order to replace the old also increases the potential for what former U.S. Commerce Secretary Peter G. Peterson calls "the economic version of MAD." In this scenario, nations and regions use trade, technology, and financial policy to fire economic missiles and to retaliate against one another. Without new thinking, new institutions, and creative responses to the challenges ahead—new software, in short—Peterson warns that "what could have been a glorious period of improved East-West relations and expansion of global markets and trade in the 1990s could become a postmodern dark age instead."

QUESTIONS REPLACE ANSWERS

Even as graffiti-covered chunks of the Berlin Wall were being carried away, a number of questions about the geopolitical future of the world were beginning to loom, replacing the simple answers of only days before:

Would a reunified Germany content itself with amalgamating East and West, or would it seek to reclaim other parts of its prewar territory? The possibility of an attempt to incorporate other German-speaking peoples from neighboring countries was not purely a paranoid fantasy of Germany's former victims. "West Germany's chancellor, Mr. Helmut Kohl, is neither a bully nor a madman, though . . . he has done a passable impersonation of both," intoned the normally reserved *Economist*.[20] Kohl had just sent shock waves through Europe by hinting that he did not necessarily accept the Oder-Neisse line as Germany's border with Poland. Later, he retracted this position. But the thought that Germany's boundaries might once again be disputed was enough to frighten even those who normally defended the Federal Republic as a pillar of democracy and stability.

What would be the impact on the world economic system as West Germany, a key capital-surplus nation with low inflation and a strong currency, undertook the task of rebuilding East Germany, a capital-intensive project that might ultimately result in inflation, rising interest rates, and volatility for the deutsche mark? The instability of the financial markets in the early part of 1990 did not encourage optimism, as the events in Germany led to a massive sell-off of stocks in Tokyo and a global race to raise interest rates.

Could Germany's new nationalist stirrings and economic vigor be given room to develop without triggering the kind of military conflicts which had pitted Germany against its European neighbors three times before in the three-quarters of a century from 1870 to 1945? "In the new, proud, united Germany, the nationalists will proclaim the Fourth Reich," predicted Conor Cruise O'Brien, giving voice to one of the world's most deep-seated if least-expressed fears. "I can see some of the consequences: expulsion of Jews . . . a statue of Hitler in every town."[21]

Would a reunified Germany remain a member of NATO? "Out of the question," declared Mikhail Gorbachev, desperately holding on to one of his last bargaining chips. A few months later, he and Helmut Kohl would strike a deal allowing the new Germany to stay in NATO in return for massive German economic support for Moscow. But that was by no means the end of the issue; Oskar Lafontaine, governor of the Saarland and Kohl's most formidable political challenger at the time, announced, "Kohl is wrong if he thinks Germany can stay in NATO."[22]

If Germany exited NATO, could the alliance survive? In any event, how much longer would the American military presence be necessary or welcome in Europe? And if U.S. troops and weapons were withdrawn, might not a militarily weak Europe someday fall victim to Soviet aggression—if not instigated by Gorbachev, then by a hard-line successor trying to keep control of the Kremlin by waving the flag of militarism?

Even if there was no chance that German reunification would call forth a new Hitler, didn't the prospect of a stronger, more nationalistic Germany threaten the tidy balance of European political forces in other, more subtle ways? As Charles Krauthammer put it in an essay discounting fears of German military revanchism or economic hegemony, the more realistic concern is that German reunification could "reverse one of the most salutary European developments of the last fifty years: the decline of sovereignty. German reunification will constitute the most dramatic rebirth of sovereignty in the postwar era. . . . [Germany] will begin to act in accord with its new power . . . with the kind of assertiveness . . . that characterizes the other great powers, notably the United States and the Soviet Union. . . . We return . . . to the old Europe, balance of power Europe, the Europe that produces more history than it can consume."[23]

Would the EC's grand plan for 1992 be derailed or destroyed by West Germany's new focus on integrating East Germany? European Commission vice president Sir Leon Brittan, speaking in Washington in the spring of 1990, refused to entertain any such doubts: "Nothing that has happened in Eastern Europe should dissuade us from our task of completing the 1992 program and nothing shall." But European business leaders were less certain. Jacques Calvet, president of Peugeot, Europe's third-largest automaker, appealed to Brussels to halt the 1992 process until changes in the East could be digested. "It would be wild madness to continue calmly writing pieces of paper and making directives," Calvet asserted. "Directives to do what? What is the common future? I don't know."[24] The acid-penned French intellectual–turned–investment banker Alain Minc was succinct on this subject: The European Community's "dream died on November 9," he declared.[25]

Would Margaret Thatcher's Britain, routinely accused of foot-dragging by the EC leaders in Brussels, now find in Germany's preoccupation with reunification a pretext for further severing itself from the EC?

Could the EC's plan for a single currency—the economic and political linchpin of the 1992 debate in the months preceding the opening of the Wall—continue to proceed as hoped if the Bundesbank, Europe's monetary center of gravity, became enmeshed in the difficult and costly effort to achieve intra-German monetary union first?

What would happen in countries such as Portugal and Spain, where support for 1992 was conditioned by the expectation of hefty West German economic aid and investment, if Germany's money now flowed to East Germany and Eastern Europe instead? What would become of southern Europe's key competitive advantage in the 1992 package—its low-cost labor—if Western European business began to tap the more disciplined, better-skilled, and even cheaper labor pools of Eastern Europe?

Would the need to make protective exceptions for East Germany and other potential new EC members emerging from socialist economies reverse the trend toward free-trading, procompetition policies in the EC as a whole? Even British leaders, who had frequently criticized the 1992 program's less-than-wholehearted commitment to free trade, began to sound protectionist. Said Foreign Secretary Douglas Hurd, "The rest of us will need protection from the entry into our markets of subsidized East German goods."[26] Would this new round of discussion revive the wider European protectionist tendencies that had earlier led Americans and Japanese to worry about the dangers of a "fortress Europe"?

Would the positive elements of the reemerging Eastern European nationalisms—so forceful that they called to mind the "Springtime of Nations" of the European revolutions of 1848—be overshadowed by their darker energies? Would Eastern nations that had been held together by the iron rule of communist dictatorships now splinter apart under the pressure of age-old rivalries—Czechs versus Slovaks, Bulgarians versus Turks, Hungarians versus Romanians—that had made the geographical term "Balkans" synonymous with fractured nations? And if that happened, would the process infect Western Europe, where it was only recently that nationalist groups like the Basques in Spain had begun to relent in their radical and separatist demands? "Our unity in the West is hard won and still surprisingly fragile," warned former French Foreign Minister Jean François-Poncet. "If balkanization occurs in the East, its poison may not be so easily contained there."

While the opening of the Berlin Wall generated a great deal of speculation about the future of Europe, the questions raised were by no means confined to that continent. In fact, some of the issues with the widest potential repercussions actually concerned those farthest from the epicenter of the quake:

How would the world adapt to the end of the bipolar structure, the blurring of the once clear-cut division between East and West, and the ensuing era of multipolarity? What did it mean that first Japan and now Germany had become new superpowers by shunning the arms race and the ideological disputes of the last two generations to focus instead on economics, finance, trade, and technology? And where exactly did that leave the United States and the Soviet Union, which had both made such huge, nationally bankrupting investments in the arms race?

What would be the future of the increasingly unhappy relationship between the United States and Japan, absent the harmonizing bottom line of a common assessment of the Soviet threat and the need to stand together against it? Would there be an inevitable American psychological desire to replace the Russians with the Japanese as chief enemy? Would the Japanese find the changed situation in the Soviet Union and Europe a basis for new alliances, partnerships, and business deals at America's expense?

If thriving parts of the industrial world such as Europe and Japan no longer needed America's nuclear umbrella, would they necessarily grow less receptive to American leadership in other areas of multilateral concern? What would become of the postwar institutional framework—GATT, the IMF, and the U.S. dollar's role as global key currency, to mention but a few of its pillars—which rested so heavily on the assumption of American leadership in a world dedicated to triumphing over the Soviet threat? And what would happen in the increasingly large areas of the third world left behind by economic development, as both Washington and Moscow lost interest in extending aid to poorer countries as a way of vying for influence and extending their client bases?

Perhaps most disturbing of all was this question: Was the world being naive in believing that military power would diminish in importance and that the end of the Cold War meant an age of peace? Hadn't the eve of World War I as well as World War II also been filled with talk of the permanence of peace?

"THE ENEMY IS UNPREDICTABILITY"

When the Berlin Wall went up in 1961, the United States and the Soviet Union were at the apex of their might as global superpowers. Few people outside Germany remember what the German political figures of those days said and did. What the world remembers is the rhetoric and imagery of the Americans and the Soviets, of Kennedy and Khrushchev.

The early 1960s was a time when John F. Kennedy could credibly speak of the United States being willing to "pay any price, bear any burden, meet any hardship, support any friend, and oppose any foe," without Congress debating the fiscal constraints of such commitments. In the deepest frost of the Cold War, the young American president went right into the thick of the crowds and, standing on the steps of the West Berlin city hall, denounced those who built the Wall. Declaring that "all free men, wherever they may live, are citizens of Berlin," he galvanized West Berlin, West Germany, Western Europe, and the entire Western world behind his leadership in what he depicted as a global freedom struggle.

The early 1960s was also a time when a bullying remark by Nikita Khrushchev—"We will bury you"—was taken seriously enough for Western experts to debate whether he meant that the Soviet Union would surpass the U.S. economically, or bury America under a nuclear cloud. Khrushchev could taunt Kennedy with predictions that West Berlin would fall "like a ripe apple from a tree"—leaving it vague whether that meant Soviet military annexation or a Kremlin-engineered set of political events that would enclose West Berlin in the surrounding East German landscape. The point was that Khrushchev controlled events on his side of the Wall. He had the power and no one doubted that he might use it.

Twenty-eight years later, however, one of the most salient aspects of the fall of the Berlin Wall was how little control over the process either Washington or Moscow had. As in the old Sherlock Holmes story, the curious thing about the superpowers in the night of November 9 was that they did nothing in the night of November 9. Gorbachev's most important action was simply choosing not to act. Making a virtue of necessity, he converted his fundamental inability to act into a "policy of nonintervention" that won him the acclaim of the world.

As for George Bush, supporters as well as critics were stunned by his seeming detachment and lack of emotion before an event which, theoretically, was a great victory for American foreign policy. For twenty-eight years, Washington had insisted that the Wall be torn down. From Kennedy's *"Ich bin ein Berliner"* to Reagan's "Mr. Gorbachev, tear down this wall!" American leaders had emphatically demanded what George Bush was now getting.

"I just can't believe it," said Republican Congressman Frank Wolf. "I took my kids to see the Berlin Wall when we were in Germany. Now, they see it coming down on television, and they're thrilled. They see it as a spectacular victory for freedom and democracy. Meanwhile, Bush is practically silent. My kids understand what's happening better than the president does!"

A *Wall Street Journal* report contemptuously derided Bush: "The television screens this weekend flickered with the images of American leaders uttering bold, inspiring words about Berlin. But those leaders were John F. Kennedy and Ronald Reagan. George Bush, by contrast, presided over the most dramatic turn in East-West relations in more than 40 years sitting behind his desk, looking at a map of Germany and saying . . . 'I'm just not an emotional guy.' "[27]

As an event that symbolized the triumph of the human spirit and celebrated the role of individuals taking history into their own hands, the fall of the Wall certainly deserved better than it received from George Bush. But in the president's impassive response there may have been more self-knowledge and a more sober assessment of reality than those who criticized him were prepared to accept. He admitted he lacked "the vision thing." His administration, former UN Ambassador Jeane J. Kirkpatrick noted, possessed "an avowed aversion to 'big think.' "[28]

One senior Bush administration official, speaking candidly about the rapidly changing situation in the East, confided, "I have spent my entire grown-up life not knowing the difference between Latvia, Lithuania and Estonia. There was never any reason to think about them."[29] Raymond G. H. Seitz, the U.S. Assistant Secretary of State for European Affairs, put the case equally frankly: "Bureaucracies are meant to operate within a framework. In terms of European policy we have had that framework established for a very long time. There was NATO, the Warsaw Pact, the Wall, the spending levels. They were all thought to be immutable. The bureaucracy is not like academe, where you are trained to question assumptions. . . . Now everything is back to square one. Nothing is immutable. It requires a total intellectual retooling."[30]

Every American foreign-policy goal of 1949 was being realized in a sudden surge of good news: An economically strong, united Europe was on the rise, Germany was reunifying, and Eastern Europe and the Soviet Union were de-communizing and democratizing. The trouble was, this was 1989, not 1949. What may have been so clearly in American interests four decades earlier was less clearly so now. Without a large measure of vision, and without some desire to engage in "big think," it would be hard to exchange the comfortable fixed realities of the postwar period for the new questions, instabilities, and chaos ahead.

The fall of the Berlin Wall was the birth trauma of a new era. The future it presages demands an activist, creative reevaluation of existing beliefs and a dramatic reconfiguring of existing institutions. For those wishing to cling to the nostalgic notion that America is still the world leader and can continue to be without submitting itself to the challenge of change, the events in Berlin were nothing to get excited about. They were to be more feared than welcomed.

Coming down from Camp David after a weekend meeting with Chancellor Kohl over the issue of German reunification, George Bush was asked who the "enemy" was in today's world if it was no longer the Soviet Union. "The enemy is unpredictability," responded the president. "The enemy is instability."[31]

It had been easier to fight the predictable, stable Soviets for the last forty-five years than it would be to fight the amorphous forces of "unpredictability" and "instability" in the years ahead. America, in fact, had become an old Cold Warrior of a nation, highly skilled at Russian-fighting. But a different set of skills, priorities, and concepts is required for leadership in the twenty-first century. Summoning up the right stuff from the wellsprings of America's rich national character to cope with an inherently—and perhaps increasingly—unpredictable and unstable world is now a crucial task for contemporary American leadership.

It is more than a little ironic that the old, tradition-bound societies of Japan and Germany, with their reputations for inflexibility and rigidity, are beginning to appear more readily adaptable to the demands of the new era than the young, dynamic United States, with its reputation for flexibility and easy acceptance of change.

In Berlin, the tectonic plates of history came together. And when the Wall fell, the Euroquake began: a sudden, shocking upheaval in the world balance of power. The superpowers were no longer as all-powerful as they had once been, and new powers were on the rise. The Euroquake was centered in Germany, but the ruptures, aftershocks, and tidal waves it engendered were headed for every corner of the globe.

=3

The Hidden History of the Third World War

Yes, there are still two superpowers in the world. But they are no longer the United States and the Soviet Union. The new superpowers are Japan and Germany.

JEAN-JACQUES SERVAN-SCHREIBER

WINNERS AND LOSERS

It was not just that World War II and the U.S.-Soviet Cold War had finally ended in Berlin in 1989. Another war was also winding down. This was a war at once undeclared and yet global. It was a war in which the body count was low but the economic and political impact enormous. It was a war so subtle that leaders everywhere could credibly deny it had even happened, yet so complex that the world may need the rest of this century to negotiate the terms of its peace. It was a cold war within the Cold War. It was fought more or less throughout the 1980s. It was, from a functional point of view, the Third World War.

The big "winners" of the Third World War were Japan and Germany—the very powers which had been the losers of World War II.

Also among the winners were some of the European and East Asian countries which had been nominal victors in World War II, but only after massive suffering at the hands of Nazi Germany or Imperial Japan. By holding their noses, taking the plunge of geo-realism, and aligning economically with their much-chastened enemies from four decades earlier, Western Europeans as well as East Asians emerged again as winners in the Third World War—with far more to show for their triumph this time around.

The big "losers" of the Third World War were the United States and the Soviet Union—the very powers which not only won World War II but became leaders of vast empires and blocs as a result. The Soviet defeat was obvious and total. Its post–Third World War future looks extremely bleak. America's defeat, on the other hand, was only partial. It left the country in a situation not unlike that of Japan and Germany after World War II. Although sectors of the American economy lay vanquished by foreign competition and in near-ruins at the end of the 1980s, the basis for revival was still solid. The necessary condition was an American public- and private-sector leadership willing to pursue in the 1990s policies as farsighted and self-disciplined as those of Germany and Japan in the 1950s and '60s.

A DECADE OF ROLE REVERSALS AND RADICAL CHANGE

The realignments and shifts of power that occurred between 1980 and 1990 were of the magnitude that has historically been associated with great wars. Insofar as American and Soviet power are concerned, the 1980s resembled nothing so much as a replay of World War II and its outcome—*only this time in reverse*. Let us recall for a moment just how radical the changes of the 1980s were with respect to economic power and global leadership, first for the United States and then for the Soviet Union:

Early '80s: The United States was the world's largest creditor nation.

End of the '80s: The United States became the largest debtor nation in history. Japan, meanwhile, replaced the U.S. as the world's leading creditor, with West Germany second.

Early '80s: Japan and the United States both suffered modest trade *deficits,* while West Germany's traditional trade surplus was reduced nearly to zero as a result of the oil crisis that followed the Iranian revolution.

End of the '80s: Japan and Germany were neck and neck in the race to enjoy the world's biggest trade *surplus.* Their positive annual trade balances have ranged from $70 billion to nearly $100 billion in recent years—far, far ahead of any other nation's. The United States, meanwhile, has consistently posted staggering annual trade deficits in the $100–170 billion range.

Early '80s: Despite a growing appetite for imported foreign goods, the U.S. was still the world's largest exporting nation.

End of the '80s: West Germany, with a work force less than one-fourth the size of America's, caught up to the United States as the world's leading exporting nation in absolute terms. German workers were out-exporting Americans four-to-one.

Early '80s: The United States dominated world trade in services and enjoyed a huge net surplus in its global investment income account.

End of the '80s: In the second quarter of 1989, the United States moved into net deficit in its global investment and services income account for the first time in modern economic history, as the weight of foreign debt service began to be felt. "More of our income in the future will go to service our debt rather than to our investment," commented policy analyst Pat Choate as this historic watershed was passed. "It means our standard of living will decline."[1] Japan and Germany, ever the obverse of the U.S., emerged in the late 1980s as large surplus countries in their global service and investment activities.

Early '80s: Americans invested twice as much abroad as foreigners invested in the United States.

End of the '80s: Foreign investors—principally European and Japanese—invested almost exactly twice as much in the U.S. as Americans invested abroad in 1989.

Early '80s: Western Europe was mired in deep economic stagnation. Its growth rates trailed America's by 1–3 percent annually.

End of the '80s: European growth rates moved consistently ahead of America's. In the fourth quarter of 1989, the annualized rate of growth for U.S. GNP was a paltry 1.1 percent, compared with 4.1 percent in West Germany and 4.3 percent in France. By early 1990, Japanese and German growth rates were both in the double digits—ten times higher than American levels.

Early '80s: The rise of the "little dragons" of Asia, such as South Korea and Taiwan, was greeted in the United States as a victory for American capitalism in the fight for ideological influence against the powerful tide of Asian communism. China was expected to be a great new market for American business.

End of the '80s: The little dragons emulated Japanese-style capitalism. Japan, not the United States, became the leading foreign investor and trading partner in almost every East Asian country, including China. The "little dragons" developed their own significant trade surpluses with the United States, as well as competitive technology-intensive industries. Korea now makes the world's microwave ovens and Singapore its disk drives. Like the Japanese, other Asians began to use financial power to acquire American companies and assets.

Early '80s: The two largest banks in the world were American—Citicorp and Chase Manhattan.

End of the '80s: The world's *ten* largest banks were all Japanese, while the biggest non-Japanese banks were French and German.[2] Citicorp, the biggest American bank, ranked only twenty-sixth in the world and was teetering on the brink of insolvency.

Early '80s: The U.S. dollar was worth over 260 Japanese yen and 3.1 deutsche marks at various points in the first half of the decade.

End of the '80s: The dollar had fallen as low as 123 yen and 1.6 deutsche marks.

Early '80s: American companies on the New York Stock Exchange represented more than half the world's stock market equity, while the Tokyo Stock Exchange represented less than one-fifth. Frankfurt was an inconsequential backwater for all but the most specialized international investors.

End of the '80s: Tokyo surpassed New York in market capitalization in 1987. Frankfurt emerged as the hottest stock exchange of 1989 and the most important new market to watch.

Early '80s: The American economy was seen as the global "locomotive." American economic trends set the agenda for the world economy—sometimes causing "shocks" in Japan and Europe.

End of the '80s: Japan and Germany were increasingly acknowledged to be the leading stimulators of the rest of the world's economy. The U.S. government became reliant on Japanese and European investors to finance a third or more of Washington's annual budget deficit. "Fed Has Lost Much of Its Power to Sway U.S. Interest Rates," declared one *Wall Street Journal* headline at the beginning of the 1990s. The article went on to explain that the power to set rates "is slipping away to markets in Tokyo and Frankfurt. As the Fed loses leverage, the U.S. is losing some of its control over its economic destiny."[3]

Early '80s: The U.S. was far and away the world's leading donor nation in dispensing international development aid.

End of the '80s: Japan became the number-one donor nation; the European Community, taken as a group, superseded both Japan and the U.S.

Early '80s: Americans enjoyed veto power over the postwar system of multilateral economic organizations such as the International Monetary Fund (IMF).

End of the '80s: The most important new multilateral organization to appear on the scene was the European Bank for Reconstruction and Development. The bank's purpose was to coordinate economic assistance to Eastern Europe. Washington found itself isolated within the group over issues such as how much aid should go to the Soviet Union. "For the first time in the postwar period, Washington is participating in the establishment of a multilateral lending institution that it will not control—reflecting the decline of this country's relative global weight," observed one news account.[4]

Early '80s: The global production of semiconductors was overwhelmingly an American business. About 60 percent of these quintessential building blocks of the Information Age were made by American companies in the United States.

End of the '80s: Japan had taken over as the world's dominant producer of semiconductors, with a 50 percent global market share for all types of semiconductors and as much as 75 percent for certain types of memory chips. Korean and other Asian companies were also serious market players. The European Community had targeted the semiconductor industry as one it would take active policy measures to foster.

Early '80s: Constellations of venture-capital-backed high-tech companies in California's Silicon Valley and on Massachusetts's Route 128 were writing a new chapter in global economic history. American capitalism seemed to be experiencing a renaissance, making a spectacular leap in its ability to innovate technologically, create jobs, and reward a wide spectrum of entrepreneurs with unprecedented wealth. Europeans and Japanese came like pilgrims to see Silicon Valley firsthand and try to figure out how to get similar results in their own countries.

End of the '80s: Some of the top American high-tech corporations went bankrupt; others moved into slow-growth phases, lagging behind traditional industries. Apple Computer, the prototypical Silicon Valley enterprise, went through a traditional boardroom struggle to oust founder Steve Jobs and get the company back into the mainstream. But its markets were contracting and global competition was heating up. Jobs, who moved on to found a new high-tech company, NEXT, was now an experienced veteran of American technology. "Will there even be a U.S. computer industry ten years from now? I'd say the odds are only fifty-fifty," he lamented.[5] Venture capital, so readily available in the early

1980s, was drying up by the end of the decade. An increasing amount of what *was* available came from Asian and European investors. Genentech, the South San Francisco–based company that had launched the biotechnology revolution, sold a majority interest to the Swiss parent company of pharmaceutical giant Hoffmann–La Roche to raise the capital to remain competitive. "European government ministers used to visit Silicon Valley in search of its secrets of success. Today, the boot is on the other foot," noted a British observer at the end of 1989. "As the U.S. semiconductor industry struggles to regain its international competitiveness, industry leaders are looking to Europe and Japan for a model upon which to base their efforts."[6]

Early '80s: Although the state of American education was already the focus of much criticism, the United States was widely viewed as the world's most advanced and capable society in terms of meeting the new requirements posed by technology and the Information Age.

End of the '80s: American high school test scores in math and science trailed those of Japan, most European countries, and even some of the "little dragons" in Asia. Although the U.S. continued to lead the world in spending on higher education, the nation's investment in the K–12 years—arguably the most important part of the learning process—trailed that of Europe and Japan.

Early '80s: With the opening of the Tevatron collider in 1983 at the Fermilab in Illinois, the United States possessed the world's most advanced facility for particle physics research.

End of the '80s: A fourteen-nation European cooperative venture opened the world's largest particle accelerator at the CERN facility outside Geneva in 1989, marking the end of half a century of American leadership in particle physics, dating back to the Manhattan Project. CERN immediately reversed the long-standing "brain drain" in the field of physics: The number of American scientists who left to work at CERN in 1989 exceeded the number of European scientists who came to the U.S. to work.

Early '80s: Despite severe problems in American manufacturing industries, the U.S. still produced more cars than any other country. American technology in areas such as nuclear power generation, jet aircraft production, and telecommunications was far out in front of the rest of the world. Most of the consumer and industrial goods needed by the domestic U.S. market were still manufactured by American companies—79 percent of machine tools, for example, 88 percent of telephones, and 60 percent of televisions.

End of the '80s: Japan surpassed the U.S. in total automobile production. The most modern automobile-assembly facilities *in the United States* were being built by Japanese companies. General Motors' share of the U.S. market fell to an all-time low. The U.S. moved into a deficit in high-technology trade with Japan, and Japanese companies outdid their American rivals even in sensitive areas of technology such as nuclear power generation, composite-materials production, and advanced-aircraft radar. With the lead in technology shifting to Japan, it was no wonder that in industries such as consumer electronics American companies found themselves unable to compete, even as the domestic market for their products exploded. Nor was it just the Japanese who were gobbling up the U.S. market. Big European electronics companies, such as France's Thomson (which bought TV-manufacturing divisions from both RCA and General Electric) and Groupe Bull (which bought Zenith's computer division), and the Dutch Philips (which owned Magnavox), were also succeeding where American companies were failing. By decade's end, Asian and European companies were responsible for 65 percent of machine tools sold in the U.S. domestic market, 75 percent of telephones, and 90 percent of televisions. High-Definition Television (HDTV), potentially a multibillion-dollar industry, was being actively developed in Japan and Europe but not in the United States. This marked the first time in the postwar era that Americans not only didn't lead but were barely present in the development of a new technology. Ian Ross, president of AT&T Bell Labs, the premier private-sector R&D facility in the world, warned that because of HDTV's likely impact on a broad spectrum of other technologies, America's failure to participate in the development race could result in the loss of *two million jobs* and a high-tech trade deficit in the range of *$225 billion* annually by the year 2010.[7]

*   *   *

If America's changed fortunes vis-à-vis its allies and partners in Asia and Europe were astounding, the Soviet Union's changed position with respect to its former "sphere of influence" was even more so:

Early '80s: The Soviet Union was in firm control of its empire. Under the "Brezhnev Doctrine," Moscow sought to *expand* its influence by invading and occupying Afghanistan, supporting Vietnam's invasion of Cambodia, and abetting Cuba's military adventures in Africa and Latin America.

End of the '80s: Practicing what Kremlin spokesman Gennadi Gerasimov called the "Sinatra Doctrine" (letting other countries do things their own way), the Soviets withdrew from virtually every foreign conflict in which they were directly engaged. They started the process of bringing their troops and tanks home from Eastern Europe, and began to shut off the spigot to former proxies such as the Cubans and the Vietnamese.

Early '80s: Any sign of independence in Eastern Europe, such as the rise of Solidarity in Poland, triggered the threat of Soviet intervention. The whole region was locked into the political and economic straitjacket of the Soviet Politburo's *diktat*. The COMECON alliance served principally to enable Moscow to exact tribute from its allies in the form of cheap raw materials and consumer goods.

End of the '80s: Six Eastern European revolutions later, Gerald Ford's absurd gaffe, made during a 1976 presidential campaign debate with Jimmy Carter—"There is no Soviet domination in Eastern Europe"—had become astonishingly true. Local support for traditional communism evaporated almost overnight in 1989. Most Eastern European leaders recommended radically overhauling or altogether scrapping COMECON. Although the process was fraught with dangers, Eastern Europe emerged as the focal point of global experimentation with new economic and political forms.

Early '80s: The Warsaw Pact was purely a rubber stamp for Soviet military and security policies.

End of the '80s: Most members of the Warsaw Pact opposed Gorbachev's policies on cutting-edge issues such as whether or not a reunified Germany could or should stay in NATO. Hungarian leaders not only wanted to leave the Warsaw Pact, they actually expressed a desire to *join NATO instead.*

Early '80s: Outside observers knew that the Soviet Union was still the same "prison house of nations" it had been when Lenin used those words to describe czarist Russia. But few in the West thought it possible that any of the fifteen Soviet republics would ever attempt to break away—let alone succeed in doing so. American support for so-called captive nations such as Estonia, Latvia, and Lithuania came mostly from aging immigrant groups and far-right-wing politicians.

End of the '80s: The Soviet empire was breaking up. Lithuania, Latvia, and Estonia all declared their independence, and nationalist movements were challenging Soviet power in most of the fifteen republics. Even leading Russian thinkers had begun to advocate the breakup of the Soviet Union. "Russia should be the first to separate," proposed economist Vladimir Kvint.[8]

PERESTROIKA FOR AMERICA

As the above account shows, the United States and the Soviet Union both experienced radical changes in their global status in the course of the 1980s. As must be reemphasized in making this comparison, there is no question but that the situation is many orders of magnitude worse in the Soviet Union. The United States does not face the collapse of its economy and the total rejection of its leadership by its allies, as does the Soviet Union. While Gorbachev races against the clock of history, with his job growing more difficult every day, the new global situation holds some promise for the still powerful American economy to renew itself.

Yet there is a reason why *"perestroika"*—a concept that to many seems inextricably bound up with the Soviet experience—has become such a popular word in the vocabulary of American economic commentators. To cite just one small example, *Perestroika for America* is the title of a recent book by Harvard Business School professor George C. Lodge, who warns that unless the United States restructures its business-government relations, it will be unable to transform its technological ability into competitive advantage and will continue its slide into economic and political decline. The point is that although the daily realities of the U.S. and the Soviet Union are worlds apart, both nations need a large-scale overhaul of their institutions, a bold break with economic and political ideas that are no longer working, and an imaginative new agenda of initiatives for the twenty-first century.

The Soviets need *perestroika* because the arrival of the Information Age made it manifestly impossible to remain competitive with an economy based on a completely constricted flow of information. Lenin, Stalin, and Khrushchev had always been able to show progress in "catching up to the West" by being super-industrializers—albeit at great human cost. But postindustrial society has new requirements. Unable to meet them, the Soviet Union has fallen further and further behind the advanced capitalist democracies in the 1970s and '80s.

The United States needs an American version of *perestroika* for a less dire but nonetheless compelling reason: Although still an extraordinarily wealthy and powerful country with high living standards for most of its people, the United States in the Information Age has begun to lose noticeable ground to others practicing advanced capitalist democracy with different emphases, priorities, and strategies, particularly in Asia and Europe.

The idea that America was facing generalized economic decline vis-à-vis other advanced capitalist nations initially met with a great deal of resistance in the business community. By the late 1980s, however, and particularly in the aftermath of the 1987 Wall Street crash—it had become the accepted wisdom that America was in decline relative to its major competitors.

The "decline thesis" has now been around long enough to have become an old truth which new contrarians seek to invalidate. The durability demonstrated by the U.S. economy in the late 1980s has given the new contrarians plenty of grist for their mill. The Wall Street crash of 1987 proved not to be the beginning of an apocalyptic end to the Reagan era's economic expansion. It ended up having less immediate impact on the real economy than experts anticipated. The much-criticized U.S. trade and budget deficits have yet to produce the systemic shock some expected by now—although many economists believe the accumulated damage of the deficits will accentuate recessionary trends and dampen full-throttle recovery throughout the '90s.

Critics of the decline thesis invariably call attention to the fact that the United States had nowhere to go but down from its "unnatural" post–World War II position of global economic dominance. Immediately after the war, in the late 1940s and early 1950s, the U.S. was the only large industrial economy that was still able to function. Under those conditions, the U.S. churned out 40–50 percent of world production. That dominance was inherently unsustainable. Today's American contribution to world output—recently running at just over 20 percent and falling—does not represent decline so much as a return to prewar normalcy, according to the critics of the decline thesis. Don't worry, they say, America isn't getting poorer. It's just that the rest of the world is now back on its feet and getting richer.

This line of reasoning has merit. The case for American decline shouldn't be overstated—yet. It does result in part from a reordering of the abnormal postwar situation. But the "anti-declinists" frequently miss a critical point: Most of the rest of the world was already back on its feet by the 1960s, or the 1970s at the latest. The Japanese, German, and other postwar "economic miracles" were very old news by 1970. The bombed-out steel mills and auto plants had long since been replaced with modern, state-of-the-art facilities.

Yet, until the mid-1980s, no one could come close to matching the United States in developing and commercializing leading-edge technologies and productive processes, or in capital formation, capital market vigor, and global investment clout. There had been some evidence of a competitiveness problem in the 1970s, but it was not until the mid-1980s that the crisis of American competitiveness really struck. Beginning then, and continuing to the present, the issue for at least some American businesses has not been the need to adjust to a more "natural" share of the market. Instead, it has been whether American companies will survive the global competition at all.

In other words, the precipitous erosion of U.S. leadership during the 1980s was indicative of something more than a simple return to a natural order. The pattern of events suggests that specific policy measures and failure to adapt to changing conditions were responsible for the squandering of economic resources in the United States. On the other hand, the implementation of different policies in Japan and Europe, and the willingness in those countries to make radical adaptations, has brought about explosive growth in their competitive power.

THE TURNING POINT: 1985

The bulk of the pioneering work in brand-new Information Age technologies, processes, services, and financial mechanisms has been done and continues to be done in the United States. But it is the Japanese—and now others in East Asia as well as Europe—who are proving to have more staying power in *commercializing* the breakthroughs in these areas, creating economies of scale to dominate the markets and building integrated "food chains" of technology that reinforce existing competitive advantages.

This reality has confounded many experts who based their projections about the American future on the seminal first half of the 1980s, when the most essential Information Age breakthroughs were first being made, when American technological innovation was at its zenith, and when Europe and Japan were still reeling from the aftershocks of the oil crisis. But the contradiction between America's enormous talent for basic innovation and its weakening ability to commercialize its own breakthroughs became inescapable in the second half of the 1980s.

The first few years of Reaganomics produced a short-term spurt of growth that took American capitalism to dizzying new heights. But after 1985, the American system began to pay the long-term—and previously concealed—price for that spurt. The erosion in American competitive powers became increasingly evident, and the new dominance of the Japanese and the Europeans began to come into view.

For Japan as well, 1985 was a decisive turning point. It was then that the Japanese first realized that the rise of the yen (forced on them as a direct result of erroneous Reaganomic thinking about how to deal with the U.S. trade deficit) would necessitate a radical restructuring of their own industries. They could see that if they got that restructuring right, they would gain a new industrial competitive edge. That edge would be enhanced still further by the power of enormously inflated financial resources resulting from the increased value of the yen. And that combination would allow Japan to internationalize its businesses as never before and emerge as a global superpower.

As we saw in chapter 1, 1985 was also the turning point for Europe. It was then that the 1992 project became Europe's conscious answer to its own lack of competitiveness. Suddenly, the United States was fighting a two-fronted economic war with two major competitors, while continuing to escalate its commitment to the Cold War with the Russians.

Something else happened in 1985: The price of oil began a precipitous slide which ended up lasting the rest of the decade. A great deal of the wealth generated in all three parts of the Triad thereafter—the best years of Reaganomics in the U.S., the buildup of financial resources in Japan, and the beginning of Europe's turnaround—was linked at least in part to the falling price of oil. Especially in Japan, but also in Europe, programs to reduce oil consumption and restructure industries continued through the second half of the '80s, even as oil costs fell. In the United States, however, conservation programs were abandoned—indeed, gas-guzzling cars became popular again—as the business world rushed to celebrate what some experts insisted was the return of permanently cheap foreign oil.

In 1990, with oil prices skyrocketing overnight once again during Iraq's aggressive rampage in the Middle East, the United States was more vulnerable to recession than either Europe or Japan. The first two oil shocks of 1973–75 and 1979–81 had had wrenching effects on all three regions of the Triad, but they had hit Japan and Europe hardest. This time, however, because of policy choices made over the last five years, it looks as if the recession of the early 1990s will take a heavier toll on the United States than on Europe or Japan.

From 1985 forward, Japan and Europe, each after its own fashion, embarked on visionary efforts to adapt their economies to the new conditions of the global marketplace. The United States, meanwhile, continued to rest comfortably on its laurels. As Alvin and Heidi Toffler have written, the grand projects undertaken by Europe, Japan, and even today's Soviet Union to remake themselves—and their belief that such reinvention is *necessary for competitive survival*—suggest that "the 21st Century has begun—everywhere but in Washington."[9]

THE STRATEGIC WEAKNESSES OF AMERICAN CAPITALISM

In Washington, of course, *competitiveness* has been a political buzzword for years. Thus far, however, most politicians have avoided addressing the strategic weaknesses of American capitalism as it is currently practiced. A brief list of the system's shortcomings would include its tendency to:

- favor short-term profit over long-term interests
- encourage immediate consumption at the expense of savings, which are needed to fund long-term private-sector investment and public-sector investment in infrastructure and education
- reward individuals exceedingly well but keep the cost of capital to industry exorbitantly high
- maintain an adversarial relationship between government, business, and labor rather than encouraging partnerships of interest
- oppose using the power of government to seed and coordinate the development of new industries
- promote service industries over manufacturing
- place greater weight on financial and marketing disciplines in corporations, rather than on factory-floor engineering, skills training, and quality control
- emphasize excellence at the top end of the educational system— college and graduate levels—while allowing the basic system of education and literacy to collapse
- make access to the U.S. domestic market relatively easy for foreign competitors while failing to aid American companies seeking to globalize and enter export markets

The above points are overly generalized for the sake of brevity. What is important to recognize is that (1) on almost every count, Reaganomics was responsible for a significant worsening of the problem, and (2) on almost every count, Japanese and German policies in the 1980s tended to be the opposite. In exactly those areas where America is weak and getting weaker, Japan and Germany are strong and getting stronger.

NEW CO-PROSPERITY SPHERES

Yet another difference of critical importance has emerged recently between the old superpowers and the new ones. As the fabric of the economic, political, and military hegemony previously maintained by the United States and the Soviet Union over their allies continued to fray in the 1980s, German and Japanese economic hegemony over new spheres of influence (Europe and East Asia, respectively) was being carefully woven together.

The physical size and resource base of the United States and the Soviet Union have always been viewed as significant factors in their rise to global power. In fact, however, the U.S. and the USSR are the *first* great powers in modern history to possess large land areas and abundant natural resources. Prior to 1945, the world's great powers were almost always small nations which managed to achieve some particular competitive advantage and to use it to build an empire. This was certainly the case for the Portuguese, Spanish, Dutch, French, and British empires. Traditionally, the need for raw materials, new markets, and new frontiers was what compelled talented nations to go abroad, leading them to sharpen their skills further and to develop global influence.

We may be returning to such a time. The sheer size of the American market has certainly been one of the chief reasons American business has *failed* to think globally in the past. With so much opportunity at home, why think about foreign markets? The rising superpowers like Japan and Germany have not been afforded the luxury of asking that question. They have *had* to think internationally. As a result, they have learned to become competitive in the extreme far beyond their borders.

Japan and Germany today are both compact, homogeneous nations. Partly as a result of their compactness and homogeneity, they can adapt to new challenges more quickly than others. Yet immediately beyond their borders, both countries have forged strategic links with large, dynamic regions offering all they need in the way of raw materials, lower-cost labor, export markets, and investment opportunities. It might be more convenient to have such assets *within* their borders, as in America. On the other hand, the need to maintain leadership in cross-border relationships is likely to keep the expanding Japanese and German empires on their toes, prevent complacency from setting in too soon, and make their activities central to all developments in the global economy.

With a gross national product of over $5 trillion, the U.S. is still the world's hugest economy—about twice as big as Japan's and four times the size of Germany's. The experts are divided over whether the *absolute size* of a nation's GNP is more important in accounting for its economic power than the *per capita GNP,* since the per capita figure is more indicative of productivity and living standards. On both scores, however, American preeminence is in eclipse.

Japan recently surpassed the United States in per capita GNP, although figures for the two countries are now so close that exchange-rate fluctuations can produce different results on different days. But given today's capital-investment boom in Japan, it is logical to assume that its per capita GNP will continue to increase more rapidly than America's in the 1990s—just as it has for most of the last thirty years.[10] Kenneth Courtis, an economist with Deutsche Bank Capital Markets in Tokyo, believes that by the year 2000, Japan may achieve a total GNP only 15 percent lower than America's—with a work force only half the size. On paper, that suggests that the Japanese of the year 2000 will be nearly twice as productive and twice as wealthy as Americans, even if the total U.S. GNP remains larger than Japan's.

The European Community's 1992 program, as we have seen, has as its central mission nothing less than creating the world's largest single marketplace. The EC is expected to have a gross product roughly equal to the U.S. total of $5 trillion by January 1, 1993, counting only those countries which are members of the EC today. But that may not be all. In projecting to the year 2000, it may be reasonable to add another $4–5 trillion to the total size of the European market. That figure is derived from a combination of likely growth rates for the EC after 1992 and increased integration with the European Free Trade Area (EFTA) and the more promising economies of Eastern Europe.

Whatever the ultimate shape of "greater Europe," it is likely to be a complex and fluid entity. Even if the 1992 program has a high degree of success, it is unlikely that Europe can become as economically integrated by the year 2000 as the United States is today. What is clear, however, is that Germany will be the dominant power in this sprawling $9 trillion-plus European economy.

It is an oversimplification, but not an egregious one, to say that today's prosperity in Western Europe—and the hope for prosperity tomorrow in Eastern Europe as well—is driven by the German economic engine. Outstanding fiscal management by Germany's Bundesbank, for example, is credited with taming previously widespread European inflation in the 1980s and reining in some of the chronic overspending by European governments. The centrality of the D-mark to the European Monetary System (where it makes up over 30 percent of the basket that sets currency rates for most EC members) has vastly improved the EC's overall macroeconomic outlook and increased the global purchasing power of most European companies.

"We're all Germans now," says Peter Ludlow, director of the Brussels-based Center for European Policy Studies. "The whole EC is obtaining German virtue—low inflation, a strong currency, and a good mix of growth and social welfare."

Even the French, historically phobic about acknowledging German superiority in any sphere, have little problem recognizing the reality of Germany's economic stewardship of Europe. Sitting in one of the grandest office suites off the Rue St.-Honoré in Paris, Philippe Lagayette, deputy governor of the Bank of France and heir to the longest, proudest government banking tradition in Europe, is candid on the subject: "After the failure of [Mitterrand's] nationalizations and socialist experiments at the beginning of the 1980s, we were able to improve a difficult economic situation rapidly by submitting ourselves to the discipline of the Bundesbank. The Germans do quite a fine job of macroeconomic management, you know."

Although former British Prime Minister Margaret Thatcher often railed against the EC's desire to establish a common currency and a pan-European central bank, she was opposing what, in many ways, were already realities. Says a former Exchequer economist now working in Brussels, "We already have a common currency in Europe—the D-mark!" The *Financial Times* already refers to the Bundesbank as "the *de facto* central bank of the Community."[11]

The investment of Germany's capital surplus has created growth booms throughout Europe, such as in Spain where Volkswagen now builds its popular Polo model. At the same time, the German market's openness to imports has become a powerful stimulant to its neighbors. "We automatically profit" from stronger growth in the German economy, notes a Dutch economist, pointing out that Germany already takes 30 percent of Dutch exports and is the Netherlands' biggest trading partner.[12]

German largesse (currently contributing a shade over 25 percent of the EC budget) has been critical to resolving some of the knottiest political problems within the Community. Referring to the "structural funds" scheme, in which the wealthiest EC members support economic development in weaker regions, Claus Haugaard Sorenson, a Danish representative in Brussels, observes pointedly, "The Mediterranean countries have agreed to implement European Community directives they never would have accepted in the past basically because they are being paid to do so by Germany." Even tourism is a major vehicle of capital recycling:

German tourists spend upwards of $20 billion elsewhere in Europe and are responsible for creating some 300,000 jobs in the holiday havens of Italy, Greece, and Spain.

A new strategic and self-interested German benevolence is now being bestowed on Eastern Europe. It was not for nothing that Václav Havel chose to make his first trip abroad after becoming Czechoslovakian president to Bonn. In Hungary, German is being taught along with English to schoolchildren. D-marks are now routinely accepted at hotels and business establishments. In Poland, hundreds of thousands of people now depend directly or indirectly on being able to work at menial jobs in Germany during their vacation weeks. A highly skilled Polish anesthesiologist, for example, earns the equivalent of three years' pay by washing dishes in a German delicatessen during the summer. He then drives back to Poland with the consumer goods his family needs to make it through the winter.

Jean-Jacques Servan-Schreiber, the French writer and futurist, comments, "How did '1992' succeed in becoming such a catchword? Why does the eradication of borders seem like such a good way to promote economic growth? Because the eradication of boundaries makes possible turning Europe into an enlarged Germany." In short, the idea of Germany as a twenty-first-century superpower rests not so much on the Germany that exists within the confines of its own borders as on its leadership role in a wider and dynamically expanding European marketplace.

"The dirty little secret is out," observes Thomas Kielinger, chief editor of the *Rheinischer Merkur,* a leading Bonn newspaper. "We revel in our elevation to superpowerdom."[13] A top adviser to Helmut Kohl concurs. "We *want* to lead," he says, suggesting that the United States ought to look after Latin America while Germany looks after the new situation in Europe.[14]

Unlike Germany, Japan *within its borders* stands a chance of becoming an economy of nearly American superpower-size. But giving Tokyo its added edge will be the enormous interest it holds in the rapidly growing economies of the Pacific Rim. This includes South Korea, Taiwan, Singapore, Hong Kong, Thailand, Malaysia, parts of China, and other emerging "little dragons," as well as large parts of the commercial zone from Sydney to San Francisco. New Japanese direct investment in Asia is now running at double the American rate, and Japan's trade with its Asian partners is only slightly less than the voluminous U.S.-Japan trade of $141 billion a year. The Pacific Rim, in short, is to Japan what Europe is to Germany.

Both Japan and Germany will play an important economic role in virtually every part of the world. But if one of capitalism's most salient characteristics is the constant jockeying for markets, then what is noteworthy here is that Germany in the 1990s will be at the heart of the developed world's largest single market (Europe), while Japan will be at the heart of the region that may eventually become the developed world's largest market (the Pacific Rim). The United States, meanwhile, will no longer be the dominant marketplace it is today. By the early twenty-first century, it might rank only third in size among world markets.

Yoshio Suzuki, a former top international economist with the Bank of Japan and now vice-chairman of the Nomura Research Institute, sheds an insightful Japanese light on all this. He believes a profound shift in the global economic balance has taken place, with the postwar *"Pax Americana"* giving way to a tripolar structure. American domination of Asia and Europe is yielding to three spheres in which a regional power will dominate—Germany in a newly opened Europe, Japan in Asia, and the United States in the Americas. Germany and Japan, he believes, are developing clear-sighted policies on how to promote growth in "their" regions. But the U.S. spends "more time lamenting its loss of influence than on articulating a new strategy for developing the Americas."[15]

Just a few years ago, those arguing that Japan was becoming a superpower were met with a flurry of objections from scholars. Aside from its number-two status behind the U.S. in total economic size, Japan's lack of military might and even its lack of an overt global "mission" would prevent it from ever obtaining American-style reach, the experts insisted. Today, however, while the world's new agenda increasingly focuses on the creation and allocation of economic resources as the central "mission" of our times, even the popular press has grasped the potential first of Japan and now of Germany to play a superpower role.

"The old superpowers, both of them bent under the costly weight of their military commitments and plagued to one degree or another by economic stagnation, will be joined at the top of the political heap by lean, mean trading machines—Japan and now Germany, one leaping the Pacific, the other astride Central Europe," declares one newsmagazine's summary of recent events. "The losers of World War II may emerge as the economic and political winners of the Cold War."[16]

WAR IN THE INFORMATION AGE

The kinds of radical shifts in national fortunes we have discussed thus far are similar to those that took place in the aftermath of the two world wars. Going back in time, one can trace how the Franco-Prussian War, the Napoleonic wars, the War of the Roses, and other notable international conflicts of the last several hundred years each brought about radical changes in the economic circumstances of both winners and losers. All these wars have complex histories and origins. But the undeniable fact is that historically, large-scale wars have erupted every twenty to forty years, as new nations with new strengths and resources have challenged the existing order of global wealth and power.

Judging by the patterns of history, a new global war was overdue by the 1980s. Numerous mainstream political science theories attempt to explain why it didn't happen. Prevalent among these is the idea that the nuclear balance of terror has made large-scale war obsolete, relegating military conflicts to the low-intensity type, to be fought out by proxies rather than through direct engagement of the great powers. A more meaningful explanation, however, may lie in the rise of the Information Age and the way it has exploded the neat, linear patterns of prior historical experience.

Ever since the rise of nation-states in the middle of the current millennium, countries have fought with one another at various times over ownership of territory; access to natural resources, sea-lanes, and markets; the elimination of adversaries from areas considered to pose security threats; and other similar issues generally rooted in the need or desire to conquer fixed geographical positions. The British empire (and later the American empire) owed most of its wealth and success to great achievements in industry, commerce, and science. But it was no mere coincidence that Britain and, subsequently, the United States were also the greatest military powers of their day. Throughout the Industrial Age, real power depended not only on the degree of a society's innovative genius but also on its ability to control the global situation to maximum strategic advantage.

These old truths about the role of military power began to change with the passing of the Industrial Age. With the exception of oil, natural resources—traditionally considered national assets—began to depreciate precipitously. Financial power, technological power, and trading

power—all increasingly derived from knowledge-based resources—
began to emerge as fluid, flexible, cost-efficient ways to enjoy national
wealth and exert global influence. Conversely, traditional military
strength, particularly vast nuclear arsenals, began to grow prohibitively
expensive and antiquated. The real threats to international security would
now tend to arise not from within the Triad but from those outside trying
to fight their way in. Nuclear stockpiles and "Star Wars" systems would
be of little use in dealing with these rogue states.

Inside the Triad, the advent of the new age meant that the purposes of
war could now be accomplished without necessarily having to shoot.
Global market share in a new industry could be obtained through means
far more sophisticated than the clumsy brutality required in the old days,
when the goal was to capture territory. Nations could now compete ruthlessly and even lay waste to large sectors of one another's economic
apparatus without having to engage in the antiquated practice of slaugh-
tering human beings.

Thus, the Japanese did not have to drop a bomb on the United States
to wipe out half the asset value of American industry in the 1980s. The
strengthening of the yen and the weakening of the dollar accomplished
essentially the same purpose. Not a single Japanese soldier had to be
sacrificed in order to destroy American competitive abilities in semiconductors. The skillful use of adversarial trade policies was quite sufficient.

Nor did West Germans have to fight a war to gain control of the East
German market. West Germany's absorption of East Germany has been
compared facetiously to events in the mergers-and-acquisitions business.
Calling German reunification "the bid to end all bids," *The Economist*
offered this tongue-in-cheek analysis: "The biggest deal of all is about to
be done. Meet Helmut Kohl the asset-stripper: raider, unbundler, and
would-be revitalizer of a badly managed, overmanned company called
East Germany."[17]

The analogy is no joke, however. West Germany *is* engaged, essentially, in the buyout and takeover of its eastern neighbor. Not unlike a
clever corporate raider, Bonn has calculated how many billions of D-
marks it will cost to assume East Germany's liabilities, and balanced
this against the country's potential value once the old "management"
is thrown out and East Germany's assets are deployed more productively. Some American financial experts are worried that Helmut Kohl
& Co. may have lost their normally cool heads by willingly committing
an estimated $30 billion a year for the next several years to bail out the

faltering East German economy and begin to bring it up to Western European standards. But viewed as a pioneering exercise in the M&A of sovereign states, the deal looks good: all of East Germany for an annual bill of not much more than New York leveraged-buyout specialists KKR paid in 1989 for a single American company, RJR-Nabisco.

Today's battles for control of tomorrow's markets are being fought, "not in khaki on the Somme or in Normandy,"[18] but at meetings in Brussels to set common standards for European technology, in lawsuits at the European Court of Justice in Luxembourg, in antidumping hearings at the U.S. Commerce Department in Washington, at GATT meetings in Geneva devoted to unfair trade practices, and in the smoke-filled meeting rooms of the Ministry of International Trade and Industry (MITI) in Tokyo.

Gorbachev is trying to bring even the Soviet Union into the new age. When Lithuania first demanded its independence, he initially countered not by sending tanks or troops, as any prior Soviet leader in his position might have done, but by demanding $33 billion in payment for the infrastructure he claimed the Moscow government had built there over the years.

The global problem-solving agenda increasingly centers on economic issues. Everywhere, there is talk of new "Marshall Plans." A Marshall Plan is needed for Eastern Europe, it is said, and another for the Soviet Union. A Marshall Plan must be developed for Latin America, and even for the war on drugs, for the battle against AIDS, and for the environment. The idea is overused and often inappropriate, but the consistency with which the Marshall Plan concept is invoked reveals a profound if simple truth: In many parts of the world, and for many different kinds of problems, the ability to concentrate economic resources and deploy them strategically—the essence of the original postwar Marshall Plan for Western Europe—has become what is needed and expected of the great global powers.

Comparing the real Marshall Plan of yesterday with the one envisioned for Eastern Europe today also reveals much about the changed role of the United States. From 1946 to 1955, Americans spent some $170 billion (measured in 1989 dollars) to promote the economic recovery of Europe. That contribution contrasts sharply with what Washington is prepared to do today for Eastern Europe. The maximum total aid package currently proposed by America comes to less than $15 billion.

Increasingly, the United States not only lacks the requisite liquid assets, but is hesitant to use what resources it has for what is perceived as a distant and complicated undertaking. When a Democratic congressman asked Secretary of State James Baker why the mighty United States government wasn't doing more to help Eastern Europe, he retorted, "You want to go out and argue for higher taxes to pay for foreign aid?"[19] But as House majority leader Richard Gephardt has pointed out, when President Truman launched the Marshall Plan, only 14 percent of the American people supported the idea of foreign aid at all. It was up to leaders like Truman to rally the country around the vision of rebuilding Europe and to support the massive commitment of resources to pay for it. Increasingly, Japan, Germany, and the EC *have* the resources to underwrite today's new equivalents of the Marshall Plan and are showing a willingness to use them.

Some economists argue that trade deficits and surpluses have become meaningless because increased economic interdependence and the changes in ownership and production methods make it harder to separate what is truly domestic from what is foreign. They would do well, however, to contemplate this "coincidence": The funds the United States spent rebuilding Europe in the postwar decade were roughly equal to a single year's trade surplus in those days, when America had the world's most remarkable positive balance of trade. The funds West Germany is now committing to rebuilding East Germany amount to roughly a single year's West German trade surplus. "When you have a large trade surplus, you can do lots of things," noted a nonchalant official from Bonn's Ministry of Economics. He might have added: When you have a large trade deficit, it is hard to do many of the things you might otherwise want to do.

Japanese and German victories in the Third World War derive from many sound choices and intelligent policies in both countries. But excellent as Japanese and German economic managers have been in the postwar period, they need not be regarded as *Übermenschen*. Both countries owe much of their current success to circumstance—particularly to the way their defeats were settled forty-five years ago. By imposing a peace that deliberately disarmed the two aggressors of World War II, the United States and the Soviet Union inadvertently laid the groundwork for their own defeat in the Third World War of the 1980s. Without the pressure or even the option to compete for world power through traditional military means, Japan and Germany were able to focus their national agendas instead on the new power to be gained from constructing supercompetitive economies. The United States and the Soviet Union, on the other hand, lost the Third World War for many reasons. But certainly the biggest single factor was their obsession with outdated military and geopolitical strategies, which ultimately resulted in the misallocation of national resources and the loss of economic leadership over their respective alliances.

THE CURIOUS PARALLEL BETWEEN REAGAN AND BREZHNEV

To return for a moment to the beginning of the 1980s, a curious parallel can be observed between the administrations of Ronald Reagan and Leonid Brezhnev. Both men presided over systems which, though still extraordinarily powerful, were clearly beginning to show signs of decline from the peak of their power a decade or two earlier. Whatever their own intellectual limitations may have been, both men were surrounded with capable advisers who could surely see that economic and technological competitiveness rather than military and ideological strength would be the most significant criteria in determining future world power. Yet both Washington and Moscow ultimately chose to make unprecedented new commitments to their military sectors. They geared up to fight World War III in traditional fashion.

In the United States, Ronald Reagan doubled defense spending between 1980 and 1987—with an 18 percent jump in 1982 alone. He engaged in a military buildup that included the B-2 Stealth Bomber, which by some accountings was costlier than its weight in gold. A massive commitment to the early stages of "Star Wars" (the costliest military program ever conceived) was undertaken. So too were major new missile systems for a Western European alliance that would, within a few years, no longer be sure where to point them. Billions of dollars in aid flowed to support American interests in low-intensity conflicts in Nicaragua, Afghanistan, and elsewhere.

The Reagan administration spent as if the United States were at war. Even more important, Washington *borrowed* as if it were at war to finance this military spending. That massive borrowing, in turn, drove up the cost of capital in the U.S. to levels that rendered American corporations unable to invest for the long term on a competitive basis with Asian and European rivals. Through most of the 1980s, the average after-tax cost of capital was 200–300 percent higher in the United States than in Japan or West Germany. No wonder Japanese and German companies began to out-invest American businesses in building the factories and industries of the future!

The Reagan administration's massive borrowing binge also prevented the U.S. government from investing in areas critical to the nation's future economic competitiveness, including infrastructure-building, education, transportation, and civilian R&D. The borrowing program made the U.S. so heavily reliant on the inflow of foreign capital that the American negotiating position in seeking better terms of trade from its European and Asian partners was seriously compromised. After all, U.S. trade officials could not take a tough stance with the very countries who were financing the American budget deficit.

Reagan-era decision-makers, unlike the architects of the successful war efforts of the past, chose to go to war without seeking any sacrifices from the American people or the American business establishment. Quite the contrary: The Republican-led White House and the Democrat-led Congress of the 1980s, despite contentious public wrangling over which special interests to favor, pursued a joint policy of *lowering* taxes while *raising* spending. The most excessive binge of consumption and private-sector debt in world economic history was actively encouraged.

Ronald Reagan told the nation that America was "strong again." He hammered home the message that the great competitive battle of our times was with the "Evil Empire" headquartered in Moscow, not with our friends in Europe and Asia. In so doing, the president gave American politicians, corporations, and social institutions a monumental excuse for *not* feeling challenged by increasingly competitive allies, for *ignoring* mounting economic and social problems, and for *opposing* proposals to adjust the system itself.

It was not just that Reagan reemphasized the supremacy of military power at a time when a less militarized world was already taking shape. The Reagan era also turned out to be one of the most ideologically driven periods of American history, at a time when the rest of the world was turning away from the great ideological battles of the past. The decision to oppose Soviet communism by making overwhelming new commitments to American military capabilities was closely linked to a relentless Reaganomic belief in the ideological superiority of American capitalism. The administration's almost religious devotion to the "free market" dispensed with the moderating influence American government had exerted since the days of the robber barons and encouraged the triumph of short-term thinking over long-term national interest.

While the situation in the "Evil Empire" may have appeared to be completely different, there was in fact a profound similarity between the Reagan era and the Brezhnev era. Brezhnev and his first two successors, Andropov and Chernenko, proceeded, of course, from an economic base far weaker than that of the U.S. at the beginning of the 1980s. But the Soviets, too, chose to reassert military power instead of attempting to overhaul their economy. They pursued this course even more suicidally than the Reagan administration did, spending three to five times as much on their military sector, when measured as a proportion of GNP. If allocating 6–7 percent of the GNP to the defense budget was severely hampering nondefense economic capabilities in the United States, the Soviet commitment of 20–30 percent of their GNP to military spending led to the complete collapse of what was once—at least in the more fortunate parts of the country—a moderately advanced economy.[20]

It makes for an interesting academic exercise to model scenarios of what might have happened if some large portion of the more than $2 trillion the United States spent on defense in the 1980s—and the considerably larger sum allocated by the Soviets—had instead been invested in domestic initiatives aimed at achieving economic renewal in the two countries. Without concurrent democratization, even that tonic would not have been sufficient to halt the Soviet slide into systemic collapse. But it is reasonable to assume that Gorbachev would have inherited a considerably healthier economy than he faces today. In the United States, too, the problems go far beyond mere overspending on the military budget. But in the American case, especially given the world-leading high-tech revolution achieved in Silicon Valley in the early part of the 1980s, it is quite possible to argue that more-rational government priorities would have made the U.S. a supercompetitive economic power today, rather than a nation caught in a crisis of competitive identity.

These "what ifs" about the U.S. and the USSR are, of course, purely matters of conjecture. What is *not* conjecture is the experience in the 1980s of Japan, West Germany, and other countries which chose to focus on competitive economics rather than military buildups. Only with great reluctance did they assume any of the burden sharing the U.S. attempted to foist on them. Maintaining low levels of defense spending (1–2 percent of GNP in Japan[21] and around 3.5 percent in Germany), they emphasized not weapons systems but advanced manufacturing systems, not strategic missiles but strategic trade and industrial policies.

THE LONG SHADOW OF THE COLD WAR

Many observers find it deeply ironic that the very nations that were America's chief enemies in World War II now seem to be outperforming the United States on so many fronts. Striking as the irony is, it is important to recognize that these developments are not some simple, perverse twist of fate. Rather, today's turning of the tables is the end product and logical outcome of conscious policy choices made in Washington, Bonn, and Tokyo.

The choices began with the onset of the Cold War in the late 1940s. The decision by the United States to expend massive resources rebuilding the industrial strength of both Japan and Germany was, as most historians agree, not principally an expression of benevolence from victor to vanquished. It was, instead, a carefully calculated strategy designed to promote American economic interests and check the spread of Soviet influence and communism into Asia and Western Europe.

A debate even took place over this strategy. The American political left of those days argued that if the U.S. was going to finance rebuilding anywhere, it should help the Soviet Union, its wartime ally, not Germany and Japan, where barely rehabilitated fascists and scarcely concealed imperialists still ran business and government. The debate culminated in 1946 when Secretary of Agriculture Henry Wallace urged President Truman to propose unilateral disarmament of the United States. Instead of incurring the costs of an arms race, Wallace said, the U.S. should give economic aid to the Soviets as a way to ensure a friendly relationship. Truman fired Wallace and put an end to the debate.

American policymakers were not so thickheaded as to fail to understand the potential for Japan and Germany to quickly become industrial giants once again. It was precisely because they understood that prospect so well that they believed U.S. aid and support could be the catalyst to rapidly turn both countries into economic bulwarks against communism. General Douglas MacArthur, presiding over the occupation of Japan, warned Americans that the work ethic he witnessed there would make powerful competitors out of the Japanese in no time. Secretary of State George C. Marshall, architect of the Marshall Plan, predicted Germany would become a world-leading economy again within a decade.

Max Kohnstamm, one of Jean Monnet's protégés in founding the European Community, recalls, "We had two great concerns in those days: how to get the economic system functioning productively again, and what to do about Germany. In Holland we knew that we could never get back on our feet again without reconstructing Germany, since the Dutch economy is so closely connected to Germany. But why build up steel production in the Ruhr again if it would just create bombs to drop on Rotterdam someday? Obviously, there had to be a strong Germany but a way to contain it as well."

Another Monnet protégé, Robert Marjolin, writes in his memoirs, "Despite the violence of my feelings towards the Germans before and during the war, I had rapidly convinced myself after the hostilities ended that Europe could not recover unless Germany were rebuilt and became once again a great industrial country."[22] Monnet and his able lieutenants had the complete support of the U.S. in pursuing this strategy. Indeed, as Marjolin notes, "no major economic decision could be taken in Europe without the agreement of the Americans."[23] Thus, with its eyes wide open, the U.S. assisted in the creation of its own future economic competitors.

But American policymakers, in their all-out desire to build a bulwark against the Soviet threat, went further still. They structured the NATO alliance and the U.S.-Japan security relationship in such a way that Washington effectively underwrote almost the entire defense burden for Germany and Japan. Washington's security umbrella thus allowed its enemies-turned-allies an opportunity the United States did not allow itself: the chance to focus intellectual, political, and financial resources almost exclusively on peaceful economic development.

As a final part of the bargain in the evolution of the Cold War strategy—to make absolutely sure capitalism would take hold and thrive—the U.S. also condoned policies under which Asian and European allies could protect their nascent markets and industries from foreign exploitation, but at the same time gain free access to the U.S. domestic market for their exports. In the current debate about protectionism and "unfair" foreign trade practices, Americans tend to forget that the double standard was built into U.S. relationships with its allies at American initiative. It was President Dwight D. Eisenhower and Secretary of State John Foster Dulles who lobbied Congress, the Commerce Department, and other U.S. agencies to help find ways to support the development of Japanese and European exporting industries. This was all part of the compensation package for what was then judged to be much more important—having pliant American allies who would lend unquestioning support to U.S. strategy for dealing with the Soviet menace.

The weakness of the Soviet Union and the near-complete evaporation of traditional communism's appeal are such obvious facts of life today that it is sometimes impossible to imagine how different the conditions were in the early 1950s. Soviet-supported communist parties in Western Europe were then strong enough to mount electoral campaigns that placed them within striking distance of political power in France, Italy, and elsewhere. West Germany nearly succumbed to the temptation of Stalin's offer of re-unification in exchange for a German neutrality pledge.

In Asia, meanwhile, Mao's revolution triumphed in 1949, and Sino-Soviet ties were close for the first decade thereafter. In Korea, the Russians and Chinese demonstrated an apparent willingness to establish communist regimes in Asia by force—even if it meant taking on the United States militarily. The French were losing to communist insurgents and preparing to abandon Indochina, while communist-led nationalists were advancing in guerrilla wars throughout Asia. Even Japan seemed vulnerable.

Although much of the talk of a "missile gap" and other supposed U.S. military deficiencies could be dismissed as Pentagon-generated hype, there were credible reasons to worry that the Soviets might be gaining the upper hand militarily. The launching of *Sputnik* in 1957 suggested that the Soviets were well ahead in at least one critical area of technology with substantial military applications.

In view of all these developments—not to mention the actual record of communist aggression, terror, and economic failure over the forty years that followed—it would be unfair to judge those in the Truman-Eisenhower-Kennedy years too harshly for having identified the Soviet Union as the principal threat to world peace and democracy, and for having developed the wide-ranging strategy they did to contain and combat that threat.

The strategy worked brilliantly. By fostering democracy and economic growth in Western Europe, East Asia, and elsewhere, the United States checked the advance of the Soviet superpower. The problem was not with the fundamental principles of American postwar strategy or even the excesses that sometimes flowed from that strategy. The problem, which worsened over time, lay in Washington's failure to update its strategic thinking as global circumstances underwent radical change.

The first clear-cut instance of misguided American policy was the Vietnam War, in which the U.S. squandered vast resources, polarized its own population, and thoroughly alienated itself from its allies. Yet Vietnam was not of critical importance to the U.S., as history has demonstrated. Fifteen years after the reunification of North and South Vietnam under communist command, not one of the serious problems the United States faces in the world today can be attributed to the fact that North Vietnamese communists won the war.

After the Vietnam debacle, there was still ample time for the United States to readapt its strategy to other changing realities. The 1970s saw the issue of foreign economic competition begin to emerge as a national-policy agenda item. From the Japanese success in introducing fuel-efficient automobiles, which Detroit had not yet even begun to design, to the nation's perilous reliance on foreign oil itself, the public perception began to spread that America was losing some of its global economic leadership.

''Competitiveness'' was born as a Republican issue, and its first presidential standard-bearer was Ronald Reagan. Reagan's 1980 campaign platform and some of the early initiatives introduced by his administration were on the right track. Attempting to balance the federal budget, a signature issue with Reagan, was an excellent idea in a world in which the U.S. was losing economic leadership, the cost of American capital was too high, and the government could no longer afford to be all things to all people. Similarly, efforts to deregulate businesses overly constricted by government bureaucracy, to dismantle elements of the U.S. welfare state that were clearly no longer working, to encourage corporate investment through tax policy, to emphasize morality in private life, and to ensure that schools provided American children with at least the ''basics'' were all worthy undertakings.

Yet most of these Reagan initiatives never came to fruition. Some—such as balancing the budget—actually turned into their opposites in the 1980s. In other cases, what began as an intelligent step in the right direction—deregulation of the financial-services industry, for example—rapidly descended into laissez-faire excess, leading to the collapse of the savings-and-loan industry, with its continuously rising bailout costs; the junk-bond-backed destruction of important American corporations; and a debt-driven economy increasingly reliant on foreign capital.

Even after Gorbachev rose to power and introduced his policy of *glasnost* in 1985, the Reagan administration waited nearly three years before thinking about using this turn of events in the "Evil Empire" to bring an end to runaway military spending. Despite the massive U.S. investment in "intelligence-gathering"—now costing an estimated $30 billion a year—the American intelligence community was incapable of detecting the substantive change effected in the Soviet Union by Mikhail Gorbachev until long after it was obvious to the rest of the world. West German Foreign Minister Hans-Dietrich Genscher implored the U.S. to "take Gorbachev at his word," but in Washington, the foreign-policy establishment, which had grown up with the Cold War's premises hardwired into its thinking, found it hard to shift course.

By 1990, most of the American intelligence community was at last willing to accept the premise that Gorbachev was for real. CIA Director William H. Webster told the House Armed Services Committee that Moscow had reached the point where only the overthrow of Gorbachev and a forced return to Stalinism could reverse the process of change under way in the Soviet Union. Even in that worst-case scenario, the CIA director noted, it was unlikely that the Soviets would threaten the United States or Europe again. Yet the Bush administration's response to that stunning new assessment was *not,* as many expected, to propose substantial reductions in the nearly $300 billion U.S. defense budget. At first, the administration suggested no more than withdrawing a previously discussed $10 billion *addition* for 1991. Defense Secretary Dick Cheney warned that even the loss of that $10 billion was dangerous. "Real trouble" lay ahead, he said, if the U.S. failed to continue increasing military spending.[24] Months later, Cheney had inched a little closer to recognizing that something had changed in the world; still, he favored only a 10 percent budget cut—to be phased in over *five years,* at 2 percent a year.

In fact, one could reasonably argue that the Soviet threat to the United States had been reduced by as much as 90 percent. Nevertheless, when Senators Jim Sasser and Sam Nunn proposed immediate cuts in defense spending levels amounting to just 10 percent, they were criticized for going too far.

Rising military tension in the Mideast in 1990 reminded Americans that the end of the Cold War with the Soviet Union did *not* necessarily guarantee an era of world peace. The ability to project American military power to disparate parts of the world was and is absolutely crucial to U.S. interests. Unfortunately, Cheney and the Pentagon seized on Iraq's aggression to destabilize the world economy as an opportunity to defend a military budget whose major programs are tied up in weapons systems aimed at the Soviet Union and the nations of the collapsing Warsaw Pact alliance. The Cold War, in other words, is still being fought, even as new security threats arise to supplant it.

While it remained remarkably easy to sell $300 billion defense budgets, allocating a mere 0.5 percent of that to support the American electronics industry's desire to become a global leader in HDTV could not win the necessary backing. When industry representatives went to Washington in 1989 with a proposal to "jump-start" a domestic American initiative on HDTV in order to better compete with Japanese and European projects already well under way, their appeal for government loans, credits, and investment was turned down flat. Ostensibly, the request was refused because the Bush administration viewed the Stealth Bomber and the vestiges of Cold War aid programs in Central America as higher priorities.[25] But the real reason was that few in Washington were ready to acknowledge that catching up to the world's new competitive realities required a break with laissez-faire American economic thinking.

Some American political leaders recognized the new competitive economic challenges but were still unable to act decisively. An October 1989 cover of *Time* told the story succinctly. It depicted George Washington shedding a tear alongside this headline: "IS GOVERNMENT DEAD? Unwilling to Lead, Politicians Are Letting America Slip into Paralysis."[26] The fault was not just with the Bush White House, although much of the blame inevitably lay there. "Congress: It Doesn't Work" was *Business Week*'s apt cover story a few months later.[27]

The public sense that government had lost whatever ability it had once had for national problem-solving was only heightened by the theater of the absurd production known as the 1990 "budget summit." With the White House and Congress now nearly unanimous in the view that the budget deficit was, indeed, a serious problem, an orgy of media-hyped conferencing, secret negotiating, political flip-flops by the president, and impassioned "soak-the-rich" speech-making by congressmen ensued. All of this presented the appearance that Washington was serious about cutting the budget deficit. Yet when the theatrics were over and the deal was signed, careful analysis of the figures suggested that 1991–92 budget deficits would be the worst on record.

In the 1990 midterm elections, few candidates spoke in any detail about the budget. Fewer still addressed the military buildup in the Persian Gulf which was just then taking place. And only a handful centered their campaigns on issues having to do with the competitive economic challenges posed by Europe and Japan. The system, in short, simply wasn't dealing with the fundamental political and economic questions of the American agenda.

Paul Craig Roberts, a staunch defender of Reaganomics in its heyday, now observes:

> The U.S. is still acting out the game plan of 1948. This plan was designed to contain communism by restoring the economic vitality of Europe and Japan while fostering economic development in other regions through foreign aid and multilateral lending institutions such as the World Bank. In effect, it was a plan to protect our interests by advancing the interests of others.
>
> Now that communism has collapsed from its own failure and our World War II adversaries, Japan and Germany, have strong economic positions, it is time for the U.S. to devise a new strategy for protecting its interests. . . . It remains to be seen whether the U.S. government can cast off the practices and attitudes of 40 years and learn to defend U.S. business interests as successfully as Japan and West Germany defend their own.[28]

In short, the Third World War is over, and the Japanese and Germans have won. It is high time for the United States to sue for peace. What is needed now—and what doesn't yet exist—is a strategic vision for domestic economic renewal as well as new burden- and power-sharing partnerships among America, Europe, and Japan that can creatively coordinate the extraordinary new opportunities for peace and prosperity while minimizing the equally breathtaking dangers ahead.

PART II

The Emerging European Suprastate

4

1992:
The World's Largest Market

If the citizens, companies and governments of Europe respond robustly to the challenge of 1992, they will propel Europe onto the blustery world stage of the 1990s in a position of competitive strength and on an upward trajectory of growth lasting into the next century. . . .

The impact of EC market integration could put between four and seven percentage points on the Community's domestic product. This vista is not a tantalizing chimera. On the contrary, it is a firm prospect. . . .

The removal of non-tariff barriers will trigger a supply-side shock. Costs will come down. Prices will follow as business, under the pressure of new rivals in previously protected markets, is forced to develop fresh responses. The downward pressure on prices will in turn stimulate demand, giving companies the opportunity to increase output, to exploit resources better and to scale them up for European and global competition. . . .

PAOLO CECCHINI, *author of the "Cecchini Report," on the costs of a fragmented Europe and the benefits of the single market*[1]

EUROPEAN UNITY AS DREAM AND REALITY

The idea of a unified Europe is anything but new. Two thousand years ago, the Romans presided over a "common European economic space" that would make today's Eurocrats envious. Roman coins functioned as a common currency. Common "technical standards"—such as the Roman alphabet, numerical system, measurements, and architectural principles—were accepted almost everywhere in the empire. The famed Roman roads and aqueducts helped develop the outlying regions and link them to the center, not unlike today's EC-backed transportation and infrastructure programs. Roman leaders even enjoyed what today's European unifiers do not dare discuss: a common language.

Several hundred years after the Fall of Rome, Charlemagne brought a good piece of European real estate back together again. The new empire he forged was an amalgam of lands which today lie on either side of the Rhine in France and Germany. Charlemagne's vision was such that eleven and a half centuries later, in the 1950s, it would still inspire French President Charles de Gaulle as he embarked on the road to the European Community together with West German Chancellor Konrad Adenauer. De Gaulle saw Adenauer as a "good German," because he was a Rhinelander, not a Prussian. And being a Rhinelander, de Gaulle said, made it possible for Adenauer to be "imbued with a sense of the complementary nature of the Gauls and the Teutons which once fertilized the presence of the Roman Empire on the Rhine, brought success to the Franks and glory to Charlemagne."[2] Together, de Gaulle believed, he and Adenauer could reestablish "*l'Europe des patries*"—the Europe of the two fatherlands that resided at the heart of Charlemagne's realm.

Charlemagne's successors expanded the boundaries of European unification still further, laying the basis for the Holy Roman Empire. But although this empire was unified in theory, its history was characterized by continuous wrestling for political control between religious and civil authorities, as well as central and local ones. As today's Eurocrats consider the problems of building a supranational organization to encompass several big nations where the drive for national sovereignty is still very much alive (Britain, France, and Germany), smaller nations whose pride is still fierce and whose economies are still deeply connected to their specific culture (all the rest of the EC's roster), and regions long accustomed to their own decentralized rule (each of the German *Länder,* Scotland, Catalonia, etc.), one can hear faint echoes from the discord of the past among the Holy Roman Empire's popes, emperors, and local monarchs.

In the early part of the sixteenth century, humanists such as Erasmus and Thomas More built an intellectual and cultural network that revived the influence of the Latin language, Roman law, and Catholicism's universalism. Their goal was not to unify Europe politically. In fact, they ended up contributing to its divisions by opposing the winds of the Reformation. But in universities, libraries, and monasteries, a common Europe of ideas sprang up.

In modern history, Napoleon succeeded in unifying Europe for a brief time. So did Hitler. And, remembering the new importance of the East as a legitimate part of European history, one must not discount the record of Byzantine emperors, Ottoman Turks, and Soviet communists as European unifiers.

One obvious lesson emerges from this quick scan of history: Unifying Europe is *not* impossible. Equally evident is the fact that whatever kind of unity Europe has achieved in the past, it has never lasted.

JANUARY 1, 1993, IS ALREADY HERE

American businesspeople tend to be pragmatists with a built-in skepticism toward grand plans. The obvious question in contemplating the 1992 program for the first time is "Will it work?"

The twelve member countries of the EC, after all, have a dozen official languages and a dozen different currencies. Even the most casual tourist making his way across the Continent cannot help but notice the abundance of sharp cultural contrasts between Catholic and Protestant Europe, Northern and Mediterranean Europe, Atlantic and Central Europe. On fundamental political, economic, and social issues—the degree of state centralization, the extent and forms of electoral democracy, workers' rights, business law, open markets versus protective regulations, sources of tax revenue, the status of women, and education policy, to name but a few— there is not one Europe but at least three or four groupings of countries, with shifting compositions depending on which issue is being posed.

As one moves from Portugal and Greece to Germany and Denmark, average income rises by nearly 300 percent. The rate of VAT (Value-Added Tax, a kind of national sales tax in European countries) ranges from 0 percent to more than 30 percent, depending on the product and the country. Spaniards pay only one-fourth of what Germans pay for pharmaceuticals, but twice as much as the British for life insurance. Some countries have always had open trucking markets, but Germany, with the biggest market, has historically insisted on protectionist rules forcing domestic companies to use domestic truckers and insurers. Thus, German trucking costs have been much higher than the Community average. In Denmark, a 200 percent tax is levied on new car purchases, while in Luxembourg it is only 12 percent. And speaking of cars, in those countries where auto markets are fully open to Japanese imports (such as Ireland and Denmark), Japanese market share ranges from one-third to one-half of the total, while in countries with protected markets (notably France, Italy, and Spain), Japanese car sales account for less than 3 percent. That is quite a stunning difference on a continent where one out of every twelve jobs depends on the good health of the European auto industry.

EC members have distinctly different emphases in foreign policy. Ireland is officially neutral. France participates in NATO but maintains its own independent military command. Germany, with the biggest European army, is fully integrated into NATO. Denmark relates closely to its Scandinavian neighbors, which are not currently EC members, Greece to the Middle East, and Germany increasingly to Eastern Europe. On many issues, the United Kingdom still has closer ties to the United States than to Europe.

In fact, Britain's Thatcher often appeared as a truculent Iron Lady standing alone in opposition to the eleven would-be unifiers of Europe. While endorsing the 1992 program in its most limited sense, she dismissed efforts in Brussels to link 1992 to broader issues of monetary and political union as "airy-fairy and absurd." She contemptuously rejected Jacques Delors's suggestion that eventually 80 percent of economic policy decisions will be made by the EC rather than by national governments. In a landmark 1988 speech in Bruges, Belgium, Thatcher declared, "We have not successfully rolled back the frontiers of the state in Britain only to see them reimposed at a European level, with a European suprastate exercising a new dominance from Brussels."[3]

Although Thatcher was alone in her overt EC-bashing rhetoric, her underlying concerns were often shared by others in Europe, especially the Dutch, the Danes, and the Germans. They, too, worry about an overly centralized, nonelected EC bureaucracy intervening too much in the marketplace.

A complete cataloging of the differences of opinion, culture, and history that exist among the various European nations would fill a good-sized encyclopedia. There is consequently not a single European leader who, when asked what 1992 will mean, does not begin by pointing out that "of course, the Germans will still be German, the French will still be French, the Italians will still be Italian," and so forth. When the heads of the twelve EC governments met in Dublin in April 1990 to appeal for more-urgent action to achieve "a political union of Europe," none dared offer a concrete description of what this union might look like. Any attempt to do so would have precipitated a schism.

Yet, despite Europe's many differences, the answer to the question "Will 1992 work?" is almost invariably an emphatic "yes." This optimism is due in part to the fact that the Europe of January 1, 1993, is already functioning in several important ways right now. It has arrived most obviously on the practical level of increased investment and economic growth.

In 1986, Lord Cockfield, the British EC commissioner responsible for developing the single market, invited former EC official Paolo Cecchini to organize the massive study cited in the epigraph to this chapter. In a Continent-wide research blitz that ended up lasting two years, a team of 200 fact finders made inquiries among 11,000 companies and produced 6,000 pages of published data; the "Cecchini Report," as it is known, surveyed what was called "the cost of non-Europe."

"The cost of non-Europe" is just one of many unique Eurospeak locutions to emerge from the growing body of EC jargon. This particular phrase is shorthand for what it would cost European economies if they did *not* complete the single-market goals. To no one's surprise, the report's findings were bullish in support of 1992—so much so that some critics dismissed the document as propaganda. By analyzing the consequences of the EC's many nontariff barriers (such as border controls, customs red tape, divergent technical standards, protectionist government procurement practices, and conflicting accounting procedures), Cecchini's team assigned an impressive cost to keeping Europe fragmented and inefficient. The *bottom line* was that implementation of the 1992 program would result in a savings of 170–250 billion ECUs (European Currency Units), roughly equivalent to 200–300 billion U.S. dollars, and would add 4–7 percent to the EC's gross product.

The methodology of this far-flung cost-benefit analysis was roundly criticized by experts, most of whom thought it was wildly optimistic.

Recent economic history, however, seems to be on Cecchini's side. Even with very few of the 279 directives that now make up the 1992 package fully implemented, Europe is *already* achieving better growth rates than it has seen in twenty years. Companies are investing in Europe as never before, adding advanced new capacity, modernizing outdated facilities, opening offices, hiring personnel, developing land, and aggressively trying to position themselves in new markets through mergers and acquisitions.

During 1988 and 1989, the realization that the 1992 campaign might actually work sank in across the Continent, creating a wave of "Europhoria" responsible for record highs on stock markets in Amsterdam, Brussels, Frankfurt, Lisbon, Madrid, Milan, Paris, and elsewhere. American and Japanese businesses also jumped on the bandwagon. Fearful at one point that they might be excluded, foreign companies rushed into new EC investments, contributing to European growth rates to an extent unforeseen by Cecchini's study. Even now that the red heat of Europhoria has cooled down to a more realistic temperature, EC growth rates continue to surpass those Cecchini had thought unreachable until the mid-1990s.

Although the "Cecchini Report" was initially criticized for being too optimistic, it has now developed a coterie of critics who think it *understated* the potential. "Cecchini assumed that the productivity and efficiency benefits of 1992 would occur once and for all," observes Charles Wyplosz, an economics professor at the INSEAD business school in France. "But we know they are bound to be cumulative and lasting."[4]

Whatever Cecchini's accuracy, the essential point is that the business community had already made up its mind that barriers were coming down. With a thousand days to go before the 1992 deadline, the EC Commission was issuing stern warnings that only half the proposed 279 directives had been drafted and a paltry 21 actually enacted by all twelve governments. But the business world was not waiting for these niceties to be completed.

"To wait for 1993 to see what the situation will be is to commit suicide," notes the sagacious Viscount Etienne Davignon, once a top EC official and now managing director of the Société Générale, a vast diversified banking and real estate conglomerate which is Belgium's largest company. "Every business leader assumes that 1992 will be successful, at least in its broad outlines. This creates a virtuous circle. Companies believe it will happen, so they begin to implement the strategies and investments that will ensure that it happens."

Americans who don't do business in Europe on a regular basis often hold outdated perceptions of the level of competence and global competitiveness achieved there. German industry is at last being taken seriously in the United States—as well it should be. The excellence achieved by German engineering and technology is amply demonstrated in the sleek Mercedes-Benzes, BMWs, and Porsches which in America have become the ultimate status symbols of the very good life. A few products of German origin are so institutionalized in the United States that most people don't realize their connections to German companies. Such is the case with the ubiquitous Bayer aspirin, whose original formula was developed by the German pharmaceutical giant of the same name. It is also true of the huge American publishing and entertainment operations acquired by the German media conglomerate Bertelsmann during the 1980s, including the Bantam and Doubleday publishing houses, RCA Music, and *Parents* magazine.

Unlike Japanese exports, however, many of Germany's most globally competitive products are rarely seen by the average consumer. The Germans excel most of all in producing machinery, machine tools, precision instruments, factory control systems, pharmaceuticals, chemicals, and other components of industrial-process technology not always obvious to the layman—but in keen demand almost everywhere in the world.

After all that has happened since the fall of the Berlin Wall, Americans are now ready, in a vague sort of way, to accept that Germany is an economic powerhouse. This is true even if they remain unfamiliar with German companies other than the automobile manufacturers and even if they know precious little about German business strategy or management philosophy. Perhaps this imperfect American understanding of German economic excellence is what prompted Volkswagen's recent advertising campaign based on the nearly unpronounceable and hard-to-define concept of *"Fahrvergnügen."* What can be inferred from the ads is that *Fahrvergnügen* results from some sort of innate German mastery of engineering and design so far beyond American norms that it has no English translation. (In an ironic semiotic comment on America's two-fronted competitiveness war, Japanese automaker Mazda has launched its own ad campaign based on the equally untranslatable—but easier to pronounce—concept of *kansei* engineering. Detroit, which once created and defined the language of the automobile, apparently no longer does.)

Important as it is that Americans develop a better understanding of

Germany in order to grasp Europe's future direction, it is equally essential that they recognize that the growing competitiveness of European business is by no means *confined* to Germany. "Many people in North America don't realize it, but the quality and productivity are not much different if you go across the border from Germany into certain parts of Italy or France," says Justus Fürstenau, director of VDMA, a trade association which represents the world-leading German machinery industry.

Italy's economy, once a strike-ridden, inflationary mess, became a mini-miracle of the late 1980s. Fiat, the Italian automaker, was in 1980 a crippled giant headed for collapse. But over the last decade, it cut 80,000 jobs, doubled production, built some state-of-the-art assembly facilities, and eventually replaced its massive debt with a self-financing cash surplus, which it is now using to move quickly into the Eastern European market.

France is not a country that most Americans would identify as a world leader in the high-technology area. And yet, the French operate a nuclear-power industry that is both more efficient and considerably safer than America's. France also builds some of the world's best and fastest forms of transportation, including the TGV (the world's fastest train) and the Concorde (the world's fastest commercial aircraft, built by an Anglo-French consortium). The French Minitel in-home computerized information system is not only the leading network of its type in the world, it is the only one anywhere to succeed in attaining wide public use.

Americans also would not tend to think of France as a champion in the highly competitive field of steel production, but state-owned Usinor Sacilor has suddenly emerged as one of the world's biggest, best, and most profitable steel-makers. After the company slashed its payroll by 100,000, shut down inefficient facilities, and introduced a new generation of technology, Usinor's cost of production, previously one of the world's highest, became one of its lowest. Second only to Japan's Nippon Steel in total output, Usinor has gobbled up a dozen other steel-related companies in Europe and is now expanding rapidly in the United States.

For companies such as Fiat in Italy, Usinor in France, and hundreds of others across Europe, it is 1992 which has provided the impetus—and sometimes the pretext—for doing what they needed to do anyway to remain competitive. "We believe that European unity is our best hope for stimulating growth and technological innovation, and for remaining an influential presence in the world," explains Fiat's chairman, Giovanni

Agnelli. The situation in Europe has reversed since the 1950s, when politicians wrote the Treaty of Rome and the business community objected. As far as 1992 goes, Agnelli believes "it is the entrepreneurs and corporations who are keeping the pressure on politicians to transcend considerations of local and national interest."[5]

The business community's perception that the old barriers are falling is not just wishful thinking. One of the best examples of the new opportunities created by these changes is EUREKA, the EC's high-tech research program responsible for launching collaborative efforts on HDTV among thirty European electronics companies.

"I was originally quite skeptical about trying to develop HDTV with thirty partners," says P. Bögels, a top Philips executive who serves as president of EUREKA's HDTV directorate. "Strange as it seems, we have succeeded. We all know if we don't work together on a common European strategy, we will lose to the Japanese."

Having worked together inside the EUREKA consortium for three years, Europe's two biggest electronics companies, the French-based Thomson and Dutch-based Philips, recently established a $3.6 billion joint venture for production and marketing of HDTV hardware. "HDTV is our industrial future," remarked French Industry Minister Roger Fauroux in announcing the deal. "This accord between two groups which have been competitors for decades symbolizes what we want to do in Europe to catch up to Japan."

In almost every business sector, 1992 has been the catalyst creating an embryonic united Europe of the boardroom. The *1992 M&A Monthly* manages to fill eight pages simply reporting the news of the prior month's cross-border deals. In a Europe where such deals were once rare, an average month now sees one to two hundred. Tabulating 1989 totals, the newsletter came up with 542 acquisitions worth 45.3 billion ECUs, plus an additional 733 transactions with undisclosed values. A conservative estimate on the values of the latter would push total deal volume over $70 billion.

M&A activity tells only a small slice of the story. Companies are also making additional billions of dollars' worth of green-field investments. This has been true of the rapidly expanding media business—a business personified by publishing baron Robert Maxwell. In 1990, he launched *The European,* an English-language newspaper designed to cover all of Europe for a Europe-wide audience, with printing plants in England, France, Germany, and Hungary. *The European* is unique in attempting to target a mass audience of ordinary people who identify themselves explicitly as Europeans. Although the betting is heavy against the long-term success of Maxwell's venture, his premise summarizes the bullish mood of businessmen on their region's blurring borders: "I dedicate *The European* to supporting the country of Europe as a home with open doors and windows, a country to which everyone, from the Urals to the Atlantic, can belong."

European Community agreements requiring that France and Italy lift remaining controls on capital have now been successfully implemented, despite predictions that authorities in Paris and Rome would not live up to these obligations. EC directives on banking have taken the Community's dozen mostly closed, fragmented financial markets and merged them into what European Commission vice-chairman Sir Leon Brittan calls (with only slight hyperbole) "the largest and most open banking market in the world."[6] As a Conservative Party lieutenant in Thatcher's campaign to privatize the British economy, Sir Leon has impeccable past credentials as a free trader. It is therefore worth taking note of his claim that the U.S. financial-services market is closed by comparison with what has been achieved in Europe. Putting the shoe on the other foot, he says he will launch a campaign to demand that Washington end various forms of financial market protectionism.

Whether the whole package of 279 directives will be accomplished by the end of 1992 is no longer the burning question it was, although it still has potent symbolic value. Obviously, if the commission succeeds in delivering its program on time, its credibility will be heightened and its mandate to continue acting boldly will be reinforced. If some of the directives have to be watered down too much in order to get out on time, and if individual countries continue their current foot-dragging on adopting each directive into national law, there will be greater room for doubt and questioning about the process.

But with $70 billion worth of cross-border corporate acquisitions being made annually, the investors are now in the driver's seat. They are unlikely to sit still for very long if the politicians fail to deliver most of what was promised in terms of an easily accessible Europe-wide market. The unambiguous reality is that it is not 279 directives which are needed to bring competition to the market, but the active participation of competitive corporate entities across the length and breadth of the market. That part of the equation—the most important part—*is* developing daily.

WHAT 1992 IS NOT

Many of the details of the single-market campaign, however, will clearly not be realized by the 1992 deadline. The sticking points are becoming increasingly apparent. A few particularly important matters the EC had hoped to resolve by the end of 1992 now look as if they will be papered over with stopgap compromises. The effort to harmonize VAT rates throughout Europe, for example, is considered crucial to the creation of a single market without nettlesome tax-related distortions. While the commission had once expected to establish EC-wide VAT standards, it now recognizes that the best it can hope for is an agreement to narrow some of the differences that currently exist.

The commission has managed to generate support for a directive that will open up the lucrative $730 billion government procurement market to pan-European competition. But this opening will be partial and phased. The directive covers only certain large sectors—energy, transportation, water, and telecommunications projects—leaving nearly half the total government procurement business untouched. As in other matters, the weaker economies of Portugal, Spain, Greece, and the former East Germany will be allowed all sorts of exemptions from the 1992 deadline. And major questions remain about how the U.S., the EC's other foreign trading partners, and the GATT will react to protectionist "buy-European" provisions incorporated into the directive.

The 1992 program was also supposed to substantially deregulate Europe's overcrowded and overpriced air routes. This is a high-priority measure, going to the very heart of the major goals of easing the movement of people and goods. Yet, with most of Europe's big airlines partially or wholly government-owned, progress has been painfully slow. "Introduce even a tablespoonful of real competition to European air traffic, and you put Alitalia and the other weak national flag carriers out of business," explains a commission staffer. "We need Italian support on too many questions to let that happen just yet." On this issue, as on others, there will be progress but no total solution.

The controversial question of import quotas on autos will not be settled by 1992, although a compromise involving voluntary restraints by Japan is likely. Countries wishing to maintain import quotas will almost certainly be allowed a transition period, which may reach into the next century, before Brussels requires them to open their markets fully. "If we completely open our frontiers in the present circumstances, we will be eliminated," says Peugeot's Jacques Calvet. "I consider it impossible that France and Europe would want their own destruction."[7]

The issue of importing Japanese autos is just one of many questions regarding access to the integrated market by companies from "third countries"—principally Japan, but also the U.S. and others. For all the talk about pulling down barriers and freeing up the marketplace, wherever large-scale European industries are threatened by qualitatively superior foreign competition, the EC will use quasi-protectionist measures to buy time for Europe to restructure. The post-1992 EC will *not* be the protectionist "fortress Europe" some Americans and Japanese had once feared. In fact, it is likely to be much more open to foreign business than it is today. But it will not be *wide open* either. (The prospects for American and Japanese access to the EC market are discussed in detail in chapters 7 and 8.)

To labor unions, the unemployed, immigrants, women, the disabled, and others among Europe's disadvantaged, 1992 has been sold as a program to create a "citizen's Europe" with a "social dimension." For part of 1989, debate focused on the drafting of a social charter which would guarantee certain rights to all Europeans. Despite opposition by Britain's Thatcher, the charter was eventually passed. It covered sweeping ground: the free movement of labor, health and safety protection for workers, the guarantee of the right to a decent wage, collective bargaining, vocational training, vacations and social security, equality between men and women, protections against abuses of child and teenage labor, the establishment of a minimum income for the elderly, and mechanisms for worker representatives to participate in corporate decision-making.

This utopian package was couched in language vague enough to make serious enforcement difficult. At the end of the day, the social charter was above all a rhetorical concession to the left's objection that 1992 was only good for big business. It did, however, demonstrate the commission's interest in social issues and established its right to initiate relevant action. Furthermore, the charter made it clear that there would be no "social dumping": The benefit-rich German work force, for instance, would not be dragged down to the level of Spanish and Portuguese workers. Instead, the future would lie in trying to obtain for the Iberian worker more of his northern European brother's blessings. But even European labor movements are aware that the commission won't seriously begin to address this basket of issues until after the single market is in place.

Even the most symbolic measure of the whole 1992 program—the end of physical frontiers within the EC and the unimpeded movement of people—may not be achieved on schedule. Some intra-EC borders are already virtually unpoliced. Passenger cars routinely pass from Germany into France or from the Netherlands into Belgium without border guards even looking up. But as 1992 rapidly approaches, the thought of dismantling those border posts permanently has made EC governments increasingly nervous.

One sign of trouble emerged when the Schengen Accord, a prototype for the overall plan to abolish frontiers, ran temporarily aground. Five EC members—Belgium, France, the Netherlands, Luxembourg, and West Germany—drew up the agreement, which declared their intention to do away with formalities at shared frontiers as early as December 1989. As new concerns about immigration from East Germany and other problems arose, signing was delayed into 1990 and implementation into 1991. The Schengen Accord is now back on track, but the fact that countries already practicing the EC's most liberal border policies had trouble taking the final step sounded a warning note to those monitoring the EC's progress toward its frontierless 1992 deadline.

The problems of how to deal with drug traffickers, terrorists, and illegal immigrants, especially in the wake of the revolutions in Eastern Europe, have proven more complicated than they first appeared. To give just a brief illustration, Spain is insisting on its right to a "special relationship" with Latin America which allows Latin American visitors to enter without a visa. West Germany has recently decided to drop visa requirements for Hungarians. Now the French worry that if the Spanish-French border is eliminated after 1992, Latin Americans—presumably including some big cocaine dealers—will automatically gain free access to France from Spain. The British are concerned that if they drop immigration and customs procedures for flights arriving at London's Heathrow from Frankfurt (because after 1992, these will be defined as domestic EC flights), then they will effectively be granting free access to Hungarians, presumably including some Soviet spies. Scare stories have circulated throughout the European press about a borderless EC that turns into a free market for the Mafia, cocaine kingpins, art thieves, and KGB agents.

Solutions to all these problems exist. Those who are critical of the rush to eradicate frontiers are also aware that today's minimal border-crossing procedures do not actually provide much of a deterrent to wealthy drug lords or clever KGB agents determined to enter a country. "Many of the world's biggest drug traffickers have so much money that they never have any trouble going anywhere they want in the world legally," observes a Spanish member of the commission staff, Damián Hernandez. "And the ones who want to go somewhere they are not welcome usually don't have any problem figuring how to do that either."

Enhanced EC-wide police and intelligence coordination would substantially ease the anxieties European leaders feel about relinquishing their last controls over the comings and goings in their countries. Such programs are already under way, but full implementation will take most of the '90s.

The list of business that remains to be concluded as 1992 approaches is not a cause for despair, however; the process, not the date itself, is what matters. The most important part of that process has already been accomplished. Now come the problems, the adjustments, and the evolution. The very fact that increasingly loud complaining about what *isn't* done will accompany the rush to the deadline reflects the fact that Europe has been sold on the importance of *getting it done*. The old protectionist, anticompetitive Europe, with its outdated industries and high unemployment rates, won't be transformed overnight into a sleek new competitive Europe of double-digit growth and marvelous high-tech industries. But it has already made more progress than most Europeans thought possible in the early 1980s—and it has already become much more competitive than most Americans realize even now.

Don't expect the world to change on January 1, 1993. It already has.

A GRAND ILLUSION?

As European enthusiasm for 1992 continued to escalate, a controversial book by the high-profile French intellectual and businessman Alain Minc launched an attack on the project's very foundations. Minc's Paris-based CERUS group is the French investment arm of Italian financier Carlo De Benedetti, who is engaged as actively as any other individual in constructing a pan-Europeanized business world.

The book, which rose quickly to the top of French best-seller charts in 1989, is called *La Grande Illusion*.[8] Its stinging thesis, as suggested by its title, was that 1992 was nothing but a psychological illusion—a desire to believe in a future that would never come. By accepting the premise of 1992, nations would be blinded to the real tasks on their respective national agendas. The promised "social dimension" of 1992 would never come to fruition. Big-business leaders (Minc and De Benedetti among them, presumably) would use the freedoms gained under the 1992 program to attack workers and further polarize the social classes. A chaotic Darwinian nightmare would follow, complete with collapses, shakeouts, and unemployment, as companies inexperienced in free competition collided.

Minc appears to have vastly overstated the dangers. It was as if he envisioned Margaret Thatcher or Ronald Reagan rather than Jacques Delors setting the agenda for EC deregulation. It is unlikely that there will be any massive, sudden deregulation of everything, any throwing open of marketplace doors overnight. The "supply-side shock" anticipated in the "Cecchini Report" will turn out to be less than shocking.

Even so, there was more truth to Minc's arguments than many European leaders wanted to admit. The process of removing barriers, encouraging competition, and discouraging state subsidies—no matter how controlled and well planned—*does* mean that some enterprises, industries, and perhaps even whole countries may end up "losers." By the end of 1990, that reality was increasingly apparent. The headiest days of "1992 fever" were over.

Companies which had expanded rapidly in preparation for 1992 were coming to grips with a slowdown in Europe-wide growth rates for 1991 and a looming recession in Britain. Oil prices and interest rates were higher than anticipated a year earlier. German investment capital was less available. "Cheap" dollar-denominated American exports were flooding the market, and the output of Japanese transplant factories was beginning to steal market share from established Europeans. Some of the EC's prized high-technology research programs faced serious difficulties as their corporate participants lost the luxury of positive cash flows with which to fund them. Profits were down at blue-chip companies. Some, like France's Michelin, the world's leading tire maker, experienced shocking losses. Massive industrial rationalizations became commonplace: In just one three-week period at the end of 1990, Philips revealed plans for the elimination of up to 45,000 jobs, Bull announced its intention to idle 5,000 workers and shut half its plants by 1992, and Olivetti unveiled a restructuring to trim its work force by nearly 15 percent.

All this bad economic news has introduced some renewed pessimism into the Community, although nothing like the profound Europessimism of the past. This time around, most European experts seem convinced their downturn will be short; that the major Continental economies will escape an actual recession; and that even if one develops, it will be milder than the severe recession they forecast for the United States. Nevertheless, economic uncertainty has injected a note of caution into corporate planning. This has been mirrored by some slowing in the Brussels decision-making process and nervous waffling on major issues such as economic and monetary union. But the march toward the common destiny of January 1, 1993, continues inexorably. The nightmare of chaos and destruction anticipated by Alain Minc has not happened—at least not yet.

A second aspect to Minc's thesis was the provocative suggestion that the most fundamental reality in Europe was not EC unification but German power and dominance. Well before the opening of the Berlin Wall, Minc argued that Germany was not only becoming a superpower, but was also following its historic *Drang nach Osten* ("drive to the East") to reclaim its natural sphere of influence in Central and Eastern Europe. The EC's idea that 1992 would somehow anchor Germany in the West, Minc maintained, was just another grand illusion. He forecast instead that a new German-Soviet relationship would arise in which Germany would obtain reunification and superpower status at the expense of neutralizing and "Finlandizing" Europe.

As with his forecast of 1992-driven marketplace chaos, events so far have proven Minc wrong about Germany. Even so, his concerns about a Soviet-German alliance may yet have validity—an issue we shall come to in chapter 6.

THE EUROVISION: SUPRANATIONALISM

Another sense in which 1993 has already arrived is in the methodical strengthening of the supranational aspects of the European Community. Without this, even the adoption of the entire package of 279 directives by every country tomorrow still would not guarantee open markets. The Treaty of Rome ended up as mere words on paper for three decades, and the 279 directives could, theoretically, meet the same fate.

It is easy to sit in the United States and pontificate on the bottomless depth of European nationalism and the irreconcilable differences between countries. "Is the grand history of British governance really going to end in a bureaucrat's office in Brussels?" asked a *Wall Street Journal* editorial recently. "Colbert, Napoleon and de Gaulle: Is the glorious tradition of French sovereignty also about to culminate in some boxlike room in the Berlaymont? Does German history also end in that squat, graceless building by the Schuman metro station?" The authors of this editorial seem to believe that the plan for European political union will get nowhere. The most difficult directives necessary for 1992 will end up dead in the water because "the nations of Europe continue to act as distinct nation-states . . . concerned above all with their own national power and security."[9]

This view is arguably a valid interpretation of certain superficial realities. But deeper down, a more important side of the story is unfolding. The collective support and enthusiasm for the 1992 program has been artfully manipulated by Delors and his commission to enhance the supranational structure of the Community. Just as important, they have begun to build this new supranational organism *without* creating much of a centralized bureaucracy.

With only a little over 10,000 employees (a pittance by the standards of most governing bodies) and a budget of next to nothing, the EC is becoming an extremely powerful institution exercising considerable authority. In this regard, Delors is again very much like his historic mentor, the Community founder and former cognac merchant Jean Monnet. To watch cognac being made, Monnet once said, is to understand how dozens of small practical steps taken in the present can add up to something grand many years later. For Monnet, the goal of the Community was always political: It would be a European union that would solve the question of Germany and keep Europe strong, prosperous, and peaceful by encouraging the interdependence of its nations. He tried to attain this ideal through a series of low-key, pragmatic measures. Tireless as he was in attending to the details of the European Coal and Steel Community, Monnet was never especially interested in coal or steel. What concerned him was making sure a structure was in place that intertwined French and German interests and made it less likely the two nations would go to war again.

For Jacques Delors, the 1992 program is the equivalent of the Coal and Steel Community of the 1950s. Despite the daily attention he lavishes on the complexities of creating the single market, Delors regards economic union principally as an appealing practical device with which to rally the Europe of today. His ultimate purpose remains to use this eminently practical program to weave the fabric of Europe ever more tightly together—to continue making the *engrenage* happen—so that a political union will eventually take root.

The key to continuing the development of a political union is to enhance European acceptance today of the EC as a supranational entity and to build confidence in its ability to carry out supranational functions in a nonbureaucratic, effective, fair, and beneficial way. And that is exactly what Delors and his commission are doing. Indeed, previously unimaginable challenges to sovereign national policies are now being made routinely by the commission as it seeks to enforce supranational rules to which the member states agreed long ago.

When the Danish government awarded a $382 million contract to a consortium of mostly Danish companies to build a bridge across the Baltic Straits from one point in Denmark to another, the EC took the Danes to court. The commission successfully argued that other bidders, notably a consortium led by the French construction company Bouygues, hadn't been given full consideration. A clause in the contract specifying the use of Danish labor and materials was a clear violation of EC principles.

Similarly, after years of failure by the U.K. to comply with a Brussels directive on acceptable drinking-water quality, the European Commission took Mrs. Thatcher's government to court to force a cleanup of domestic British water supplies. "The environment and the good health of consumers cannot rely on promises by the British government," declared Carlo Ripa di Meana, the EC commissioner for the environment.[10] Thus, Europe was treated to the spectacle of Thatcher insisting Britain would never submit to rule by European bureaucrats, while in fact, an Italian EC commissioner from Brussels succeeded in ordering her to clean up her water because he believed the British public was entitled to better standards.

On the other hand, England's crumbling medieval Lichfield Cathedral is being repaired with nearly $2 million in aid from the EC's Regional Fund—a small slice of $2.5 billion worth of EC aid that will go into renovating Britain's roads, bridges, and outmoded industries over a three-year period. The cathedral qualified for assistance on the grounds that if it closed, tourism would decline and jobs would be lost. Mrs. Thatcher did not criticize the "loss of sovereignty" entailed by such munificence from Brussels even though the EC's flag flew over Lichfield's scaffolding, as it typically does at project sites where Community funds are used.

With Greece in political chaos and its economy drifting further away from EC norms recently, Jacques Delors saw no reason to worry about appearing to undermine Greek sovereignty. He penned a dire public warning to Greece about its future, which he knew would be interpreted as support for the conservative New Democracy party of Constantine Mitsotakis. The strategy worked; according to one news account, "Just enough Greek voters took Mr. Delors' implicit advice to enable Mr. Mitsotakis at last to form a government."[11]

The commission has not just gone after governments, however; it has also taken on some of the largest private-sector corporations in Europe. When Brussels launched an investigation into possible cartelization of PVCs and polyethylene by German chemical industry giant Hoechst, for example, the company was less than cooperative. The EC's investigators eventually staged a dawn raid on the company's Frankfurt offices to get the relevant documents. Hoechst complained that its rights had been violated because the EC had, in effect, sidestepped the German national system for obtaining court-ordered search warrants. The high court in Luxembourg, however, upheld the commission's right to carry out such investigations.

The European Commission has also exercised its supranational authority to seek to do away with the subsidies received by prominent and politically sensitive "national champion" companies such as Renault in France. It intervened in the takeover of British Caledonian by British Airways—which had already been approved by British antitrust authorities—and insisted on freeing up some of the routes that would otherwise have been monopolized. It has challenged the discriminatory policies of soccer teams in Spain and Italy, which allow only one or two players from other European countries to join. It has taken on powerful state monopolies such as the Dutch post office, which it alleged was getting preferential treatment in competing against private-sector companies in the burgeoning express-delivery business.

Brussels is in no position to contest the hundreds of violations of EC law which go on constantly in virtually every EC member country. But the commission is again and again making its point that over time, European governments will have to live up to the European commitment they have undertaken, even when it goes against their own national or political interests. The countries and companies that have been targeted by the EC have, of course, often fought back—and sometimes won—in court. But win or lose, the very process of contesting their cases in the

European Court is part and parcel of the acceptance of the EC's supra-national power.

Less dramatic but no less important elements of supranationality are being woven into the basic fabric of the EC's institutions. "When I was first elected to the European Parliament," recalls Enrique Baron, now the parliament's president, "I was told I was being deported from the Span-ish political scene to an elephant burial ground. But today, the parliament is gaining legislative power, and we will have more in the future. We have British Tories working together with Italian Communists on matters of mutual concern. We have seven or eight former prime ministers from different countries as members. Nationality and even party lines are dis-appearing in this parliament. Someday we will be the legislature of a federal Europe."

In meetings of the Community's finance authorities, national curren-cies are periodically realigned in value to the ECU (European Currency Unit). When this process first began, it made headlines worldwide. At times it still involves heated political clashes. But by and large, coordi-nation of the EC's Exchange Rate Mechanism has become a highly pro-fessional microeconomic management function. It is now so routine that, interestingly enough, no one any longer questions the right of a supra-national authority heavily influenced by Germany to tell most of Europe what its money is worth.

TOWARD A COMMON CURRENCY

The debate about whether or not Europe will adopt a common currency is frequently misunderstood as an all-or-nothing question. Outsiders seem to think that an EC "yes" on the issue of a single currency means that Europe's unification will continue apace, while a "no" will signal the failure of the program, the weakening of the EC, and the reassertion of national power.

The reality is much more complex. Ever since the "Werner Report" of 1970, the EC has been in favor of Economic and Monetary Union, or, as it is more familiarly known, EMU. Consistent low-level progress toward EMU has been a hallmark of Western European financial history over the last twenty years. Going backward to a completely *disunified* European monetary structure is simply not a realistic prospect. The debate, there-fore, is not about *whether* monetary union should take place. Rather, it is over how much unity is to be achieved, how fast, through what structures, and with what larger purpose in mind.

One of the best arguments for convincing reluctant European central bankers of the merits of EMU is neatly framed this way by a top French banker: "In reality, there are only two choices about monetary union. If you say you are against it, what you are really saying is that it will be all right with you if the Bundesbank as it is now constituted—with an all-German membership making its decisions in secrecy in Frankfurt—remains the de facto central bank of Europe. If you say you are for monetary union, then what you are really saying is that you think the rest of us in Europe should at least get some seats on the board, get some advance warning of what's going to happen next, and not let the Germans control *everything*."

It is an argument to which even the Germans are increasingly sympathetic. Not unlike America in the 1950s, on questions of power, the new Germany generally favors solutions in which German policies predominate, but are bolstered by the appearance of multilateralism and the support of Germany's European allies.

In any event, the quiet emergence of the ECU as an increasingly viable common European currency speaks volumes about where the debate over monetary union is headed. Originally the ECU was designed to be what economists call a "notional" currency (i.e., an accounting device); hence, there are virtually no "retail" ECUs—no bank notes or coins—to be used by the man in the street. You can't hear the confident sound of ECUs jingling in your pocket, you can't take an ECU down to the *pâtisserie* on the corner to buy a *baguette,* and you can't stuff them under your mattress if you fear a run on the banks. Basically, the ECU is just a calculation. It represents a "basket" of EC currencies periodically adjusted to reflect the relative strength of each member nation's economy. Thus, for example, after one recent adjustment, the deutsche mark made up about a third of this basket, the French franc slightly less than 20 percent, the British pound 13 percent, the Italian lira 10 percent, the Dutch guilder 9 percent, and so on down to the fractional percentages represented by the Greek drachma and the Luxembourg franc.[12]

When the ECU was invented in 1978, it served initially as a common accounting unit for the European Community's own financial operations. It offered a standardized way for Brussels to calculate the budget contributions of individual member states and to allocate funds for its various programs. It made possible a common statistical framework for collecting economic data, setting agricultural prices, and settling cross-border customs and VAT reimbursements.

In the last few years, however, the ECU has become much more than that. Today, the EC and its agencies issue ECU-denominated bonds, as do many European governments and businesses. Even non-European institutions entered the ECU bond and swaps business in the 1980s. The result of all this activity is that the ECU now ranks fifth among all world currencies used for international bond issues, with a 6 percent global market share. Not bad for a currency which doesn't really exist!

Furthermore, the ECU figures increasingly in the interbank operations of Europe. It has become one of the major reserve currencies of the world, with EC central banks depositing 20 percent of their gold and U.S. dollar reserves in the European Monetary Cooperation Fund and drawing out ECUs in return. The central banks use these ECUs to intervene in the currency markets and support the value of their national currencies whenever necessary.

Even without the backing of a venerable institution such as the U.S. Federal Reserve, the Bundesbank, or the Bank of Japan, the ECU enjoys international acceptance. Norway, which is not yet a European Community member, has already decided to link the value of its krone to the ECU. Even far from Europe, Japanese, American, and other big market players find ECU-denominated instruments useful tools to hedge against currency swings in dollars and yen.

A new element in the ECU picture is that it has begun to show indications of catching on as a retail currency—the kind of currency you *can* take to the corner to buy bread. Luxembourg experimented recently for an entire month during which ECU payments were accepted at every business establishment in the Grand Duchy, via VISA and EUROCARD credit cards and the Eurocheque check-writing system. Spain issued a gold ECU coin which sold out quickly in a wave of Europhoria around the time the Spanish peseta officially entered the Exchange Rate Mechanism in 1989. A recent survey conducted by Ernst & Young among 209 European companies and 47 banks found widespread support for making the ECU the chief European currency by 1997.[13]

"Even if the EC as a whole never agrees formally on having a single common currency, the ECU will start to move in that direction," observes John Heimann, chairman of Merrill Lynch Europe. "First, the four-star hotels and restaurants will start taking ECU credit cards. This will give ECU payment a bit of cachet. To travel around with an ECU credit card will start to mean you are very sophisticated, very international-minded, very European. Pretty soon the airlines and the airport shops will start encouraging ECU credit card payment—after all, it could make their life easier, too. Early in the twenty-first century, it will filter down to the corner grocery store. By that time, paper money may be a thing of the past anyway. You might be able to skip the whole debate about whose picture to put on European currency and just go right to a plastic money solution.''

More likely than not, however, there *will* be an officially sanctioned common currency. And it is probably coming sooner than many people think. An undeclared global contest to determine its name is already under way. Some have suggested the ''Monnet,'' combining homage to Jean Monnet with a near homonym for the French and English words for ''money.'' Others are bullish on the ''Francfort,'' which has a pleasant Carolingian ring of strength. It also links France, Belgium, Luxembourg, and Switzerland—all of whose existing national currencies are based on ''francs''—with the German city of Frankfurt, where the Bundesbank and the biggest German private banks are now headquartered.

The less poetic European Currency Unit, is still the front-runner, however. Less poetic, that is, until you recall that *écu* (meaning ''shield'' in French) was the name given to French gold and silver coins in the days when France was the world's greatest power. . . .

WILL THERE ALWAYS BE AN ENGLAND?

To argue that some form of economic and monetary union is now virtually inevitable is not to deny the importance of the current debate. Among today's issues are how and when to make the leap to formal EMU, how to structure the proposed ''EuroFed'' system of central banks, and whether to create a single, exclusive currency for the EC or to allow existing national currencies to continue to be used as well. If national currencies are to be maintained for any period of time, should their exchange rate with the ECU—or whatever unit is chosen—be fixed once and forever, or should they have zones of fluctuation and undergo periodic revaluation? Considerable debate also revolves around how much say-so the new EuroFed system should have over budgetary goals and deficit financing in each country. This is especially sensitive since the biggest immediate impact of a single currency would be to curtail the ability of individual countries to solve fiscal problems by printing money.

These issues have many ramifications, but two in particular are worth focusing on here. The first is that, unlike the much longer-range process of political union, the road to EMU is relatively clear-cut. Although it involves enough economic complexities to keep a roomful of banking experts arguing all night, few would disagree that EMU is readily feasible and possesses obvious benefits. From a purely technical viewpoint, EMU could be up and running within a very short time. Precisely because it is so immediately realizable, the debate over when and how to start down that road has also become a test of the members' true feelings about the European Community. The question of EMU, in fact, has come to represent a number of other issues—specifically, the degree of supranational authority the member states really want to vest in Brussels, their confidence in one another, and their ultimate willingness to relinquish some important appurtenances of national power for the collective good.

The second point is that the basic idea of a European monetary union necessitates a Europe-wide break with the entire history of the Anglo-American banking tradition and Anglo-American capitalism more broadly. EMU represents formal acceptance of a very Germanic approach to public finance. Outwardly, this meant defeating Margaret Thatcher. But the reason Margaret Thatcher became so problematic is that she was such an unequivocal proponent of the historic premises of Adam Smith's capitalism. These premises worked extraordinarily well during two centuries of economic development in English-speaking countries. Moreover, they exert a significant influence, even if it is a secondary one, in the economic life of virtually every other European country, especially those with a dominant Protestant tradition—such as Germany, the Netherlands, and Denmark.

No matter how independent the EuroFed of the future turns out to be, and no matter how decentralized it appears to be, EMU by definition involves a substantial degree of economic direction and management, as well as explicitly coordinated intervention in the marketplace. Bearing in mind that the marketplace under discussion involves the well-being of more than 340 million people and a gross product of almost $5 trillion, one could argue that EMU represents the largest-scale marketplace management policy ever attempted in the capitalist world. Such an idea is inherently discomforting to British leaders, just as it would be to American political leaders of the Reagan-Bush era.

EMU is thus testing not only levels of commitment to a supranational community, but also support for a powerful "visible hand" in the European economy of the future. Ultimately, the debate over EMU will determine whether European capitalism will move more in the direction of the Japanese or the American model. In view of its momentous consequences, this dialogue merits our special attention. So too do the positions and strategies of its principal combatants who engaged in high-profile battle over this issue from 1989 to 1990, Margaret Thatcher and Jacques Delors.

On the one hand, there is the "Delors Report" of 1989, which sets out a clear, stage-by-stage path to EMU. It argues that "a single currency, while not strictly necessary for the creation of a monetary union, might be seen—for economic as well as psychological and political reasons—as a natural and desirable further development. . . . A single currency would clearly demonstrate the irreversibility of the move to a monetary union, considerably facilitate the monetary management of the Community and avoid the transaction costs of converting currencies. A single currency . . . would also have much greater weight relative to other major currencies. . . . The replacement of national currencies by a single currency should therefore take place as soon as possible. . . ."[14] The "Delors Report" then goes on to present a scheme for linking Europe's existing central banks together into an EC-wide central banking system. In 1990, the report's basic conclusions were reaffirmed in a commission working paper that was more explicit in calling for the ECU to become the single currency. This paper also offered a more detailed plan for the functioning of the EuroFed and backed away from one of Delors's most controversial suggestions—that there be binding limits placed on each country's deficit spending.

Delors contends that the lack of a common currency creates an ongoing nontariff barrier and will render the new single market less efficient. Suppose, for example, company X makes its products in England and company Y makes comparable products in Germany. Both try to sell their products in both countries. If the pound depreciates against the D-mark, then company X gains a competitive advantage over company Y with respect to pricing. This will occur, not for the virtuous reason that X has found a way to make its products more efficiently, but because Britain is following questionable financial policies and engaging in currency juggling to paper over the declining competitiveness of its industries.

Furthermore, the Delors camp argues, the lack of a common currency discourages businesses from expanding on a Europe-wide scale. The transaction costs and uncertainties involved in developing a pan-European company that must constantly plan salaries, expenses, marketing, and pricing in a variety of fluctuating currencies make many businessmen prefer to stay home. A common currency would eliminate most of those headaches. In addition, it would encourage the free flow of people back and forth across Europe's borders—the factor that many see as the most crucial of all in promoting European unity. Presumably, people would travel more readily than they now do across borders—even for an evening or a weekend—if they didn't have to change their money and lose a percentage of it to the bank.

Finally, although it is not much discussed, Delors is aware of yet another advantage of having a single currency: It would endow the EC with considerable new power in the international financial community. The passage in the "Delors Report" cited earlier briefly notes that a common currency would have "much greater weight relative to other major currencies"; what this subtly implies is that the ECU could become the *world's leading currency*. If a single European ECU is adopted, it will, in fact, be more important than either the dollar or the yen in terms of its role in trade and the volume of its use in financial markets. And if world financial leaders ever finally meet to seek an end to today's global currency-rate casino, it will probably not be at Bretton Woods, under the benevolent gaze of American officialdom, but in Europe, at the invitation of the EC president and the chief of the EuroFed.

Despite the many benefits of creating a single currency and a EuroFed, Margaret Thatcher remained an implacable foe: "I neither want nor expect ever to see such a bank in my lifetime, nor, if I'm twanging a harp, for a long time afterwards."[15] Her opposition to complete monetary union was based on ideological grounds as well as short-term political considerations. The main ideological reasons were (1) her belief that market forces, not central bankers, should determine currency values and related elements of monetary policy; (2) her view that if central bankers rather than the marketplace are to influence policy questions, they should at least be responsible to democratically elected national governments— not to EC authorities, who would be "an amorphous group of people with no public accountability";[16] and (3) her conviction that monetary policy is one of the ultimate expressions of sovereign nationhood.

"If you hand over your sterling, you hand over the powers of this parliament to Europe," Thatcher declared in her last speech on the subject of EMU, shortly before her resignation.[17] Even as support for that position eroded in the British business community, Thatcher knew how to incite the xenophobia of the British masses. Immediately after her speech, the sensationalist *Sun* tabloid called upon its four million readers to face France at noon and yell, "Up yours, Delors!" The paper encouraged Britons to tell the "feelthy French to frog off," to urge Delors to "stuff his ECU," and to let him know that "he will never run our country."[18]

Thatcher's views, although often carried to rhetorical extremes, were much more than mere rhetoric. Her philosophical argument took as its starting point the absolute good of marketplace freedom and the need to choose it absolutely over all types of social direction. In this Anglo-American interpretation of capitalism, decentralized power—with all its attendant chaos—is preferable to more-centralized levels of control. Thatcher actually believed she was fighting for British freedom and sovereignty, and in a way she was: Had the EuroFed envisioned by Jacques Delors been in place in the late 1980s, Thatcher's "sovereign right" to run an irresponsible fiscal policy of high interest rates and high inflation would, no doubt, have been seriously curtailed.

Jacques Delors understood that his argument with Thatcher was not a clash of personalities but a clash of belief systems and values. "I am not fully against Mrs. Thatcher," he said in 1989. "She has administered a tough remedy for Great Britain. But a tough remedy alone is not a sufficient project of a society. In the other eleven European countries we have a very similar conception of the socioeconomic system. We all believe more or less that while the market should be the basis of the economy, the market does not have the possibility in itself to solve all the problems of economic and social policy. Therefore in each European society we are a kind of mixed economy. Germany is a good example. No one can contest the liberal, open character of the German market and the success of the German economy. But if you look at the role played by the state and the central bank in Germany, it is to make sure that it is not only a market economy but what the Germans call a *social* market economy. In this conception, all of us in Europe have very strong differences with the Thatcherists."

Jacques Delors and Co. responded to Thatcher's opposition to EMU in what can only be described as Machiavellian fashion. They held out the prospect of a "two-speed Europe"—where the U.K. would remain a member of the EC but would not be forced to accept all the programs to which the other eleven would move on. That idea then worked its way back into British domestic opinion, where the Labour party was able to exploit it to rekindle its electoral hopes. Not wanting to be left behind in Europe's "slow lane," the majority of decision-makers in Thatcher's own party began to break ranks with her—first in a trickle and then in a torrent.

Thatcher's supporters in the financial community were among the first to criticize her EC-bashing. Fearful that failure to endorse EMU would undermine the City of London as financial capital of the New Europe, *The Economist* editorialized as early as 1988 that the threat to the City's role was no longer from tax-raising, regulation-minded politicians of the left: "Today, the biggest threat to the City comes from a tax-cutting, free-market Tory—but one whose nationalism has blinded her to the way Europe's financial system is moving." On EMU, she was "repeating a bad old British habit: fighting yesterday's battles, while tomorrow's chances slip away."[19] Two years later, the magazine's editorialists had grown more impatient and more explicit: "There is fog in the Channel, and once more the Continent is cut off. This time, however, the fog is being generated in Downing Street. Britain is in danger of becoming an irrelevance on the world stage, largely because its foreign policy emanates from the gut of Mrs. Thatcher."[20]

Sir Leon Brittan, a man who might be prime minister someday, warned that Thatcher's position on EMU was harming all of British business: "Every month that goes by confirms the advantage that our European competitors have against British firms."[21]

Michael Heseltine, the kinder, gentler Tory who was the first to issue a public challenge to Thatcher from within the party, brilliantly picked apart her views on Europe, calling her opposition to EMU a "dangerous infection." Heseltine appealed to his countrymen to "commit all our national energies to the enterprise of Europe." Dismissing the very idea of sovereignty as "illusory" and "impotent," Heseltine distanced himself from Thatcher with this perspective: "There are those who fear that in moving closer to Europe, Britain will lose her identity. On the contrary, I believe that within the Community she will find a greater one."[22]

The resignation of Sir Geoffrey Howe as deputy prime minister in November 1990 was the straw that broke the Iron Lady's iron grip. Howe was the last Thatcher loyalist remaining from her original 1979 cabinet. He had stomached much, but he could not abide Thatcher's above-quoted speech to parliament on EMU. With his prime minister accusing Britain's partners of living in "cloud cuckoo land"[23] on the issue of EMU—at the very moment when the rest of the EC was uniting on a decisive course of action and timetable for monetary union—the affable Howe at last broke ranks. His resignation, in turn, set off a chain of events which, within three weeks, forced Thatcher herself to resign and brought her little-known protégé, John Major, to power as the new prime minister.

The strategy concocted by Jacques Delors had worked. By making the issue of EMU such a critical touchstone, he did not have to press for final victory over Margaret Thatcher. He gave her enough rope to hang herself—and she complied. Her own party took care of removing her as an obstacle.

It is still unclear if Britain will be fully involved in the next stage of the Community's monetary union. Ironically, the reasons have more to do with the thinking at the Bundesbank about how best to manage economic convergence than with British politics and John Major's neo-Thatcherian preference for a "hard ECU" instead of a genuine common currency. But the important point is that with Thatcher gone, the Community and the British government can move toward a cease-fire in the ideological debate over the issue, and focus on the pragmatic details.

The national identity so treasured by Mrs. Thatcher is not and has not been the real issue. What the very nationalistic French, the increasingly nationalistic Germans, and all the other member states of the EC recognize is that their national identities reside in their culture, language, life-style, history, and in many other areas no one is asking them to change—but not in their economies, which have become inextricably interdependent. Eleven members of the EC—each with its own reasons to hesitate—have come to believe that the next step is more integrated economic, monetary, and political coordination.

Post-Thatcher Britain is likely to concur eventually, although it would be naive to assume that the Iron Lady's departure alone is sufficient to bring about that change. By the end of her career, however, it had become clear that Thatcher, the supreme populist, was out of step with majority opinion in her own country. One could see this, if not in the view of the *Sun,* then in the considerably more credible estimate of the London *Sunday Times:* "There is little enthusiasm for her brand of Euro-bashing. On the contrary, Europe is actually quite popular these days. People cross the Channel more than ever before and they like what they see. There is no longer a feeling that 'abroad' is a place where you should boil the drinking water and spread newspaper on the beach before you sit down. Nowadays, it is our water and beaches which are the dirt-iest. Europeans are richer than us. Their towns are cleaner. Their schools are better. State subsidies for the arts and the universities are not given grudgingly as they are here. Their constitutional rights are better protected. Even their political systems are fairer.''[24]

Culturally, there will, of course, always be an England. But as the Channel Tunnel readies to open in 1993, providing the first-ever fixed physical link to the Continent, Britain will no longer be an island. It too will be swept up in the stream of European integration. That's where the new power, the new money, and the new British future can be found.

Although the situations are not directly analogous, it is quite possible that in Mrs. Thatcher's defeat there are lessons worth studying by those in the Bush administration who still cling to the Reaganomic illusion that a laissez-faire America can help pull the rest of the world in a laissez-faire direction. As Thatcher's debate with her EC colleagues shows, even those who are legitimately serious about removing barriers and freeing markets (as Delors's EC Commission is—and as the Japanese now are too, for that matter) do not propose to do it our Anglo-American way. They will rely on their ''visible hand'' of leadership and governance while we continue to put our faith in the ''invisible hand'' of the marketplace. The 1990s will tell much about the relative competitiveness of the two different approaches. What is instructive is that so many of Mrs. Thatcher's Tory colleagues—whose belief in the renaissance of Adam Smith a decade ago was purer, more consistently implemented and less corrupt than its Reaganomic reflection—now believe they know the answer. They are choosing to look to Europe as the only way to ensure a competitive future for Britain.

The German Question and the German Answer: Europe's Stormy Rite of Passage

> If tomorrow the politicians of the first rank in Germany say it's possible to have reunification, the English will be afraid. The French will return to their worst attitudes of provincialism and anti-Germanism. The construction of Europe will be in danger.
>
> JACQUES DELORS, September 1989

> In five years, it will be completely evident that a German union will mean a push and not a decline for the Community.
>
> HELMUT KOHL, March 1990[1]

AGAINST ALL ODDS

A myriad of obstacles lies ahead on the road to 1992 and to constructing the steadily more integrated European Community of the future. On any given day over the next few years, progress may appear imperiled. None of us should be surprised to awaken some morning to newspaper headlines announcing yet another difficult new challenge unfolding in the drama.

Against all odds, however, the European unification project is likely to continue to succeed. To better understand why, it is worth reviewing the severe tests the EC has already faced and how it has withstood them. In tracing this recent history, moreover, we will see the profound power shift within the Community as it makes room to accommodate the unavoidable reality of the new German giant in its midst.

The events of 1989–90 represent a watershed in European and perhaps even world history. The way German reunification thrust itself onto center stage in the fall of 1989 presented an opportunity—indeed, even an invitation—for Europe to be torn asunder by internecine rivalries. The fact that this has not yet happened implies a significant break with the historic force of nationalism.

"A unified Germany will be very strong, but there is no point in trying to avoid it as de Gaulle once did," says Simone Weil, the French philosopher and former president of the European Parliament. "We cannot maintain the nations of long ago. Today, most European nations have no choice about whether or not to be part of Europe—not even the U.K. Germany is the only one strong enough to have a choice, and it is choosing Europe."

That the French, Dutch, Belgians, British, and others recognized reality sufficiently to see the pointlessness in waving their national flags on a backward march to a weak and fragmented Europe is one half of the story. That the Germans were able to navigate the road to subsuming European interests under their own national interests without, at the end of the day, antagonizing their neighbors too much in the process—at least not yet—is perhaps the more important half.

Thus far, postmodern German nationalism looks as if it will be relatively diffuse, sophisticated, and benign—in other words, nothing like what Europe has seen before. *If* Germany can content itself with being the senior partner in a pan-European alliance composed of many diverse partners, it will give European unification a solid foundation and catapult the New Europe to an extraordinarily powerful position in the world. Should Germany seek a greater, more overt role than that, it will destroy the unity of Europe and perhaps itself as well.

The evidence of the last two years indicates Germany is headed in the former direction rather than the latter. Despite Germany's overbearing history, despite the "heaviness" of German culture as compared with the "lightness" of the Japanese, it appears the Germans will play a role quite similar to the Japanese in the future: Tomorrow's Germans will assert their will over others quietly, patiently, and by amassing such overwhelming superiority that friends see no advantage in challenging them and foes have no ability to do so.

A NAIVE SUMMER IN THE EUROPHORIC SUN

The spring of 1989 was the high tide of Europhoria. The 1992 program picked up momentum with each passing week. Bourses were cresting across the Continent. Giant pan-European business deals made daily headlines. Special issues of leading magazines flooded the kiosks with excited commentary about the New Europe. Americans and Japanese paid the EC the highest compliment by monitoring with unprecedented attention every straw in the Brussels wind.

The European Parliament, the only democratically elected supranational political body in the world, held elections on June 18, 1989. It was the first time these elections were taken seriously by significant numbers of voters. As a matter of fact, it was the first time many of them even became familiar with this often quixotic parliament, which makes sweeping declarations about European unity but is itself unable to agree on such a simple question as where its own headquarters should be. (Currently, the European Parliament maintains offices and headquarters in Brussels, Strasbourg, and Luxembourg, requiring its members to engage in what Enrique Baron calls "constant political tourism.")

In June 1989, however, this sometimes surreal parody of a parliament suddenly offered a glimpse of what a Federal Europe might look like in the future. In every constituency, the question of the direction to be taken by Europe formed the basic election theme. As TV anchormen reported the election-night results, with news flashes first from Paris, then from Rome, Bonn, Copenhagen, Lisbon, or Dublin, no one watching could miss the Continent-wide enthusiasm for 1992.

In that naive summer in the sun, the storms of revolution had not yet broken across Eastern Europe. German reunification had not yet returned to haunt the EC as a major political issue. European leaders could believe they had finessed the ultimate juggling act. They had laid the most solid groundwork ever in four decades of attempts to create a unified Western European market big and attractive enough to anchor West Germany firmly within its boundaries, yet balanced with a sufficient array of counterweights to preclude German domination. They had at last developed the critical mass for this European Community to be recognized as more than the sum of its parts—especially when it came to the deep-seated desire to obtain a voice in global decision-making fully independent of the United States. They had brought business and labor together in support of the 1992 program with a unity of purpose unknown since World War II. And they had managed to construct the framework for a strong New Europe with Moscow's tacit blessings, despite the historic Soviet hostility to the idea of a "United States of Europe," which had begun with Lenin and continued unabated for seventy years.

An amazing juggling act, to be sure. As we now know, it was small change compared with the challenges that would soon arise. That summer, though, it seemed to many Europeans that the hardest part was already over. In June 1989, it was still widely believed that the pace of change in the East would be slow, incremental, and evolutionary. Western Europe, it was assumed, would have plenty of time to build its orderly, tidy dream house of a unified market by the end of 1992 before having to consider seriously how it might interact with a changing East.

EIN DEUTSCHLAND?

Even during the sunny days of Europhoria, there was a whiff of explosive powder in the air. I noticed it as soon as I arrived in Brussels that June to begin on-the-ground research for this book. My instinct told me that no matter how many times I heard the 1992 program called "irreversible," I would do well to search for factors that could derail, transform, or even destroy it.

Gorbachev had just visited Bonn, where he had been received like a rock star. Reporters dubbed this unprecedented enthusiasm "Gorbymania"; Europe, they wrote, was in the throes of a "Gorbasm." Indeed, the Soviet leader was accorded nothing less than the most emotional, evocative, and welcoming embrace given any foreign leader anywhere in the world in the 1980s.

The intrepid *Economist,* a magazine known for its thought-provoking covers, used the occasion to run its most provocative cover ever. Against a field of tricolored stripes resembling the German flag, a simple question was printed in classic Fraktur type: *EIN DEUTSCHLAND?* ("One Germany?").

Half a year later, of course, that profoundly shocking question would shock no one. The very design and wording of that particular cover would be repeated almost identically on the covers of *Time, L'Express,* and other international newsmagazines. But when the June 17, 1989, issue of *The Economist* appeared, the question it raised seemed absolutely outlandish even to the best-informed experts on European affairs.

At the U.S. embassy, I was told *The Economist* was off its rocker. How could there be a reunified Germany? The Soviet Union, even under Gorbachev, would never tolerate it. Nor, for that matter, would Britain or France. Any pro-unity rhetoric coming from Bonn was just a sop thrown to the right wing of Kohl's coalition, to take the issue of nationalism away from the tiny but growing neo-Nazi Republikaners, who'd recently scored some upsetting gains in local elections. Besides, my source asked, did I seriously believe the pragmatic, inflation-phobic bankers running the West German economic miracle would voluntarily assume the full cost of bringing their Eastern brethren out of the communist muck and up to Western standards? Impossible!

Almost everywhere I went in Brussels, the same argument was presented to me: West Germany supports the European Community. Any serious move toward German reunification will wreck the EC. Therefore, German reunification is not possible. The frequency with which I heard this analysis led me to question its veracity.

One evening, I arranged to meet a brilliant young German economist who had recently arrived in Brussels to work on the staff of Martin Bangemann, a former high-ranking West German official who was now one of the key members of the European Commission. Bangemann himself—much praised in the United States as a free trader who would resist the temptation of a protectionist "fortress Europe"—had been unable to see me. Instead, his office had suggested I meet Dr. Reinhard Büscher.

We agreed to meet at a café near the Berlaymont. He didn't remember the name but told me the street corner and said the café had a sign advertising the Belgian beer Loburg. He added that I would recognize him because he would be reading *The Economist.*

As fate would have it, the cafés on both sides of the street had Loburg signs. Unsure which one Dr. Büscher meant, I walked from one to the other, looking for him in the clutter of café tables where small groups of Eurocrats huddled together speaking a variety of European languages, drinking espresso, beer, Campari, or whiskey, and arguing from time to time over an item in *Le Monde, El País, La Repubblica, The Independent,* or *Die Welt.* At last, my eyes fixed on a solitary figure reading *The Economist.* It was the very issue whose cover called attention to the return of the German question.

Dr. Büscher and I exchanged pleasantries. The conversation quickly turned to the article in *The Economist,* and he explained to me the thinking in Germany since Gorbachev's visit to Bonn the week before. "This business of the European Community and 1992—it's all quite well and good," he began. "But it is basically a pocketbook question—a few more percentage points of economic growth, some more jobs. . . . Okay, everyone wants that, and so do the Germans. But you know, we in West Germany are already quite rich. Maybe you do not know about this. Americans sometimes do not understand just how wealthy Germany has become. Actually, we are quite satisfied from the point of view of material things. But Gorbachev! *Ach!* Gorbachev! Now there is something for the German heart, for the soul, for the spirit! What is happening in the Soviet Union is certainly more exciting to most Germans than what we are doing here in Brussels.

"This European Community . . ." he went on. "Why these particular twelve nations and not others? Do you suppose we Germans have that much in common with Dublin or Lisbon? Actually, we know almost nothing about those places. But Budapest . . . Warszawa . . . Praha . . . even Moskva . . . we know very much about these places and we understand them quite well!"

What about German reunification, I asked? Even the outspoken Dr. Büscher demurred. The *"ein Deutschland"* scenario reflected fears in some European quarters more than it related to real-life possibilities in Germany. But he did not rule it out—and that was important to me. I had done dozens of interviews thus far, and every time German reunification came up, the expert I was interviewing would dismiss it completely. Dr. Büscher offered a different perspective.

"A powerful nation must be inspired by a vision," he explained. "Its leaders must give the people something to dream about. They cannot just dream about a few points of economic growth. West Germans now are *dreaming about East Germany.* And through East Germany, they are dreaming of the links to all of Eastern Europe and the Soviet Union.

Henry Kissinger is right: The unfulfilled ambitions of the Germans lie in the East.''

That was the "aha!" moment in which I felt my own foggy vision of Europe's future snap into sharp focus. The center of gravity of the New Europe would be the new German superpower. Despite the various reasons experts were then giving for why it could never happen, I suddenly knew German reunification was inevitable. And the reunification process was, in turn, the explosive factor I had been trying to uncover that could completely transform the orderly rules of the 1992 game.

Whether Europe would be transformed for better or for worse was not then clear to me. One possibility was that reunification would wreck 1992 and European unity, just as almost everyone seemed to think. But another was that it would be responsible for bringing the New Europe out from under all the Eurocratic talk about harmonizing insurance regulations and standardizing pasta ingredients. The new Germany, especially with its ambitions in the East, was the force that could put the real meat of history on the technocratic bones of 1992. And in doing so, it could thrust Europe visibly, if also volatilely, onto center stage in the global power balance.

I went back to my hotel room and reread the well-crafted opening lines of the *Economist* editorial:

> One Germany. Tear down the Berlin wall. Build a common European house. For 40 years leaders in East and West have intoned such words at varying times and with varying motives. West Germans, in their national anthem, sing about a united German fatherland; so did East Germans, until the state told them to forget the words and hum the tune. A common thread ran through every wish: the wishers did not mean it. Or rather, they did not need to wonder whether they meant it; *for it could not happen*. This comfortable hypocrisy is no longer available.[2]

Indeed. From here on in, building the New Europe was not going to be as simple as some people in Brussels thought. On the other hand, the New Europe they would be building would be that much more important and powerful if they succeeded. . . .

POKER IN MADRID

Jacques Delors, the student of Jean Monnet's theory of *engrenage*, understood the threat posed by even the first few whispers of German reunification. The German question was such a huge, "big-picture" topic that the mere act of opening it up for discussion would be enough to halt the progress on every practical front of the 1992 program. A serious debate over Germany could bring a swift end to 1992 and the dream of a united Europe.

"It is the bicycle theory," a Delors aide confided. "Right now, we know where we are going. If we stop pedaling and start thinking about our direction, we will all fall off." While the wind of history was at Europe's back, Delors did not want to lose momentum. Keeping Europe focused on practical issues was critical. And continuing the process of weaving Germany more consistently into the EC fabric was now more urgent than ever.

One way to keep the enormous challenge of the German question at bay was to notch up the level of difficulty in the unification project. By adding a new challenge, Delors could refocus the debate in the Community before it drifted East with the Germans. With the single-market program moving along so well, the time was ripe to press ahead on economic and monetary union.

Delors had little trouble enlisting the support of French President François Mitterrand and Spanish Prime Minister Felipe González. Aside from the fact that Delors had strong ideological bonds with both men—they were the three most powerful Socialists in Europe—the leaders of France and Spain were the official agenda setters for the EC during 1989. In the first half of the year, González was taking his turn as the president of the European Council. He was therefore in charge of coordinating high-level policy decisions. The French turn at the presidency would follow next, and Mitterrand would preside in the second half of '89. With their cooperation, Delors believed he could up the ante considerably and launch the EC on the road to monetary union by the end of the year.

Traditionally, the outgoing president of the European Council hosts a summit meeting in his country toward the end of his term. Thus, González convened a summit in Madrid at the end of June. The centerpiece of discussion would be the "Delors Report"—the basic blueprint for launching the EMU process.

Margaret Thatcher made no secret of her opposition to the report. The rhetoric on both sides grew inflamed as Thatcher declared, "There is no need for a single currency," and said she refused to be dragged "pell-mell into something called economic and monetary union."[3] Mitterrand castigated her as a "brake on European integration," and Thatcher shot back, "That's rich. He's barely got in the car yet," referring to the fact that France had yet to lift its own remaining controls on the free movement of capital.[4]

It was a poker game. Delors's strategy was to turn up the pressure on Thatcher by showing her to be outnumbered 11 to 1. As Delors himself said, the key question for the heads of government at the summit was, "Do they accept the report? Yes or no."[5]

The overt part of the strategy was to make Thatcher appear weak and isolated. An 11–1 vote would send the signal that Europe was ready to proceed without Britain. This would undermine Thatcher's importance and erode the credibility of her views within the EC. Delors and Mitterrand also hoped it would encourage pro-Europe voices in Thatcher's own party to force her to become more conciliatory—or even to replace her.

But Madrid was not as simple a poker game as it appeared. Delors had a more subtle purpose in mind than excoriating Margaret Thatcher. He was even more concerned with ensuring that Germany, Denmark, the Netherlands, and even Luxembourg, for that matter, all fully subscribed to monetary union. These countries had expressed some reservations about the haste with which the plans for EMU had been drawn up. Danish Prime Minister Poul Schluter admitted that his own feelings were "somewhere in-between" the positions of Thatcher and Delors.[6]

As for Germany, Foreign Minister Hans-Dietrich Genscher supported EMU, while the powerful chief of the German Bundesbank, Karl Otto Pöhl, was against it. Pöhl was putting pressure on Chancellor Kohl to oppose any rush to proceed on EMU at Madrid. Kohl himself was said to waffle from moment to moment, depending on whether he had talked last to Pöhl or to Genscher. "The clash you will see at Madrid," said one German economist, "will look like a fight between Thatcher and Delors. To be more precise, it is a battle between Genscher and Pöhl for who will control Kohl's ear."

By isolating Thatcher, who had made herself an easy target, and forcing other leaders to choose sides, Delors believed he could shore up support for EMU among the Germans, the Danes, and any other recalcitrants. The EC unity steamroller he had built around 1992 would thus continue to gather speed. Bigger political issues about the changing conditions in Europe would be kept off the front burner by the need to focus on practical matters concerning EMU.

Mrs. Thatcher, however, proved not to be such a bad poker player herself. Desperately casting about for a monkey wrench to throw into the machine at Madrid, she came up with the idea of tentatively agreeing to enter the first of the three phases of monetary union proposed in the "Delors Report," but buying time by demanding that Britain have a chance to present alternative views on how to proceed further along the road. It was an acceptable compromise.

Both sides claimed victory after Madrid. Delors succeeded in isolating Thatcher and forcing Kohl and other fence sitters to endorse EMU. But Thatcher won too. As John Kerr, her European affairs specialist at the Foreign Office, remarked a few days later, "We've stopped the steam-roller in its tracks. We snookered our friends across the Channel. It looks like they won—but we've slowed down the whole process. We've bought time to present more reasonable alternatives."

Kerr was right, although the alternative the British ended up proposing at a subsequent finance ministers' meeting in Cap d'Antibes was anything but reasonable. It was such a radical example of free-market thinking that it embarrassed most British free marketers. The essence of the U.K. "alternative" was to allow EC currencies to compete with one another by making them all legal tender throughout the Community. The free market would then carry out a Darwinian selection of Europe's common currency by choosing to use strong currencies while shunning the weak.

The finance ministers could hardly believe their ears. Was Mrs. Thatcher's government, which so strongly favored "rolling back the state's intervention in the marketplace," really championing a proposal which would force the corner pub in London to accept Greek drachmas in payment for a beer? Was this British prime minister, usually such a staunch defender of national sovereignty, ready to walk down the road that, faster than any other, could lead to the British pound disappearing from circulation and the deutsche mark becoming the European standard?

The officials quickly recognized that the whole proposal was a bluff— and an outrageous one at that. Yet it worked. Thatcher got what she wanted. The unbridled Europhoria of the preceding months died down. Even if other European leaders disagreed with her, they recognized that the dangers she spoke of were real. By forcing the EC to look before it took the next leap, she introduced doubt and caution into a process where those ingredients had been surprisingly absent.

In October 1989, the finance ministers were still chortling over the absurdity of the U.K.'s "alternative." The heads of government were just beginning to think seriously about their tactics for revisiting the EMU question at their next summit, scheduled for December in Strasbourg.

This one would be held under the French presidency of the council. Mitterrand, one of EMU's greatest enthusiasts, would therefore be in control. He was sure to isolate Thatcher further and force the question of convening an Inter-Governmental Conference (IGC) to amend the Treaty of Rome, as would be necessary to move to a single currency and other parts of the EMU plan.

But as the Foreign Office's Kerr pointed out, the point of Thatcher's "buying time" in June was that "anything could happen" by December. And anything did: Suddenly, the Berlin Wall was falling. Revolutions swept Eastern Europe. And the question of German reunification was thrust before a European leadership which had fully expected never again to have to deal with that most profoundly divisive of all European issues.

ANGST IN STRASBOURG

The immediate result of what happened in Germany in November was that the EC temporarily lost its rudder. The 1992 program suddenly seemed pale by comparison with the world-historic opportunities afforded by the massive wave of change in the East. Debates about a common currency seemed beside the point when the whole post–Cold War order was at stake. And above all, there was the German question.

The nightmare scenario went something like this: Germany's new strength wrecks the delicate balance of power in the EC. Bonn becomes so preoccupied with reunification—and with its future as a Central and Eastern European power—that it ceases to provide the economic glue necessary to hold Western Europe and the 1992 program together. France, Britain, and other EC members grow so paranoid about a newly powerful Germany that they begin to block with one another to stop German reunification. Germany becomes enraged by the attacks of its allies and is driven farther and faster to the East. The fabric of European Community history, from Jean Monnet to Jacques Delors, is ripped apart. The Germans pick up anchor from the West and head east, nationalist impulses flare up across the Continent, and Europe is fragmented into new divisions and haunted by new fears.

It didn't happen, but it came close. In London, Germanophobia was intense. Britain's last claim to geopolitical empire was its role as keeper of Europe's balance of power—a balance now being overturned completely by Germany. Mrs. Thatcher convened a meeting of some of the world's top experts on Germany. Later, a summary written by Thatcher's private secretary, Charles Powell, leaked out. The document included this choice listing of elements of the German national character: "angst, aggressiveness, assertiveness, bullying, egotism, inferiority complex, sentimentality." Powell's report concluded, somewhat more diplomatically: "We should be nice to the Germans. But even optimists had some unease, not for the present and the immediate future but for what might lie further down the road than we can yet see."[7]

The lightning rod in the British discussion of Germany turned out to be Nicholas Ridley, who served as trade and industry secretary and was ideologically close to Thatcher. He would be forced to resign from his post in 1990 after expressing himself a bit too candidly in an interview with *The Spectator* about reunification and Germany's growing power in the EC: "This is all a German racket designed to take over the whole of Europe. It has to be thwarted. This rushed takeover by the Germans on the worst possible basis, with the French behaving like poodles to the Germans, is absolutely intolerable." Ridley went on to say he preferred the chance to fight Hitler militarily to being "taken over by economics." Helmut Kohl, he predicted, would soon be "coming here and trying to say this is what we should do on the banking front and this is what our taxes should be. He'll soon be trying to take over everything."[8]

In France, the politicians were scarcely less fearful when the reunification issue first surfaced. There was Mitterrand, so recently arm-in-arm with Helmut Kohl in a zealous round of Thatcher-bashing at Madrid, now cooing softly in the direction of London as he discussed with Mrs. Thatcher ways to set up a British-French dialogue on NATO, disarmament, and nuclear weapons—a thinly veiled agenda aimed at containment of Germany. On the eve of the Strasbourg summit, Mitterrand was suddenly running to Kiev, of all places, for a tête-à-tête with Mikhail Gorbachev. Their meeting dramatized shared fears of German unity and focused on ways to slow down reunification momentum. There was *Le Figaro* arguing that German domination would destroy the EC. François Mauriac's barbed aphorism from the 1950s was back in vogue: *"J'aime tellement l'Allemagne que j'en veux deux"* ("I love Germany so much that I want there to be two of them").

Suddenly, even Delors and Thatcher appeared to be in agreement. They both feared the possibility that German reunification would upset Western equilibrium. Along with other European leaders, they tried to encourage some sort of vague road to unity of the two Germanys "within the *EC*''—a euphemism for opposing real German unity in the form of a single nation.

''If the Germans in the West want to have a close relationship with another part of the German people, the best solution is not a German state, but the construction of Europe,'' argued Delors. Turning conciliatory toward Thatcher, Delors held out an olive branch just before the Strasbourg summit. The political cohesion of the Community, he acknowledged, was more important than immediate progress on monetary union. EMU was no longer the urgent take-it-or-leave-it issue he had made it out to be in Madrid. Now it had become a ''train journey'' with ''frequent stops at which passengers can get out or seek to reroute the train. There's nothing automatic.''[9]

In Brussels, the official line of the Eurocracy was that German reunification and revolutions in the East made the 1992 program and the collective action of the EC more necessary and urgent than ever. ''Deepening'' the Community—seeing 1992 through to the end, moving on to EMU, and beginning to work for political union—was the best response to the chaos in Eastern Europe. This stood in opposition to those who wanted to shift course and ''widen'' the Community to include Eastern countries breaking free from communist rule. It was also the riposte to Thatcher and others who saw in the topsy-turvy political situation of Germany and the East a new argument for going slow on further EC unity measures.

When Mitterrand convened the December 1989 summit of EC leaders in Strasbourg, the situation was still very much in flux. ''History at present could go one way or the other,'' he said, sounding an uncharacteristic existentialist note. Unless the pace of European integration accelerated, Europe risked seeing the reemergence of centuries-old disputes and warring nationalisms. ''We just don't know which way it is going to go.''[10] Delors, too, had lost his usual optimism. ''I have a fear that the conference may end in bitterness,'' he intoned.[11] Just before the Strasbourg meeting opened, Chancellor Kohl sent Mitterrand a letter saying that, while he continued to support the general idea of monetary union, he thought the pace should be slowed down, not accelerated. In any event, he would not be prepared at Strasbourg to agree to a date for the requisite IGC to begin.

French officials seized on the Kohl letter as evidence that Bonn was more interested in German reunification than European integration. Mitterrand intimated that Franco-German relations were heading toward rupture. A deep crisis of identity wrenched every European leader. Every one of them had been reared on what had always been seen as the immutable lesson of the Munich Pact half a century earlier: It was Europe's appeasement of Germany and concessions to its territorial demands which had emboldened Hitler to embark on his war against Europe. Would history judge the European leaders of 1989 guilty of making the same mistake—and find them doubly guilty for having ignored the lesson of experience taught to every schoolchild? No matter how strong a pillar of democracy and prosperity West Germany had been for the last forty years, might not a reunified Germany revert to its past ways? Would the process of reunification unduly provoke the Soviets or otherwise drown Europe in the very sort of deluge the Community had been set up to prevent?

Rarely have modern political leaders been called upon to think through the historic consequences of their actions to the degree the European leadership was in the fall of 1989. If they were going to pursue the sensible course of realpolitik and tolerate German reunification, they would have to put aside the distrust inculcated by their past history and their past national experience. And this is what they chose to do in the end.

When the angst cleared in the wintry winds of Strasbourg, the nightmare didn't come true. The EC didn't split. The bitterness was no greater than at Madrid. In fact, there was a greater spirit of reconciliation in some ways, based on the common understanding of how much higher the stakes now were. What was surprising, given the radical realignments that took place in Europe in the weeks preceding the Strasbourg meeting, was how much its outcome resembled that of the Madrid summit—at least superficially.

"EC Heads Isolate Thatcher," declared a headline in the *Financial Times*, which ran over a front-page photo of the British prime minister alone, huddled in her overcoat, nearly being blown off the embankment into the Rhine.[12] Thatcher was more isolated than ever. Her eleven partners—including Helmut Kohl—had voted to convene the IGC debate on monetary union in December 1990. They had also voted to adopt the social charter that she opposed. But there was little inflammatory rhetoric and certainly no open break. "The Community is immensely strengthened," declared Irish Prime Minister Charles Haughey as he prepared to assume the next rotation of the council presidency.[13]

The story that got the most press attention, as usual, was the titanic clash of the large personalities. No journalist could ignore the chance to focus on the human drama of one tough British lady sticking to her guns against eleven European men. As usual, however, the subplot at Strasbourg was more important than the main event.

What had happened to all of Europe's fears about Germany? What had come of all the public statements of European concern about reunification that had been made in the weeks before Strasbourg? And why had Kohl changed his mind and agreed to the December 1990 start of the IGC, when just a few days earlier he'd said he couldn't accept a specific date? The answer was that a tacit deal had been cut. It was a deal that would slowly begin to shape the rest of the EC's development.

In principle, the bargain went like this: Helmut Kohl would continue to deliver on German commitments to the West. He would not allow the reunification process to deter Germany from the cause of European unity. Not only would he deliver, he would become a more passionate "European" than ever. To bear immediate witness to this covenant, he once again resisted high-profile pressure from the Bundesbank and came down firmly on the side of EMU. He reversed the stance taken in his letter to Mitterrand and was willing to support a specific date for opening the IGC process.

At first blush, Kohl got little in return. All he asked was that the IGC be pushed back from an initial target date in the first half of 1990 to December 1990 so that it would begin after the German elections. This was accepted by most observers as natural enough. In fact, however, it was a power play.

By requesting that Europe postpone a conference perceived in Paris and Brussels as urgent, Kohl was asking his EC colleagues to take a backseat to domestic German politics. Mitterrand and Delors went for it because it seemed a small price to pay for what they wanted. With this seemingly minor concession, they were able to put away almost all the frightening scenarios that had sprung from Pandora's box in the last month. The Wall had fallen, the world had changed, the EC had come to the brink of failure. But now, Mitterrand could close the session in Strasbourg by declaring it a "great moment and a decisive event," in which "huge decisions" with few parallels "in the history of the Community" had been made.[14]

Helmut Kohl would make a crucial trip to Brussels and London in March 1990 to cement the deal. In Brussels, he met behind closed doors for three hours with the members of the European Commission. What he said is not public knowledge, but the implication was clear: As long as Europe didn't stop Germany from its rendezvous with its greater destiny, Germany would continue to play its locomotive role in pushing Europe toward its own rendezvous with its collective destiny.

After the session, Kohl appeared before reporters to reaffirm his intention of keeping Germany anchored in the EC and pressing on simultaneously with the dual Herculean tasks of European unity and German reunification. "We don't want to be a Fourth Reich," he swore. "We want to be European Germans and German Europeans," he said, invoking the old appeal against German nationalism coined by novelist Thomas Mann.[15]

From Brussels, Kohl went to London for a meeting with Margaret Thatcher. Certainly, there was no love lost between the two of them. Thatcher had been more dramatic than Mitterrand in warning of the dangers to European stability posed by German reunification. She had underscored this by making the most of Kohl's ambiguous statements about whether or not the reunified Germany would accept its existing border with Poland. Thatcher and Kohl had even engaged in a messy, gossipy battle in the European press over Thatcher's allegation that she had heard Kohl, at a dinner in Strasbourg, state that the border question was open to renegotiation. It was a charge Kohl flatly denied.

Thatcher's opposition to reunification was inspired by historic considerations rooted in Britain's World War II experience and the Cold War aftermath. But history was a thin cosmetic for more profoundly nationalist considerations. The German newspaper *Die Zeit* was on target when it called Thatcher a "little Englander" whose British nationalism would not brook the thought of a Europe dominated by a united Germany.[16]

In spite of all that divided them, Thatcher and Kohl were fellow conservatives. Together, they represented the political right among the EC-12. Kohl was by no means as extreme as Thatcher, but they were both more vociferously in favor of free markets and free trade than most of their colleagues. Through sometimes covert machinations, Germany had occasionally blocked with the U.K. to keep the EC from going too far too fast down the road to what Thatcher viewed as the most "airy-fairy" parts of the Brussels program. As one of her top advisers had remarked a few months earlier, "Provided Germany remains in the liberal [i.e., free-market] camp, we can always gather a blocking minority in the council on the really important questions. Besides ourselves and the

Germans, all we need to stop Delors's mischief is one small country—and we can always get either the Danes or the Dutch to go along.''

When Helmut Kohl went to London in the spring of 1990, however, it was to tell Thatcher that the game was up. Germany would not be part of the blocking minority anymore. He was ready to proceed full speed with what Thatcher viewed as the worst mischief of Delors: monetary and even political union. If she wanted to remain a credible force in Europe, it was time at last to recognize the reality of German and continental European power and to cease being so obstructionist.

Thatcher got the message. In a press conference at the end of her talks with Kohl, she reluctantly acknowledged, ''We have to get used to having one country in Europe that is far stronger than the rest. Everyone has to accept that there is a bigger Germany.''[17]

Over the next few months, the decisive power shift within the EC would become clearer. It had always been assumed that Germany's wartime history would prevent it from ever becoming a political leader. ''We have what you might say is an arrangement,'' observed Edith Cresson, the French minister for European affairs at the time of the Madrid summit. ''Germany provides the economic energy for a united Europe, and France provides the political leadership.''

That arrangement was fine until the Berlin Wall fell and the reunification rocket took off. Kohl, Genscher, and even their domestic political opponents in the Social Democratic Party realized they had on their hands a totally unprecedented opportunity to unify Germany, provided they moved decisively and quickly. If they waited for the support of their European friends and allies—the ones who liked to invoke Mauriac's cynical ''love'' of Germany—they might miss out on more than just the ideal conditions for reunification. They might end up waiting forever.

FORWARD FROM DUBLIN

Helmut Kohl, often derided by fellow European heads of state as a dolt, a bumbler, and the embodiment of why Europe needed non-German political leadership, in this instance proved himself the shrewdest European leader of them all. *He called Europe's bluff.* Knowing just how dependent Europe was on Germany, and how much the 1992 program rested on German support, Kohl simply ignored the dire warnings of his colleagues on the dangers German reunification posed to European stability. Three weeks after the Wall fell, with all the other leaders of the EC convinced that going slow on reunification was infinitely preferable for Europe, Kohl put forward his ten-point program for German unity without consulting anyone in Brussels. A rush of other bold plans followed, serving as magnets to suck in East Germany before there could be any further questioning of the matter.

Although EC leaders kept insisting that the Community must be involved at every stage in the process of reunification, Kohl's actions were essentially unilateral. He tipped his hat to the Allies by creating the ''2 + 4'' formula. Under this plan, East and West Germany (the ''2'') would negotiate their reunification first. Then, the United States, Britain, France, and the Soviet Union (the ''4'') would have final approval over those issues that would end their occupation of Germany and Berlin. But Kohl and Genscher took pains to stress that the formula was ''2 + 4,'' not ''4 + 2.'' This emphasis on arithmetic nuance was meant to notify all concerned parties that the important part of the equation was *what the Germans decided,* not what the former Allies wanted.

Kohl's unilateralism continued to trigger complaints by his EC colleagues that he was bungling one issue after another—the Polish border, intra-German monetary union, the timetable for unification, and other sensitive matters. But he was not actually blundering. Although his ambivalent statements about Germany's frontiers enraged the Poles, the Soviets, the French, the British, the Americans, the Jews, and most of the rest of the world that still remembered World War II, they went over quite well *inside* Germany. Kohl, it must be remembered, was facing declining electoral popularity at home. Aside from making an appeal to latent German nationalism in general, there was substantial political favor to be curried on the border issue among the eight million Germans with family ties to disputed areas in Poland or Czechoslovakia that had once belonged to Germany. Even when he finally agreed to accept the definitive nature of the present German-Polish border, Kohl still managed to convey his sympathy with the right wing's view that Germany had been victimized after World War II. ''The truth,'' he maintained, was that ''the expulsion of Germans from their native regions was a grave injustice.'' He was conceding on the border question, not because he agreed with the Polish and European positions, but simply for the sake of expediency—so as ''not to gamble away the chance of German unity.''[18]

Kohl succeeded in getting the rest of Europe to swallow its pride and let him handle the German reunification process more or less as he pleased. It was the most sensitive issue the EC had ever faced, but there would be no real supranationality involved in its resolution. Germans alone would solve the German question. Europe would get a *fait accompli*.

Shortly after Strasbourg, an emergency EC summit was scheduled for April in Dublin to deal with what was then seen as the urgent need to craft a collective approach to the question of reunification. But by the time April 1990 arrived and the leaders prepared to gather around the lunch table in Dublin Castle, Kohl had taken full control of the process. His fraternal Christian Democrats had just won the March elections in East Germany's first free vote, providing a ringing endorsement of Kohl's strategy of quick reunification. There was no longer any point in debating when the train should be allowed to leave the station, because it was already hurtling down the tracks. The shocking, frightening, unimaginably dislocating issue of German reunification, which had been the cause of such great angst at Strasbourg, had already been settled by the time the EC's leaders gathered in Dublin, only five months later.

Recognizing that there was nothing left to discuss about Germany, Delors and Mitterrand decided to use the Dublin meeting to launch an appeal to proceed not only toward monetary union, but toward a separate Inter-Governmental Conference on political union as well. This would mean collecting from Kohl the rest of their payment for having stood aside on the reunification issue. And Kohl, proving once again more clever than many thought, was happy to give them what they wanted. After all, it was not in Germany's interests to be perceived as opposing or drifting away from Europe.

Thus, all of a sudden, Helmut Kohl, the "European German," was not only a great proponent of moving decisively toward EMU, he was also in favor of political union. He gladly joined Mitterrand in signing the letter inviting the EC clan to gather in Dublin, not to focus on German reunification, but to begin to consider how to proceed with Europe's largest goal—political union. Kohl, who just a few months earlier had wavered on whether Germany supported an IGC focused on EMU, suddenly seemed ready to go the whole nine yards, supporting an additional, simultaneous IGC, to be convened on political union. Margaret Thatcher scoffed at the idea, but, humbled somewhat by Germany's powerful new position, even she didn't issue a categorical no.

Kohl emerged as the de facto helmsman of the European Community after the Dublin meeting in April. By November 1990, with the two IGCs set to convene in Rome at the end of the year, he was urgently needed to steady the unity ship through its next difficult passage—the confusion and doubt following the onset of the Persian Gulf crisis in August.

The British, still trying to stop the rush to EMU, proposed a somewhat more credible plan than the ludicrous "competing currencies" they had put on the table in 1989. John Major, then Thatcher's Chancellor of the Exchequer, presented a scheme for what he termed a "hard ECU"—a thirteenth currency, to exist side by side with national currencies indefinitely. Carlos Solchaga, the Spanish finance minister, appeared to endorse parts of the "hard ECU" proposal as he lobbied for slowing down the EMU timetable. Other weak-currency EC members—Portugal, Greece, and Ireland—joined Solchaga and Major in raising questions about the speedy schedule demanded by Delors. The Bundesbank reverted to its instinctive fear of EMU, as Karl Otto Pöhl wondered out loud how Europe could commit to specific near-term dates for the various phases of monetary union when economic circumstances in Europe were so different from one country to the next. Sounding suspiciously sympathetic to Mrs. Thatcher, Pöhl declared, with obvious reference to Britain, "A country with an inflation rate three times as high as Germany's cannot link its currency to the deutsche mark without mass unemployment and enormous payment problems."[19] For very different reasons, Pöhl and Thatcher shared the tactical desire to keep EMU vague and far off. Both were taking advantage of another moment of European disarray to press again for the go-slow approach.

Like all other debates over EMU, this one had its own logic rooted in the details of economic issues, yet served simultaneously as a referendum on the wider picture of European unity. That the consensus on EMU which had seemed iron-clad at Strasbourg and Dublin now showed signs of breaking up underscored new, widespread jitters over European unity induced by the Persian Gulf crisis.

Pöhl's implicit sympathy for Thatcher was so disturbing to Jacques Delors that he responded by publicly disparaging the German position. "Do the Germans really want economic and monetary union? Quite frankly, I often wonder. Quite frankly, I am . . . disoriented by the contradictory statements sometimes coming from the same mouths over a short space of time."[20]

Enter Helmut Kohl. Rising to the bait from Delors, he proceeded to sort out the confused signals from Germany (where, as usual, the thinking in Bonn was conditioned by whether it was Pöhl or Genscher who was exercising the greatest influence on the chancellor at the moment). First, Kohl made use of the Bundesbank's technical objections to the "hard ECU," encouraging Pöhl to dismiss the British proposal as "the worst possible recipe for monetary policy in Europe."[21] He thus made it clear that the "hard ECU" was an unworkable diversion. But he made it equally clear that Europe needed to recommit itself to the essentials of the Delors plan. He resisted the Bundesbank's advice to avoid setting specific dates and proposed January 1, 1994, as the start of EMU's all-important "second stage" when the groundwork for a common currency and European central bank would be laid. The 1994 date was a year later than Delors had originally envisioned. By pushing the timetable back, Kohl made a modest concession to the Bundesbank view and again showed that resolution of major debates in Europe took a backseat to internal German politics. But the delay of a year was not substantive. In fact, given the confused economic environment following the Iraq crisis, only a hopeless idealist would have argued that Europe was even capable of moving toward EMU at the originally planned speed. The main point was that by stepping into the confusion and proposing a specific date for EMU's second stage, Kohl renewed Germany's commitment to EMU and kept the whole process from disintegrating under new pressures and fears.

Next, the chancellor boldly enunciated concrete ideas about political union, such as expanded powers for the European Parliament. He spoke out on the urgency of making tangible progress toward common foreign and defense policies. This provided focus for the otherwise amorphous discussion of political union.

Finally, Kohl and his countrymen began demonstrating that, despite all the scare stories circulating in prior months about the potential for runaway inflation in Germany, massive capital shortages, and economic collapse in the east, the reunified economy was working. Germany was emerging nearly as growth-oriented and dynamic as optimists had hoped, and certainly much more vital than pessimists had feared. The problems in absorbing the eastern half of the country were real, but they were being brought under control. By the end of 1990, it was evident that the economic leadership the EC so badly needed from Germany was not in jeopardy. It was also increasingly clear that having integrated the former East Germany into a unified political system and a unified economy with one currency and one central bank, the Germans knew what they were talking about on the subjects the rest of the EC would begin discussing in Rome: economic union and political union.

*   *   *

Two conclusions present themselves based on the stormy passage of a year's events from Madrid to Strasbourg to Dublin:

First, Delors's *engrenage* is still working. The European Community has been tested by extreme pressures and tensions. Somehow, it has managed to push on successfully. Its track record would seem to minimize the likelihood that future storms in the '90s will blow the Community apart.

Second, the EC has now accepted not only economic leadership but a measure of political leadership as well from Germany. The ideal moment for resisting greater German influence has passed. A German-led Europe is thus being born, comfortably wrapped in the cloak of the Paris-Bonn axis and speaking through the collective voice of the EC-12 in Brussels. Confounding Germanophobes inside and outside Europe is the prospect that, at least in the short run, German leadership is likely to be a positive factor ensuring Europe's success in the global economic competition.

"To formulate a question is to resolve it," wrote Karl Marx in *On the Jewish Question*—an essay whose title was later played on by nineteenth-century German political philosophers in coining the phrase *"die deutsche Frage"*—the German question.[22] Now, nearly a century and a half later, the German question has an answer: There *will* be a German superpower, and it will be the leading force in the New European order now being created.

6

The Birth of the New German Superpower

West German wages top the charts, per capita income is near the top, and West Germany leads the world in exports.

Given the above, why does a computer search reveal so little material on West German management? Why don't the bookstore shelves at Stanford contain a single volume on West German management practice?

TOM PETERS, author of *Thriving on Chaos* and coauthor of *In Search of Excellence*[1]

WHAT MAKES GERMAN POWER SUPER?

Why did West Germany's intent to absorb East Germany inspire such a broad global discussion on the "Germany-as-superpower" theme? Skeptics argued at the time that the acquisition of East Germany was more a liability than an asset. What West Germany got in this deal, they reasoned, was 16–17 million people, most of whom fall below the West German poverty line and many of whom need costly welfare benefits. The initial price tag for rebuilding East Germany was set at $70 billion in the form of the "German unity fund" created by the Bonn government. But most German leaders knew at the time that was only the down payment on much, much more—even if they professed surprise later at the skyrocketing cost.

The land area acquired leaves the unified Germany still only two-thirds the size of France. Yes, there's cheap labor, but if you want cheap labor, there are lots of places to go without also having to take responsibility for restructuring hundreds of inefficient industries which cough up nightmarish levels of pollution. Anyway, East German labor is not all that cheap. For years, the East German government imported Vietnamese workers in order to have a pool of really cheap labor.

Compare German reunification with other vaguely possible expanding-nation scenarios. If France, for example, were to be reunited with Quebec—a more attractive asset than East Germany, in some people's eyes—would magazine covers around the world be pondering the new French "superpower" as a result? China will actually absorb Hong Kong in 1997. But no one thinks the addition of Hong Kong will fundamentally change China's role in the world—even though Hong Kong's economy is far healthier than East Germany's, its technological base is superb, and it has some of the world's most active financial markets.

So what *is* it about the German question that set the world abuzz? At the psychological level, of course, there are the old fears that Germany could become expansionist, fascist, anti-Semitic, and even militaristic again. Such fears make German reunification more fascinating as well as more frightening. The ascendancy of a Fourth Reich in Berlin may be an extremely unrealistic scenario. But even forty recent years of West German stability and democracy cannot completely undo what went before. The mere fact that German power is waxing once again is enough to get the world's attention.

The merger of the East and West German armies will result in the biggest army in Europe occupying the most-central parts of Europe's geography. This is no trivial matter, even in a demilitarizing world. Many worry that Germany could become a "loose cannon," threatening the stability of the Continent. No matter how often political leaders in Bonn swear their intention of remaining in NATO, the ultimate result of German reunification could be military neutrality. Alternatively, with American and Soviet forces withdrawing from Central Europe, Germany could end up being not only the area's dominant economic power, but its greatest military power as well. That prospect gives modern Germany geopolitical and strategic clout it has never before had. The Soviets spoke out loudest and most consistently on their concerns about this combination of German economic and military might. Actually, though, their fears were shared in many quarters.

But fear does not explain why, just twelve days after the Wall opened, the *International Herald Tribune* ran a story headlined, "Superpower Status for Bonn?" or why three months later, *Newsweek* felt confident enough to remove the question mark and simply declare: "A United Germany: The New Superpower."[2] While fear may *dramatize* the German story, it doesn't alter its basic plot.

Nor do the short-term benefits of adding East Germany to the overall German economic pie. The East's $200 billion GNP was probably greatly inflated by the old regime. Even taken at face value and added to West Germany's trillion-dollar-plus annual output, it really just pushes Germany a little further ahead of France and Britain than it already was, while leaving it still well behind Japan and the United States. The East German population also counts for something by virtue of its sheer size. Previously, the populations of the major Western European economies were virtually identical (61 million for West Germany, 58 million for Italy, 57 million for Britain, and 56 million for France). Suddenly, with 78 million citizens, a united Germany will stand a full head taller than its partners. No doubt this will matter someday in calculating mechanisms for majority rule in the European Community, apportioning representation to the European Parliament, and making budget allocations.

But although the East will add mass and weight to the unified German economy, it still falls short of providing the full answer to why Germany, so little noticed until recently, has suddenly commanded the world's attention as a new superpower. In reality, there are four more answers to this question:

- The first is that West Germany *already was an economic superpower* long before reunification was put on the table. Most Europeans, living in close proximity to the *Wirtschaftswunder,* understood this. The fact that every single member of the EC suffered a trade deficit with West Germany reminded them of this "miracle" constantly. It took the fall of the Berlin Wall, however, and the media focus on Germany that followed to cause Americans to become aware of Germany's recent achievements.

- The second answer is that while the addition of East Germany itself may not have an overwhelming impact on the unified nation's strength and position, the world can now see clearly that this is only the first stop on the overall road of Germany's *Drang nach Osten* (''drive to the East''). Moving on to capture the markets in the rest of Eastern Europe and to play the leading role in rebuilding Czechoslovakia, Hungary, Poland, and parts of the Soviet Union carries far more economic significance than simply absorbing East Germany. Along with reunification comes the prospect of Germany's establishing a de facto sphere of influence from the Elbe to the Urals to add to the sphere it already dominates from the Atlantic to the Elbe.

- The third answer has to do with Germany's immense capital surplus. In the era of financial power, money talks as never before. The ''bottom line'' of all the competitive features of German society is its huge reservoir of surplus capital, augmented annually by a trade surplus of $80 billion. This puts Germany in an exclusive league of global financial superpowers whose only other member is Japan. The U.S. has temporarily quit this league, and the bankrupt Soviet Union is not likely ever to join. This year and next, much of Germany's capital surplus may go to rebuilding East Germany. But what about the year after that and the years beyond? Like Japan, Germany has translated its industrial edge into a surplus-capital machine. The power to invest massive sums across borders is the equivalent of yesterday's ability to occupy foreign countries militarily. As the U.S. and the Soviet Union withdraw their antiquated armies, the Germans and Japanese use their D-marks and yen to gain influence more efficiently.

- The final answer lies in a Germanic version of the Frontier Thesis elaborated long ago by American historian Frederick Jackson Turner. Although modern writers have tried to debunk Turner, his essential argument remains inescapable. The push west in nineteenth-century America and the constant expansion of new frontiers promoted the continuous invigoration of American capitalism and helped make it the most dynamic system in the world. John F. Kennedy was a deep believer in Turner's thesis. Kennedy's New Frontier of the early 1960s, replete with his call to develop the science and technology necessary to put a man on the moon by the end of that decade, represented the last conscious American effort to foster the frontier spirit in a country which had completed the task of exploring and developing its physical hinterland.

Eastern Europe is now West Germany's frontier. It is, of course, quite possible that the Germans will fail to tame this hinterland, just as it was always possible that the new American nation could have failed to win the Indian wars, been unable to lay train tracks across the Rockies, or lost the battle with lawlessness and anarchy in the Wild West. For Germany to succeed, it must develop world-leading social software and physical hardware. In rising to that challenge, Germany could go so far as to become the world's leading power.

In the next four sections of this chapter, we will take a closer look at each of the above four facets of the new Germany.

ALREADY A SUPERPOWER: THE MIRACLE, THE *MITTELSTAND*, AND THE SOCIAL MARKET

Shortly after the fall of the Wall, a wise British writer remarked that Germany is not "going to 'become' the dominant economic power of Europe; it already is."[3] This fact of life, increasingly evident to Europeans throughout the 1980s, was largely concealed from American view. Americans tended to be so infatuated with the enormity of the economic story entailed by the Roaring Eighties and Reaganomics at home that they paid scant attention to such distant matters as the ascendancy of Germany.

To the extent that Americans concerned themselves at all with foreign business affairs in the 1980s, they considered the big story to be Japan. This was natural. The rise of Japanese financial and economic power was and continues to be even more stunning than the "miracle" in Germany. It is Japan which represents the greatest long-term challenge to America's position in the world, regardless of what happens in Europe. More to the point, Japanese businesses in the 1980s, unlike their German counterparts, posed direct competitive threats inside the American market to the biggest domestic American industries (such as automobiles) as well as to those deemed to have the greatest potential for the future (such as microelectronics).

The American focus on Japan was therefore understandable. In essence, when the media covered Japan, and when corporate leaders and politicians spoke out on Japanese industry, they were really addressing the American crisis of competitiveness. They erred only in the single-mindedness of their preoccupation with Japan. The question of how the United States stacks up competitively against Japan is more or less the same issue as how it compares with Germany. Naturally, the permutations and nuances are quite different when the focus is on Europe rather than Asia. But the basic challenge facing America is similar in both cases.

A very different and much graver error made by the media, think tanks, economists, and politicians in the 1980s was their tendency to concentrate more on the U.K. than on Germany. A sampling of a typical month of business news in 1986 underscores this trend: Nine stories about Britain appeared for every one on Germany. Until the very end of the 1980s, the average reader of American financial pages could be forgiven if he drew the conclusion that the biggest business story of the decade in Europe was Thatcher's turnaround of Britain.

Mrs. Thatcher served as mentor to the Reagan administration on the art of privatization and deregulation. She was often able to state the ideological case for marketplace freedom better than the "Great Communicator" himself. As a result, her regime's victories represented news that Americans of the 1980s very much *wanted* to hear. The unleashing of the City of London to do as it pleased in financial markets fit in very well with what was happening on Wall Street in the 1980s. Thatcher's antiunion, antiwelfare rhetoric was almost identical to Ronald Reagan's. Her willingness to risk big trade deficits, a weak currency, intensified social polarization of the haves and the have-nots, and Japanese takeovers of large parts of British industry flowed from the same economic reasoning that was then in vogue in Washington: Create an atmosphere where the free market can work its wonders, and all problems can be solved.

By contrast, the developments in West Germany conveyed messages Americans did *not* want to hear. The German experience was showing that it was possible for an economy to offer its citizens one of the world's best social-benefit programs, pay extremely high labor costs, shorten the workweek, and extend vacation time, while still remaining in the front ranks of global productivity and competitiveness. Engineering such a system, however, required different policies from those of the Anglo-American model of the 1980s. West Germany's high taxes, disciplined government spending, closely regulated financial system, and large trade surplus were antithetical to the economics of Reagan and Thatcher. So too was Germany's emphasis on labor-management partnerships, social investment in skills training for the workplace, and capital investment in manufacturing.

Even before Reagan's election, the systemic differences between Anglo-American and European capitalism were in evidence; the Reagan era would simply magnify them. In a 1980 *Harvard Business Review* article, professors Robert Hayes and William Abernathy argued that American productivity and technical innovation were declining relative to Japan as well as Europe. Moreover, they claimed that blaming America's problems on factors such as the size of government bureaucracy, the excessive tax burden of businesses, the high cost of labor, and the high price of oil—explanations that would so often be proffered in the Reagan era—simply didn't wash with the international experience. "A German executive . . . will not be convinced by these explanations," they noted. "Germany imports 95% of its oil (we import 50%), its government's share of gross domestic product is about 37% (ours is about 30%) and workers must be consulted on most major decisions. Yet Germany's rate of productivity growth has actually increased since 1970 and recently rose to more than four times ours."[4]

But only when the bright lights of the American videocameras shone on the Berlin Wall did Americans begin to see a glimmer of just how successful West Germany was. Long accustomed to Washington's line that budget deficits and spending constraints made new initiatives impossible, Americans were shocked to realize that West German business and the Bonn government itself were not blinking at assuming the enormous costs of de-communizing East Germany.

"West Germany has the highest rate of savings in Western Europe. We have enough capital to finance the reconstruction of the East German economy all by ourselves," an expert in Bonn cavalierly announced.[5] Or, as Chancellor Kohl put it, "If we can redirect a small part of our trade surplus into East Germany, if we succeed in making a small part of our capital export available to East Germany, then this alone will be enough to give a strong start to the economy there."[6]

The sense of shared national purpose also stood out, in contrast to the fractured American debate on economic matters. Reunification, according to Daimler-Benz's Edzard Reuter, was "politically correct and we all have to support it," regardless of the sacrifices.[7] The degree of political unanimity was so high, in fact, that the worst thing the opposition SPD could say of Chancellor Helmut Kohl on the reunification issue was that he was "plagiarizing their ideas."[8]

As Americans watched the new German superpower use its wealth so boldly to achieve its aims and demonstrate the ability of its consensus-making machinery to resolve complex questions smoothly, there was a sense that we had seen this movie before. Not the old World War II movie—although there were abundant allusions to that as well. The film the new German drama most resembled was the one that might have been called *The Japanese Story*.

Throughout the second half of the 1980s, West Germany was quietly becoming very much like the Japan that was, in many people's eyes, the world's most excellent and voracious economic machine. Like the Japanese, the Germans began running current-account and trade surpluses unprecedented in economic history. Today, Germany's trade surplus actually *exceeds* Japan's.

The German social system, like Japan's, was gaining steadily greater advantage over countries such as the United States thanks to its long-standing emphasis on education and training. Like Japan, Germany had come to believe in long-term stable partnerships between management and labor. These were working so well that even after the American labor movement had practically ceased engaging in large-scale strikes, the number of man-days lost to labor disputes in West Germany remained an order of magnitude lower.

As in Japan, German corporations remained insulated from the kind of quarter-to-quarter profit pressure generated in American companies by stockholders. They tended to avoid the whirlwind of LBOs and debt-driven acquisitions in the 1980s and to focus instead on long-term growth and development. "We have the room to think really strategically, long-term," said Edzard Reuter.[9] It was a statement few of his American counterparts could make.

Like Japanese financial authorities—and decidedly unlike policymakers in Washington—the German Bundesbank paid great attention to the stability of the financial system. Together with the Japanese, in the second half of the 1980s, the Germans maintained the industrial world's lowest inflation rates, the lowest cost-of-capital structures, and the soundest, most dramatically appreciating currencies. As in Japan, these policies encouraged and enabled German businesses to invest for the long term in R&D, expansion of capacity, and capital equipment. The opposite policies in the United States had the opposite effect.

German regulators, like their Japanese counterparts, were willing to tolerate highly monopolized businesses enjoying vast economies of scale and stable cross-shareholdings without launching the kind of antitrust actions that have dogged American business. In return, German and Japanese corporations were able to demonstrate that big wasn't inherently bad or anticompetitive. Given the right social conditions, in fact, "big" would help make German companies *highly* competitive in the global battle of businesses.

In both Germany and Japan, economic planners found themselves regularly surprised by the robustness of their economic growth. For much of 1988–89, the reality consistently proved *better* than what had been forecast. While Americans fretted over larger-than-anticipated budget deficits, the Germans in 1990 discovered that higher-than-anticipated revenues slashed the projected deficit by nearly 20 percent.

Finally, although the German market for goods is far more open than Japan's, the German and Japanese business communities both hold a strong intuitive belief that their companies are *national assets,* which should not be freely bought and sold by foreigners. As in Japan, the economic miracle the Germans have created is chiefly for the benefit of their own people. Even those outsiders who can afford to buy into it find a myriad of barriers preventing them from doing so. This domestic practice, needless to say, has not stopped the Germans from joining the Japanese in actively acquiring very large companies in countries where the investment market is open.

Germany, of course, is not a carbon copy of Japan. Each society has achieved its disproportionate share of global wealth and economic power for its own specific reasons. Germany trails Japan in several extremely important economic respects that are almost certain to be at the cutting edge of twenty-first-century global competitiveness. Germany's high-technology infrastructure, for example, doesn't even come close to Japan's. Its microelectronics industries are far behind those of both Japan and the United States. Although German companies are export-oriented in their strategic thinking, many are still focused almost exclusively on Europe. Very few have emerged as integral players in all three major regions of the Triad, as Japanese companies have done.[10]

On the other hand, the German system enjoys attributes which can only be envied from a distance by the Japanese. In particular, Germany has managed to achieve many of the same economic successes as Japan— such as a huge trade surplus—without incurring the kind of resentment and international hostility encountered by the Japanese. Part of this difference undoubtedly is owed to thinly concealed racism and Eurocentrism. Because Germany is a European country with a European history and culture, Europeans as well as Americans tend to feel less threatened by Germany than by Japan—even in spite of Germany's horrific wartime record. German acquisitions of American companies scarcely attract notice, but similar acquisitions by Japanese firms inspire panicky headlines.

Racial factors aside, however, Germany gets better reviews in large part because the Germans have cultivated a role for themselves as positive global partners. Germany's home market *is* more open to foreign goods than Japan's. Its financial aid to its neighbors is perceived as generous, whereas Japan is still trying to shake the image of stinginess. In NATO and in the EC, Germany has established a long record of willingness to sacrifice and compromise for the common good of its allies. Japan, of course, is moving in all these directions, but it is not yet there.

Both Japan and Germany enjoy labor peace, a high degree of social harmony, and a political consensus that functions efficiently from the top of society to the bottom. But Germany has managed to obtain these blessings while offering its average citizens more personal freedom and choice than is typical in Japan. It also allows them a much greater slice of the miracle pie: Germans work 450 hours a year less than the Japanese (and 200 hours less than leisure-loving Americans!). Germans take the longest vacations in the industrial world, whereas the Japanese must try to refresh themselves with the shortest. The status of German women outstrips that of their Japanese sisters by light-years. These are important considerations because they represent areas where Japanese society is only beginning to face up to demands for change. How Japan deals with these challenges may well affect its competitiveness as a society. Germany, meanwhile, has already found the way to share the wealth and broaden the franchise of empowerment without diffusing its economic strength.

One of the few popular American analyses of the German economic miracle has recently been completed by management consultant *extraordinaire* Tom Peters. Since his findings have yet to appear widely, they are particularly useful to summarize here. Below are the eight factors Peters cites as helping to make the German miracle so miraculous:[11]

1. Training. "The Germans are training fanatics." Each year, a million young people, "from bankers-to-be to machine-tool makers," enter a three-year program in which they divide their time between working for their companies and attending highly respected vocational training centers. The implication for American managers is this: "The days of narrow specialization and unskilled labor are past. Relative skill will determine the futures of developed, high-wage nations—their ascendancy, stagnation or decline. The Japanese, Koreans, Taiwanese, Singaporeans and West Germans clearly understand this. We don't."

2. Labor Harmony. German workers, the highest-paid in the world (when wages as well as fringe benefits are calculated), are also among the most productive. They have already won the thirty-eight-hour week. They enjoy an amazing average of thirty-nine holidays and vacation days per year—nearly twice the American norm. "Paradoxically, the high pay and short hours may be a boon, not a millstone." Knowing they have to compete globally with lower-wage economies, Germans work hard and smart during the fewer hours they *are* on the job. The system of "codetermination," by which workers participate in all major management decisions through their Works Councils, reinforces the cooperative spirit between management and labor.

3. Quality, Perfectionism, and Constant Improvement. "Even more than the Japanese, the Germans make up for not being first by persisting until matchless levels of productivity, quality and efficiency are reached." German managers are obsessed with manufacturability as well as constant product improvement.

4. Niche Markets. Unlike giant American companies, which find $5–50 million markets unattractive, many German companies are perfectly content to pursue global leadership in relatively small niche markets. More than two-thirds of industrial machine goods—Germany's biggest export item—come from "one-of-a-kind products."

5. The *Mittelstand*. Germany's midsize companies, known as the *Mittelstand*, are actually the heart of the economy. They dominate Germany's world-leading machine-tool industry and produce 75 percent of the German chemical industry's output—even though that sector includes three of the world's biggest chemical firms, BASF, Bayer, and Hoechst. Flexible, fast-moving generalists, the *Mittelstand* are more likely to think global than midsize companies in the U.S. or Japan. "A majority eat, sleep, and breathe export." They also provide the competitive antidote to big, centralized German companies in a culture known for its hierarchies.

6. Export Orientation. When it comes to exporting, "The *Mittelstand* worry about it as much as Volkswagen and Siemens do, [and] unions worry about export competitiveness almost as much as management does." Thus, Germany as a nation is constantly thinking about what it can sell to the rest of the world and how it can improve what it already sells. The result is that 62 percent of German autos, 60 percent of machine tools, and 50 percent of chemical products are exported. This brings in the capital surplus that allows Germany to make the long-term investments in its own future.

7. Innovation. Yes, the Germans are far behind the Japanese and Americans in most high-tech industries. But they are "world leaders in *applying* high technology." They may import semiconductors from Japan, but when it comes to using advanced chips in factory automation technology, they do a world-class job.

8. Fiscal Conservatism. Inflation-phobia, inherited with the collective memory of the Weimar Republic hyperinflation that helped pave the way for Hitler, makes Germany extremely prudent in monetary and fiscal matters. Its economy is ultrastable as a result—"the anchor of Europe, and to some extent the world." Against this backdrop of stability and steady growth, German firms are able to take the long view in their planning. The German system's weakness is that so much stability diminishes the entrepreneurial impulse to take risks and leads to a "risk-averse attitude at a time when the world economy is changing and risk-taking is a must." This contrasts sharply with the American system. Peters concludes that "the West Germans need to loosen up a bit and we need to tighten up a bit." With their vast gamble on East Germany—even at the expense of rising interest rates and a major increase in the money supply—the West Germans show signs of heeding Peters's advice to carry out some healthy loosening up.

Several factors cited by Peters are part of the larger German concept of the *social market,* whose principles were first expounded by Ludwig Erhard, the economist who supervised postwar reconstruction in the '50s and served briefly as chancellor in the '60s. Practicing a finely tuned balance between an open market and a system of state regulation and social benefits, Germany's latter-day practitioners of the social market believe the state should define the framework for the economy, and then allow competition and individual enterprise to flourish within those parameters. This orientation is widely shared by Germans on both the left and the right, although with different emphases. The most successful blend of the state and the market seems to have been recently achieved by Kohl's Christian Democrat–Free Democrat coalition government, which has implemented a circumspect program of carefully monitored deregulation and modest tax cuts.

Kohl is routinely labeled a conservative in the American press, and that is exactly what he is in the German spectrum. Yet he fully supports a German system of business-labor codetermination that, were it to be proposed by an American political leader today, would be too far to the left to be considered a mainstream political idea. "Chancellor Kohl is a great believer in promoting the cooperation of labor and business," notes one of his advisers, Rüdiger Thiele. In 1989, Kohl held a series of conferences focusing on the "dangers and opportunities" in the new European situation, to which he invited business, trade-union, and government leaders. "Everyone at these meetings has agreed that the social dimension of 1992 is just as important as the economic dimension. If we keep our social peace, we will keep our competitiveness," says Thiele.

It is not only "conservative" German political leaders who support this unusual mix of marketplace freedom and state agenda-setting that lies at the heart of the social market. So, too, do captains of German business and industry.

"There should always be regulation of deregulation. Whenever we deregulate, it should be done very carefully; otherwise, there will be an explosion," observes Bertelsmann's CEO, Mark Wössner. Prior to the Time-Warner merger in 1989, Bertelsmann was the world's biggest media company. It remains the world's most successful book publishing company, doing 65 percent of its $7 billion annual business in thirty countries outside Germany. Wössner's predecessor and mentor, Reinhard Mohn, was the architect of Bertelsmann's growth from a small Bible-printing company in the mid-German town of Gütersloh to a global giant. He has written one of the few easily accessible books on German management by a prominent German manager, *Success Through Partnership*. While reflecting Mohn's own unique credo, the book is nonetheless perfectly German in its endorsement of what Mohn calls "a free-market economy with social responsibility."

"The purpose of business activity is no longer maximizing profits but making the greatest possible contribution to society," Mohn writes.[12] He is a certifiable free marketer, critical of German unions, in favor of tax reductions, and against government bureaucracy. At the same time, he believes in the concept of "corporate social policy." Bertelsmann has made a lavish commitment in that direction, with a rich profit-sharing plan, a corporate constitution spelling out the staff's right to control many aspects of its working environment, and a policy that encourages each employee to gain as much training as possible and to pursue "self-fulfillment" within the corporation.

The social market is costly to maintain. Yet the system manages to deliver benefits that warrant the price. Thus, even foreign investors who have the option of selecting other, lower-cost locations are investing heavily in Germany. Ford, for example, had at one time planned to make its Bridgend, England, plant the key center for an extensive overhaul of engine production for its European cars. But in 1990 Ford announced it would do most of the work in Cologne instead. Costs were lower at Bridgend, but productivity was estimated to be at least 10 percent higher in Cologne, and labor relations were much better in Germany than in England. Opting for the German location, moreover, gave Ford an opportunity to invest in the expanding, post-reunification economy. "In the mid-1980s Bridgend may have looked like an attractive gateway to the post-1992 market. Now it looks a long way from Berlin," concluded the *Financial Times* ruefully.[13]

Another valuable institution of the social market is the system of dividing leadership responsibilities between two boards of directors—one for daily operations and a second, "supervisory board" to oversee the way management manages. Instigated by the Allied victors after World War II, the supervisory board was intended to prevent reconcentration of power by keeping companies on a short leash and holding them responsible not just to themselves but also to larger public constituencies—labor, the community, and the banks. The free-market-minded British journalist Norman Macrae admires the system of German supervisory boards as "the most stringent possible watchdogs for stockholders," and jokes that what every U.S. corporation today needs is a steel-hearted German banker on its board. After witnessing the shortsightedness of American boards in the 1980s, Macrae concludes, "European boards may be slow moving and rigid, but they have done a much better job of preparing their companies for the tough global marketplace of the 1990s."[14]

Still another key ingredient of Germany's social market is its mix of centralization and decentralization—which also has its roots in Allied-occupation policies. In most European nations, economic activity has become prohibitively centralized, often focusing on only one or two cities. The Parisian region casts a dominating shadow over the French economy, and the same is true of the greater London area in Britain. In contrast, Germany has developed a wide variety of distinct economic centers—Stuttgart, Munich, Cologne-Düsseldorf, Frankfurt, Hamburg, Berlin—and now several more are emerging in the East. Each of the German *Länder* (states) has its own independent regional policy.[15] Yet in critical areas of economic management, the central state apparatus has little trouble asserting a unified policy. This combination of decentralized development and central control calls to mind the United States of more-efficient days.

A VOLKSWAGEN ENGINE IN A TRABANT BODY

As the euphoria surrounding the fall of the Berlin Wall dies down, more and more voices in the U.S. are expressing skepticism about real-world business prospects in the formerly communist world. Eastern Europe, says outspoken stock trader–turned–Columbia Business School professor Jimmy Rodgers, will be "the next South America rather than the next Southeast Asia."[16]

The Germans, however, seem to know quite clearly what they are doing in Eastern Europe—beginning, of course, with East Germany. Years before the Wall fell, the network of East-West business contacts was already extensive. Even the old Honecker regime had begun to encourage the rudiments of joint ventures. But when the Wall opened up, the rush began. *The New York Times* captured the mood of unbridled, hasty optimism in this conversation with a Western businessman visiting the East German town of Magdeburg:

> Outside the City Hall, a Jaguar sports sedan disgorges a West German in a shiny gray suit, alligator briefcase and heavy diamond ring. "I probably should not talk to you," he said with a conspiratorial wink, "but I'm here to set up a casino and some video game parlors." But what about the absence of laws on foreign investment? "If you wait for those to start, you'll be the last in line," he said, walking off briskly down Karl-Marx Street.[17]

At stake in East Germany, of course, is much more than video-game franchises. The West German business community, while cognizant of the time and the cost it will require, is confident it can create an economic miracle in East Germany. The profits will be substantial—and so will the overall contribution to the competitiveness of the German system.

To begin with, the drive to rebuild East Germany will exert a powerful "pull" factor stimulating almost every sector of the German economy. Machinery sales from West to East could triple in two or three years, according to the VDMA trade association. A Ministry of Finance official predicts West German gross domestic product will grow by 1 percent or more annually simply to satisfy demand in East Germany.[18]

The demographics are especially appealing to German businessmen—in particular the idea of replacing immigrant Turks, Slavs, and other "guest workers" in West Germany with literate, skilled, "disciplined" East Germans. The importation of foreign workers has been a necessary evil of the West German economy's rapid growth, but it has led to unrest on an otherwise tranquil social scene. In the eyes of many Germans, the presence of more than 1.5 million foreign laborers—constituting over 6 percent of the work force, the highest ratio of any major economy in Europe—has harmed rather than enhanced the overall competitiveness of German society. Turkish workers are now being offered cash incentives of thousands of marks to go home and make way for the much preferred East Germans.

Racism mixes with realism in the business outlook on this issue. "Just think of it!" exclaims one German chief executive with glee. "It is as if you Americans could send your Mexicans home and replace them with well-educated, hardworking, highly skilled New Englanders whose native language was English—and who were willing to work for even less than Mexicans!"

For companies such as Volkswagen, tapping the new labor market will be relatively easy. VW's main production facility, in Wolfsburg, is barely ten kilometers from the East German border. It has procured headlights and other parts from suppliers in East Germany for several years. Company chairman Carl Hahn, who was himself born in an area that later became part of East Germany, has announced the most ambitious East German deal to date: a $3 billion pact to built VWs at factories where Trabants are now assembled.

Companies with historic roots in East Germany are particularly eager to reconnect with their past. Dresdner Bank's Wolfgang Röller insists that the East German city of Dresden "has always remained our hometown," even during the two generations in which the bank was confined to the

West. In a dramatic homecoming, the bank held a board meeting on a train while passing from West to East Germany and chartered two jets to bring in financial journalists to cover its return to Dresden. BMW, Daimler-Benz, Hoechst, Krupp, Siemens, and Veba have all expressed interest in new ventures involving their former facilities in East Germany, outmoded as they now are.

Prior to reunification, West Germany's population was shrinking. The country faced the prospect of becoming one of the Triad nations earliest and hardest hit by the burdens of supporting a "graying" population. Now, the youth-skewed demographics of East Germany are likely to ease that crisis.

Quite a few East German assets also have considerable intrinsic value. East German property is, after all, prime, centrally located European real estate on an intensely overcrowded Continent. The parts of it that aren't polluted beyond recognition—most of it, fortunately—are massively undervalued only by virtue of the economic policies pursued by the state that owned them. The Bundesbank can be confident the exchange of worthless ostmarks for D-marks will not be as inflationary as predicted, thanks to the great secret resource of East German property. Rather than fueling runaway inflation in the West, most of the newly issued D-marks will be soaked up as apartment dwellers in the East buy the flats they live in and workers or their pension funds buy shares in the factories that have employed them.

The industrial assets are also worth noting. While most contemporary East German manufacturing is woefully beneath world standards, certain sectors—for example, machinery-building and the production of printing equipment and precision instruments—live up to German traditions of excellence. Firms such as Meissen (the famous ceramics maker) and Carl Zeiss Jena (a renowned optics and instruments company) are world-class by anyone's definition. Polygraph, a state-owned printing-machinery firm, has sold one-fifth of its output to the United States in recent years and has earned enough foreign exchange to embark on a $35 million acquisition of a New York–based marketing company. At least fifteen East German companies are said to be worth over half a billion dollars each.

Americans may be cynical about how good a deal the East German buyout is, but Germany's European competitors are not. Sir Denys Henderson, chairman of ICI, Britain's largest chemical company, sees the writing on the wall: Reunification "will make German competition tougher because the German market will be an even bigger market," he says. "In a decade when demography is going to be a problem in terms of getting new skilled workers into the economy, it will give the Germans access to a very skilled work force. We will have to run like mad to improve our productivity, our technological base and international presence to compete satisfactorily.[19]

A complete inventory of the most attractive assets in East Germany's economy would demonstrate conclusively that West Germans have not lost their heads to romantic nationalist notions. In buying out East Germany, they are pursuing a sound long-term investment strategy. What's more, the investments being made in East Germany are springboards for future expansion throughout Eastern Europe. Announcing Volkswagen's plan to retool the old Trabant factories, Carl Hahn declared, "We see this as a European car project, with Poland, Hungary and Czechoslovakia just around the corner."[20] And Wolfgang Röller, reporting that Dresdner Bank would be opening thirty-five new branches in East Germany, also used the occasion to state his interest in expanding into Hungary, Poland, and Czechoslovakia.

East Germany was the most successful socialist country in history. It provided automobiles, trucks, agricultural implements, factory machinery, tools, office equipment, and consumer goods to the Soviet Union and other Eastern Bloc countries. The quality may have been poor by Western standards and the productivity low, but East German enterprises were at the heart of a marketing pipeline. Robotron, for example, East Germany's largest industrial conglomerate, sold 60 percent of its computers and office equipment to Eastern neighbors. West German entrepreneurs are now in a position to exploit these old marketplace connections and use the pipeline to deliver revamped, upgraded products.

"The Soviet Union's largest East European trading partner is East Germany and its largest Western trading partner is West Germany," notes Sovietologist Charles Gati.[21] The point is that East Germany should not be considered as a market unto itself. It is more properly viewed as a German-speaking, German-cultured bridge into the entire process of developing the East.

"German unification is bound to be the first step toward building a great, united Europe, East and West," observes Lars Ramqvist, CEO of the Swedish telecommunications giant, Ericsson. "This united Europe will be 700 million people, according to the old definition of Europe from the Atlantic to the Urals. In the beginning, it will be tough to do business in East Germany, but long-term it will open up . . . the first step in a bigger Europe.''[22]

Germany's central role in determining the shape of this bigger Europe makes it extremely powerful. When Mikhail Gorbachev came to Washington in May 1990 for four days of summit meetings with George Bush, the agenda was nominally focused on arms control, trade, and other bilateral matters. But everyone knew the key issue lay elsewhere. ''You want to know what this summit is about? The core, the gut, the center of it is . . . Germany,'' said CBS News anchorman Dan Rather.[23] U.S.-Soviet summitry had already taken on ''the air of an antique,'' said the *Wall Street Journal*. The Washington-Moscow dialogue had moved to ''the periphery of events now driving the world.'' The cameras might still focus on Bush and Gorbachev, ''but the real game is elsewhere.''[24] Without Germany—and without Japan, for that matter—one could no longer speak meaningfully of a ''superpower summit.''

DEUTSCHE MARK!

The strength of the deutsche mark is the most obvious sign of the German economy's global competitiveness. The D-mark is also becoming the German business community's chief tool in expanding its interests abroad. Helmut Kohl said as much when he announced, early in 1990, that intra-German monetary union—making the D-mark legal tender in both Germanys—was the very first step necessary in the reunification process. Kohl explained, ''We want to associate our compatriots in East Germany directly with what we have built up in the Federal Republic over the decades—the D-mark.''[25]

As with the remarkable surge in value of the Japanese yen, the story of the D-mark is a virtuous circle, at least as far as German interests are concerned. The D-mark first rose in value because the German economy was gaining strength, the trade surplus was growing, and the Bundesbank was pursuing monetary policies aimed at maintaining a strong currency. In 1985, at the insistence of the United States and as a direct result of concerted central-bank intervention orchestrated by the Reagan administration, the D-mark was driven rapidly upward in value against the dollar. This was part of the severely flawed Reaganomic strategy of attempting to rein in the mushrooming U.S. trade deficit through currency-rate juggling. White House economists expected the strong yen and strong

D-mark to make Japan and Germany less competitive internationally, while the weak dollar would increase American competitiveness. This thinking, however, proceeded from outdated economic assumptions.

In fact, what occurred was just the opposite of what the White House expected. In this new age, where the flow of capital counts more than the flow of goods, a strong currency in the right hands is not a liability but a highly competitive asset.[26] Both the Japanese and the Germans managed to combine the rising value of their currencies with economic policy adjustments that ensured them the best of both worlds: They restructured their industries to make them that much more competitive internationally—and to make their trade surpluses that much fatter. At the same time, they took advantage of the new high value the outside world put on their money to buy foreign assets at bargain prices, thus taking a quantum leap in their international influence. Completing the circle, the intelligent management strategies employed by central bankers in Tokyo and Frankfurt gave the global currency markets even more confidence in the yen and the D-mark. They became institutionalized as strong currencies, backed by sound money policies and steady economic growth. The dollar, meanwhile, depreciated into a chronically weak currency, constantly subject to the pressures of America's deficit-driven economy.

"The strong D-mark has been a major factor in our increasing competitiveness in recent years," explains Richard Kudis, an economist with BDI (German Federation of Industries) in Cologne. "We cannot expect to sell our goods internationally simply because they are cheap. We have to be successful on the basis of productivity and quality. A strong currency is a real asset when you are importing a lot of raw materials and components but exporting a lot of capital equipment, as we are in the Federal Republic. It allows us to buy what we need cheaply. As for our exports, if no one else can compete on quality, then it doesn't matter if the strength of our currency makes the price go up."

The Reaganomic attack on the dollar, combined with the sound fundamentals of the German and Japanese economies, resulted in what was quite nearly a *doubling* in value of every deutsche mark in Germany and every yen in Japan. The United States, once the world's leading creditor nation and "banker to the world," suddenly traded places with Japan and, to a lesser extent, Germany. The U.S. became the world's largest debtor nation, with over half a trillion dollars in net external debt today. Japan became the world's biggest creditor, with some $400 billion in net external assets today. Germany emerged in second place, with $200 billion.

The D-mark, already a tower of power, seized the spotlight in the feverish aftermath of the Berlin Wall. During the three-month-long "re-unification rally" that followed, the D-mark shot up another 15 percent in value as the DAX index of Frankfurt stocks jumped nearly 20 percent. The Japanese, who recognized a phenomenon similar to their own experiences of 1985–87, were often more bullish than the Germans themselves, "buying marks, German stocks, and funds like there's no tomorrow," according to one Frankfurt broker.

The Germany Fund jumped to a 37 percent premium over its net asset value. The telephone lines to Deutsche Bank's New York offices were jammed with calls from American investors seeking information on how to buy stock in the company. "The mark will be the currency of the 1990s," announced New York foreign-currency expert Al Soria.[27]

"Deutsche mark fever is gripping the world's currency exchanges," declared *Business Week*. "Surging economic growth and euphoria over reunification with the East are prompting investors from all corners to pour billions into the mark. 'It's the D-mark over every other currency in the world,' says Barry M. Gillman, CEO of Prudential Insurance Co.'s international money management unit."[28] The deluge of foreign investment represented "one of the most dramatic shifts of capital flows into a country in recent history," observed Salomon Brothers economist Nicholas P. Sargen.[29] Salomon itself took full-page newspaper ads to trumpet the opening of its East Berlin office. The Rothschilds, the world's most legendary banking family, chose this time of deutsche mark fever to put the scars of World War II behind them and reopen a long-closed office in Frankfurt.

The D-mark's popularity spread rapidly through Eastern Europe. As soon as the Soviets got wind of the intra-German agreement on monetary union, they began pressing East Germany to pay for Soviet oil not in the USSR's own nearly worthless rubles but in D-marks. From Warsaw to Sofia, a thriving black market arose. With the mark replacing the dollar as the hard currency of the East, noted *Business Week*, "West Germany's power to control currency values and interest rates throughout Europe will be unchallenged."[30]

Even bad news about the deutsche mark—of which there may be more in the future—only served to illustrate its importance to the world economy. In March 1990, foreign bond markets began to get the jitters about what was perceived as the runaway costs of German reunification. The bill seemed to be mounting every day as things turned out to be bleaker in East Germany than they had looked in the initial months of euphoria. Foreign experts, who had speculated that the West German authorities might exchange East German ostmarks at conversion rates ranging from 2:1 to 7:1, were dumbfounded by the politically driven notion of 1:1 currency-conversion rates between the D-mark and the ostmark. They were particularly alarmed when Bundesbank chief Karl Otto Pöhl, in whom they had so much confidence, began expressing skepticism about Bonn's plans for monetary union. Clever foreign analysts began to calculate what would happen to global liquidity if Germany began borrowing heavily in world markets to finance its redevelopment program in the East.

The analysts didn't get too far with their calculations before they triggered a sell-off in financial markets all over the world. For a few weeks, international investors braced for a steep plunge to the bottom, and Japan actually experienced a near-meltdown. Eventually, the roiled markets becalmed themselves, in no small measure because German bankers and economists went on the offensive, explaining to foreigners that the reunification process was firmly under control. What looked like exorbitant costs to some American eyes, they said, were really quite manageable to a rich country like Germany. What appeared dangerously inflationary actually wasn't—*if* you had the wise men of the Bundesbank deciding precisely when to ease and when to tighten. What looked like pressure on the D-mark was only a momentary fluctuation. In the long run, so many people all over the world would be buying D-marks that the small number of East Germans who were to receive a few thousand each in exchange for their country would be just a drop in the capacious economic bucket of the new Germany.

Offering an instructive glimpse into German thinking, the Bayerische Landesbank took out advertorials in financial journals to insist that fears about radically rising interest rates and a weakening D-mark were unjustified. Their commentary dismissed such notions as a "purely psychological phenomenon" defying "logical" and "sober" arguments.[31] World financial markets, of course, are not known for their loyalty to logic and sober reasoning. But the good folks of the Bayerische Landesbank seemed to think they could prod the world into shaping up and flying right on the German question. Amazingly, they and the rest of the German banking community succeeded.

By summer, the world was ready to accept that the July 2, 1990, monetary union between the two Germanys and the one-to-one conversion rate were not as crazy as they at first seemed. The cult of the deutsche mark was only growing stronger. As befits a superpower in an age defined by financial power, the Germans had the best-managed financial system in the world.

A HINTERLAND AT LAST: THE FRONTIER THESIS OF ALFRED HERRHAUSEN

As I interviewed Alfred Herrhausen in September 1989, our meeting was probably being watched by the terrorists who would assassinate him two months later. Already they were tracking the banker's every move. The terrorists murdered Herrhausen for the same reason I wanted to interview him: He was the perfect symbol of the new Germany. Herrhausen epitomized his country's potent new dynamism as an individual, in his corporate role as the chief executive of Deutsche Bank, and above all, in his ideas about the future of Germany and its place in the world.

As a personality, Herrhausen defied the outdated stereotypes of Germans still so prevalent in the United States and elsewhere. Ruggedly handsome, trim and suave, impeccably tailored, charming, and utterly searing in his intellect, he came across as the consummate Continental, not the overbearing boor foreigners often expect to find in German executive suites. His English was not only fluent, he was capable of using it to express the full gamut of his intellectual pursuits. The microeconomic details of daily banking operations certainly occupied much of his mental shelf space. His concerns about macroeconomic issues ranging from a common currency for Europe to third world debt and the future of the yen-dollar relationship took up even more. But there was still plenty of room for phenomenology and modern philosophy, the political situation in the Soviet Union, and German neo-expressionistic painting. His taste in art was not just modern but postmodern. Each floor of the Deutsche Bank's gleaming twin towers—the dominant landmarks of the Frankfurt skyline—is decorated with the work of a different avant-garde German artist. Herrhausen's own office featured the work of the East German émigré artist A. R. Penck—the toast of New York's SoHo in the late 1980s.

As speaker (CEO) of Deutsche Bank, Herrhausen gave the lie to the trite image of the dull, plodding German manager. He moved with the speed of a panther through the global jungle of international finance, acting with a decisiveness that was extraordinary by American banking standards and altogether staggering by those of the big Japanese banks with which Deutsche Bank is more properly compared. "Herrhausen Swallows a Bank Before Lunch," headlined the *Financial Times* shortly before his assassination, as he swooped in for a press conference to announce Deutsche Bank's $1.5 billion acquisition of Morgan Grenfell.[32]

Herrhausen also possessed enormous political influence. He was a confidant of Helmut Kohl and a consultant on important economic issues. Kohl, by no means a sentimentalist, nearly broke down while giving the eulogy at Herrhausen's funeral.

As a corporation, Deutsche Bank epitomizes German economic prowess just as Herrhausen typified the new generation of brilliant German managers. With nearly $200 billion in assets, Deutsche Bank is the biggest bank in Germany—but that does not begin to tell its story. Nor is it enough to say that in a profit-squeezed global banking industry, Deutsche Bank is one of the best-performing financial institutions in the world, with a 1989 operating profit of nearly 4 billion marks.

The real story of this bank lies in its system of cross-shareholdings and minority investments, which place it at the heart of a network connecting many of Germany's most important enterprises. It owns a controlling 28 percent stake, for example, in Daimler-Benz. Partly as a result of Herrhausen's persuasive lobbying at the highest levels in Bonn, Daimler-Benz was allowed to push the limits of German antitrust law to acquire MBB, one of Europe's biggest aircraft manufacturers and defense contractors.

Deutsche Bank also owns 10 percent or more of over a dozen other German companies, including the Karstadt retailing group, Heidelberger Zement (cement), Südzucker (sugar), Philipp Holzmann (construction), and other firms with interests from household appliances to oil trading. If participations under 10 percent are counted, then Deutsche Bank's portfolio includes holdings in at least four hundred other companies. About 40 percent of all new stock issues in Germany are underwritten by Deutsche Bank's securities operation.

The recent outward thrust of Germany's long domestically oriented financial institutions has been led by Deutsche Bank, which now has branches in more than thirty countries. The bank has also built up a presence in the U.S. government bond market and other global financial-service activities of a wholesale nature. Its Tokyo subsidiary is one of the most profitable foreign institutions in Japan.

Beginning with Herrhausen's purchase of the Bank of America's Italian subsidiary in 1986 and continuing through to the big Morgan Grenfell deal in 1989, a stream of foreign acquisitions positioned the bank not just for 1992 but for the globalized banking environment of the '90s in general. These included a number of small and midsize firms well situated in various niches such as trade financing, investment banking, securities dealing, and in some cases, retail banking: Antoni, Hacker in Austria; MDM Sociedade de Investimento in Portugal; Banco Comercial Transatlántico in Spain; H. Albert de Bary in the Netherlands; and McLean McCarthy in Canada.

Deutsche Bank's list of cross-border investments also includes a 3 percent interest in automaker Fiat, Italy's biggest company. The two firms have recently teamed up to market a jointly owned credit-card operation in Italy. And any day now Deutsche Bank is expected either to acquire or enter into a joint venture with a French bank, something Herrhausen was considering just before his death. And, according to one well-informed New York investment banker, "the chief executives of the four biggest New York banks are all dreaming that Deutsche Bank will somehow rescue them from their present crisis."

While European and American politicians were still discussing the merits of economic aid for the Soviet Union, Deutsche Bank opened a Moscow office—the first big Western bank to do so. Its privileged position is symbolized by its claim to be the only foreign bank which owns its Moscow office building. To date, Deutsche has done more business in the Soviet Union than any other foreign bank. Herrhausen helped finance the giant Soviet gas pipeline project. Shortly before his murder, he put a new credit line of 3 billion D-marks at Mikhail Gorbachev's disposal. Herrhausen was also the Hungarian government's principal private-sector banker.

An ardent spokesman for both the economic and political value of reunification long before it became a fashionable subject, Herrhausen moved swiftly the moment the Berlin Wall came down. His personal intervention helped ensure that there would be an adequate supply of cash for the throngs of East Germans who lined up at West Berlin banks to collect their 100 marks in "welcome money." Consequently, the greatest run on banks the world has ever seen happened not only quietly and smoothly but without a hint of stress to the German financial system.

By February 1990, three months after the opening of the Wall, Deutsche Bank had established ten branch offices in East Germany—some temporarily housed in hotel rooms until suitable office sites could be found. By April, a high-level joint venture had been negotiated with East Germany's Kreditbank, the former state-owned banking monopoly, which will create a network of one to two hundred East German branch offices. Meanwhile, Herrhausen directed Deutsche Bank's real estate managers to begin buying up property in Berlin with the clear intention of moving the headquarters there someday. Bonn, Herrhausen believed—as do many influential Germans—was not a suitable capital for Germany. Even Frankfurt's emergence as a world financial center did not make that city attractive enough to be a great bank's permanent home when compared with Berlin.

Herrhausen was not bashful about Germany's new self-confidence and the dream of a reunified country whose capital might once again be an undivided Berlin. Long before the Berlin Wall fell, he was encouraging reunification. "Can you imagine that West Germans identify themselves with Bonn as our capital? The answer is no. Can you imagine that people in East Germany identify with East Berlin as their capital? Again, the answer is no." A single Germany would have a single Berlin as its capital, Herrhausen was certain.

Radical leftists scrawled graffiti on the Berlin Wall in November 1989 urging East Germans to say "no to the dictatorship of the three D's: Deutsche Bank, the Deutsche mark, and Daimler-Benz." They might as well have spared the spray paint for the second two D's. Herrhausen's Deutsche Bank controlled Daimler-Benz and held more sway over monetary policy and the D-mark's value than any other institution save for the Bundesbank itself.

Jealous domestic rivals criticized Herrhausen for being too aggressive and too powerful. Some leaders of the SPD and the Free Democrats seized on the growing concentration of power by German banks in general—and Deutsche Bank in particular—as a national political issue. "The best thing the Americans did after the war was force the breakup of big, centralized German companies," remarked one Socialist politician. "Now, the banks control too much, and Herrhausen controls most of all." The press referred to Herrhausen with bitter irony as "Almighty Supreme Being"—an appellation which irritated him. Nevertheless, it was obvious to all observers that this already mighty man, "who many people say [was] Europe's most powerful banker," was "eager to become even mightier."[33]

In his very quest for power, Herrhausen also symbolized the new Germany and its relationship to Europe. He loved competition, he loved being the best, and he saw no reason not to wield the power he had won fairly through competitive excellence. Some of those who argued that he and his bank were becoming too powerful could play successfully on public fears about what *might* happen in the future. But none of his critics could point to evidence of any adverse consequences that had actually arisen from this concentration of power.

Unlike those who hemmed and hawed about Germany's future when speaking in public (while usually exhibiting no such reticence in private), Herrhausen expressed the same opinion both in public and in private. The world, he said, would just have to get used to Germany's playing a leadership role commensurate with its economic strength. Europe, he insisted, must allow Germany to regain "what every other country has, namely, a national identity." Herrhausen's vision of the future is particularly important to the discussion in this book because it tells us much about the new Germany. Just as his personal career paralleled Germany's success, his ideas formed an elegant distillation and creative synthesis of the most dynamic thinking around him.

Just what did Alfred Herrhausen understand about the future? Like most German businessmen, he believed in the importance of the conspicuous market immediately across the false border: 17 million German-speaking consumers in need of everything from refrigerators to automatic teller machines—and willing to work hard to get the goods and services they desired. Like most of his colleagues, Herrhausen saw the attractiveness of playing the "east card" to solve West Germany's chronic labor shortages. And of course, better than most German businessmen, he understood that East Germany's process of economic transformation would have a substantial impact on Hungary, Poland, Czechoslovakia, and the more economically attractive parts of the Soviet Union.

But Herrhausen also sensed some things that were not always so well understood by his peers. In particular, he believed that the "big vision" of national purpose can stimulate economic growth in mysterious ways economists have never been able to quantify. Absorbing and integrating East Germany into a single German economy, he said, would be a "challenge" but certainly not a liability. Indeed, he relished the prospect. "I do not hesitate to state that Germans still know what it means to work hard. They still love it. With such a national aim, they would do their utmost in a short time. After the war, we proved this was possible. . . ."

The very difficulties of rebuilding East Germany, Herrhausen believed, would shake out any remaining stodginess in German industry. The task would call forward a new generation of entrepreneurs. Some of them, no doubt, would be found among the youth of East Germany, who, unlike their Western brethren, still recognized what it meant to risk their lives and to struggle to survive. Reunification would rid Germany of any tendency toward smug complacency, which has been the undoing of so many successful societies in history, including the United States. The combination of the internal challenge of rebuilding East Germany with the external challenge of Europeanizing German companies in preparation for 1992 was a dream come true for a man who believed that tough challenges brought out the best in his society. A Germany that was already growing by leaps and bounds would thus have the chance to engage in a constant process of renewal and reinvention lasting into the next century.

It was in this vision that Alfred Herrhausen articulated a critical truth that lies at the very heart of the global competitiveness race. The Triad has become an extremely wealthy, affluent world. Within it, the struggle for basic necessities of life has recently ceased to propel social progress as it did for countless centuries before. Poverty, hunger, and homelessness still exist—but these arise primarily from contradictions and imperfections in social, political, and distribution systems.

Under those circumstances, how do societies maintain their forward motion? What compels them to continue changing, evolving, and progressing? Herrhausen, his colleagues in Germany and elsewere in Europe, and many people in Japan and East Asia looked at the American experience in this regard and found it wanting. No intelligent person, least of all Alfred Herrhausen, would question the immensity of American wealth, resources, and power. What Herrhausen wondered was whether American society still had the capacity and the will to use this abundance as a platform for further evolution, or whether Americans had come to accept a long, slow erosion as inevitable. Why weren't American leaders instilling a sense of purpose in their people? Where was the vision? To Herrhausen, being a leader meant setting a bold, visionary agenda and then organizing and motivating followers to push the limits of their abilities in order to live up to that vision. That was what he intended to do in Germany. . . .

SPRECHEN SIE DEUTSCH?

Germany is back. It is a superpower once again. Because of the way World War II expunged almost everything positive about Germany from view, it is sometimes hard for those of us born in the postwar era to realize that it is normal for Germany to be a great power.

Emphasizing Germany's military past, we tend to forget the powerful role it has played in economic history. The Germany described by John Maynard Keynes seventy years ago is remarkably similar to the nation of today: "Round Germany as a central support, the rest of the European economic system grouped itself, and on the prosperity and enterprise of Germany, the prosperity of the rest of the Continent mainly depended." Recalling that Keynesian wisdom, Kemper Financial Services economist David Hale observes:

> The great tragedy of German history in the 20th century is that she was on her way to achieving a powerful, if not dominant position, in the affairs of Europe through peaceful means when militarism diverted her onto a destructive course. In the late 19th century, Germany led the industrial world in the introduction of universal education, technical training for workers, unemployment insurance and the provision of other social services designed to enhance national productivity. As a result of Germany's success in both diffusing knowledge and applying technology, her share of world industrial output overtook Britain's in the first decade of the century.[34]

Ideas, philosophies, schools of thought, and cultural trends that have their roots in Germany (or at least in the German-speaking world) form much of the bedrock of contemporary Western civilization. Germany's record as a global power is not just that of Hitler and the Nazis, as we have tended to think for the last four decades. Germany is also Bach, Beethoven, Brahms, and a preponderance of the great composers. It is Luther, Kant, Hegel, Marx, Weber, Nietzsche, Husserl, Wittgenstein, Freud, and a preponderance of the leading philosophers and social thinkers. It is Einstein, Heisenberg, Planck, and many of the great physicists of the twentieth century. It is shrewd political power brokers from Metternich to Bismarck, towering literary figures such as Goethe, Mann, and Brecht, and important architects such as Mies van der Rohe and Walter Gropius. It is inventors from Johannes Gutenberg, whose movable type planted the seed of the Information Age, to Karl Benz and Gottlieb Daimler, whose internal-combustion engines laid the basis for the automobile industry two decades before Henry Ford founded his company.

The list goes on and on. But while we recognize these names and know their work, most of us outside Germany have been trained *not* to think of these people as especially German. We have been steered away from contemplating the idea that, as a group, they represent the excellence and talents fundamental to one of the world's richest and greatest societies. Until recently, the unstated assumption in America was that German history had come to an end with the Nazis and the Holocaust. The horrors visited on the world were sufficient to justify not only the Allied neutering of the German state but also the retrospective excising of German culture from world history.

Today, Germany is back in our field of vision whether we like it or not. And it is not just the great German economic machine. Germany is now beginning to manifest all the signs of a multifaceted, advanced, creative, and progressive society.

A renaissance is taking place in German physics, for example. Every year since 1984, a German has won or shared a Nobel science prize, some of them for work in the hottest fields of discovery, such as superconductivity.

The German painter Anselm Kiefer is esteemed by many American critics as the single most important artist on the contemporary scene. In a recent review, Peter Schjeldahl called Kiefer ''the world's most prepossessing artist,'' and declared West Germany ''the most successful national culture in contemporary art.''[35]

When the New York Philharmonic recently searched for a successor to music director Zubin Mehta, it reached into East Germany's most globally competitive realm—its classical music culture—to recruit conductor Kurt Masur. On the international cabaret scene, meanwhile, the West German chanteuse Ute Lemper is often compared to Marlene Dietrich. Her sensational international appearances are reminding the world that being a sex symbol and being German need not be a contradiction.

Some of the best indicators of the robust health of German society are found in athletics. In 1989, just as the flow of East German refugees was beginning to create the pressure that would ultimately bring down the Wall, a momentous event took place on center court in Wimbledon: Two Germans, Boris Becker and Steffi Graf, won the men's and women's singles championships, the two most coveted titles in tennis.

The upcoming summer Olympics will likely have substantial symbolic implications. They will take place in 1992, Europe's fateful year, in Barcelona, one of the hot cities of the New Europe. Had the two separate German Olympic delegations been unified in 1988, they would have won 142 medals, compared with 132 for the Soviets and 94 for the Americans. Although the East German sports machine has lately been thrown into chaos, a sweep by a unified German team in '92 is still possible. It would certainly be a telling sign of the times.

A world-leading German fashion designer? Yes, said *Manhattan inc.,* describing Hugo Boss—although Boss recently sold a majority interest in his company to a Japanese group. The "Bossing of America" is now alleged to be taking place, "with Bosswear already turning up in such bastions of yuppie chic as *L.A. Law* and most mornings on model anchorman Bryant Gumbel." The Boss line owes its success in part to the fact that the Berlin Wall is coming down, Europe is consolidating its power, and "Germany is getting a lot of good press."[36]

In film, directors such as Rainer Werner Fassbinder and Wim Wenders have brought to the postmodern German cinema some of the distinguished tradition of modernist innovation that originated with Fritz Lang. Wenders, says *Newsweek,* "is the sort of film visionary who might help bring the golden age of cinema back to the future German capital."[37] Meanwhile, Berlin is teeming with cultural activity in general. West Berlin cultural official Anke Martiny explains, "By the time the European free market comes about in 1992, we must present a united European front against U.S. domination of our screens and airwaves."[38]

Although West Germany was not widely thought of as a leading global political power until 1989, its political traditions—and even its protest movements—exerted ever greater influence beyond its borders throughout the 1980s. German opposition to nuclear weapons helped focus world attention on the idea of ending the Cold War, while the Green movement launched environmentalism into the political mainstream all over the globe. The Bundesbank, regarded so highly throughout Europe for its financial achievements, is now also admired for its political structure, emphasizing decentralized independence within a federal whole. Germany's system of education and skills training is constantly invoked as a model elsewhere in Europe. Peter Morgan, a former IBM executive who is now director general of London's prestigious Institute of Directors, waxed so dramatic on this theme at a recent institute luncheon that indignant editorial writers inferred he was suggesting "Britain should emulate West Germany in every respect"—perhaps beginning with a national campaign to eat wurst.[39]

Even the German language is enjoying a modest but strategic revival. Routinely studied as a great world language by American college students of the 1920s and '30s, German was once a requirement at many American medical schools. After World War II, however, the worldwide German language-learning industry collapsed. Beginning in the 1970s, it began its comeback as hoteliers from Torremolinos to Bali sought to learn the language of the German clients descending in droves on these resorts. The decisive moment confirming Germany's arrival as a superpower may have come in February 1990 at the annual World Economic Forum in Davos, Switzerland. The Davos event is the premier regularly scheduled conclave of global capitalism's elite, bringing together the CEOs of the world's biggest businesses, finance ministers, and celebrated economists. The 1990 session turned out to be the biggest gathering ever. Some seventy ministers, prime ministers, and heads of state jammed into the conference hall along with hundreds of CEOs. When Klaus Schwab, the forum's president, began the meeting by giving his "address in German, and not, as usual, in determinedly international English," *The Economist* viewed it as proof positive that "the decade of Germany" had officially begun.[40]

Suddenly, the Bundesbank's Karl Otto Pöhl, extremely fluent in English, was giving speeches at international conferences in his native German. German representatives in Brussels were demanding that more official EC business be carried out in German as well as French and English. The Brussels branch of the Goethe Institute reported a 13 percent jump in enrollment in its German classes in 1990.

"The Germans are no longer on probation and many feel liberated from constantly having to prove their internationalist credentials," said newspaper editor Thomas Kielinger in explaining why so many English-speaking Germans were using their native tongue at the 1990 annual Anglo-German Königswinter Conference.[41]

In Eastern Europe, the German language has been growing increasingly popular for some time. Alfred Herrhausen told the story of meeting the former Hungarian leader János Kádár, who informed him that Hungarian children were being required to learn two languages, one "Western" and one "Eastern." Herrhausen assumed Kádár meant English and Russian. "No," said Kadar, "the Western language is English, and the Eastern language is German.'' After the events of 1989, German began to spread like wildfire through Eastern Europe. The Bonn government is actively encouraging this trend. It has increased its annual budget for German cultural activities abroad to almost a billion marks and is opening new German language and cultural centers in Moscow, Warsaw, Prague, and Sofia.

Czechoslovakia is currently debating whether its school system's second language should be English or German. Rita Klimova, Czechoslovakia's ambassador in Washington, senses German will win out: ''The German-speaking world will now achieve what the Hapsburgs, Bismarck and Hitler failed to achieve: the Germanization of Central Europe—through peaceful and laudable means of course. And by the logic of commerce rather than conquest.''[42]

Germany, in fact, will most likely exert more than just a linguistic influence on the changing societies of Eastern Europe. Bartold Witte, head of the West German Foreign Ministry's cultural department, explains, ''This is not just because of centuries of cultural and linguistic relationships with Eastern Europe, it is because we West Germans have built up a democracy after the catastrophe of totalitarianism.'' Germany's' ''reformed capitalism'' offers the attraction of a ''third way'' to Eastern Europeans eager to put their socialist past behind them but not ready to embrace ''the excesses of Anglo-U.S. liberalism.''[43]

SHOULD THE WORLD FEAR THE NEW GERMANY?

In the space of a year, the non-German world's thinking on the German question evolved as follows: In July 1989, the idea of German reunification still seemed too improbable to merit serious discussion. By October, it had become possible, but those who advocated a quick timetable were accused of provocation and adventurism. In November, it began to seem likely—and therefore became a cause for panic, as the world considered the many problems that might ensue. By December, every fear about Germany that remained in the world's collective memory had bubbled back up to the surface. Some of these worries seemed particularly well founded in view of the pushy conduct and unilateralism exhibited in Bonn; especially worrisome was Kohl's apparent willingness to reopen the Polish border question. But by March 1990, Kohl had made amends on the Polish issue and had cemented his deal with his allies in Paris,

Brussels, and London. All concerned breathed a deep sigh of relief. By April, the world had resigned itself to accepting German reunification as inevitable. Some of the naysayers of months past even busied themselves with explaining why it would be good for Europe and good for the world. By July 1990, the first stage of reunification—intra-German monetary union—had actually begun. Three months later, German reunification became an accomplished fact. The issue of reunification had proceeded so definitively from the realm of the impossible to the realm of the real that by the time it actually happened it was pure denouement. If one had suggested in July 1989 that on October 3, 1990, Germany would be reunified and the outside world would find it only the second most important news story of the week, one would have been thought quite mad. That, however, was exactly what happened. The actual day of German reunification turned out to be a non-event for the outside world, over-shadowed almost completely by the crisis in the Persian Gulf. Besides, the world had made its peace, more or less, with the new German superpower.

In an effort to dispel remaining fears, or at least contain them, the "don't worry about Germany" school took up its cudgels. The German establishment led this mission, arguing that Germany had accumulated more than enough credentials to prove it is one of the most stable, prosperous, and pacific democracies in the world. Despite its growing involvement in the East, there is no need to anchor Germany to the West, they said. Germany *is* in the West, and the Germans have no desire to go elsewhere. The American political leadership firmly backed this view. President Bush raised no substantive questions about Germany, and offered nothing but praise for Kohl's handling of reunification. Even when it looked as if Kohl might be making his own private deal with Mikhail Gorbachev—announcing their agreement on reunification on Gorbachev's home turf—Bush rushed to insist that neither he nor the United States was being left out of the process.

A wide array of credible analysts have argued that to fear Germany is to look backward at what it once was, and to ignore what it is today. "Europe need have no fear of a democratic Germany. It can be as large as it wants," declared Václav Havel as he welcomed West German President Richard von Weizsäcker to Prague. Von Weizsäcker's visit took place exactly fifty-one years to the day after Hitler arrived in Czechoslovakia to subjugate the country. It was purposely scheduled that way by Havel to "cancel the memory." To condemn today's Germans simply for being the children of yesterday's Germans, said Havel, "is the same thing as to be anti-Semitic."

Historian Henry Ashby Turner challenged what he termed the "hackneyed idea" of a warlike "national character" innate to all Germans. He called attention to the irony that in the early nineteenth century, "the Germans were widely considered a quaint, impractical 'nation of poets and thinkers,' whereas the French were feared as Europe's most bellicose people."[44] Times, conditions, and peoples change, Turner insisted. The factors that once made the Germans militaristic are now gone. In fact, it is the Germans who have taken the lead in surrendering national sovereignty to the European Community, and they have shown no noticeable military zeal in recent years.

Writing on the so-called character issue, Robert Kaplan said the Germans have not only parted with their past ways, they have been reborn, with a new and utterly benign character. Germany, he asserted, may be the most developed mass democracy in the world. The extremes of wealth and poverty that afflict America are absent there. Unlike the Germany of the 1920s, which was racked with unemployment and hyperinflation, today's Germany has achieved an evenly distributed prosperity. Kaplan described the nation as a "single sprawling version of Shaker Heights or Chevy Chase." The Germans, he concluded, are indeed on the threshold of "*their* century," but instead of a time of conquest, it will be an age in which Germany exerts a "positive moral influence," especially on Eastern Europe.[45]

These arguments make intellectual sense. The fact that reunification has taken place without any visible negative consequences is assuaging some of the world's fears. But none have gone away. Indeed, depending on the run of events, they might yet again merit our attention. It is therefore worth listening now to some of those who have voiced the gravest misgivings.

"All peoples, especially those of the Soviet Union, must have a guarantee that the war threat will never come from German soil," said Soviet Foreign Minister Eduard Shevardnadze as he launched a campaign to protect Moscow's interests during the reunification process, which unfolded at a time of extreme political vulnerability in the Soviet Union. Warning against "sinister shadows of the past" which could return to haunt the future, Shevardnadze went so far as to demand that those countries which had suffered from German aggression be permitted to hold a referendum on reunification.[46]

Deep-seated fears about Germany prompted a few normally objective voices to allow themselves the rare privilege of speaking from the gut. Former French prime minister Michel Debré delivered an emotionally charged explanation of his countrymen's concerns: "We French who know our neighbors well, how can we not remind all Europeans and the world as a whole of the need to guard against abuses which Germany commits in all areas where it sees an opportunity?"[47]

No pundit spoke more from the gut than A. M. Rosenthal of *The New York Times*. He challenged the sterile clinical talk about reunification, both inside and outside of Germany, and noted the absence of certain important and highly charged words from the discussion—words such as "Jew, Auschwitz, Rotterdam, Polish *Untermenschen,* Leningrad, slave labor, crematorium, Holocaust, Nazi." Those words, he said, are "still part of every European, American and Soviet mind and memory. . . . Did not the two earlier German unifications lead to war? Is there not a terror in millions of human minds and hearts that the nightmare visage of the past may be the face of the future?" In Rosenthal's opinion, it would be better to wait twenty or thirty years, until the last of the Nazis are dead, before allowing Germany to reunify. He urged that individuals of moral authority—not the State Department—play a role in shaping the U.S. response to what will probably become "the most powerful nation on earth."[48]

Playwright Arthur Miller, one of those individuals of moral authority called upon by Rosenthal to comment, did so in a thoughtful essay. Germans have never won a revolution, Miller noted. Since Bismarck's day, their social welfare benefits have been bestowed from above. Today's highly successful West German political structure was largely imposed by the Allies. While West Germany is now as democratic as any society—Miller called it "less repressive and all-controlling than France"—what concerned him was the fact that Germans themselves did not have to fight to create this democracy: "No German soldier can say, 'I fought for democracy.' " As a result, Miller argued, no one can determine just how deeply the democratic experience of the last forty years has really taken hold.[49]

These fears are shared by some German intellectuals. "German unity is a sleeping dog today, a barking dog tomorrow and, the day after that, a biting dog," said screenwriter Wolfgang Kohlhase.[50] Novelist Günter Grass called on the world to oppose reunification: "There can be no demand for a new version of a unified nation that in the course of barely

75 years, though under several managements, filled the history books, ours and theirs, with suffering, rubble, defeat, millions of refugees, millions of dead, and the burden of crimes that can never be undone." To Grass, reunification implied "an alarming excess of power, swollen with the lust for more and more power."[51]

Columnist William Pfaff, one of the keenest American observers of the European scene, invoked Alexis de Tocqueville's assessment, made in 1856, that the Germans "possess the particular talent of becoming obsessed with what they take as abstract truths, without considering their practical consequences." But aren't the Germans the very paradigm of practicality? Be careful, warned Pfaff, they can become so attached to an idea that they have violent and extreme reactions when circumstances change. It was such responses, in a climate of global instability, which contributed to two world wars. Pfaff cautioned against the easy way the world has declared geopolitics and war "out of fashion," and urged that Germany's centrality to both not be forgotten.[52]

Asked in early 1990 if they feared a reunified Germany becoming the dominant power in Europe, 50 percent of Britons said yes, 50 percent of the French, 69 percent of Poles, and 29 percent of Americans. A *majority* of people in Britain and Poland were worried about the possibility of a German return to fascism.[53] In Britain, France, the United States, and most of the rest of the world, early misgivings receded as German reunification and German power became more visible realities. For the Soviet Union, Poland, and the international Jewish community, however, the new Germany presented a particularly uncomfortable and frightening specter. The fears of these groups will continue to make news for some time to come.

As for the Soviets, a Machiavellian Moscow consistently tried to cut a better deal than the one first offered in return for its acquiescence on the German question. It tapped the world's sympathies over the 20 million Soviets who died in World War II and asserted a moral and political imperative to find ways to make sure a reunified Germany would not be a threatening Germany in the future. Gorbachev's rhetorical flourishes have been impressive—on one occasion, he threatened the West with something it feared even more than a single Germany: "The same day the reunification of Germany is announced, a general will be sitting in my armchair."[54] That, of course, didn't happen. But it would not be surprising to see Soviet leaders try to capitalize on world fears about Germany again as events unfold.

While feelings about the Germans run deep in the Soviet Union and memories there seem to have lasted longer than in most other places, Gorbachev's position is conditioned less by sincere political beliefs than by the knowledge that, as the lone substantive roadblock to Germany's dreams, the Soviet Union ought to get something valuable in exchange for standing aside. A man of Gorbachev's negotiating skill is likely to continue to exploit Moscow's "right" to oppose a strong Germany—until the last dollar, the last D-mark, and the last demobilized NATO soldier have been squeezed out of the deal.

Poland also finds it difficult to countenance the idea of a reunified Germany. Some 50 percent of Poles surveyed said they believed a re-unified Germany *would* try to expand territorially—and that Polish lands would be Germany's first target. This distrust is not a product of Poland's long history of victimization by its expansive neighbor. Even Helmut Kohl's dance of ambiguity over whether or not he would accept the Oder-Neisse line as a definitive boundary doesn't entirely explain it. The Poles also know that inside Germany, many political leaders favor re-gaining what Finance Minister Theo Waigel called "eastern German territories" lost after the war—that is, the quarter of present-day Poland which was in German hands before World War II.[55] Kohl might have to accept the Oder-Neisse line as a compromise today. But what about tomorrow's German leaders?

Finally, there are the fears in the world Jewish community, which may linger the longest of all. Few Jews can look with complete dispassion on an expanding Germany, even if the causes and means of the expansion are completely different today from those of half a century ago. Hitler, the Nazis, and the Holocaust are inextricably identified with Germany. The passage of a mere four decades cannot erase *those* memories—especially when "Deutschland, Deutschland Über Alles" is being sung again at rallies, and politicians all over Germany once more routinely invoke the idea of a glorious German Fatherland. Schooled in the premise of "never again," taught above all never to forget the victims of the Holocaust, even those Jews who identify little with organized Jewry know that if they wait to speak out until neo-Nazis or anti-Semites are in power again in Berlin, it will be too late.

Aside from expressing a general distrust of Germany, Jewish critics have tended to focus on two specific concerns. One is that reunification is making Germans more nationalist in their thinking. Now that their country is strong, this new nationalism may allow Germans to lose sight of their guilt and responsibility for the horrors of the Holocaust, which they only accepted with reluctance when they were weak and needed the world's support. Helmut Kohl is the chancellor who encouraged Ronald Reagan to visit the Bitburg cemetery where SS soldiers are buried. Jews were not necessarily being paranoid in wondering if the "Jewish question" might arise again, when Kohl hinted that the Polish border question might be reopened or made statements such as "I always believed that Germany would rise again as one nation—history is fulfilling itself."[56] This is a particularly deep concern at a time when instability in Eastern Europe has opened the door to a wave of anti-Semitism of an intensity not seen there since World War II.

A second Jewish concern is more specific. While West Germany can point to a long record of confronting, debating, and publicly dealing with its Nazi past—although those efforts have not always been as extensive as some Jews would have liked—*East* Germany has virtually exempted itself from that process. Of course, Hitler and the Nazis have always been excoriated in East Germany's teaching of history, and great sympathy has been expressed for the loss of life and sacrifices experienced by the Soviets during the war. However, "in East German textbooks and novels, there has been hardly any treatment of the Holocaust and crimes of the Third Reich against the Jews," notes Robert Gerald Livingstone of Johns Hopkins University.[57] Following the opening of the Berlin Wall, in fact, some long-suppressed neo-Nazis became active in East Germany, holding anti-Semitic demonstrations and wearing Nazi uniforms.

Rabbi Marvin Hier, the dean of the Simon Wiesenthal Center for Holocaust Studies in Los Angeles, wrote to Chancellor Kohl to ask what special measures he planned to take to preserve the memory of Nazi crimes in a unified Germany. Kohl's reply did little to reassure concerned Jews. He stated that the existing West German laws against crimes of hatred, which would apply in a united Germany, were sufficient; no special measures were necessary. Indeed, in his letter to the rabbi, Kohl actually went on the counteroffensive, arguing that the real problem is not Germany but those outside Germany who fail to appreciate how much his country has done to support Israel and to inform its people about the history of Nazi tyranny.

Kohl's failure to reassure those concerned with the Holocaust issue called to mind his waffling on Poland. Why would a savvy politician seeking to allay the world's fears about a united Germany not address these questions more positively and forthrightly? Why didn't Kohl *insist* from the beginning that he would never allow a united Germany to infringe on the territory of others? Why didn't he, in his very first speeches on reunification, promise that the new Germany would have a special commitment to the Jews, the Poles, and all the others in Europe who had suffered so much? Why did he speak about these issues only when asked—and even then make veiled or direct criticisms of those doing the asking?

The simple answer was that Kohl believed Germany had grown powerful enough to disregard most of the outside world's protests. He concentrated instead on playing to the political audience at home. And much of that audience—particularly on the right—not only continues to harbor anti-Semitic sentiments but also is deeply resentful that Germany has for so long been obliged to lie low and accept the countless criticisms of outsiders.

Thus far, Kohl has been an effective manager of these dangerous trends of thought on his right. He has told the right-wingers just enough of what they want to hear to rein them back into the political mainstream, which is democratic, centrist, and stable. It is interesting to note, for example, that the neo-Nazi Republikaners, who attracted considerable attention with their surprisingly strong electoral showings (7 percent of the vote in the 1989 European Parliament elections), have been declining in popularity ever since the Wall opened. Led by former Waffen SS sergeant Franz Schönhuber, the Republikaners claimed to be Germany's only true nationalist movement. This pretense is now gone. Kohl's Christian Democrats have seized the nationalist mantle. By bringing about the reunification of the German Fatherland, they have carried out the boldest nationalist strategy imaginable. The Republikaners are now racked with internal contradictions. They are splintering and disappearing at a time when, theoretically, the social dislocation of reunification should be providing fertile ground for them to recruit new followers.

Will Kohl and his successors be able to manage the tension between the far right and the center with such good results in the future? The answer isn't clear. What is clear is that outsiders who continue to position themselves as watchdogs are under increasing pressure to get out of Germany's way. Heinz Ruhnau, the chairman of Lufthansa, is one of those losing patience. He dismisses foreign fears of a unified Germany by saying, "It's the same whether we have 60 million or 76 million people." If reunification has negative consequences—in other words, if it *does* lead to an ugly new German nationalism—it may be the foreigners' fault for not supporting today's German leadership heartily enough. "Not only the Germans murdered the Weimar Republic," Ruhnau says, emphasizing that the failure of foreigners to support German moderates in the 1920s helped bring on Hitler.[58]

The world ought not accept that kind of pressure. Reunification should be supported, as should all other aspects of German self-determination. The world should make more room for the Germans, who have done and achieved so much. But that doesn't mean we should overlook German weaknesses. Outsiders need not have a holier-than-thou attitude. Right-wing movements, anti-Semitism, and dangerous nationalisms exist everywhere, including in the United States and, increasingly, in the Soviet Union. The neofascist Le Pen movement in France garners more votes than Schönhuber's Republikaners. Any genuine democracy is bound to have fanatics and hate groups on its fringes. But there is a difference in this regard between Germany and most other democracies: The fact is that democracy once failed in Germany and the fanatic fringe managed to gain power. Germany need not be on trial forever, but it is certainly worth waiting another decade, to see how it deals with reunification and its greatly enhanced power in the world, before closing the case.

It is, in fact, extremely unlikely that Germany will head in a fascist, expansionist, anti-Semitic, or martial direction. Certainly it is worth watching out for these dangers, but it is doubtful they will come to pass. There *is* a streak of authoritarianism in German culture, and the world— especially Germany's partners in Europe—will see plenty of this in various ways over the coming years. But authoritarianism is only one aspect of the German personality, and even at its worst, it is not necessarily related to fascism. A world that has learned to deal with "ugly Americans" and "ugly Japanese" can surely manage to withstand what may be an increasing number of affronts by "ugly Germans."

There *are* some undeniable German yearnings to incorporate greater territory. But if Germany takes back parts of Poland, it will probably be done with deutsche marks, not Panzer divisions. Many people in Poland may be happy to make the deal.

There *will* be German economic domination, as well as complaints about it. But German economic domination is already a fact of life in Europe, and most people appear ready to accept or even welcome it. Unlike the Japanese, the Germans have shown a greater propensity for sharing the wealth and leaving tangible benefits on the table for others to take home. As long as they continue in this way, they are likely to be alternately admired and muttered about, but should not become a source of major conflict.

So when all is said and done, should the world fear the new Germany? The short answer is yes—but not for the reasons most people cite. The biggest dangers come not so much from the old issues that are so much discussed, but from new questions that are only rarely mentioned. Consider the following:

- What happens if Germany is *not* able to deliver a new miracle to East Germany—or at least not as quickly as East Germans are expecting? How stable, prosperous, and democratic will Germany be with thousands of East German workers, who formerly held secure if not terribly lucrative jobs, wandering around unemployed? What will become of the million or so communist cadres in the East, who may have lost their faith and their credibility but not their skills at organizing?

- The roller-coaster ride experienced by world financial markets in March 1990 was triggered in large part by fears about German inflation and the high costs of reunification. Those issues are now downplayed by the wise men managing Germany's economy. But what if circumstances change? What if even the brilliant managers of the Bundesbank can't check inflation? With so much of the world, especially Europe, now basing so many of its economic assumptions on German stability, that's a serious risk.[59]

- Should Germany have its own nuclear weapons? Today, in a time of optimism about nuclear disarmament, this question is dismissed as irrelevant. But other trends—the crisis over NATO's future, the impending American troop and weapon reductions in Europe, etc.— may eventually make the idea of German nuclear capability seem desirable. It could be a very real issue by the end of the decade.

- What if the Soviets are much shrewder than we think? What if they continue to press for concessions that end up undermining NATO, severing Germany from it, and eliminating the U.S. military presence in Europe? The Soviets, of course, will have to withdraw, too—but they will still be "in" Europe, even after they've returned to their own territory. By the year 2000, Germany could be effectively neutralized, Europe largely disarmed, and the Americans gone, while the Soviets could still have a forceful military presence on Europe's periphery. German business, meanwhile, will probably have made huge investments in Eastern Europe and the Soviet Union. At that point, it may not be a question of Germany picking up anchor from the West and turning East, it may be that a German-dominated Europe as a whole will find itself forced into a Soviet alliance.

· Finally, there are the specific implications for American business of a bigger, more powerful, more competitive Germany—especially one that dominates the European marketplace and makes alliances with the Japanese. The two-fronted war American companies are now trying to fight with Asian and European competitors is going to get much tougher the more powerful Germany becomes and the more global the reach of its companies grows.

The above short list represents just a few of the dimensions of the ''new German question.'' The world need not take its eyes off the old questions to contemplate these. But Helmut Kohl is almost certainly right: He is not building a Fourth Reich, and no one likely to come to power in Germany intends to do so. What Kohl and his colleagues *are* doing is changing the global balance of power. And that process deserves much more than a watchful glance. It demands extremely careful strategic thinking on the part of all those who wish to remain competitive and influential in the world of new superpowers.

PART III

Storming the Fortress: Americans and Japanese in Europe

7

A Seat on the Concorde: The New American Atlanticism

The tumbling of barriers between the two halves of Europe and the end of the Cold War have widened the Atlantic. Europe seems farther away to the U.S. and vice-versa. The notion of being a European and a Westerner used to be the same because the threat was the same. Now, there is a difference.

Dominique Moisi, French Institute for International Relations[1]

A GREAT EUROPEAN NATION: THE USA

Quick—which nation has made the greatest cumulative investment in Europe outside its own borders? Which nation made more cross-border acquisitions in Europe during 1989 than any other? Which nation's corporate subsidiaries employ the greatest number of Europeans outside the parent company's home country?

The nation that fits this description is *not* the powerful Germany described in the last chapter—at least not yet. The answer to all the above questions is: The United States of America, in its role as a great European power.

American companies have made over $180 billion worth of direct investments in Europe.[2] For some perspective on that eye-popping number, it might be useful to think of it as *three times* more than all the Japanese direct investment in the United States, which has rightly attracted so much attention in recent years.

One of the big American investors in Europe is IBM. Massive as IBM's business is in the American marketplace ($25.7 billion in 1989), its revenues in Europe are almost as large ($23.2 billion). And its European business is growing nearly five times faster.

Another big investor is the Ford Motor Co. Its 12 percent market share makes it as integral a player as any in Western Europe, the world's largest automobile market. "We have historically approached Europe as a single market," says Andrew Napier, the British-based director of Ford's 1992 task force. "Nineteen ninety-two implies many challenges for us, but becoming pan-European is not really one of them. I think it is fair to say we are the most pan-European of all the automobile companies in Europe."

The European Community is America's biggest trading partner, accounting for roughly one-fifth of all foreign trade in which the U.S. is involved. Most important, it is the biggest buyer of American goods, absorbing 23.3 percent of all U.S. exports in 1988, compared with Canada, which took 21.5 percent, and Japan, which took only 11.7 percent.

Subsidiaries of American manufacturing firms in EC countries are estimated to do over $375 billion worth of sales annually. Adding the revenues of service firms, the "American" sector may account for as much as one-tenth of the entire EC economy. Beyond the enormous scope of this transatlantic economic relationship, of course, are thousands of political, cultural, and military-strategic ties which bind the United States and its European partners.

Until recently, American power, leadership, and vested interests in Europe were so obvious that they scarcely merited discussion. It was shocking *news* when Toyota captured 10 percent of the American automobile market. But the fact that General Motors has long enjoyed more than a 10 percent share of the European market (chiefly through its Opel division) is deemed "natural."

The United States, then, is a major European power. What happens in

Europe, both positive and negative, will have deep repercussions on the U.S. domestic economy and on the business plans of American companies. These will be felt with a special intensity because Americans have become so accustomed to the status quo of the U.S.-Europe relationship that they have forgotten or ignored the possibility of dramatic change.

But there is another crucial detail to be added to this brief sketch of the American presence in Europe. Substantial as it is today, it is not as important, and certainly not as dominant, as it once was. The United States has descended far from the heights it occupied in 1956, when Paul-Henri Spaak, Belgium's foreign minister, declared, "There is no motor car manufacturing firm in Europe which is big enough to take full advantage of the most powerful American machinery. No country on the Continent can build large airliners without outside assistance. In atomic science, the knowledge that has been acquired in European countries equals only a small fraction of what the United States is now putting at the disposal of its industries."[3]

American power in Europe reached its zenith in the 1960s. It was then that Jean-Jacques Servan-Schreiber wrote his famous book, *Le Défi américain* (The American Challenge). A best-seller all across Europe, the book lucidly explained the growing role of the American financial, industrial, and technological colossus which was winning one competitive battle after another in Europe. The profits of American businesses in Europe were then half as much as total profits for all European-owned businesses—and rising. High technology was in its infancy, but U.S. companies already controlled 95 percent of the European semiconductor market and accounted for 80 percent of computer sales. Americans, according to Servan-Schreiber, had "gauged the terrain" and were now "rolling from Naples to Amsterdam with the ease and speed of Israeli tanks in the Sinai desert."[4]

One of the key ingredients in this U.S. corporate dominance of Europe was the aggressive American willingness to take advantage of the Common Market. Nine years after the Treaty of Rome, "this European market is basically American in organization," Servan-Schreiber wrote. It was Americans, not Europeans, who were building Continent-wide businesses. "This is true Federalism—the only kind that exists in Europe on an industrial level. And it goes a good deal farther than anything Common Market experts ever imagined."

Citing studies showing that American investment in Europe was growing twice as fast as American investment in the U.S., Servan-Schreiber forecast that the world's third-largest industrial power (after the U.S. and the Soviet Union) would, within fifteen years, be *American industry in Europe*.

It didn't turn out like that. Along the road, American business lost its way. Before fifteen years had passed, the U.S. began posting a series of staggering annual trade *deficits* with Western Europe that would grow to $30 billion by 1987. Much of what Servan-Schreiber had said about American technical and managerial leadership in the 1960s had, by the 1980s, become more applicable to the Japanese.

American business withdrew considerable resources from Europe over the course of the 1970s and '80s. In part, this was due to generalized economic decline in Europe. It was also attributable to protectionist measures instituted by European governments alarmed by American dominance of their markets, and it owed much to the emergence of better opportunities elsewhere in the world. But the principal reason was that American business was losing its nerve as a global leader as it found itself increasingly obliged to refocus its once globe-conquering vision on mounting problems back home. Chrysler, for example, pulled out of Europe entirely when its U.S. parent company nearly went bankrupt in the late 1970s.

Something else eventually happened, too: Europe found its way. Two decades after Servan-Schreiber urged Europeans to use the Common Market for their own benefit instead of leaving it to Americans to create pan-European enterprises, the EC's 1992 program has at last provided a meaningful response to "the American challenge."

The ability of American business to dominate Europe and other global markets in the 1950s and '60s was a major factor in the explosion of wealth and competitive economic power experienced by the United States in that time period. It is no coincidence that American living standards rose most rapidly during those decades when leading American companies also dominated the European market in most industries.

It would be foolish to think that at this late date measures to promote American competitiveness can restore America's past economic hegemony. The rest of the competition has simply grown too strong and is gaining ground too rapidly. But two vital competitive issues are at stake in Europe today. In the first place, the U.S. must adequately defend its powerful remaining economic interests against what now will be ferocious German, pan-European, and Japanese competition. Second, if American companies and Washington decision-makers play their cards right, they may be able to take advantage of the real strengths Americans still have in Europe to gain back some of the competitive ground they have lost. The European economy has become so big and so dynamic that even a modest improvement in the U.S. position there could have a substantial impact. If pursued properly, the new opportunities in Europe could be exploited to forestall an otherwise likely implosion of the U.S. domestic economy and to buy some time for the long-term program of American renewal.

THE RISE AND FALL OF "FORTRESS EUROPE"

"Fortress Europe" is dead. There will be no protectionist European Community bureaucracy sitting in Brussels conspiring to close the doors of its market to foreigners. But, since most outsiders originally feared that the 1992 program would lead to the creation of a fortress Europe, it is useful to review how the idea rose and fell.

As the European Commission went about its work of fleshing out the details of the single-market program during 1985 through '87, the United States seemed largely unconcerned. Europe's dormant economy, combined with the EC's constant infighting, generated enough foreign ennui about the Community to suffocate almost all news coming out of Brussels. Discussion of the future of Europe, remarked columnist William Safire, "usually causes great, jaw-locking yawns in the U.S."[5] The EC's grand plans for unifying Europe had been heard all too many times. "For the most part, U.S. companies seem alarmingly unaware of the coming changes," reported *Newsweek* in 1988. When the magazine asked a top executive of a medical equipment manufacturer based in the Midwest about 1992, his response was, "We lost our marketing director recently and no one else at the company knows anything about the subject."[6]

Yet from the spring of 1988 through the fall of 1989, Americans heard plenty about the 1992 program—most of it about the impending threat of a fortress Europe. A few examples will serve to recall the mood:

"Forget about smashing Japanese radios with sledgehammers on the lawn of the U.S. Capitol," began a typical *Wall Street Journal* news article. "A new trade villain is about to take over in Washington: *Europe*." The article then quoted U.S. Trade Representative Clayton Yeutter, who declared, "The implications of 1992 for the U.S. are far more serious than people realize. In the next few years, Europe will be a tougher nut to crack for us than Japan.'' Yeutter said Brussels was already drafting rules which could deny market access to U.S. financial institutions, automakers, and other industries.[7]

Alfred H. Kingon, then the U.S. ambassador to the EC, struck a similar note: ''There is a real risk that Europe will turn into a protectionist entity as 1992 comes more and more into being.''[8]

Financial scenario modeler Paul Erdman declared 1992 a doomed attempt to fight Eurosclerosis with ''Europrotectionism.'' He predicted that Europe after 1992 would be a ''regional bloc that will be almost totally self-centered, one designed to divert trade inward . . . and one that will represent a serious threat to the . . . ultimate goal, universal free trade.'' Erdman proposed putting ''a tough guy in charge'' to formulate an aggressive U.S. response to European protectionism, namely, Lee Iacocca. ''Let's sic him on the Europeans.''[9]

A Düsseldorf-based American consultant, John Meyer, spoke for many Americans when he said in an interview, ''I don't like the way things are going at all. As the walls go up, U.S. companies will be frozen out. With 1992, trade disputes will be enormously magnified. The prospect is for feuding trade blocs—the U.S. against Europe, the Europeans versus the Japanese. Businessmen will be caught in the middle.''[10]

Some thirty-three U.S. government agencies launched their own separate studies on the impact of 1992. The House Subcommittee on International Economic Policy and Trade issued a report warning of numerous decisions being made in Brussels with potential restrictive impact on U.S. business. The new U.S. trade representative, Carla Hills, assumed her post announcing she would use her ''velvet crowbar'' to crack open fortress Europe. Sniffing a campaign issue for the presidential election of November 1992, Senator Lloyd Bentsen returned from a fact-finding trip to Brussels declaring that the 1992 program sounded to him like a case of Europe trying to close its markets. ''What we see the Europeans saying is that if you want to trade in our country you have to accept restrictions.''[11]

In an influential 1988 speech in Davos, Lester Thurow, dean of MIT's Sloan School, predicted that the EC's 1992 plan would be ''the event that visibly destroys the post–World War II GATT era.''[12] GATT, he announced unceremoniously, was ''dead.'' Regional blocs were the way of the future. In Thurow's opinion, 1992 would hasten the formation of such blocs in other parts of the world. The rudiments already existed in the form of the U.S.-Canada Free Trade Agreement, and there had been talk about a Japan-led trading zone in the Pacific.

Other analysts took Thurow's conclusions one step further toward the precipice, arguing that the simultaneous rise of these three regional blocs would lead to global trade wars. A *Forbes* article with the fearsome title "Sons of Smoot-Hawley" declared: "Europe, cocky over the prospects of 1992, is clearly in the mood to listen to protectionism. . . . Unless something can be done to stop it, international trade will soon have degenerated from relatively free exchange to a system of three separate trading blocs. This is not just a threat. It is an emerging reality."[13]

Fortunately, this apocalyptic vision has not come to pass. In spite of many ongoing trade disagreements and considerable acrimony in the GATT talks, the chances of "Smoot-Hawley"-type protectionism and trade wars are lower today than they were in the late 1980s. While the world *is* moving toward intensified unity within particular geographic groupings—and the EC is leading the way—there is little indication thus far that this process will bring trade to a halt among the three major regions of the Triad.

Since the early part of 1989, in fact, American fears about fortress Europe have steadily diminished. Commerce Secretary Robert Mosbacher made a high-profile visit to Brussels and returned home declaring he was satisfied American voices would be heard as the EC moved to harmonize product standards and rules. In July 1989, George Bush put the presidential seal of approval on 1992: "Let me say clearly a stronger Europe, a more united Europe, is good for my country." Bush and Jacques Delors developed a good working relationship, meeting four times during 1989 and agreeing in general that the United States has special interests which need to be considered as EC policies evolve.

Rather than railing against protectionism, most American companies are hoping to pursue the opportunities presented by the New Europe. Arthur Davie, president of AT&T Europe, typifies the more upbeat attitude that now prevails: "The first thing you have to understand about 1992 is that there isn't going to be any such thing as a fortress Europe," he says. AT&T, of course, is an American company that *has* world-leading technology. Its technology leadership, moreover, is in an area where many European countries remain backward.[14] In a completely free and fair market, AT&T would likely become a European giant overnight. Davie favors lobbying for greater liberalization and ensuring that the EC observes its stated commitment to opening up its markets. But he has no illusion that AT&T will get a huge amount of business quickly, or that it will be easy to win bids when competing against long-protected European "national champions." AT&T, in fact, has bought stakes in some of those national champions and created joint ventures with others in order to get better access. Yet Davie doesn't dwell on those elements of the market that still remain either explicitly or implicitly protected. "The new reality for us," he notes with equanimity, "is that we are able to do a reasonable level of business in countries that used to be completely closed and dominated by government monopolies."

In the corridors of the Berlaymont, theories vary as to how the term "fortress Europe" came into parlance among Americans and Japanese in the first place, and why what the EC now insists was always a plan to liberalize trade was initially interpreted by outsiders as an attack on the global trading system. These explanations range from the ridiculous to the sublime.

One EC staff economist blames the whole notion of a fortress Europe on the consulting industry that has grown up around 1992, noting that "without the fear factor, the idea of paying for advice on European unity would have sounded terribly unnecessary in a boardroom back in the States." It is true that the big international consulting firms have opened or expanded their Brussels offices, as have global law firms, accounting firms, and public-relations and marketing-communications companies. In fact, more people in Brussels are being paid to dispense advice on 1992 than are actually involved in the creation of the program itself. Nevertheless, the consultants didn't create the issue; the issue created the need for the consultants.

Another theory blames the media, especially an alleged misunderstanding of a speech given by Delors. A high-ranking commission staffer recounts this anecdote: "What Delors said was that 'Europe should be neither sieve nor fortress.' But the word for *sieve* in French is obscure, and the American reporters probably did not understand it. They just took away the idea that Delors was talking about a fortress. That was a lot sexier for American newspapers and magazines, anyway." The idea of a single phrase misheard around the world makes for a nice legend, but lacks credibility. The press corps in Brussels is extremely diligent. They do a thorough job of their work and generally don't invent what isn't there.

A self-critical explanation is offered by veteran European Commission diplomat Hugo Paeman. "We made a serious mistake at the beginning phase of the 1992 project. We were so caught up in our own internal discussion that we ignored how we might be perceived outside and how the rest of the world would react.'' Americans first began to hear about the single market in 1988, at a time when the United States was feeling seriously threatened by Japanese trade policies. ''In that atmosphere,'' says Paeman, ''it was easy for the United States to assume 1992 was just another threat.''

Still another popular theory in the Berlaymont alleges a Japanese conspiracy. According to this line of reasoning, the Japanese deliberately incited fears of a fortress Europe in order to enlist American support to prevent the EC from taking tough measures aimed principally at Tokyo. No concrete evidence is offered to support this theory. The circumstantial case, however, is good: In 1987, while Americans were mostly ignoring the Single European Act, the Japanese *were* beginning to become disturbed about its implications. The Community was aggressively bringing antidumping cases against Japanese manufacturers of products from photocopiers to computer printers. These actions were seen in Japan as a ''deliberate campaign to encourage increased investment in the Community's manufacturing,'' according to journalist Kenjiro Ishikawa.[15] In effect, the EC was threatening to close the door to Japanese goods unless they were manufactured *inside* Europe.

The Japanese were damned if they did and damned if they didn't. In some cases, Japanese companies set up simple final-assembly operations in a cosmetic attempt to comply with European rules on local manufacturing. But Brussels sought to impose antidumping duties on such goods anyway, dismissing the facilities as ''screwdriver'' plants whose production was insufficient to qualify as local manufacturing. Even when the Japanese made heavy investments and employed thousands of workers, they still faced exclusionary policies. France, for example, refused to accept Bluebird cars manufactured by Nissan at its Sunderland, U.K., facility as British. Nissan had invested a billion dollars in the plant, the work force was British, and Mrs. Thatcher herself defended the cars as thoroughly British. But the French wanted them designated ''Japanese''—and therefore still subject to highly restrictive French quotas—on the grounds that Nissan was a Japanese company and the ''EC content'' of the auto parts wasn't high enough.

As if all these tactics for dissuading Japanese companies from entering Europe were not enough, in 1987, EC officials began insisting more and more on what they called ''reciprocity''—a highly charged code word referring to a policy whereby the EC would allow companies from foreign countries access to its market only if those countries had fully opened their markets to European participation.

The increasing talk of reciprocity was cause for alarm in Tokyo; the policy could be used as a blanket tool for excluding the Japanese from almost every European business, since an interested party could reasonably argue that almost any sector of the Japanese domestic economy was not fully open to foreign participation. What's more, the Japanese feared that if the reciprocity principle was a success in Europe, Americans might also begin to adopt it as a weapon in their own trade battles. Astute Japanese trade experts reasoned that their best hope was to urge the U.S., while still under the sway of a free-trading Reagan administration, to join forces with Japan and lobby Brussels against reciprocity *on principle*.

Commissioners in Brussels tried to keep Americans from taking the bait. They explained with a wink that when they said "reciprocity" was aimed at "third countries," they meant only Japan. But Washington didn't buy that logic. American trade officials rushed to support the Japanese in their battles with Brussels on everything from screwdriver plants to Nissan Bluebirds.

In a memorable rhetorical flourish, John Heimann, chairman of Merrill Lynch Europe, predicted that even if the Europeans intended reciprocity as "a missile aimed at Tokyo," it would nevertheless "land in New York and explode on Capitol Hill."[16] He was right. For one thing, the Reagan-era ideologues, who relished their role as the police of free trade's global politics, believed it was their duty to oppose European protectionist tendencies, regardless of whether they were directed at Japan or the U.S. For another, they mistrusted the socialist-led EC bureaucracy in Brussels and were inclined to believe whatever evils Margaret Thatcher ascribed to it. On the other side of the aisle, the emerging trend of "economic nationalism" among congressional Democrats led to fears that EC-92 might well result in the creation of "the next Japan"—another institutionalized force for unfair trade harmful to American interests. A number of leading Democrats were eager to make their mark early in the battle with Brussels.

"Americans were fooled by the Japanese into fighting all their battles for them," concludes French senator Jean François-Poncet. "If you look at some of the biggest efforts the Americans have made in Brussels, almost all of them are about the rights of the Japanese . . . Japanese cars, Japanese photocopiers, Japanese banks—I would say it sometimes looks as if the Japanese have turned the American government into their lobby-ists.'' That may be an overstatement. Yet Japanese perspectives clearly played a role in ringing U.S. alarm bells over a fortress Europe.

The Japanese, however, did not invent the EC's protectionist tenden-cies, and the American concern about them was not wholly misguided. In fact, amid all the explanations and theories, the most obvious reason for American anxiety about a fortress Europe is the one that goes least men-tioned in the Berlaymont. And that is that after the EC first reached general agreement on the single-market concept in 1985, the early pro-posals on how to implement it *did* have a strong protectionist bent.

Some Eurocrats today would like to deny this history. They smugly insist that Americans simply misunderstood and are only now coming to realize that the EC never intended to use 1992 to create an import-resistant fortress. ''I don't know where Americans ever got this idea of 'fortress Europe,' '' says Willy de Clercq, a Belgian member of the European Parliament. Yet it was de Clercq himself who, during his tenure as the commission's chief of external affairs, gave speeches and inter-views suggesting that American and especially Japanese global trading strength might make it necessary to build a European fortress.

''We see no reason why the benefits of our internal liberalization should be extended unilaterally to third countries,'' he announced at one point. If third countries wanted access to the big European market, they would have to earn it by negotiating ''reciprocal concessions.''[17] ''Is there any political, moral or legal obligation on us Europeans to just open all the gates of the 1992 gold mine without asking anything in return?'' he asked pointedly.[18] And commenting on the Japanese appetite for en-tering European finance, de Clercq warned that Europe ought to study the incoming Japanese wave, ''understand its dimensions and organize our defenses. The challenge to all of us is to construct those defenses in time. Before the wave strikes.''[19]

A non-European could be forgiven for taking that kind of talk to mean that Europe would soon become a trade ''fortress.'' The whole package of ideas being proposed at Berlaymont on matters such as reciprocity, local content, and rules of origin suggested the EC was indeed poised for a serious turn inward. Suddenly, officials were questioning those provi-sions in the Treaty of Rome which granted locally incorporated subsid-iaries of American companies all the rights and privileges of other European companies. Rumors flew around Brussels that only those com-panies established within the Community before December 31, 1992, would be treated as "European." Latecomers would have to negotiate their way in.

In view of the conditions that prevailed in 1985–87, the case made by economic nationalists for fortress-building had an undeniable appeal:

- Diminishing the foreign share of European business offered a logical possibility for indigenous growth at a time when the EC was still suffering from low growth and high unemployment.
- Threatening to implement measures that would close Europe off could frighten foreign exporters into locating their manufacturing facilities inside the Community. This would provide a shot in the arm to EC growth and jobs—even before the measures actually had to be adopted.
- In the GATT's Uruguay Round, the Reagan administration was zeroing in on Europe's agricultural subsidies and other sensitive policies. The EC had few bargaining chips with which to respond; the threat of European protectionism enhanced its negotiating position.
- The U.S. domestic experience of those years suggested that there was no upper limit to the rapaciousness of Japanese export industries. Thus, leaving markets wide open looked like a losing strategy to the Europeans, whose economies were not even as competitive as America's.
- A number of European countries had simply had too little experience with the positive effects of deregulation and market liberalization to believe that competition could help solve their low-growth problems.

The protectionist conception of Europe may have represented only a minority of the total discussion. Those backing such ideas may have accounted for only a minority of votes. Quite naturally, however, Americans, Japanese, Koreans, Australians, and other export-oriented foreigners perceived a serious threat. Had history taken another course, that threat might have become reality.

Events, however, moved in a different direction. The rapidity with which Europhoria replaced Eurosclerosis made the EC much more self-confident and less fearful of open markets. The immense surge of American and Japanese investment, despite serious concerns about the latter, provided exactly what the protectionists were hoping for—a shot of adrenaline to get the heart of Europe pumping again. Inside Europe, a more liberal view on dropping trade barriers came to predominate. A "free-trading troika" arose within the European Commission, made up of those who held the three most important posts under Delors: Leon Brittan, Mrs. Thatcher's appointee, who was in charge of competition policy and financial services; Martin Bangemann, the German responsible for the internal market and industry; and Frans Andriessen, the Dutchman heading up external affairs and foreign trade policy.

On most occasions during 1989 when a bellwether issue presented itself to the Community, Delors, together with this free-trading troika, managed to achieve a consensus in favor of a more open vision of the New Europe rather than a more closed one. The watershed was the "second banking directive"—perhaps the most closely watched of all EC directives because it affected international financial institutions and capital flows so directly. It was in the debate about the banking directive that the issue of reciprocity manifested itself most forcefully.

At one point, the EC seemed inclined to seek strict reciprocity (also known as "mirror-image" reciprocity) in banking. Under that rubric, American or Japanese financial firms, emanating from home markets that didn't exactly mirror the EC, could have been denied full access to Europe. Brussels might have seized on American interstate banking laws to argue, "If you aren't going to allow European banks to open retail branches in all fifty states, we aren't going to allow American banks to open retail branches in all twelve countries of the Community." Americans could have argued back, "Yes, but under our law, if we deny your banks access to the whole fifty-state market, we are just treating your banks the same way we treat our own. If, on the other hand, you deny our banks access to the twelve countries of the Community, then you will be discriminating against us, because you will *not* be giving our banks the same rights you give your own."

After much debate, lobbying, and behind-the-scenes maneuvering, it was concluded that the second banking directive would not be based on strict reciprocity. Instead, the EC came out in favor of "national treatment." The essence of this approach is that as long as European financial institutions enjoy "national treatment" in the United States (i.e., the same rights as domestic institutions, which they currently have), American institutions will be accorded full rights in the EC. Certain caveats to this principle are still contained in the new directive, and frictions could arise that might lead European regulators to abuse their powers in a protectionist manner. But the same theoretical problem exists in national banking systems everywhere else, including the United States. What the new directive has done is substantially raise the threshold for triggering a penalty against foreign financial firms.

The new directive is more problematic for Japanese financial institutions, since Brussels can make a case that EC firms do *not* enjoy national treatment in Japan. But since enforcement power is in the hands of Europe's elected political leaders, not the commission, since there is a mandate to attempt to negotiate solutions to problems before taking any action, and since the Japanese and other foreigners retain the right to take their side of the story to the European Court of Justice, it is hard to imagine this directive being implemented on a protectionist whim.

In one stroke, the banking directive excised the most often cited single specific basis for foreign worries about a fortress Europe. The much-feared reciprocity principle lost its precedent-setting edge. Instead of heading backward into a closed financial market, the EC clearly chose to move forward to a more open and internationalized one.

From the American viewpoint, the next major litmus test after the banking debate was a Brussels directive relating to TV broadcasting. The commission was considering a proposal to restrict foreign (which mostly meant American) television programming to fixed quotas of total European airtime. U.S. Trade Representative Carla Hills singled out these proposed TV quotas as a symbol of the fortress Europe mentality. But when all was said and done, her case made better rhetoric than reality.

The final directive stipulated only that a "majority" of programming hours be reserved for European-produced shows. These would be broadly defined to include programming produced by subsidiaries of U.S. companies in Europe and U.S.-European joint ventures. The directive deliberately left holes big enough to drive many additional hours of American programming through by stating that airtime would be reserved for European shows only "where practicable" and "appropriate." Even without those loopholes, the directive still allows American penetration of the EC broadcasting market to make a quantum leap. From a 1987 share of 28 percent of 250,000 hours of EC airtime, U.S. programming would be permitted to rise to 49 percent after 1992, when total programming hours—largely as a result of 1992's deregulatory thrust—are expected to jump to 400,000.

In an economic sense, Hollywood certainly has a right to demand that its highly competitive exports be allowed access to 100 percent of the European market, not just 49 percent plus whatever else is "practicable and appropriate." Jack Valenti, the American entertainment industry's chief spokesman, has continued to criticize the EC's policy vociferously. But how much of a trade issue can really be made of the fact that reruns of *Dallas, Miami Vice,* and *Cosby* may be confined in the future to "only" 49 percent of European broadcasting, when that enables Americans to nearly double their large existing market share? If the American public were to awaken one day to find 49 percent of U.S. airwaves suddenly occupied with European or Japanese programming, one could expect legislative restrictions to follow in short order. Even the free-trading Martin Bangemann chided the U.S. for failing to recognize that Europe's desire to protect its culture is not the same as protectionism in the case of manufactured goods.

Minimizing neither the economic importance of the entertainment industry nor American exporting strengths in this sector, one is still forced to conclude that if EC broadcasting policy is the most salient example of fortress Europe, as Carla Hills declared it, then it is at least a fortress with wide-open gates.

All of this is not to suggest that Americans are no longer worried about EC policies. Monsanto's chairman, Richard J. Mahoney, believes Brussels is deliberately creating new barriers to exclude his company's animal hormones—particularly BST, which is used for dairy cattle. Health objections have been raised by European regulators, but Mahoney suspects the real issue is simply that productivity gains on European farms would wreak havoc with tenuous EC compromises on subsidizing agriculture. "They've introduced an unprecedented new issue into the regulatory process," says Mahoney. "Now, a new product must not only be safe, but it must fill an economic need. With this criterion, Europeans are basically saying they have the right to bar products that promote efficiency, because they might also upset the economic balance. The assumption is that the reality of 1989 is perfect and anything that changes it is bad."

Other worries abound. American Airlines chairman R. L. Crandall rails against Europe's refusal to deregulate its skies more extensively, noting that his company simply can't get access to the routes it would like to fly, even though service is badly needed. "They say they want people to be able to travel around Europe freely," muses Crandall. "So why are they keeping air travel so heavily regulated and refusing to build new airports?" One reason Crandall cites is the political clout of European airlines, which he asserts are "run more like national employment agencies than businesses." Another is what Crandall sees as the EC's thinly veiled industrial policy bias, which favors developing high-speed trains rather than building the airports, runways, and terminals so many European cities need.

The U.S. electronics industry is critical of domestic-content rules that are having the effect of encouraging American firms to locate production sites within the EC instead of shipping to Europe from Silicon Valley. An EC ruling on semiconductors is particularly troublesome. It specifies that the "diffusion" part of the manufacturing process—the crucial step in which electronic circuitry is placed onto a semiconductor wafer—must take place *inside* the EC for the chip maker to avoid a 14 percent import duty. J. Michael Ferren, an outspoken U.S. Commerce Department official, says that Intel Corporation, which has decided to build a $400 million semiconductor plant in Ireland, was "literally kidnapped into Europe by this procedure."[20]

Congressional activists concerned with trade issues are also worried. Connecticut's Sam Gejdenson (the first American elected official to have made EC-92 a principal preoccupation) fears that a transatlantic drift of jobs and investment could occur as a result of European policy decisions. Simply to satisfy their own narrow interests, American companies may bow to EC pressure to move production to Europe. "It may not make any difference to them whether they make it in Norwich, England, or Norwich, Connecticut, but it matters to me."[21] Gejdenson has developed a long bill of particulars concerning 1992. Prominent among the items he finds objectionable is the government procurement directive, which he forecasts will leave only 25 percent of EC government contracts open to American bidding. By contrast, he maintains, European bids are accepted on more than 80 percent of U.S. government contracts. As for agriculture, it is clear that there will be no open market for non-European farm products anytime soon. As the Uruguay Round of the GATT talks headed to its dramatic climax, French and German political leaders appeared perfectly willing to let global trade liberalization run aground rather than disrupt politically sensitive European agricultural subsidy schemes.

Undoubtedly, Americans (as well as Japanese, Koreans, and other non-Europeans) will continue to have disputes with the EC over specific market-access matters. Undoubtedly, various sectors of Western European economic life will remain effectively protected from foreign competition by subtle nontariff barriers. But while the list of American complaints may be long as well as valid, it is important to remember that these are all *specific* issues. Even taken as a group, they do not imply a blanket policy of protectionism any more than do all of Western Europe's complaints about the crazy quilt of American trade policies. Most of the problems are still the object of ongoing negotiations, and it is reasonable to hope for intelligent compromises. Recent economic growth has been so strong, and future prospects in many parts of Europe are so attractive, that even fervent economic nationalists have begun to accept the idea that open, competitive markets are a worthy goal—if not in all aspects of European life, then at least in most.

Arguably, for the same reasons that the idea of a fortress Europe seemed plausible two years ago, the tide could shift again and European opinion might once more favor protectionism later in the 1990s. Today's support for a progressively more open EC has yet to be tested in the face of three inevitabilities: an economic downturn at some point in the '90s, a widespread shakeout of noncompetitive European companies, and the opening up of some long-protected sectors to intense American and Japanese competition. It will therefore be essential to carefully monitor the new trade trends as they emerge from the EC.

For the present, however, the opening of the Berlin Wall and the revolutions that ensued in Eastern Europe seem to have eviscerated any remaining support for a more overtly protectionist Europe. While Western European leaders are taking the initiative in rebuilding Eastern European economies, they want and need active American and Japanese support for that cause. Even the most protectionist-minded among them know it would be difficult if not impossible to construct a fortress in the West while appealing for foreign involvement in the East. Indeed, the myriad issues raised by the end of the postwar era—whether *perestroika* will last, whether the time is ripe for massive Western investment in the Soviet Union, whether meaningful disarmament is a possibility, what will become of NATO in the future, how to defend the industrial world's oil supply, how to handle the desire of Eastern European countries to join the EC—will all require a great deal of international dialogue and negotiation over the next few years if workable solutions are to be found.

In sum, when the broad outlines of the 1992 plan were first suggested, it may have been possible for economic nationalists to imagine the single market as a tool for minimizing the foreign presence in Europe. But now that the major geopolitical and geostrategic issues of our times have become inextricably linked to 1992, such a position has become untenable. As the Berlin Wall crumbled, it also destroyed the last rampart of fortress Europe—and, at least for the foreseeable future, no one intends to rebuild either edifice.

The additional good news is that absent a European fortress to catalyze the process, the world is much less likely to break up into antagonistic regional trading blocs. Certainly, Europe, North America, and East Asia will continue moving toward greater unification of their respective geographic markets. But for now, this process appears to be taking place in more or less peaceful conjunction with the expansion of world trade.

The fact that the twelve disparate countries of the EC have been able to harmonize so many of their trade-related rules and establish a supranational market is, in a certain sense, an inspiration to the rest of the world's negotiators trying to make the GATT system work, even if it is the Europeans who appear to Americans as the uncompromising antagonists destroying the Uruguay Round. The fact that the Soviet Union and other Eastern European countries now want to join the GATT club, meanwhile, is a reminder that the expanding global trading pie may provide ample room for newly muscular economic powers without igniting trade wars over access to existing markets.

EIGHT WAYS AMERICAN BUSINESS CAN WIN IN EUROPE

Enormous opportunities lie ahead in Europe for American business and American national interests. The savviest companies and the shrewdest investors are sure to find plenty of profit in the New Europe. A larger and more open question is whether the United States will manage to turn the many tactically advantageous circumstances into strategic gains for the next century's global competitiveness race. Let us outline some of these opportunities and look at what Americans are doing to capitalize on them:

1. American companies are already pan-European in their thinking and management. The large American multinational companies operating in Europe today are following the pan-European trail blazed by American managers in the 1960s. Four or five managerial generations ago, as Jean-Jacques Servan-Schreiber pointed out, Americans were building Continent-wide corporate structures while Europeans were sticking to the narrow comforts of their own national markets. This American corporate network is not as powerful or dominant as it once was, and many key American players have lost their footing along the way. But the most excellent American companies are today more sophisticated at playing the pan-European game than many of their European competitors.

A good example is American Express. No European company can begin to compete with its product mix and expertise in both travel and financial services. "We've been in Europe for a hundred years," says CEO James Robinson III. "Tourism is already the world's biggest industry, and it's growing in Europe. The European financial-services market will now become much more integrated. I would venture to say that few developments could play better to our unique corporate strengths than 1992."

Adds Joan Spero, an Amex vice president who put together a veritable "diplomatic corps" inside the company to deal with issues relating to EC-92, "American businesses are used to dealing with many different European markets at once and operating across borders. The 1992 program will make it that much easier for them to access an even larger European market. More European consumers are going to have more money to spend on exactly the kinds of products and services American Express offers." All over Europe, financial institutions are trying to find ways to build a pan-European customer base. American Express already has one in place.

"American companies have always had a *Europe-wide* strategy which gives them common management methods, budgeting, accounting, and information systems right across Europe," says Eric Friberg, managing director of McKinsey & Co.'s Brussels office. Even more important than this valuable pan-European infrastructure, he believes, is the human dimension: "American companies have spent twenty to thirty years creating a cadre of multilingual, multicultural managers. This is the greatest strength of American business. Sometimes it scares Europeans."

Friberg's point is well illustrated by the case of Transmanche Link, the British-French construction consortium building the tunnel under the English Channel. As Transmanche grew increasingly desperate about cost overruns, delays, and engineering problems involved with the $12 billion project, it sent out an SOS to Egon Zehnder International, the Zurich-based international head-hunting firm, to find the world's best project manager to bring in as chief executive. The man they got was Jack Lemley, an American, who has done a stunning job of getting the project back on track.

Friberg's view is no mere self-congratulatory celebration of the virtues of American managers. Most of the human resources he speaks of are not Americans at all, but European nationals working for American firms. Big U.S. multinational firms, in fact, have been the chief consumers of talented Europeans with multicultural management abilities—or those on a track too fast for some of continental Europe's staid business communities. A typical example is Eckhard Pfeiffer, the German manager of Compaq Computer's European operations. When Wall Street analysts want to know about Compaq's future prospects, they trek to an industrial park on Munich's Elektrastrasse. There, Pfeiffer plots the pan-European strategy responsible for over a billion dollars' worth of Compaq's annual sales—almost half of all Compaq's revenues. Pfeiffer's operation, says *Business Week,* is "Compaq's engine of growth."[22]

As for Hewlett-Packard, its personal-computer business is so much stronger in Europe than in the United States that it took the unprecedented step in 1990 of moving its worldwide PC headquarters out of Sunnyvale, California, to Grenoble, France, under the stewardship of a talented Frenchman, Jacques Clay.

All of this is to say that in terms of their operations as well as their management, many American companies are already well positioned in Europe. While growth in the Japanese market remains difficult for Americans to convert into opportunities, European growth is playing to American strengths. Barring management missteps and corporate crises at home, most of the big U.S.-based multinationals already present in Europe should do very well there in the 1990s.

2. Business alliances are the way of the future. New conditions in Europe are prompting once self-sufficient American companies to seek joint ventures, marketing agreements, and strategic alliances with European partners. At one end of the spectrum there are big, visionary pacts such as the IBM-Siemens joint quest for next-generation technology, or AT&T's equity stake in the Italian phone company Italtel, which facilitates joint pursuit of Italian and European telecommunications opportunities. Ford and Fiat are cementing a $5 billion partnership in farm equipment that basically lets Ford get out of a business in which it was doing poorly, while keeping a finger in it for the future.

At the other end are more-focused and lower-profile collaborations. For example, Chrysler plans to reenter the European market by producing minivans at the facilities of Austrian specialty vehicle-maker Steyr-Daimler-Puch Fahrzeugtechnik, and Scott Paper (the U.S. company which is Europe's leading tissue manufacturer) is creating a joint venture with the German-Swedish paper group Feldmühle to gain better access to the German and Dutch markets. American Airlines has taken on a European collaborator, too, establishing a marketing agreement with the French railway system to link air reservations in and out of Paris with rail travel to other parts of France.

Faddishness helps to explain some of this recent spate of cross-border alliances, and not surprisingly, a few of these marriages have already begun to unravel. A much-touted strategic alliance between AT&T and Olivetti ended in high-profile friction, Daimler-Benz had a falling-out with General Electric which almost led to an international lawsuit, and a joint venture between Chrysler and Renault to build four-wheel-drive vehicles in France was jointly terminated.

But the principle of global partnerships will endure. American companies have powerful assets to bring to the bargaining table in forming such alliances, not the least of which is the access they can provide to the U.S. domestic market. Given the erosion of manufacturing competitiveness at home, developing a system of alliances with other global leaders may be the most appropriate and advantageous course for many U.S. firms.

3. American companies speak English! A considerable competitive advantage resides in the fact that managers of U.S. companies—whether American or European by birth—speak English, since this has emerged as the common language of European business. Local languages may remain extremely important within individual countries, and German may be gaining some popularity. But as far as pan-European business is concerned, English—the medium for conducting 50 percent of the world's business deals and storing 80 percent of its computer-based information—is indisputably the way of the future. With native speakers of English in the U.K. and Ireland, and a vast number of Continentals who speak it as a second language, English has emerged as the single most widely spoken European language.

Even the French, who are notoriously chauvinistic about their language, have begun to recognize this fact of life. ''French is dead as a world language,'' concedes Yves Sabouret, a top executive with the giant French publisher Hachette. ''If you are in the media, information, and entertainment businesses, you cannot doubt that English is the language that will experience the most future growth.''

4. European profits can be reinvested to enhance the overall global competitiveness of American business. Increased revenues and profits from the European market can be plowed back into improving the general competitiveness of American companies. Digital Equipment has survived rough weather recently in its domestic U.S. business by riding the back of a huge boom in Europe—now the company's fastest-growing region and the source of 45 percent of total corporate revenues. The biggest U.S. company of all, General Motors, has adopted a similar strategy. GM now sells 30 percent of its total auto production in Europe and earns 50 percent of its worldwide profits there. The European operations are doing so well that GM plans to expand production by 25 percent, even as it closes U.S. facilities.

"I don't think one can overestimate the importance of GM Europe to the entire GM organization," says Maryann Keller, the world's leading GM watcher. Europe, she explains, "is where the cash is coming from for investment in GM North America."[23] In other words, despite woeful management mistakes and a precipitous loss of market share to Japanese rivals at home in the U.S., the European business is healthy enough to provide GM the reinvestment cash it needs to attempt a domestic turn-around.

5. Europe may help the American growth businesses of the 1980s to continue growing in the 1990s. As a result of the unusually long period of sustained U.S. economic expansion in the 1980s, many American companies have been left with the capacity and staff necessary to satisfy a continuously growing market, at a time when many sectors are facing saturation and even contraction. The U.S. computer business is one of the best examples, and as we have noted, companies such as IBM, DEC, and Compaq are easing the transition by turning to Europe for revenues and profits.

Real estate developers and construction companies, facing the aftermath of American overexpansion, plummeting real estate values, and the collapse of the S&Ls, are looking to Europe for opportunities. While office space is oversupplied in many major U.S. cities, it is desperately short in much of Europe. "There is more economic activity now than I've ever seen in Europe," says Donald Williams, CEO of the Trammell Crow. "The 1992 unification is a reality."[24]

Household appliance makers, which did record domestic business in the expansion of the 1980s, are also shifting their sights toward Europe.

Whirlpool spent $470 million in 1989 on a majority stake in the European appliance business of Philips, anticipating consistently stronger growth in Europe during the '90s than in the United States.

The "baby Bell" telephone companies have a similar outlook. "Europe is where we see the most potential," says Eugene Sekulow of Nynex.[25] U.S. government restrictions still prohibit baby Bells from entering businesses such as telephone-equipment manufacturing, cable TV, and long-distance telephone services inside the U.S. In Europe, however, they face no such constraints. Nynex, which serves New York and New England, now owns half the local telephone company in Gibraltar, provides network management services in the U.K. and France, and is helping to upgrade systems in Poland and Hungary.

Investment bankers also smell money in Europe, although none of the smart ones expect Europe's deal-making ever to match that seen on Wall Street in the 1980s. While the art of the deal is slowing down in the U.S., it is heating up in London and European points beyond. Jeffrey Rosen, of the New York investment-banking firm Wasserstein, Perella & Co., complains that striking up conversations with potential clients on the Concorde's swift ride across the Atlantic has become tougher recently. It seems too many rival American bankers are trying to do the same thing. "They race to either end of the aisles," says Rosen. "Nobody gets to eat anymore, because everyone's so busy trying to do business."[26]

The Concorde trips seem to be paying off for Wasserstein, Perella, however. Despite some early stumbles, the American takeover specialists teamed up with A&P to win a stake in a high-profile war of nerves for control of Gateway, Britain's third-largest food-retailing chain. Together with Paribas, the big French bank, Wasserstein, Perella has created a pan-European acquisition and buyout fund to take American-style deals further into Europe.

The danger exists, of course, that U.S. strategic planners may overestimate Europe's potential or attempt to move too quickly without establishing sufficiently deep local roots. But if exploited judiciously, the European market could serve to carry many American companies through what would otherwise be a traumatic contraction at home.

6. American businesses lead the world in sectors likely to experience robust European growth. Although U.S.-based companies have lost global leadership in manufacturing, they are far out in front in many areas of the emerging service economy, such as finance, software development, information-systems management, communications, entertainment, leisure time, and franchising, among others. In all these sectors, the outlook for Europe in the '90s is bullish.

A number of excellent services originally developed for American domestic consumption are now finding new markets in Europe. Ted Turner's Cable News Network has won a loyal audience in several European countries, and the *CBS Evening News with Dan Rather* has become popular in France. More American films and television programs are now being developed with the European market in mind than ever before. The quirky *Twin Peaks* TV series was as popular on videocassette in Europe as it was in the U.S. on network TV. The European video even had its own ending that answered the question "Who killed Laura Palmer?" long before American audiences would find out.

The enthusiasm that greeted the Euro Disneyland project has led other American companies into developing theme parks and new entertainment ventures all across a continent that, from an American viewpoint, is seriously underserved when it comes to leisure-time facilities. Toys "R" Us stores are sprouting up at prime locations off the German autobahn as America's master toy marketers cash in on the European baby boom. Even something as uniquely American as the National Football League is cultivating a European market. NFL exhibition games are now played annually in cities such as London, Paris, and Berlin, while domestic games are regularly televised in the U.K.

U.S.-based accounting firms are already the leaders in cross-border accounting worldwide and are now experiencing rapid European growth as the EC moves toward standardizing its financial rules and procedures, as well as certain taxes. For American international-law firms, advertising agencies, public-relations companies, and executive recruiters, Europe is now perceived as a new frontier.

7. Europe offers American businesses new strategies for dealing with Japanese competitors. From the standpoint of business strategy, one of the most promising aspects of Europe's new economic vitality is the potential trump card it offers Americans doing battle with Japanese competitors. Whether American companies will choose to play this card remains to be seen, but a few are already trying.

IBM and Siemens, as noted earlier, have teamed up to try to catch Japanese leaders in the race for mass production of the next generation of computer memory chips. On another front, Philips and Thomson, already allies in European HDTV ventures, have formed a special U.S. consortium with NBC to try to outflank Japanese efforts to capture the American HDTV market.

"The best tactic for American companies worried about the Japanese is to make alliances with European partners," says Edith Cresson, France's combative prime minister. "Americans and Europeans complement each other's strengths and weaknesses very nicely. We both face the same problem with the Japanese. Why not solve it together?" It is a tempting offer, although the simplicity of the idea belies the complex mechanics and conflicting interests involved in putting such deals together. Nevertheless, the European "trump card" holds a great deal of promise as a much-needed new strategy for countering Japanese competition.

8. Americans can be leaders in creatively developing the Eastern European and Soviet markets. Although Germany may be inclined to regard all of Eastern Europe as its natural home market, there is no fundamental reason why Americans can't be very successful between the Elbe and Urals. So far, certain American companies are showing a healthy interest in Eastern Europe, and even seem willing to take big risks for the sake of getting in on the ground floor of this complicated but exciting market. PepsiCo exhibited daring as well as a flair for creative bartering when it entered into a $3 billion deal to provide the Soviets with bottling plants that can churn out as much as 75 million cases of Pepsi a year. In return for all those soft drinks, PepsiCo will get Stolichnaya vodka and Soviet-built oceangoing freighters and tankers. Philip Morris, meanwhile, is finalizing a barter venture that may net it up to one-fifth of the Soviet cigarette market in a country which has twenty million more smokers than the United States. It is not yet known exactly what Philip Morris will get in this barter deal, but oil, gold, and diamonds have been mentioned as possibilities. The international strategists at Philip Morris certainly know a good market when they see one: In the Soviet Union, health concerns take a distant backseat to the desire to inhale an American cigarette, and workers spend a phenomenal 10 percent of their income on tobacco.

Other American firms have been equally creative, albeit on a smaller scale: Ben & Jerry's will build ice-cream-making facilities in the Soviet Union in return for a supply of honey, walnuts, and Russian *matrushka* dolls. Rodale Press will publish a magazine for Soviet farmers, operating a Soviet sausage factory and selling ad space back home in the U.S. in order to pay for it.

General Motors, meanwhile, managed to talk Moscow into paying a billion dollars in hard currency for auto parts. GM Europe president Robert Eaton believes Europe as a whole will be the key battleground in the international auto business of the 1990s, and that the Soviet and Eastern European markets in particular will be the critical platforms for growth. (Analysts expect those markets to triple in size from today's 2.4 million annual car sales to more than seven million by decade's end.)

Time Warner is cognizant of the fact that the Soviets are the world's biggest moviegoers. The average Soviet citizen sees fourteen films a year in cinemas. (Americans, who have so many other entertainment alternatives, make an average of only four trips per year to the movie theater.) Consequently, Time Warner has created a joint venture with Soviet film authorities to build two of the world's biggest and most spectacular multiplex cinemas—a 4,000-seat, ten-screen complex in Moscow and a 3,400-seat, nine-screen theater in Leningrad.

Chevron, together with the Soviet ministry of oil and gas, is working on plans for what could be the biggest, boldest East-West joint venture yet—development of the Tengiz oil fields. At 25 billion barrels, the estimated reserves of Tengiz make it "probably the single largest field discovered in the last decade," according to Richard Matzke, president of Chevron Overseas Petroleum.[27] If the estimates are accurate, Tengiz would hold two and a half times as much oil as Alaska's Prudhoe Bay, which now accounts for 20 percent of U.S. oil output.

The Soviet Union desperately needs American technology, although it generally has little hard currency with which to buy it. But the Soviets also have some technology of their own that may prove to be marketable. The Bechtel Group has undertaken a feasibility study for converting a government research center outside Moscow into a prototype American-style cluster of high-tech enterprises. Arthur D. Little, Inc. has entered into a joint venture with the prestigious Soviet Academy of Sciences to commercialize technology developed by leading Soviet scientists.

"It costs $250,000 to $300,000 a year to support a top-level scientist at major American corporations," says Barney O'Meara, a consultant on East-West technology trade. "You can have the same caliber of talent, complete with overhead, lab space, and graduate students in the East for $25,000 to $30,000."[28] Monsanto is sponsoring ten Soviet bioengineers working at Moscow's Shemyakin Institute; according to a Monsanto spokesman, the scientists are "some of the finest minds on earth."[29]

In a 1990 survey, 70 percent of American senior managers said they were preparing new business strategies based on the revolutions in Eastern Europe and were developing plans to enter those markets. OPIC, the U.S. government agency that provides political risk insurance to U.S. companies abroad, reports American investments in Eastern Europe rising from a base of zero in 1988 to $500 million in 1989 and $1.5 billion in 1990.

One of the countries with the best outlook is Hungary. R. Mark Palmer, the U.S. ambassador to Hungary and a career foreign-service officer, believed prospects were so exciting that he resigned his ambassadorship to manage a consortium of North American financiers interested in doing business. Backed by the likes of Ronald Lauder and Albert Reichmann, the group purchased a 50 percent stake in Budapest's General Banking and Trust Co., one of the last remaining financial institutions with a reputation dating back to before World War II.

George Soros, one of Wall Street's most legendary fund managers and a Hungarian by birth, organized a Hungary investment fund to operate as a venture-capital-style company in the uncharted waters of private-sector development. Schwinn's Budapest bicycle factory has become the case study in successful capitalist management of a failing communist plant. And GE's $150 million acquisition of a majority interest in Tungsram, the largest light-bulb manufacturer in Eastern Europe, is the prototype for future M&A deals involving former state-owned enterprises.

Commenting on the Tungsram deal, GE executive John Opie says, "We're looking at this as a manufacturing entry into Europe, not Western Europe or Eastern Europe, but Europe."[30] Tungsram already does $120 million worth of business annually in Western Europe. With Hungarian wages at less than a dollar an hour, GE believes it can now be competitive at the low end of the European lighting market, whereas previously it was focused almost exclusively at the high end.

Speaking at the inaugural dinner of the fifty-seven-company American Chamber of Commerce in Budapest, Palmer, the ambassador–turned–venture capitalist, said, "If you stand in the lobby of the Forum Hotel you are lucky not to get knocked down. The gold rush is on in Hungary. Budapest is a boom town."[31]

Even before the Berlin Wall had fallen, Coca-Cola had begun handing out free Cokes to East Germans crossing the border. Now the company has followed up with a $140 million capital investment program to provide bottling plants, trucks, and vending machines for what was formerly East Germany. Coca-Cola already derives a hefty 12 percent of its worldwide revenues from West Germany. The pent-up demand in the East is enormous, especially since East Germans have watched Coke ads for years on West German television and have never been able to buy the stuff. With the U.S. domestic beverage market nearly flat, Eastern Europe presents a market opportunity that will have a direct impact on revenues in the short run.

EUROPE'S NINE FUNDAMENTAL CHALLENGES TO THE UNITED STATES

Against the positive backdrop of an increasingly dynamic marketplace that is likely to be more open and internationalized after 1992 than it is today, the New Europe poses far more subtle and complex challenges to the United States than the simplistic protectionism envisioned in the "fortress Europe" scenario. Even the many opportunities cited above could backfire, producing negative consequences, if Americans fail to play their cards wisely.

Political pundits have acknowledged recently that it was easier to be *against* the Soviet menace during the Cold War than it is to determine what to be *for* in the post-postwar era. Similarly, it may prove far more difficult to formulate competitive American economic strategies in a world that includes a relatively open, dynamic, and powerful Europe than it was to simply castigate the real or imagined bogeyman of a fortress Europe.

Let us now consider some of the challenges and dangers that the New Europe may present to American competitiveness:

1. European business will become more competitive *everywhere*. This simple fact is the basic *raison d'être* of the whole 1992 project. The economies of scale now being built by European firms suggest they will emerge from their home markets as leaders of the world market. Americans already find themselves confronting these new competitors not only in Europe but also in Japan, at home in the United States, and elsewhere in the global marketplace. It is interesting to note, for example, that in Japan, the single foreign market Americans have expended the most political energy to penetrate, Europeans are garnering a disproportionate share of the imported-goods sector now that the Japanese domestic market has begun to finally open up.

While Americans have not been shy about acquiring European companies and positioning themselves for the post-1992 marketplace, Europeans have been buying American companies at an even more breathless pace. Most of the largest U.S. corporate acquisitions by foreigners have been made *not by the Japanese but by Europeans:* British Petroleum's $8 billion purchase of the half of Standard Oil of Ohio that it didn't already own, Grand Metropolitan's $6 billion takeover of Pillsbury, Hoechst's $3 billion buyout of Celanese, and Rhône-Poulenc's $3 billion merger with the Rorer Group. French-based Michelin paid $1.5 billion to buy Uniroyal-Goodrich, becoming the largest tire company in the world as a result. Renault holds a major stake in Mack Trucks; Fireman's Fund was sold to Allianz, the German-based giant of European insurance, for $1.1 billion; and specialized American companies from Motel 6 to F.A.O. Schwarz are being gobbled up by rich European investors. Precisely because 1992 is liberating them from their past inward focus, European companies are now prepared to use their vast capital assets to improve their global position.

German business is building economies of scale and moving offshore as never before. The watershed was the takeover of aircraft maker MBB last year by Daimler-Benz. Just before his death, Alfred Herrhausen confided that his goal in putting together this deal was nothing short of rendering MBB an effective competitor to Boeing, the world's biggest aircraft manufacturer. To Herrhausen, the key was not his bank's prodigious capital resources or the much-vaunted technological prowess of Daimler-Benz. Developing MBB into a global leader, he said, would be possible only now that Germany could consider all of Europe its "home market." "In the European context and under the European dimension," he said, competing with Boeing was a realistic ambition.

Simply put, American companies, which have grown used to thinking of "competitiveness" chiefly as a battle with Japanese and Asian rivals, must now prepare for the added squeeze of aggressive new forces emerging in Europe.

2. Americans are falling behind in the race to develop Eastern Europe. Certain brave and aggressive American companies are playing a leadership role in opening up Eastern Europe, as noted above. Yet there is a growing perception that the U.S. government isn't doing what it needs to do—or what other governments are doing for *their* businesses—to ensure a long-term competitive position for American business in the expanding Eastern European marketplace.

"Will Eastern Europe be a market for everyone, or only for those companies whose governments extend credits to enable those in the East to buy?" asks Monsanto's Mahoney. "We could sell $2 billion worth of products a year if the U.S. was in a position to offer the credits the Germans are offering."

Aside from IBM, Coca-Cola, and a few others, American firms are moving too slowly in East Germany, the most immediately promising market and the one with the most strategic significance to Europe as a whole. "Where are the Americans?" asks Deutsche Bank's Kurt Kasch, who is spearheading his company's drive to the East.[32] British, French, Dutch, and Swedish firms are all said to be more active. This pattern is attributed not only to the individual business strategies of various companies, but also to policies in Washington which have failed to encourage bank financing and other mechanisms to smooth the way for American companies.

The pattern, moreover, extends throughout Eastern Europe. A single West German deal—Volkswagen's $3 billion program to build factories in East Germany—represents a commitment of 150 percent greater than the value of all U.S. business deals in East Germany, Poland, Hungary, Czechoslovakia, Romania, and Yugoslavia during both 1989 and 1990 combined.

Thus, while opportunity abounds—and some Americans are seizing it—there is also danger. "If the Americans don't get involved now, in ten years we will see Germany completely dominating Europe economically," predicts Martin McCauley, a professor of economics at London's School of Slavonic and East European Studies. "Then the Germans will begin talking very tough indeed to the United States. And they may not be asking; they may be demanding."[33]

3. Japan will be a powerful new competitor in Europe. It will undoubtedly take years for Europe to fully relax its prevalent Japanophobia and for the Japanese strategy in Europe to become clear. But several trends are already noticeable.

First, the well-established American multinational giants in industries such as automobiles and computers will face serious competitive pressure from Japanese rivals entering Europe in a big way for the first time. A company like Ford may benefit greatly from harmonization of European standards on emission controls and auto safety. But in the long run, Ford's biggest competitive battle may not be so much with European manufacturers as with the Japanese. The idea of being able to take one approach to the EC instead of twelve has immense appeal in Tokyo, even if it means making concessions to EC negotiating positions on "local content" or joint-venture investment.

Second, Europe today offers an attractive alternative to the United States for Japanese investors. Although the capital markets are not yet as large and liquid as those in the U.S., Japanese money is flowing there in sizable streams. Americans comforting themselves with the thought that Japan has nowhere to invest its capital surplus besides the U.S. may soon discover that the Japanese have developed a strong position in Europe which can be leveraged a number of ways. If Japanese bond buyers shift even a small portion of their attention from American to European debt, it could drive up U.S. interest rates. It is also likely that U.S. equities, real estate, and other financial assets which enjoyed strong Japanese interest in the 1980s will now have to prove themselves as outstanding performers, not just convenient parking places, to attract a continued flow of funds from Japan.

Third, through sophisticated use of its financial assets in Eastern Europe and through strategic targeting of its job-generating and technology-locating investments in Western Europe, Japan could eventually outflank the United States and develop a close political relationship with European countries. With American policymakers constantly demanding in the late 1980s that both Tokyo and Bonn act to raise discount rates, stimulate domestic economies, consume more, import more, and save less, it is not surprising that Japanese and German central bankers found themselves more frequently in agreement with each other than with the Americans. American investment banker Jeffrey E. Garten notes that it "would be a major mistake to dismiss the pressure Tokyo and Bonn could exert on the United States in concert."[34]

4. Europe's newly competitive companies will benefit from the powerful tool of industrial policy. Whether one agrees or disagrees with the theoretical underpinnings of industrial policy, the rise of Europe means a global economic environment in which Japan and Europe will *both* be practicing various forms of industrial policy, while the

United States will not. Tokyo and Brussels are racing ahead with projects to support and encourage the emerging High-Definition Television industry, while the Bush administration is deliberately emasculating all government-sponsored R&D in the U.S. on the grounds that it is not Washington's place to "pick winners and losers" in the American economy.

The United States on the whole remains technologically far ahead of Europe, even as it is beginning to trail Japan in key areas. Yet if the array of new technologies that are proving too expensive for single American companies to develop alone should meet with the same governmental indifference as HDTV, it is not inconceivable that American business could fall behind Europe as well as Japan.

Apart from backing its own indigenous industries, EC industrial policy is also working to increase employment, technology transfer, and regional economic development, using "local content" and "rules of origin" regulations to spur foreign investment in Europe. Most of what is still seen as European "protectionism" is not protectionism per se, but manifestations of industrial policy. What Europe wants—and what it is getting from Japanese and Americans alike—is large-scale integrated facilities that will augment the amount of R&D and high-value-added production taking place within the Community.

Debate about trade issues is increasingly evolving into debate about investment issues as it becomes clear that cross-border investment is a new weapon in the competitiveness battle. But because foreign investment has only recently come to the fore as a powerful competitive tool, it is subject to few international agreements. Instead, conflicting national philosophies and strategies are virtually at war with each other in the marketplace.

The EC is thinking critically about what kinds of foreign investment it favors and opposes. In Japan, the same thought process is taking place, although less transparently and certainly without the favor to foreigners of establishing clear-cut rules, as Brussells is now trying to do. But the Reagan and Bush administrations have explicitly chosen to prevent the United States from developing a national strategy on foreign investment.

America has already paid a price, with the decline of its global competitiveness, for its naive and at times downright blind faith in its particular vision of the free trade in goods. The U.S. may end up paying an even greater price if it insists on a similarly laissez-faire approach to foreign investment in a world where few of its competitors are similarly cavalier.

The appalling irony, of course, is that the U.S. government does have an industrial policy, so to speak. Unfortunately, though, it is a negative policy of default rather than proactive and positive. The decisions made in the early 1980s about deregulating the savings-and-loan industry, for example, ultimately necessitated one of the most massive government interventions in the marketplace ever. A decade ago, deregulation was widely hailed as a sensible way to get government out of the banking business. However, the net result of the process has been to force the government into what amounts to a nationalization of the S&L business—at a cost to taxpayers of half a trillion dollars or more.

The issue, then, isn't whether or not the United States should have an industrial policy, the issue is what kind. Should it be a policy of corruption and benign neglect that transfers half a trillion dollars' worth of national wealth to a small number of speculators in the savings-and-loan, real estate, and junk-bond businesses? Or should it be a creative, "postindustrial" policy that develops workable American strategies for competing with the Europeans and Japanese, especially in developing and commercializing the new technologies and export products of the future?

5. There are dangers for American business both in underestimating Europe—and overestimating it. While the EC has certainly captured a much greater share of the American mind in the last two years, on the whole the United States is undercommitted to Europe, particularly in view of the importance of what will happen there in the 1990s.

One good indicator is the staffing of the U.S. mission to the EC in Brussels. Only twenty-three American diplomats were accredited there in 1989. The Japanese, with a team of twenty-five, seemed to be somewhat more interested. Even Canada, with an economy less than one-tenth the size of America's, was represented by a diplomatic corps of twenty-one. The majority of the $200 million total spent in 1989 by foreigners on Brussels-based lobbying and public-affairs campaigns came from the Japanese, not the Americans.

House Majority Leader Richard Gephardt laments the lack of knowledge on the part of the various U.S. agencies which ought to be concerned with the European Community, such as the State Department, the Commerce Department, the Treasury Department, and the Office of the

U.S. Trade Representative. Referring to 1992, Gephardt said, "Up-to-date information is more easily obtained from the *Wall Street Journal* than the U.S. government."[35]

Another small sign of the times is America's attitude toward the 1992 World's Fair, to take place in Seville, Spain. Initially, Congress refused to appropriate funds for a U.S. pavilion, citing the need to make deficit-reducing cuts. "It all seems inconsequential and almost amusing now," said Alfred Heller, an American expert on world's fairs. "But come 1992, and here is a major world event, with more nations participating than ever before, during the year of Europe when, perhaps, a good number of Eastern Europeans could be traveling to the West for the first time, and here is *the great democracy* too preoccupied to participate."[36]

American thinking about Europe still tends to be disproportionately Anglo-centric. Although U.S. companies led the pack in cross-border investments in Europe during 1989, 75 percent of those deals were in the U.K. It is easier, of course, for American companies which have decided to upgrade their European presence to do so in and around London. But the heart of the coming European boom will be in continental Europe, and American business needs to be there to take maximum advantage of it.

Burned by the shakeout that followed the "Big Bang" in London and facing severe problems at home, most leading American banks have reacted with disinterest to the emergence of Europe's integrated financial market. Even Citicorp, which at first had bold expansion plans throughout Europe, has begun selling assets and subsidiaries. As the *Wall Street Journal* notes, "many U.S. banks are pulling in their horns. . . . Meantime, Japanese institutions are steadily increasing their presence as the prospect of 1992 lures more of their domestic clients to Europe."[37]

A trap is emerging for American companies which already own strong businesses in Europe: The increasing economic vigor of the marketplace and the new desire of Europeans to build Continent-wide organizations are combining to increase the value of American assets. This, in turn, is encouraging American businesses to sell off their European divisions at just the time when their importance as global beachheads could pay off most. These deals are particularly attractive to American companies strapped by LBO-laden debt from restructurings in the 1980s. RJR-Nabisco, for example, sold off five European businesses for $2.5 billion, which it needed in order to pay down its mammoth debt. BSN, the most aggressive European food company, snapped them up (although two were later acquired by PepsiCo). ITT is under intense shareholder pressure to dump its remaining minority interest in Alcatel, the French telecommunications company formed in 1986 largely on the basis of ITT's European telecommunications operations. Alcatel is now very successful in both Eastern and Western Europe. Yet key U.S. stockholders have indicated they would rather cash out now than wait for future profits. And, as part of Pan American's desperate bid to stay aloft, the airline's management felt compelled to cash out of its highly valuable operations within Germany, spinning them off to Lufthansa just weeks before reunification.

Just as undercommitment to Europe is an error, so too are corporate strategies which go too far in the opposite direction. Europe will be the biggest global growth market of the first half of the 1990s and perhaps beyond. But long term, the potential in East Asia remains even greater. Some American companies are giving up costly and frustrating efforts to do business in Japan in order to redirect their international energies toward Europe. This is a serious mistake which they will pay for later in the decade, when the new global economy will begin to punish those who cannot compete in all its major markets at once.

6. American society has not yet begun making the necessary structural adjustments to the multipolar world which 1992 will usher in. "Global markets" and "global competitiveness" have become buzzwords in America. Despite the rhetoric, however, the United States has yet to implement the requisite changes to adapt to these new realities. The need for well-coordinated U.S. trade policy, for example, has never been more visible. Yet, although a massive trade deficit remains and numerous excellent proposals for reform have been advanced, neither the way in which American trade policy is shaped nor the relevance of the policy goals themselves has been improved.

A perverse paradox is that American markets are unwittingly on their way to becoming as partially and subtly protectionist as Europe's—but to little avail. Special-interest groups continue to lobby for the kinds of protection that allowed James Baker to once boast that Ronald Reagan "granted more important relief to U.S. industry than any of his predecessors." These protectionist measures, however, are not part of an overall plan or strategy to boost American competitiveness; in the end, they amount to little more than a crazy quilt of political favors.

At the same time, those in the Congress who are seriously concerned about the erosion of the U.S. trade position have fought for and won legislation that, while well intentioned, accomplishes little and is sometimes even counterproductive. Many congressional activists had hoped the "Super 301" provision of U.S. trade law (which authorizes the president to monitor the trade practices of foreign countries and take retaliatory measures against those deemed unfair to the United States) would force Japanese and European markets to open up more extensively. But it is such an explosive instrument, it has proven too dangerous to be used against the EC and Japan. As a result, the Bush administration ended up in the pathetic position of applying Super 301 only against India in 1990—hardly America's most vital trading partner.

Although Tokyo and Brussels have eluded the reach of Super 301, both have been able to use the legislation to depict the United States as the new "bad guy" of international trade—the country which is turning toward protectionism, unilateralism, and closed markets even as Europe and Japan are opening up. The EC, for example, has denounced Super 301 as being "wholly at variance with the aim of reaching multilateral agreements in the GATT." Brussels now issues an annual report on the unfair practices of the United States. The 1990 edition catalogued fifty tariff and nontariff barriers maintained by the U.S. and declared Washington guilty of many of the same sins against free trade that Americans normally associate with Europe and the Far East. The propaganda effort is having the desired effect: In a recent survey of senior executives from twenty-three industrial countries, the U.S. was ranked as the third-most-unfair trading nation, after Japan and South Korea.

Almost every important study on the issue of American competitiveness has recommended that the United States implement certain basic changes. The most common suggestions include: raising the savings rate and lowering the cost of capital; developing incentives, through tax policy and other means, for greater investment in civilian R&D, capital equipment, and export industries; modifying antitrust legislation to permit more-extensive industrial partnerships and consortia; overhauling the basic educational system, and establishing programs for skills training in the workplace. In all of these areas, the United States faces a widening competitiveness gap, not only with Japan, but now with many European countries as well. Yet so little is changing on these fronts that one is forced at times to wonder if Americans have somehow lost their famed national traits of flexibility and adaptability.

The United States has yet to undertake even the most obvious and low-cost steps to prepare for the multipolar world order of the future. In the area of foreign-language learning, for example, despite some recent improvements, the U.S. still lags woefully behind other nations; luckily, Americans enjoy the benefit of speaking the world's most common language. And, while corporate awareness of the increasingly international nature of business has become nearly universal, American companies have actually *reduced* their expatriate staff by 25 percent over the last three years.

7. The dollar is on its way out as the leading global currency. In a world of strong yen and strong deutsche marks (with strong ECUs looming on the horizon), it is unlikely that the weakening U.S. dollar can remain the global key currency, especially now that European and Japanese macroeconomic policies are converging with each other while *diverging* from the American norm. These factors, coupled with concerns about the frightening volatility displayed by financial markets in the 1980s, are creating greater international demand for a new currency agreement. Whether the world of the year 2000 ends up with a dollar-yen-ECU basket, a formalized G-7 exchange-rate mechanism, or a single world currency, the U.S. dollar will no longer enjoy the preeminent role it has played since the end of World War II.

As the dollar falls from grace, the already high cost of capital in the U.S. will rise in its wake. The Treasury will no longer be able to issue most of its bonds in U.S. dollars, but will have to move more ambitiously into foreign-currency offerings. New costs and volatility will confront small and midsize American business operations, which until now have been shielded from the vicissitudes of the currency market. And perhaps most significantly, the United States will surrender the leverage it has squandered in the last six years to use the dollar's value as a tool for achieving macroeconomic policy goals.

8. With respect to major issues from world trade to NATO, Washington's agenda is a twentieth-century antique, ill-suited for the new millennium. On those issues over which Washington has chosen to face off with its capitalist allies in Europe and Japan, it is fighting losing battles which will ultimately jeopardize its leadership role and harm domestic U.S. economic interests.

Here, for example, is how Trade Representative Carla Hills states the fundamental goal of her office: ''The one essential target of our strategy is to get government out of business: out of the business of making steel, selling grain, growing beef, building ships, and the hundreds of other areas in which governments distort trade. This goal drives all of our recent trade actions.''

The obvious question is "Why?" If government involvement with business is as costly, backward, and inefficient as free traders like Hills claim, why do Americans care if foreign governments intervene in their private sectors? And if government involvement is capable of enhancing competitiveness rather than promoting inefficiency, why wouldn't Americans want to emulate those results? At a time when the American economy is crying out for intelligent, creative government leadership, it seems that Hills and the Bush administration are committed to a course that would make government unable to form partnerships with business under the rules of international trade.

Following this ideological agenda, American trade negotiators have fought for an end to government subsidies in agriculture. Their actions are angering America's allies in Europe and fueled the breakup of the GATT talks in December 1990. The EC's fragile compromise on agricultural policy entails subsidies so heavy they consume most of the Brussels budget, yet Europeans have agreed to this compromise to keep the political peace. Why does Washington feel it must shatter that peace?

The answer from the Bush administration is that if foreign governments eliminated their agricultural subsidies, American farmers could sell many more of their products abroad. That is no doubt true—although a number of U.S. senators and congressmen from farm states oppose abolishing U.S. government agricultural subsidies just as vehemently as the Europeans oppose ending their own. Nebraska's Senator Bob Kerrey, for example, has argued that fellow Nebraskan Clayton Yeutter, now U.S. secretary of agriculture, is selling out the interests of farmers by supporting the administration's effort in the GATT debate to reduce subsidies. In any event, making a major global issue out of farm exports seems an extremely antiquated platform at the end of the twentieth century, when farming is an area of American business with little value added and a sector that employs a continuously declining fraction of the U.S. work force.

Washington's views on the future of NATO are similarly outdated. Secretary of State James Baker has called for a "new European architecture" in which NATO would still play a leadership role, evolving from a military alliance to a more political one. The idea makes sense in the abstract. But it is being overrun by European events.

Despite some political trappings, NATO is fundamentally a military alliance designed to fight the Cold War. One of the best demonstrations of NATO's inflexible institutional role was its irrelevance in the Persian Gulf crisis. Even with its members sharing wide political agreement on the Gulf, and even with many of its members committing troops to the multilateral force in Saudi Arabia, NATO itself was a nonentity. The official explanation for this was, of course, that NATO's charter limits the scope of its activities to the North Atlantic and European theaters. But if ever there was a dramatic issue which showed the need for NATO to reconsider its charter and its purpose, it was the Persian Gulf crisis. Yet there was no motion in that direction whatsoever.

NATO simply cannot continue much longer in the absence of a military threat to Europe. The military strategists of the alliance have already declared that the Warsaw Pact no longer presents a threat. As a result, NATO is moving to abandon its historic doctrine of "forward defense." But when you begin to retreat from the front lines, the commitment to holding the back lines tends to weaken as well.

Readiness, preparedness, and the regular allocation of new resources to manpower and weapons systems have been constant centrifugal forces binding NATO together over the last decade. Remove the discipline of that structure, and the conflict between American and European interests that has always existed within NATO comes immediately to the surface. Germany has accepted a watered-down membership in NATO to placate Moscow. France, urged to reconsider its long-standing Gaullist independence from NATO's integrated command structure, has indicated it is unlikely to do so. Belgium began making unilateral cuts in its NATO commitments the moment the Berlin Wall fell. The last true NATO enthusiasts in Europe are the British—who just happen to be off the mainland and the most isolated politically—and even they are warming to the idea of a European defense union to eventually replace NATO.

While Europeans may be willing to go along with a political NATO for a while, they now have the historic opportunity to create their own defense arrangements—and they won't pass it up. They will pursue an EC defense union, which may begin as the "European pillar" of NATO but will end up in practice as a NATO without Americans. Those who doubt that Europeans desire control over their own security strategy would do well to listen to Roger Fauroux, the outspoken French minister of industry, who noted in the wake of the Gulf crisis, "If we want to exist in future conflicts, and not have the Americans run our affairs, we need rapid economic and monetary union, and then political union."[38] A

European defense union is now the next logical vehicle for promoting the goal of pan-European integration.

Few among today's European leaders believe their nations will ever have to fight again in Europe, yet none would be so foolish as to favor unilateral disarmament and demobilization. Those two propositions yield two conclusions: (1) The American military presence is dispensable, and (2) to the extent that Europe needs its own independent military force, its equipment and procurement should be Europeanized as much as possible.

Inasmuch as a political forum for peacekeeping will be needed to complement any military union, most Europeans prefer institutionalizing the Conference on Security and Cooperation in Europe (CSCE) rather than adapting NATO for that purpose. The CSCE, which comprises virtually all European countries as well as the U.S., Canada, and the USSR, has the virtue of being a political institution that promotes a highly inclusive pan-Europeanism. It extends Europe's political and strategic definition to the Urals, rather than reinforcing the Atlanticism of NATO.

Even former NATO Secretary-General Lord Carrington has admitted that he sees little future need for NATO. Its best role at the moment, he argues, is to help organize a new European Community defense system together with an enhanced CSCE. He urges Europeans to try to mind Washington's sensibilities, however: "You've got to make the Americans *feel* it's still NATO," he says.[39] Americans, in other words, should be humored into believing that NATO is being maintained, even as it is being dismantled.

While Europeans humor Americans on NATO, Americans will be humoring Europeans about U.S. support for the CSCE. Few Bush administration officials believe the CSCE can be workable, with its thirty-five-nation membership that spans East and West and includes socialists, communists, and neutralists. But as long as the military threat in Europe continues to dwindle, Americans will be on the losing end of this mutual humoring society. NATO will become less and less relevant, while an EC defense union and the CSCE become increasingly central to Europe's new architecture.

The Bush administration's extreme caution in reaping the "peace dividend" is yet another example of Washington's chronic lack of forward thinking. This is the time for the best and the brightest in the Pentagon to design a whole new conceptual approach to U.S. security—to create a defense system that can be vigilant, mobile, and responsive to a wide range of scenarios, likely or unlikely, without requiring the fixed troop strengths in Europe and the costly nuclear weapons programs of today's system. At the moment, the U.S. is neither taking advantage of the cost savings that should result from the diminished Soviet threat, nor developing the new military mechanisms to cope with the escalating regional conflicts, in the Mideast and elsewhere, that are now likely to pose the greatest security threat.

In the absence of a comprehensive approach to the "peace dividend," its potential value as a tonic to reawaken American competitiveness may be squandered. Military bases will be shuttered in the coming years instead of being offered as low-cost facilities for entrepreneurs, as they were after World War II. Air Force bases that could be developed into badly needed civilian airports will instead be closed down. And the money the U.S. saves on defense spending will be frittered away. Most likely, it will be used to pay the bills of the S&L bailout and ballooning entitlement programs, rather than being reinvested in programs to improve education and rebuild the foundation of the American economy.

9. The "vision thing" (or the absence of it) has economic consequences. The New World and Old World are undergoing a curious role reversal. Until recently, America was the place where everything was possible. In Western Europe, conversely, opportunity was seriously curtailed by the weight of tradition and the narrow confines of nations, religions, and social classes. In Eastern Europe everything was impossible.

Now the revolutions in Eastern Europe have forcefully demonstrated that anything is possible. In Western Europe, meanwhile, the process of developing the single market and a supranational Community has provided a sharp break with the constraints of the past and triggered a multifaceted wave of dynamism. Suddenly, it is in America that the sense of the possible seems to be losing its heartbeat. Even the self-confidence of "Morning in America" (however illusory the foundations of Reaganomics may have been) is now gone. Politicians refuse to invest in the future, citing the limits posed by the deficit, yet gridlock among interest groups prevents choices from being made so that the deficit can be resolved and the country can move forward.

President Bush himself acknowledges that he lacks the "vision thing." He has won considerable admiration for his competence, professionalism, and seeming ability to get along with everybody. But one of the reasons he gets along so well with so many is that he has no workable vision with which to challenge the thinking of other leaders. He is indeed the consummate international "cruise director," as he has been dubbed because of his predilection for one-on-one diplomacy with foreign leaders in relaxed settings. But it is a cruise to nowhere.

While the chaos of Ronald Reagan's White House would occasionally set off some alarms, George Bush's operation is smooth and seamless. He is presiding over the waning of American influence with such aplomb that it is easy for his domestic audience to be lulled to sleep without noticing what's happening.

A sense of the possible, a belief in the future, a vision—these are unquantifiable yet essential forces in the global competitiveness battle. Indeed, these forces drove the American economy for two hundred years, as the nation advanced from the frontiers of the West to the New Frontier of the space program. Now, however, it is old, mature Western Europe which finds itself imbued with the frontier spirit.

The millennium approaches. The ancient, tradition-bound societies of Japan and the "little dragons" in Asia have now been joined by the Europeans in welcoming the future and planning for it with specific dreams, visions, and goals. Can the United States really afford to rest on its laurels and ignore this challenge? Can the American economy remain a global leader if there is no bold American vision of the future?

Perhaps those who support the status quo will be proven right. Perhaps America really is so wealthy, so rich in assets of all kinds, so large-marketed, resource-blessed, and innovative that it need not make the arduous choices and changes that would otherwise appear to be mandated by the shifting winds of global power and competition. Or perhaps Western Europe's economic success, coupled with the de-communization of Eastern Europe, will simply contribute to the expanding global economic pie, with American business getting its share, the peace dividend minimizing the nation's fiscal problems and newly wealthy allies allowing America to become more competitive by assuming more of the burdens of world leadership. Or perhaps 1992 will fail, the attempt to rebuild Eastern Europe will bankrupt the soundest Western European financial institutions, Gorbachev will be overthrown, the zone from the Atlantic to the Urals will once again be ravaged by nationalism, and Americans will be quite happy to be far away and safe, so lucky to live on the bedrock, however flawed, of the world's strongest, most stable democracy.

Such scenarios are plausible. Unfortunately, however, they are also much less than probable.

8

The Sun Is Still Rising:
Japan's Empire Moves to Europe

The preoccupation with Europe is understandable. Yet it risks distracting attention from what remains the foremost economic challenge for America in the '90s: restoring competitiveness in the face of relentlessly efficient Japanese companies. A senior foreign diplomat in Tokyo jokes that he feels sorry for the Japanese, because "with all the chaos in Europe, they can't get anyone to pay attention to them, even though they are slowly taking over the world."

BILL POWELL, *Newsweek*[1]

A SNAPSHOT FROM JAPAN'S GRAND TOUR OF EUROPE

To begin to draw this account of the New Europe's impact on the global economy to a close, we must now turn our attention to Japan. Despite a mutual disinterest and distrust throughout much of the postwar period, Japan and Europe are now inextricably linked.

265

Japan's impact on Europe becomes daily more dramatic. From Notre Dame to the Alhambra, from Trafalgar Square to the remnants of the Berlin Wall, one cannot stand in front of a single tourist site anywhere in Europe very long without encountering a Japanese tour bus. Similarly, Japanese capital, technology, and industrial expertise are now at work in one way or another at many critical junctures of the European economy.

The invisible hand of Tokyo's economic planning (invisible to foreigners, that is) now pursues the pattern, pioneered in the United States, of recycling Japanese trade surpluses. Almost all of Japan's $20 billion-plus trade surplus with the European Community for 1990 is expected to come back to Europe in the form of new investment in 1991. Europe, like the United States, is providing Japan the capital needed to buy up its prime assets.

For those not familiar with the stake Japan has already acquired in Europe, a quick snapshot is in order. Japanese money is flooding into big, high-profile, and sometimes controversial investments such as state-of-the-art automobile, semiconductor, and consumer-electronics factories; famous old London buildings; Eurodollar and Euroyen financial instruments; Scotland's distilleries; German stocks; and French couture houses. It is also seeping quietly into the less well publicized crevices of European economic life. In tiny Luxembourg, for example, cumulative Japanese investment of over $1 billion calculates out to $3,000 for every man, woman, and child.

At least sixty Japanese banks are active in London, and the total count of Japanese financial institutions there is upwards of two hundred. The annual ranking of Eurobond underwriters—dominated by American and European firms in the early 1980s—was headed at the end of the decade by Japan's Big Four securities houses—Nomura, Daiwa, Yamaichi, and Nikko.

"Frankly speaking, if the Japanese were all to go home tomorrow, London's role as an international financial center would collapse," says Minoru Mori, a razor-sharp thinker who presides over Daiwa Europe from a glorious old building on King William Street in the City of London. "Of course, we don't intend to leave," he adds with a smile.

Yet while Mr. Mori smiles, Japan's Ministry of Finance sometimes flexes its muscles. As foreigners have long demanded, Tokyo is deregulating its financial markets. Japanese firms which were once forced to go to London to do certain kinds of deals—such as issuing and trading equity warrants—are increasingly able to complete these transactions in Tokyo.

The perverse result is that London panics whenever Japanese financial authorities appear to be thinking of calling their business home. "We are fighting the greatest threat to the market since its inception," declared Christopher Heath of Baring Securities when reports circulated indicating that Tokyo's Ministry of Finance was planning to stanch "the flow of Japanese equity warrants that has been the market's lifeblood."[2]

Japanese banks now control about 11 percent of all European banking assets. Most of the business they do is institutional. But some Japanese banks have begun offering home and auto loans in the U.K. and private client fund management in Germany. Japan's leading credit-card issuer, JCB, is aggressively trying to sign up a quarter million European cardholders.

Venerable European financial institutions are selling minority stakes to and creating partnerships with Japanese firms. Italy's Monte dei Paschi di Siena, one of the world's oldest banks (founded in 1472), sold an interest to Japan's Taiyo Kobe Bank; Britain's Hambros took on Mitsui Bank as its partner; Spain's Banco Bilbao Vizcaya has teamed up with Nippon Life; and Banco Santander has gone with Nomura—which also bought a slice of the German investment bank Matuschka. Crédit Agricole, the French banking giant, has formed a strategic partnership with Daiwa to pursue the European-Japanese M&A business. Guinness Mahon, a British merchant bank, was acquired by the Bank of Yokohama.

In the industrial suburbs of Barcelona, around Düsseldorf, in South Wales, and elsewhere, "Nippon Valleys" are springing up as Japanese companies bring their assembly lines to Europe. Fujitsu is constructing an advanced $680 million chip-making facility in northeast England that may someday be expanded into the biggest semiconductor manufacturing facility in the world. Mitsubishi Electric is building a similarly integrated plant near Aachen, and Hitachi plans to follow suit at another German site in Landshut.

Toyota has broken ground on a $1.2 billion auto factory in the British Midlands, emulating Nissan, which has had success in Sunderland. When all the auto plant construction is finished in the mid-1990s, Japanese companies will have a European manufacturing capacity of over a million units a year to add to the 1.2 million cars they now export to Europe from Japan.

Sony is so well accepted as a "British" company that it has been cited three times for a Queen's Award for helping to minimize British trade deficits through the export of its British-assembled Trinitron televisions.

Altogether, Sony now operates eight European factories and is building a new one in Barcelona capable of producing 600,000 TV sets annually. Recently, Sony reached a historic milestone by selling more electronic equipment in Europe than in the United States—a further demonstration, considering Sony's ubiquitous presence in the U.S., of the European market's importance and of Japan's intention to make the most of it.

Numerous well-respected European brand names and franchises are now owned in whole or in part by Japanese interests: Jean-Louis Scherrer, Aquascutum, Hugo Boss, Virgin Music, Laura Ashley, F. G. Reporter, Carita hair salons, and Louis Royer cognac, to name a few. Japanese investors own 6 percent of Rolls-Royce's shares and 1.5 percent of Hermès, and have acquired some of Europe's most celebrated hotels. Lucas-Carton, the three-star Parisian restaurant, is now Japanese-owned. So, too, is a big chunk of the real estate around the renowned Parisian quarter of Les Halles. Outside London, David Puttnam is developing a series of films bankrolled by a $100 million investment from Fujisankei, Japan's most ambitious media conglomerate. The Frankfurt Messeturm, Europe's tallest skyscraper, is partly Japanese-owned.

Wacoal, the Kyoto-based lingerie firm, is building its own plant in France and plans to go after the high-end European lingerie market. Dainippon Ink, which bought the Spanish company Prisma, is now the leader in the European ink market. Trading house Marubeni and department store Mitsukoshi have formed a consortium to provide popular Japanese TV shows via satellite dish to the estimated 200,000 Japanese nationals now living in Europe.

With a few notable exceptions, the Japanese have not attempted to acquire large European companies whole. Instead, they have made minority investments in big companies (such as Honda's 20 percent interest in British Rover in 1989, Idemitsu's 9 percent stake in Statoil, the Norwegian state-owned oil firm, and C. Itoh's 6 percent equity position in German steelmaker Klöckner). Otherwise, most of their takeover activity has focused on friendly acquisitions of medium-size European companies, such as Nippon Seiko's $239 million purchase of United Precision Industries (the largest British-owned manufacturer of ball bearings) or Sankyo Pharmaceutical's purchase of a majority interest in German drugmaker Luitpold-Werk for $129 million.

Positioning themselves as good corporate citizens, Japanese companies have also taken up philanthropy in Europe. NEC and Fujitsu are supporting R&D facilities at Edinburgh University. Sharp and Yamanouchi Pharmaceutical have contributed to projects at Oxford. Toshiba sponsors a wing at London's Victoria and Albert Museum, while NHK, the leading Japanese TV network, is underwriting the restoration of the Sistine Chapel.

In Eastern Europe, Japanese Prime Minister Toshiki Kaifu made a splash when he visited the Berlin Wall in 1990 and pledged a $2 billion package of loans, guarantees, and technical aid for Poland and Hungary. Suzuki is working on a plant in Hungary that could eventually produce 50,000 minicars a year. Toyota is contemplating a venture to modernize BAZ, an outdated vehicle plant in Bratislava, Czechoslovakia. Fuji Bank, through its U.S. affiliate, the Heller Group, has invested in a Hungarian trade-financing company while Nomura has joined with the World Bank to help seed an investment bank for Hungary. Casio plans to increase its exports of hand-held calculators to Eastern Europe by 60 percent, and Citizen Watch, which is creating its own marketing organization in East Germany, expects to triple exports to the region to 100,000 annually. Nissan is opening thirty-six car dealerships during 1990–91 in East Germany.

On the whole, however, Japan's private sector has been cautious about investing in the East. With time, there is sure to be increasing involvement, since virtually every large Japanese company is carrying out a careful review of Eastern European opportunities. But Japan appears likely to wait for Germany to pioneer the path and create the infrastructure. Eastern Europeans, however, are hoping the Japanese will come soon. "We desire to be the Japan of Europe," Lech Walesa declared as he greeted Prime Minister Kaifu in Poland. Or, as a Czech journalist observed wryly, "the best thing Havel can do is to call in the Japanese. If we gave them a ten-year management contract, I am sure they could turn Czechoslovakia into a rich, productive country by the year 2000."

MEANWHILE, BACK IN TOKYO . . .

No intelligent person anywhere in the world can be oblivious to the vast financial, technological, and trading-state resources Japan has accumulated in recent years. Yet a denial syndrome still prevails in much of the West. Too many people continue to wishfully regard Japan's success as only a temporary aberration, dismissing every new indicator of mounting

Japanese competitive prowess and seizing on every Japanese weakness as evidence the miracle is drawing to an end.

The rise of the New Europe has buttressed the denial syndrome in some quarters. "See," say the skeptics, "there isn't going to be a Pacific Century after all—the future is in Europe."

Those bearish on Japan's future had cause for celebration at the beginning of 1990. The Nikkei index of leading Japanese stocks, which had reached its record high on the very last trading day of 1989, proceeded to enter the decade of the 1990s with a spectacular crash. Day after day for months, Tokyo stocks plummeted—4 percent in one session, 6 percent in another, 2 percent in a third, and so on until the rolling crash had wiped out over 30 percent of the Tokyo Stock Exchange's value. The yen fell precipitously against the dollar. Even Japan's low cost of capital looked doomed as yields on bellwether Japanese government bonds floated upward toward American levels. "Japan: Can It Cope?" inquired a *Business Week* cover story that seemed to jump right off American newsstands with the good news that the Japanese bubble might be bursting at last.[3]

"Japan's trade and current account surpluses will disappear. . . . With them will go Japan's role as an exporter of capital," declared journalist Bill Emmott in *The Sun Also Sets: The Limits to Japan's Economic Power*.[4] Emmott's book arrived in Japan just as the Tokyo stock market crashed. In one of their not-uncharacteristic moments of self-doubt and gloom, the Japanese snapped up 300,000 copies. They were dying to know how much longer it would be before they would sap their savings through new consumption; exhaust their surplus capital through expansionary borrowing; become a nation of pensioners, too demographically gray-haired to be productive; and, in general, end up where Emmott suggested they would: in economic history's "dustbin." The answer, according to Emmott, was 1995, or 2000 at the latest.

Eventually, however, the stock crash bottomed out. The yen firmed. Interest rates came under control, albeit at higher levels. Not only had the real economy remained unharmed as the crash ripped through Tokyo's Nihonbashi financial district, first-quarter statistics showed that Japan was actually growing at an annualized pace of 10.4 percent!

"Fears of the demise of the great Japanese economic expansion look premature," concluded *New York Times* economic columnist Leonard Silk. "It was founded on hard work, high educational standards, high rates of savings and investment, and a creative use of technology. When the stock market slide ends, those factors will still be in place." In June 1990, the *Wall Street Journal* announced, "The bulls are back in Tokyo. A growing herd of money managers and analysts are predicting that the Japanese stock market, which earlier this year looked like a meltdown, will turn into a meteor."[5]

That meteor has yet to be sighted as of this writing, chiefly owing to the uncertainty that has dogged world financial markets since the onset of the Persian Gulf crisis. Even though Japan is much better positioned to weather a sharp spike in oil prices than it was during previous "oil shocks," a sustained price of $30 per barrel or more will take its toll. That cloud hangs over all forecasts about the profitability of Japanese corporations, the size of the trade surplus, liquidity in the system, the cost of Japanese capital, and the value of the yen. A sustained Tokyo Stock Exchange rally has thus been hard to engender, despite the best efforts of Japan's official and unofficial market manipulators.

Yet for those who look closely, the most instructive story about the Persian Gulf crisis with respect to Japan is just how strong the real economy has remained in the face of oil price run-ups and threats to long-term supply. In a nation which imports nearly all its oil, the ability to absorb the Persian Gulf crisis with scarcely a hiccup testifies to the rising sun that is still shining on Japan.

Among American watchers of Japanese stocks, Paul Aron, vice chairman emeritus of Daiwa Securities America, is the most sagacious veteran. His optimistic forecasts about the Tokyo market have been met with American skepticism for more than two decades. Yet he, and not the skeptics, has generally proved right. Even with the Nikkei index down over 10,000 points from its record high, Aron disputed the "gloom and doom scenario." The bears were rushing to "outdo each other in predicting lower equity prices," Aron said. As for himself, he calmly forecast "a probable restoration of upward market momentum."

Aron also offered another piece of advice. Those giving up on Japan in order to search out "the next Japan" were missing the obvious reality in front of their noses. The most competitive economy of the future would be the one with "a highly educated and a highly motivated labor force that can operate and improve the new technologies," where large quantities of capital were available for deploying new technology, and where long-term thinking guided investment decisions. Thus, Aron concluded, "the next Japan will be Japan itself."[6]

The 1990 meltdown on the Tokyo Stock Exchange will quite possibly be "good" for Japan in the long run. Since the markets had inhabited stratospheric heights for too long and become far too speculative, the crash was actually welcomed by some authorities in the Ministry of Finance who had long maintained that excessive market levels were not healthy. Even the big Japanese securities firms were not panicked by the crash. "I would interpret the stock market drop in Tokyo as a welcome return to reality," observed Stephen Axilrod, vice chairman of the U.S. subsidiary of Nikko Securities, one of Japan's largest brokers.[7]

Foreigners looking forward to an ultimate day of arbitrage between overvalued Japanese markets and the rest of the world must have been sorely disappointed. When the crash finally ended, the price/earnings ratio of an average Tokyo stock had fallen to a "mere" 40—still nearly three times higher than the average New York Stock Exchange multiple of 14. In other words, investors in the world's largest stock market were still confident that a Japanese company was worth at least three times what a comparable American company was worth, simply because it was *Japanese*.

But while the great Tokyo crash of 1990 may not have ushered in doomsday for Japanese economic power—and may indeed have reined in its speculative excesses with some healthy discipline—the shocking decline was not exactly devoid of adverse consequences.

For one thing, while financial regulators may have been happy to see a little speculative froth blown off the market, they were most definitely *not* happy to see such a large drop. They intervened feverishly to try to halt the skid, only to find they could not. Japan—and the world—had changed since the Wall Street crash of October 1987. Back then, the Ministry of Finance had been able to prevent Wall Street's cataclysm from infecting the Japanese market, simply by corralling the heads of the big financial-service firms and offering them a bit of so-called administrative guidance: *Stand firm. Don't sell.*

In 1990, however, the forces of reform and deregulation within Japan, combined with the diffusion of Japanese financial assets to every corner of the globe, had begun to create what Washington's negotiators had always said they wanted—and what Tokyo's authorities had always admitted they feared: real interpenetration and even a degree of arbitrage between Japan's historically insular financial sphere and the rest of the global marketplace. When the Tokyo Stock Exchange began its nosedive, the principal cause was not that the fundamentals of the real economy had changed. On the whole, Japanese fundamentals were solid during the period of the crash.

Instead, the factors responsible for the crash originated in Germany in December 1989, when the flow of Japanese money seeking to get in on the post–Berlin Wall "reunification rally" suddenly turned into a deluge. Next, fears of German inflation drove yields on German bonds temporarily above American Treasury rates. This made them spectacularly attractive to Japanese investors, many of whom were already infatuated with Germany anyway. The yen depreciated by 18 percent against the D-mark between November 1989 and April 1990, as the Japanese sold their own currency to get in on the action in Germany.

On the days when the Japanese were not euphoric about opportunity in Germany—and concentrated instead on potential dangers and instabilities in Europe—they reminded themselves that the United States, despite its problems, was still the safest and most stable international destination for their money. Acting on that impulse, they bought dollars. As a result, the yen declined by almost 11 percent against the U.S. currency during the first few months of 1990.

A decade earlier, the Ministry of Finance and the Bank of Japan had believed a strong yen was dangerous for Japan. But by the end of the 1980's, they had successfully restructured the Japanese economy around a strong currency. The rapid, dramatic declines in the yen's value in early 1990 were therefore extremely troubling. The financial authoritites, as inflation-phobic as anyone at the Bundesbank, did not want to raise interest rates. Yet that was the only way to stop the run on the yen. These mixed feelings—which even led to a rare public display of opposition between the MoF and the Bank of Japan—caused the rates to be raised too little and too late. Indeed, the hikes achieved the opposite of what was intended. Japanese investors, knowing that interest rates would ultimately have to increase in Japan, kept moving their money abroad to take advantage of higher foreign rates in the meantime. Thus, the twin pressures of a weakening currency and impending interest-rate increases continued to weaken the yen and drive the stock market lower.

An aggravating factor was the growing tension over the intractable $50 billion annual U.S.-Japan trade imbalance. American political leaders seemed to be talking tougher than ever about retaliation against Japan in the spring of 1990. Most influential Japanese understood that the Bush administration was not very likely to actually *do* anything. But there was a strong sense in Tokyo that the end of the '80s signified the end of

Japan's relentless accumulation of trade and current-account surpluses at America's expense. In this new and tougher decade, Japan might actually have to make some meaningful, perhaps even painful, economic concessions to the United States to prevent a further poisoning of the transpacific political waters. Thus the acrimonious context of the U.S.-Japan relationship became yet another factor battering the stock market.

The bottom of the crash trough corresponded roughly with the growing certainty in Germany that the Bundesbank would be overruled in its opposition to 1:1 currency conversion of deutsche marks and ostmarks. The Bonn government was apparently willing to proceed with a currency union that could cause alarming levels of inflation and destabilize the D-mark's international value. Japanese investors were shocked. They had been bullish in the extreme on Germany and had felt that with the Bundesbank running the show, their money was in good hands. Now they were asking how the Germans could possibly accept such a reversal of sound money policies. Many Japanese portfolio managers didn't wait for an answer, moving their funds immediately back to Japan. A crashing Tokyo market and a falling yen were still preferable to the uncertainties associated with German monetary union. Although the sums were not massive, the net inflow to Japan was enough to break the back of a crash that was already beginning to wind down.

Meanwhile, the storm clouds over Japan's relationship with the United States passed. In the end, the Americans accepted a package of Japanese market-opening gestures that were as vague as usual. The few specifics to which Japanese negotiators did commit themselves would be costly to some companies and industries but beneficial in the long run to Japanese interests. This package appeased Carla Hills enough to call off threatened Super 301 action against Japan. Instead, she and George Bush were now taking pains to stress in public how much progress Japan had made.

In a psychological sense if not a technical sense, the Tokyo crash was the result of momentary fears that Japan might be on the verge of losing its supercompetitive edge in the world. Opportunities suddenly looked better in Europe. Germany seemed more powerful than ever, and the yen was being overshadowed by a D-mark the Japanese didn't understand very well. Meanwhile, the Americans seemed angry enough to take injurious action against Japanese interests.

But after a few months, the panic subsided. The new world situation began to come into focus. Yes, Europe would offer new opportunities and Germany would be very powerful, but these factors were not necessarily bad—*if* the Japanese were able to understand this new order and develop responsive strategies. No, Americans probably would not be as passive in the '90s as they had been in the '80s about their vital economic interests. But a U.S. political consensus on how to organize the American economy for serious and successful competition with Japan was probably still very far off. In the long term, if not immediately, the post-postwar world order actually favored Japanese strengths.

The Japanese may be increasingly arrogant, but they have not yet lost their capacity to thrive on adversity and to adapt to new challenges as the outside world presents them. The crash was Japan's intuitive response to the explosive power of the Euroquake. The secure, comfortable world Japan had known in the 1980s had cracked apart. The Japanese would no longer be waging a unidirectional battle for global economic leadership with an America whose system was self-defeating and progressively less able to withstand the competition. For Japan, too, the three-way battle of the capitalisms had dawned.

It took them a few months, but the Japanese now appear squarely focused on turning the new world situation to their maximum advantage. And the first major task on their agenda is to position Japanese business better for the opportunities that lie ahead in the New Europe. . . .

TAKING THE FORTRESS BY STRATEGY

Had there been no Japan, there might have been no 1992 project in Europe. A great many factors went into making 1992 happen. But in the early days, Europe's fear and envy of Japan were particularly visceral catalysts.

Wisse Dekker, the Dutchman so instrumental in rallying European business to support 1992, explains the role of the Japanese threat this way: "If we did not build the single market, the Japanese would take over European industries one by one. Ultimately, we would be faced with this question: Are we ready to abandon our high standard of living and our social welfare states in northern Europe? Because if we didn't build the single market, that would be the only other way to compete with the Japanese. That, of course, would be completely unacceptable politically."

Edith Cresson, the French minister for European affairs, concurs: "Building a strong European market to stop the Japanese is a question of defending our civilization. French workers have their private life, their holidays, their social protections, their quality of life—their imagination! To try to compete with the Japanese without making a big change in Europe means you must become like ants, like them!''

And Jacques Delors didn't stand on the diplomatic ceremony of his office when the subject of Japan came up. If the Japanese weren't stopped, he warned, their ''new imperialism will be very dangerous in ten more years. There is an extraordinary parallel between the Japanese military strategy of the 1940s and the economic strategy of today.'' The best and only defense, he said in 1985, was the 1992 program.

No European could fail to be intimidated on learning that a single Japanese company—Nippon Telegraph & Telephone—enjoyed a stock-market capitalization greater than the combined values of all the stocks traded on the Paris *and* Frankfurt bourses. Yet while Europeans feared this looming power, they were also impressed by the progress the Japanese had made since a quarter century earlier, when Charles de Gaulle had dismissed Japan as a ''nation of transistor salesmen.''

Thus, along with fear of Japan, there was also envy. Could the European Community, made up of old, mature societies, like Japan, ravaged four decades earlier by war, like Japan, lacking key natural resources, like Japan, protected by the American military umbrella, like Japan, not also produce a latter-day Japanese-style miracle and climb back to the center stage of the world economy? And could that not be accomplished, in part at least, by borrowing some of the approaches to business, technology, and trade perfected by the Japanese?

And then there was the question of geostrategy. Europe was being left behind not only economically and technologically, but in geostrategic terms as well. The idea of a Pacific Century was certainly not appealing to Europeans, most of whose Pacific connections had been severed at least half a century before. While Americans may have thought themselves locked in a fractious and tense relationship with Japan, Europeans perceived U.S.-Japanese amity as too close for comfort. No matter how strident the war of words between Tokyo and Washington might become, the volume of transpacific trade had surpassed the volume of transatlantic trade. Americans and Japanese alike were brainstorming about a U.S.-Japanese condominium to lead the world. Dozens of articles and think-tank reports appeared discussing the merits of a U.S.-Japan ''G-2'' as the core of world leadership. It wasn't that those thinking along such lines were deliberately trying to offend European sensibilities. In the period

1985–88 it simply seemed an obvious reality that Europe would not be much of a leader in a twenty-first-century world centered around the Pacific Rim.

Ronald Reagan endorsed the notion of the coming Pacific Century on numerous occasions. In George Bush's first month as president, he held not one but two summit meetings with the Japanese prime mininster. His first trip abroad was a tour of Tokyo, Beijing, and Seoul. Europeans, in other words, had good reason to fear a geopolitical order that was leaving them out. It was hoped that 1992 would serve as a new Atlantic magnet, exerting a counterforce to what might otherwise be an overwhelming American attraction toward the opposite side of the Pacific.

When it came time to develop the specifics of the 1992 program, Japan was certainly the chief "third country" EC officials had in mind when they discussed various measures that smacked of protectionism. Ambassador Andreas van Agt, the former Dutch prime minister who served as the EC's ambassador to Tokyo and later to Washington, makes no bones about the origins of the "reciprocity" idea. "An undeniable misgiving about Japan prevails in Europe," he said in 1989. "In southern Europe, in particular, there is much concern about Japanese industrial-economic-financial hegemony. The perception of Japan as a threat is reflected in the idea of 'reciprocity' in the drafts of the 1992 program."

Ironically, though, 1992 revolutionized the Japanese relationship with the EC in ways few could have anticipated. Although 1992 derived some of its energy from the impulse to keep the Japanese *out* of Europe, it produced exactly the opposite effect: The 1992 program made Japan not only more conscious of Europe, but more determined than ever to move *in*. The possibility that Europe would be closed to them in the future created a rush among Japanese companies to get in before it was too late. "For us, the pressure from the EC merely accelerates an evolutionary process that was already under way," declared Sony chief executive Norio Ohga.[8]

Minoru Akimoto, the London-based managing director of the giant Japanese trading house C. Itoh, explained, "If the EC puts up a barrier, we try to go around the barrier. That's what business people do. There are no barriers for businesspeople."[9] Adds Tadashi Natori, who runs the London branch of the Industrial Bank of Japan, "Europe is very important to us in the medium and long term. Personally, I think we'll see an 'age of Europe,' and there will be plenty of room for growth."

In the end, no matter what inventive schemes Brussels developed to proscribe their activity, the Japanese found a counterstrategy. The net effect of this *pas de deux* is that under dark skies of public acrimony and openly expressed European paranoia about Japan, the hard ground of the European continent is dotted with Japanese businesses. The reality, as observed by *Newsweek*, is that European barriers are tolerable for Japan: "Japanese companies simply have the money, the technology and the production power to absorb all the rules and still flourish."[10]

A review of some typical cat-and-mouse gambits between the European Community and Japan bears this out:

"Just Because It's Made in England Doesn't Mean It's European." Japanese business had already established a substantial presence in Great Britain prior to the emergence of the 1992 issue. The British way of doing business, the legal structure, the life-style, and especially the language were similar to those of the United States, where Japanese companies had developed much of their foreign operational experience. Thatcher's United Kingdom offered the same kind of warm welcome to foreign investors and traders that Ronald Reagan's United States had offered—perhaps even warmer.

Japanese investment was actually a key part of the plan for rebuilding the British economy undertaken by Lord Young, head of the Department of Trade and Industry. In some notable cases, British authorities offered financial-incentive packages worth up to $85,000 per job created to attract Japanese industry.

Many continental Europeans did not appreciate the warm welcome Britain was extending to Japanese investors. "Thatcher is the Japanese Trojan horse for the invasion of Europe," declared Madame Cresson. Other countries tried to discourage the U.K. from granting financial incentives to Japanese investors—but to no avail. The big test came over the Nissan Bluebirds manufactured at Sunderland, which France wanted to continue classifying as Japanese and make subject to French quotas. Mrs. Thatcher went to the mats with Brussels to defend the "Britishness" of the cars and Nissan's right to export them freely throughout the Community. Nissan claimed the local EC content of the Bluebird was already 70 percent and would be increased to 80 percent. Faced with a highly nationalistic prime minister insisting the cars were British, the evident fact that thousands of British workers were employed at Sunderland, a local-content commitment of 70–80 percent,[11] and U.S. trade negotiators waiting in the wings to join the fray (in part to help set a precedent that would establish the "Americanness" of Hondas exported to the EC from assembly plants in Ohio), France backed down from a threat to take the issue to the European Court.

The Bluebird affair was a turning point. On the one hand, it affirmed the Japanese strategy of using the U.K. as a hospitable base from which to penetrate the rest of the EC market. But it also forced a change in the thinking of French, Italian, and other officials who had previously been resistant to Japanese investment. If locally manufactured Japanese products were going to flood the EC anyway, why should Thatcher's government be the only one to benefit from the new jobs, investment, and technology transfer Japanese businesses would bring with them?

"It's essential that we attract Japanese investors to France rather than have them go to neighboring countries," declared Roger Fauroux, the French minister of industry, in 1989. "It is better to have Japanese investment in France than unemployed people."[12] His comments represented a break with the prevailing anti-Japanese sentiment in Paris. Immediately thereafter, both France and Italy began taking unprecedented steps to woo the very kinds of Japanese industrial investment they had previously opposed.

Today, every EC nation is eager to get plum Japanese business. The competition among countries and regions to offer the best incentives has begun to resemble the war among American states to attract Japanese factories. One German city offers to build a Japanese school if a big Japanese project is sited there; an Italian government mission flies to Tokyo to offer reductions in quotas on Japanese goods in a last-minute sweetener to attract a new plant; representatives of Catalonia and Wales sip tea in the waiting rooms of Japanese companies, hoping for a few minutes of executive time to make their pitch about why their region and not the other should be selected. Back home in Tokyo, MITI's powerful planners are working to ensure that Japanese investment is deployed in a politically balanced way throughout the Community, not just in the U.K., where it was always welcome.

Screwdriver Factories. The Brussels "screwdriver" ruling of 1988 came about at a time when the EC was using antidumping investigations as a tool to curb the swelling tide of imported Japanese electronic products. Japanese manufacturers of fax machines, photocopiers, computer printers, VCRs, CD players, and other products were all targets, as were Korean, Taiwanese, and Hong Kong companies.[13] When the Japanese tried to circumvent antidumping provisions by importing nearly finished products from Japan and then quickly completing their assembly locally, Brussels responded with its "anti-screwdriver" legislation. This enabled the EC to extend antidumping duties to products whose final assembly had been done in Europe, but more than 60 percent of whose component value came from abroad.

The real purpose of the anti-screwdriver legislation was to force Japanese and other Asian companies to bring full-scale manufacturing facilities to Europe. Publicly, the Japanese complained that such pressure made them more suspicious of the EC and less interested in locating there. Privately, however, Japanese businessmen realized that Brussels was in fact simply prodding them to do what would ultimately be in their own interests anyway. In the year after the ruling went into effect, the number of Japanese manufacturing plants in the EC rose from 411 to 529.

While the Japanese recognized the business and political value of establishing a greater manufacturing network in Europe, they did not like the EC's pressure tactics. As a result, they took their complaint about the screwdriver ruling to the GATT for adjudication. It was the first time the Japanese had ever brought such a case before the GATT. To the world's surprise, the GATT found in Japan's favor, sending Brussels a message to tone down its blatantly anti-Japanese policies.

Diffusing the Technology. Japanese semiconductor firms have essentially agreed to an EC requirement that the critical "diffusion" step of the manufacturing process be done at facilities within the Community. At least $2 billion worth of Japanese semiconductor plants are now under construction in Europe. "Our basic position is that we want full production in the EC by 1992," a Toshiba spokesman says. After all, there is no reason why Japanese companies couldn't dominate the European semiconductor market from *inside* Europe instead of through exports from Japan.

A watershed high-technology issue was Fujitsu's acquisition of 80 percent of ICL for $1.3 billion. ICL is the only remaining British-based manufacturer of mainframe computers and the chief supplier of computer equipment to the British government. With a 5–10 percent market share in Western Europe, ICL ranks as the fifth-largest indigenous computer company in the EC—and the most profitable. It is also a leading participant in several of the biggest pan-European technology ventures established for the express purpose of developing a competitive response to the

Japanese and receives several million dollars a year in EC subsidies for its role in these projects.

The Japanese investment in ICL prompted executives of the French-based Groupe Bull to say they would oppose ICL's involvement in new EC research projects and would ask Siemens to reconsider the Bull-Siemens-ICL software collaboration already under way. Yet Bull may not get too far; even Siemens is reported to be interested in selling a small equity stake to Fujitsu. Meanwhile, ICL chief Peter Bonfield is confident he can still give his new Japanese owners the desired channel into the European marketplace—including participation in advanced research. Challenges to ICL's European bona fides may ultimately go the same way as the Nissan Bluebird case. With 18,000 British jobs at stake in ICL, and an all-British management team at the helm of the company, Brussels will have a hard time excluding ICL from European projects on the grounds that it is "Japanese." What's more, several of the biggest indigenous proponents of European high technology—companies like Philips and Thomson—have recently found themselves caught in cash squeezes and expensive restructurings that have caused them to question their once axiomatic commitment to big EC-sponsored technology research ventures. As a result, while some Europeans continue to insist on a "techno-nationalist" policy, other influential voices have begun to argue that gaining access to Japanese investment and technology is the *best* way to keep Europe in the high-tech race. Thus, for all the stated concern about developing and safeguarding an indigenous high-technology base, the EC appears ready to let the Japanese fox into the European henhouse.

Japanese Auto Exports. Brussels continues to fine-tune a compromise on the knotty question of auto exports from Japan to the EC. The focal point of concern has been the extremely restrictive quotas on Japanese imports maintained by France, Italy, and Spain. This issue is seen by some as the ultimate test of just how open the European market will be after 1992. The automobile industry is one of Europe's largest businesses, and it has been among the most protected. At Fiat, Peugeot, Renault, and other companies, there is a consensus that throwing the doors wide open to Japanese imports would spell death. Even the German luxury-car manufacturers have lost some of their former self-confidence and are now expressing concern about an influx of Japanese luxury cars such as the Toyota Lexus.

"Yes, we are for free trade," says a senior European Commission staffer working on the Japanese auto-import issue. "But I don't mind making some exceptions or contradicting myself a bit to say that Europe won't be ready for totally free trade in automobiles by 1993. I am not so loyal to the phrase 'free trade' that I will let thousands of European autoworkers be thrown out of work, or allow the destruction of the most politically important companies in Europe, such as Fiat and Renault."

Obviously, Japanese automakers would benefit enormously from a completely liberalized European car market. According to one study, they might double their share to upwards of 30 percent in as little as two years if all European quotas and restrictions were lifted. But MITI has counseled patience and urged Japanese companies to avoid the appearance of an aggressive stance on this question for fear that it could quickly rekindle the "fortress Europe" mentality. Aside from a few outspoken comments by Yoshikazu Kawana, president of Nissan Europe (the European motor industry, he lectures, can "become competitive in world terms only after it also accepts competition in its home market"[14]), auto executives have demonstrated Japanese fortitude in keeping quiet on a subject so close to their commercial interests and their hearts. In the meantime, they are leaving the battle to open Europe's car market to Martin Bangemann, the leader of the minority faction in the European Commission that supports rapid movement toward free trade in autos.

Although negotiations are ongoing, Tokyo has already agreed in principle to restrain its exports to the EC at least until the end of this decade. The Japanese experience with voluntary restraints in the U.S., after all, was immensely positive: adopting them guaranteed a certain market share and allowed profit margins to grow. But however the current negotiations turn out, there is almost no way the Japanese can lose. No Brussels stratagem can permanently compensate for the gap in financial, technological, and global marketing power between the Japanese and European car industries. At the negotiating table, Japanese manufacturers are sure to win at least marginally enhanced European acceptance of their exports. They may even succeed in getting a date for full liberalization of the market set earlier than 2000. At the same time, they will continue building local plants in Europe and creating local joint ventures. Daimler-Benz is already cooperating with Mitsubishi, as is Volvo. The Volvo-Mitsubishi tie-up indirectly involves Renault, since Volvo and Renault are now partners. And Honda is the equity partner increasingly setting the agenda for Rover's future.

By the time the European auto market is finally open, even the zealous nationalists of Fiat and Peugeot may have taken on Japanese partners to accomplish the technological renovation and global expansion they desire. In short, when the European auto fortress finally lets down its gates, there may be no need for excessive Japanese imports. Japanese interests will already be thriving from inside Europe.

THE PATIENT VISION OF THE YEN

The EC has not made it easy for the Japanese. Plenty of obstacles have been put in their way. Even so, "for the Japanese, who denominate vision and ideas in yen terms, these are merely challenges to be dealt with and overcome," says Sumito Takahashi, the London correspondent for *Nihon Keizai Shimbun*.[15]

Japan is no longer the uninvited guest at the 1992 feast. European businessmen are beginning to get a taste of the premium prices the Japanese are willing to pay for well-established assets; European governments are increasingly hospitable to the idea of importing Japanese capital and technology, and Eastern Europe continues to hope that a big dose of Japanese aid will come its way. "Japan is now doing what the United States did over 20 years ago," says Naoya Takebe, author of a study on 1992 undertaken for the Industrial Bank of Japan. Japan, he explains, is now in the process of "becoming part of the economic landscape in Europe."[16]

More than a third of leading European companies are already looking forward to mergers or joint ventures with Japanese firms, according to a study conducted jointly by the *Wall Street Journal* and the consulting firm of Booz, Allen. "Neither trade protectionism, established European positions, nor cultural barriers seem likely to slow the Japanese," the study reported. Japanese businesses are determined to move not just into obvious areas such as high technology and automobiles, but also into unexpected sectors such as services, retailing, transportation, and utilities.[17]

The sheer relentlessness of the Japanese expansion, coupled with its seductive potential for stimulating the economy, is breaking down Europe's will to resist. EC industrial policy no longer aims to block Japan's entry, but to obtain the maximum benefit for Europe from Japanese investment.

"I cannot understand why Americans let Japanese companies destroy American industry without even getting *anything* in return," says Madame Cresson. Ultimately, Europe may prove no more capable than the U.S. of resisting the tide of Japanese involvement in its economy. But the EC *is* likely to drive a harder bargain and get a better deal.

Europe is trying to steer the Japanese colossus toward:

- high-value-added production that generates well-paying jobs
- investments that help rebuild industrially depressed areas
- the establishment of R&D centers and other kinds of technology transfers that will enhance local skills and knowledge levels
- joint ventures, rather than 100 percent acquisitions, which will help make European companies more competitive while keeping them at least partially European-owned
- improved European access to the booming Japanese market, where many consumers have shown a greater willingness to buy European than American goods.

"The Brussels bureaucrats are so well trained in the art of negotiation, it's really quite incredible," declares Makoto Kuroda, a former vice-minister of MITI and a formidable negotiator himself, who was once greatly feared by American trade officials. "The Europeans are not at all like the Americans. Once they think they have some leverage, they use it very cleverly."

Europeans appear to be succeeding in their "steerage" strategy. But part of their success derives from the fact that the Japanese are willing to be steered. Although more tough negotiations lie ahead and tension between Japan and the EC is sure to flare up now and again, Japan is basically committed to entering Europe on Europe's terms.

"Europe has gone to school on the U.S.," notes Chrysler's Lee Iacocca. Europeans, he says, "will not allow the Japanese to do what they've done [in America], getting nearly 35 percent of the industry in a decade. There will be competition, but it will be honest competition. It won't be 'send us all you want and rape our market.' "[18]

Although Europeans are taking a sober, careful approach in an effort to contain Japanese power, the Japanese may still end up getting the best deal of all.

THE COMING JAPAN-EUROPE ALLIANCE

On the first weekend of March 1990, in the secrecy of Singapore's tropics, one of the most important cross-border joint ventures of all time was born. Edzard Reuter of Daimler-Benz and Shinroku Morohashi of Mitsubishi Corporation—along with the heads of their firms' automotive, aerospace, electronics, financial, and trading divisions—hammered out the framework for a wide-ranging alliance between the biggest industrial company in Japan and the biggest industrial company in Germany.

This was not simply a happenstance of global deal-making. Indeed, the Mitsubishi-Daimler pact gives new meaning to the concept of a *strategic* alliance. Even if Herr Reuter and Morohashi-san were loath to say publicly exactly what their strategy was, it was self-evident. The two corporations were teaming up to outflank American industry in its last bastions of global leadership, particularly aircraft manufacture. The capital resources, productive excellence, and long-term planning capacities of both Japan and Germany would be structurally linked and optimized.

Whatever cultural differences and misunderstandings may usually stand between Europe and Japan, these two leading private-sector companies realized they actually understood each other very well. Together, they could do great things. Whether or not they will, of course, remains to be seen. But the Mitsubishi-Daimler pact offers dramatic evidence that the idea of a Japan-Europe alliance is not so farfetched. Today, the United States remains closer to both Japan and Europe than Japan and Europe are to each other. But as with so much else in the post-postwar world, it would be a serious mistake to assume that this situation will not change.

"An old Japanese saying holds that when three people gather, it is natural for two of them to be closer to each other," says master negotiator Makoto Kuroda. "Most Japanese want to remain closer to the United States. But the U.S. is making it very difficult for us." Shintaro Abe, one of Japan's leading politicians, has publicly suggested that a way to tone down excessive U.S. demands on Japan would be to cooperate more with the EC on global trade issues.

The truth is that Japan and Europe each need the United States less today than at any other point in the last fifty years. With the Cold War fading, the nuclear umbrella becoming less relevant, and the military threats to their security abating, the Japanese and Europeans have new options.

Of course Japanese and European companies hunger for the expansive American market. None of them would deliberately harm their access to it. But the experience of the 1980s has suggested that the U.S. lacks the political will to act against foreign exploitation of its market. And in any event, for the first time in modern economic history, the United States is no longer the be-all and end-all of large consumer marketplaces.

Within the Triad, a subtle shift is taking place. The strongest bond, based on a perception of dependence, may become the one between Japan and Europe. The Europeans need the Japanese principally for their technology, and secondarily for their capital. Although European technology is likely to improve significantly in the next few years, its infrastructure is too weak in key areas such as microelectronics to deliver the high-tech miracle European leaders and visionaries hope for in the 1990s.

One of those visionaries is Jacques Attali, François Mitterrand's long-time right-hand man and now the first director of the new Bank for European Reconstruction and Development, which will coordinate the flow of capital to Eastern Europe. Attali predicts that the future world economy will be "hyper-industrial" rather than principally service-oriented. As he sees it, services will not be freestanding, but will themselves be transformed into mass-produced consumer goods:

> The most vital economic growth is now taking place in areas where new products based on the microchip are replacing the costly, debt-incurring, time- and labor-intensive delivery of services: communication, management, information processing, food preparation, health and education. The cellular telephone, the fax machine, the ready-teller machine at banks, the portable computer, the portable compact disc-player, answering machines, auto-diagnostic medical devices, VCRs, intelligent controls for cars, robots, the microwave oven for cooking food industrially prepared in advance—all vastly increase the productivity of services. [By leading the development of this hyper-industrial society, Europe can become] the core of the new world order.[19]

The major obstacle to the fulfillment of this vision lies in the level of European technological development, which continues to trail that of the United States and Japan in almost all the fields Attali suggests are crucial to the hyper-industrial order. Currently, both Japan and the U.S. have what Europe lacks technologically. But Americans, having lost their world-conquering vision, are less enthused and increasingly less able to make the necessary investments in and technological transfers to Europe. When it comes to the most advanced new technology, Japanese companies are outpacing their American competitors even in the U.S. The three companies that have been awarded the most *U.S.* patents in recent years have all been Japanese—Canon, Hitachi, and Toshiba. Almost all the most advanced American auto plants are Japanese-owned, while most of the reinvigorated U.S. steel mills result from infusions of Japanese technology and investment. Even some of the most creative American "software" enterprises are now thriving in large part because of the deep pockets of their Japanese owners. Such is the case with MCA, now owned by Matsushita. In short, the Japanese play an important role in keeping advanced sectors of the *American* economy functioning at their high performance levels.

This technological prowess, combined with Japan's world-leading factory-floor processes and management techniques, is helping to establish the Japanese production system as the de facto global standard. If the strength of that system is brought to Europe (on a joint-venture basis, of course) and added to Europe's existing assets in the atmosphere of an expanding marketplace, Europe would at least have a chance of becoming the hyper-industrial society imagined by Jacques Attali.

Japanese companies have powerful incentives to go along with that plan and move some (though certainly not all) of their best technology to Europe. They are still on the upswing of their world-conquering vision. To them, the possibility of using technological know-how to tap the huge and expanding European market is enormously exciting. Certainly, the Japanese are more feared in Europe than the Americans, and that presents problems for their expansion. But they are also more admired. It is the Japanese who are perceived as having the magic elixir Europe wants. "Never mind that American-owned companies employ 530,000 Britons to Japan's 30,000, or that there are more French and German companies than Japanese in the part of southeast Wales now known as Nippon Valley," noted *Fortune* magazine. "When polltakers asked the citizens of Luton, home of a big GM plant, if they'd be better off with a different owner, 60% knew what they'd prefer—a Japanese company."[20]

Small straws in the wind tell a big story:

- The EC's annual "Europalia"—a month-long festival celebrating the culture of one particular European country—was broadened beyond Europe for the first time in 1989. The featured country was Japan.
- *The Economist* has begun to speak of a shared "Japano-Teuton" financial culture linking Japan and Germany. It stands in contrast to the "free-wheeling Anglo-American style of finance, with its obsession for quarterly earnings and a planning horizon the length of an analyst's nose."[21]

- Liquid Japanese investment has made a clear departure from its former one-sided emphasis on U.S. financial markets. According to *Asset International,* Japanese investors are making a "shift away from the long-favored U.S. fixed income market and into European—particularly German—securities."[22]
- The young executives in the chairman's office at Compagnie Financière de Suez, the French financial-services giant, say the goal of their business strategy is to turn their firm into a Japanese-style *zaibatsu*—a cluster of diversified enterprises grouped around a financial center. It is not the American model that attracts young European technocrats anymore, it is the Japanese.
- European luxury goods continue to be the rage in Japan—Chanel dresses, Mercedes and BMW cars, French cognacs and wines, Burberry raincoats, Hermès scarves, Louis Vuitton luggage, etc. The success of such items in Japan is no economic trifle. German auto exporters are actually selling 120,000 cars a year in Japan—five times what American automakers are selling. "Behind these products Japanese people see a European culture of quality and high values," explains a Japanese salesman in a Mercedes dealership.
- The Japanese are also counting on working closely with Europe to pioneer the opening of the Soviet business and investment channel. As Ambassador van Agt has observed of his stint in Tokyo on behalf of the EC, "The Japanese want to have a substantive dialogue with the European Community. And the number-one question they want to put on the agenda is Gorbachev. They want to know: 'Should we invest in the Soviet Union now? Should we come to Gorbachev's aid economically?' They are trying to decide who is right—the euphoric Europeans or the cynical Americans."
- Japanese social critics are recognizing more and more cultural similarities between their own nation and Europe, and are speaking on that theme more frequently. "To a greater extent than we know, Europeans and Japanese are alike," says Naohiro Amaya, the visionary thinker and former MITI vice chairman who now heads the Dentsu Institute of Human Studies. "Our societies are more closed and less flexible than America's. From our own experience, we Japanese can understand why Europeans want 1992 to benefit themselves first and foremost. This doesn't surprise us, the way it surprises Americans." Masami Teraoka, a Japanese-born artist who worked in Los Angeles for more than twenty years, adds, "When I compare

Japan with European countries, there are quite a number of similarities. Europeans have long traditions and seem to have a lot of feeling for a caste system and for family and ancestors. Also, Japanese and Europeans have a more reserved attitude than Americans. So after all my travels in Europe and America, I find the most strikingly different countries are Japan and America.''[23]

· Haruki Kadokawa, a Japanese businessman who believes that Christopher Columbus was really looking for Japan in 1492, now hopes to complete the Genoan navigator's mission for him. Kadokawa is building an exact replica of the *Santa Maria* and plans to sail from Spain to Japan and parade down Tokyo's Ginza sometime in 1992. In one symbolic swoop, the voyage of his *Santa Maria II* will celebrate the five hundredth anniversary of Columbus's discovery of the New World, the launch of the EC's Project 1992, and the Barcelona Olympics. But it will also be one of a growing collection of signs suggesting that the transatlantic relationship pioneered by Columbus five hundred years ago may someday be supplanted by a more vigorous European-Japanese relationship.

JAPAN AS NUMBER ONE?

If the Japanese can continue to do all the things they have been doing right for so long *and* seize the opportunities that lie before them in Europe, then they are sure to grow even more influential than they are today. It is even conceivable the Japanese will become the *most* influential society on earth.

If, on the other hand, Japan fails to adapt to the requirements of the new age—especially if it mismanages its relations with the U.S. and Europe, overstepping sensitive boundaries and triggering the protectionist onslaught it has thus far avoided—the Japanese will suffer along with the rest of the world.

So far, the outlook for Japan is good. Rather than being merely excellent competitors as they were in the 1980s, the Japanese appear poised to emerge in the 1990s as *supercompetitors*.

For Japan, supercompetitiveness means not just having better products, but being a full generation or two ahead of the competition across a broad range of technologies. It means not only maintaining a presence in all the major markets of the world, but enjoying a *dominant* presence. It means not just being a trader and marketer, but a major investor, financier, manufacturer, and employer in all parts of the world. It means being not only a "hardware"-intensive society, but one that generates world-leading technological and social software as well. And it means exercising a leadership role in constructing a new global order in which Japanese power is institutionalized in such a way that it benefits not only Japan but also the rest of the world.

Even prior to the Euroquake, Japan was well on its way to making this transition. Some of the factors for Japanese supercompetitiveness already in the works are these:

- Japanese industry leads the world in capital spending. Japan's businesses are expanding plant capacity, modernizing equipment, adding to the world's biggest robot population, moving into new products and business lines, and committing ever greater resources to R&D. Annual Japanese capital investment is nearly three times that of America on a per-capita basis, and is $250 billion greater in the absolute. It is also twice the German per-capita level, and dwarfs Germany in absolute terms.

- The yen is becoming institutionalized as a strong currency. Even when the exchange rate fluctuates down to ¥150 = $1.00, the yen is still strong by historic standards. The same is true for Japanese financial power in general. Even at 20,000, the Nikkei Index represents stratospheric values. More important, Japan is *using* its financial strength strategically to acquire assets abroad and to make its companies the world's most globally integrated.

- Japan's ongoing domestic consumer boom has made its businesses less reliant on export-led growth in general and on the U.S. market in particular. Domestic spending has become a powerful stimulus to corporate creativity. In the past, Japanese companies often developed new products for the American market first, before introducing them domestically. Today, it is the other way around.

- Continued investment, innovation, and long-term planning have combined to allow Japanese companies to overtake American competitors at the highest levels of technology and manufacturing—in crucial sectors such as supercomputers, advanced semiconductors, X-ray lithography, luxury automobiles, and HDTV, among others. Japan is now virtually alone in its leadership of what economist Kenneth Courtis predicts will be the "megaproducts of the 1990s," such as personal portable telephones, fax machines, and integrated computer/ fax/copier/scanner devices for the desktop.

- Leading Japanese corporations have diversified out of hardware businesses and become active on the "soft" side as well. Sony is the classic case in point. Having emerged as the world's preeminent manufacturer of consumer electronics, it purchased Columbia Pictures and CBS Records in order to link its hardware to world-leading entertainment "software." Other Japanese companies are following similar strategies, using financial assets to buy abroad what Japanese society has not yet generated internally.
- Politically, Japan has pulled the rug out from under many of its American critics. Real changes have been made in the way Japan does business, both domestically and abroad. The Japanese market *has* become more open than it once was. Sophisticated lobbying, corporate philanthropy, and subtle use of Japanese money have also been tools in this process. Most effectively of all, Japanese exports of goods and ownership of American assets have become institutionalized with a broad base of American support to countervail the antagonism they stir up. Thus, even though the U.S.-Japan trade deficit is scarcely better than in the past, Washington is making much less fuss over it now. Even Japan-bashers have been forced to accept the reality that the trade problem is no longer fueled chiefly by Japanese "unfairness," but by the decline of American competitiveness.
- Investing heavily in the Asia/Pacific region, Japan is taking advantage of lower labor costs. It is sourcing raw materials and components, stimulating the growth of equities markets, and creating thriving consumer markets for the export of its own goods. In East Asia—still the world market with the greatest long-term growth potential—Japan is investing four times as much as the U.S. and eight times as much as Germany. Although U.S. companies abandoned China after the Tiananmen massacre, Japan quickly resumed its dealings with China a few months later.

To these features of the Japanese system, add corollary benefits generated in the wake of recent events in Europe:

- The end of the Cold War means that it is only a matter of time before the Soviet Union and Japan begin to develop a closer relationship. The Soviet leadership will find it useful to return Japan's four northern islands, which remains the most contentious issue preventing a thaw in the Tokyo-Moscow cold war. The Japanese will proceed cautiously, to be sure. But the commercial potential of a Japanese-Soviet relationship, involving enormous swaps of raw materials for technology, is staggering.

- Although fears of a fortress Europe are waning among all of Asia's exporting nations, the 1992 program has bolstered the desire of many Pacific Rim nations to develop their own loose regional economic alliance. Indeed, the idea that the global economy of the future will be organized into European, North American, and Asian regional groups is widely accepted throughout East Asia. This line of reasoning is being used to forge closer links between Japan and neighboring Pacific Rim countries and to overcome the latter's lingering distrust of Japanese intentions.

- The rise of the D-mark and the ECU makes possible a future U.S.-Europe-Japan currency-rate agreement in which the yen would be confirmed as a leading global currency at a strong value—without having to absorb all the burdens and costs of being the *single* key currency, as the dollar was.

- The potential size of the European market now offers Japanese investors a real choice as to where their surplus capital will flow. Partly, this will simply make them better global investors. As the U.S. dollar plummeted in 1986–87, for example, some managers of Japanese life-insurance portfolios commented that they had little choice but to sit and watch the value of their U.S. Treasury bonds fall. There was simply no other practical place to move so much money. Now they will be able to move investments back and forth between Europe and America as various opportunities and risks emerge. Even more important, the rise of Europe will increasingly allow the Japanese to call Washington's bluff when it makes excessive demands on matters of trade and finance. If Americans continue to bash and pressure Japan, the Japanese can now realistically threaten to go elsewhere. That possibility should serve to heighten the American public's awareness of the extent of U.S. dependence on Japan and to discourage any emotional attacks on America's chief banker.

- Finally, as the EC emerges as a coherent economic *and* political force, with a Europe-wide central bank, a common currency, and a shared foreign policy, the overall global balance of forces is becoming more conducive to the exercising of Japanese power. Today, one of the principal checks on Japanese assertiveness is the troubling appearance that every step forward comes at America's expense. If the Japanese want the yen to play a greater role in global finance, for example, the public sees that as a desire to devalue the dollar. If Japan wants to build its own fighter planes and, in the process, develop a civilian aerospace industry, that is seen as a direct challenge to the primacy of American companies in this field. But as the EC comes more to the fore and the economic world begins to look outwardly more three-cornered, perceptions about U.S.-Japanese competition are being blurred and confused by new issues about the U.S.-European competition, making it easier for Japan to assert its interests.

Can Japan really become number one? It is unlikely to develop into the kind of dominant power the United States has been for the last half century. Probably no single country or region will again hold that degree of economic hegemony in the world for a long time to come. But American economic leadership—and, with it, the global political dominance of the U.S.—is almost certain to erode further. The attractiveness of America's market, its technological innovativeness, and the appeal of its particular forms of democracy and capitalism are being meaningfully challenged elsewhere for the first time. Although the United States will probably remain a superpower, it is not likely to influence the rest of the world as profoundly as it did in the past.

There can be little doubt—as evidenced by the many factors examined in this book—that the New Europe will be another superpower. It will have a deep impact on other parts of the world—most notably on the Soviet Union and the many other countries that are connected to Europe by language, history, and geography. Full integration, however, will be a lengthy process and is likely to absorb most of Europe's prodigious new energies over the course of the 1990s. Even with a superpowerful Germany at its core, Europe may remain too diffuse and decentralized to act as a single force in the global economy for some time to come.

Certainly, events in Europe will go a long way toward determining the institutional makeup of the post-postwar order. The supranational structure that Europe is evolving, its ''social-market'' philosophy, its approach to environmental problems, and its quality of life in general will serve as models as the world constructs the borderless economy of the twenty-first century. And of course, the size of the European consumer market, the growing importance of the ECU, and the opening of the East—which will extend the definition of "Europe" to its broadest and most populous limits—will have profound consequences for the world as a whole.

What happens in Europe—the policies that are developed, the extent of economic growth, the level of foreign participation, the degree of political union that is achieved, the speed of disarmament, the new security order that emerges, and the destabilizing effects of the dangers on the European periphery—will influence the strategies of the United States, Japan, and most other countries in substantial ways. For all these reasons, Europe is sure to be regarded as a superpower in the twenty-first century. Over time, in fact, it may even become the power that most decisively influences world politics and the agenda of international diplomacy.

However, current readings of the global landscape suggest that Europe as a whole is unlikely to quickly evolve all the kinds of supercompetitive economic muscle that Japan is already beginning to exhibit. Over the next decade and beyond, Japan may pull even further ahead of the rest of the world in the most critical sectors of economic power, although Germany will not lag far behind. But it is Japan, not Europe or even Germany, that will probably be the world leader in creating new technology and manufacturing systems, in generating financial surpluses, and in carrying out the "global localization" of its "armies"—the Japanese corporations which even now are moving faster and deeper through the rest of the world than those of any other nation or region.

Already completely dominant in its own huge market as well as elsewhere in East Asia, and extremely powerful in many areas of the American market, Japan is now proceeding with alacrity into the European theater. By the year 2000, of the three capitalist giants, Japan is likely to be the best positioned across the whole spectrum of global markets. That positioning, in turn, may well turn out to be the key to global power in the post-postwar era.

"The strategic imperative for Japanese companies now is full participation in all three regional economies," says Paul Summerville, chief economist at Jardine Fleming securities in Tokyo. "The strategic question for everyone else is, 'Who can keep pace with this principle?' "[24]

If—and we must remember that it is a big *if*—economic competitiveness rather than military or ideological issues continues to play the dominant role in shaping the world, then it is quite possible that the particular kinds of supercompetitive economic power wielded by Japan will establish it as the first among several roughly equal giants in the twenty-first century.

The most critical question for Japan is just how thoroughly it will be able to penetrate Europe and hence benefit from the opening and explosion of that market over the next decade. Despite some initial problems, the prospects for Japan now appear favorable. In one of history's great ironies, then, the 1992 project, which was originally conceived as a way to protect Europe from Japan, may finally bring about the decisive change in the world's balance of economic power that will allow Japan to become, after its own fashion, number one.

PART IV

Fast-Forward to the Future

9

The End of History or the Battle of the Capitalisms?

From the viewpoint of the year 2020, what will economic historians say about the 1990s? They will describe it as a time when the shift from national economies to a world economy took place and when the U.S. changed from being the dominant global economy to just another competitor.

Historians will date this change to December 31, 1992, when the European Community became the world's largest economy. Like the storming of the Bastille, what actually happens on that date will not be terribly significant, but it will be a symbol. The rise of the European Community will make it increasingly clear to Americans at all levels that they have to change. The only question is when that process of change will actually begin.

LESTER THUROW, Dean of the Sloan School of Management,
Massachusetts Institute of Technology

FUKUYAMA'S NERVE

Those who believe that individuals, ideas, and the printed word can still make a difference should take great encouragement from the experience of Francis Fukuyama, the former RAND analyst who is now a State Department policy planner. In the spring of 1989, Fukuyama wrote an article entitled "The End of History?" Although the piece originally appeared in an obscure American journal with only a few thousand subscribers, it managed to provoke people all over the world into denouncing its author.

With the incredible events of 1989 just beginning to unfold, Fukuyama dared to suggest the following interpretation: "What we may be witnessing is not just the end of the Cold War, or the passing of a particular period of postwar history, but the end of history as such: that is, the end point of mankind's ideological evolution and the universalization of Western liberal democracy as the final form of human government."[1]

In Fukuyama's view, the "North Atlantic world" (which presumably includes Western Europe as well as North America), Japan, and the new industrial economies (NIEs) of East Asia all make up a single global culture. Communism had posed the last great challenge to this system, and it had failed. The zeal with which communism's new reformers were now embracing the "Western"-style marketplace provided the final affirmation that no better social system could be found than the liberal democracy practiced in the Triad.

Fukuyama borrowed the theme of the "end of history" from an obscure argument made by Hegel, the German philosopher, who as early as 1806 had declared history to be over. Although the idea became less prominent in Hegel's later work, it was resuscitated and further expounded in the 1930s by the brilliant though obscure Russian-French philosopher Alexandre Kojève. Despite these rather esoteric origins, Fukuyama's musings on the "end of history" actually became cocktail-party chitchat in New York and Washington, and his article was debated in the op-ed pages of all sorts of publications, from the straitlaced *New York Times* to the progressive French daily *Libération*, in England's *Encounter* and in various Dutch, Italian, and Japanese journals as well.

Fukuyama had touched a raw nerve. One wave of intellectuals rushed to denounce "The End of History?" because it seemed to ignore the plight of the world's billions who have not achieved the benefits of Western liberal democracy. A second group feared that if Fukuyama's proposition were accepted, the West would let down its guard against the danger of reversal in communism's reform process. A third rejected the Eurocentric assumption that Western liberal democracy was *the* culmination of the planet's ten-thousand-year search for workable social systems.

The biggest body of criticism came from those who were particularly miffed by Fukuyama's provocative assertion that the end of history would be a "very sad time." He forecast that the much-desired victory of Western liberal democracy would bring an end to the grand struggles of earlier ages, which had called forth daring, courage, imagination, idealism, and even the willingness to risk one's life. Future human challenges—economic, technological, environmental—simply would not have the romance of the life-and-death struggle against communism and fascism. Fukuyama dared to admit publicly that he was already nostalgic for the Cold War before it had even passed from the scene. Without communism to fight anymore, he maintained, the posthistorical world would be faced with "centuries of boredom," in which man's highest purpose would be to watch whatever might be on the VCR.

Of all Fukuyama's flights of fanciful reasoning, however, his most basic error went largely unchallenged. Underpinning his entire theory was the belief that today's Triad represents a single, homogeneous world of democracy, capitalism, and consumerism.

Aside from the great struggles for human progress yet to be waged in the developing world, and aside from the enormous courage, daring, and imagination the world will still require to grapple with the challenges of the twenty-first century, the most obvious reason why the future is not likely to be "boring" and why history isn't yet finished is that the Triad does *not* consist of a single universal economic and political system. In fact, it includes at least three very distinct systems and philosophies, each of which believes its approach is the best, and each of which has materially different interests.

Released from the ties that bound them together in their common struggle against communism, these three *very different* forces within the Triad are now free to turn their full attention to competing with one another. They are doing exactly that, and the contest they are waging will only grow more intense over the course of the 1990s.

LIVING IN THE GREAT ECONO-TECHNO MULTIPOLAR MARKETPLACE

The fact that the United States, Europe, and Japan inhabit the same global marketplace and have agreed to operate under certain shared rules should not be taken to mean that their competition won't be ruthless, far-reaching, devastating, and at times possibly even violent.

The fact that people in any of the Triad's great cities may have their choice of burgers, pizza, or sushi at any time of day or night, or that they watch the same American movies on their Japanese VCRs while sipping the same French wines tells us only that there is today an increasingly common level of prosperity for a certain stratum of powerful, influential, and visible people within the Triad. But such indicators reveal very little about how that prosperity is generated, or about the past and future trends associated with it. The talk of a Triad-wide consumer culture, in fact, masks two especially significant facts: (1) Until recently, only in North America could it be said that a mass consumer culture embraced the vast majority of the population; and (2) while Europe and Japan are currently enfranchising steadily greater percentages of their populations with enhanced consumption power, the United States, for the first time in its history, has *disfranchised* a large group—the underclass—and is now beginning to exclude the lower-middle classes as well from the prior basic "birthrights" of American capitalism, such as home ownership, education, and medical care.

The idea of a global marketplace sounds very nice. But it is most agreeable for those who are winning the global competition, and not pleasant at all for those who are losing. Indeed, a world organized around ferocious, intensifying intracapitalist economic competition will be characterized by constant "creative destruction"—a process that is good for human progress as a whole and excellent for those doing the creating, but dire for those who must suffer the destruction. Want to know what a global marketplace can look like?

- Take a took at Detroit. Today, a local saying goes, "Don't call it Detroit, call it destroyed." This destruction, of course, has a number of explanations. But the principal factor depressing this once-proud American industrial city and turning parts of it into a desperate war zone is this: There *is* a global marketplace in automobiles, and the Japanese have outcompeted the Americans in it.

- Or another image: Wall Street on the days of its two biggest crashes, October 1987 and October 1989, when Japanese financial power was seen most graphically. In the first instance, the technical factor triggering the 508-point drop of the Dow-Jones Index was a medium-size movement by Japanese investors out of U.S. Treasury bonds. Their exit drove yields over 10 percent and ignited sell programs in the stock market as portfolio managers headed for the safety and comfort of rising bond rates. In the second case, two Japanese banks, Sanwa and Sumitomo, decided not to provide as much capital as American managers had expected for an attempted LBO of United Airlines. This signal caused a panic on Wall Street as investors contemplated what would happen to the LBO wave—and to stock market values— if the Japanese withdrew from other leveraged deals. A decision made in Tokyo one day *not* to lend $2 billion to the UAL deal wiped out $200 billion of NYSE value the next day.

- Take a walk on Fifth Avenue in New York. In 1989, Mitsubishi Real Estate provided yet another reminder of Japanese economic preeminence when it bought its highly publicized stake in Rockefeller Center. The Rockefellers were happy; they got the money. But the American man in the street was angry; a disturbing gut feeling told him that this particular parcel of real estate, emblematic of the zenith of American wealth in the twentieth century, was a trophy seized by the Japanese to mark their conquest of America. . . . Across the street stands the Trump Tower, the flagship property of onetime billionaire Donald Trump, who in turn symbolized the aggressive entrepreneurship of the '80s that many Americans regarded as the best hope for reviving the nation's competitive prowess. By 1990, however, Trump's empire was coming unstuck, and he was forced to refinance the Trump Tower. In the end, it was Japanese and German banks that had the power to say yes or no to this man on whom American popular mythology had previously conferred omnipotent status. . . . And on your way out of the Trump Tower, watch the teenage Japanese girls who fill the designer boutiques, scooping up Tiffany jewels, Hermès scarves, and Chanel dresses. They are the envy of even the most affluent women in New York. At the corner of Fifth Avenue and Fifty-seventh Street, there is a faint but distinct whisper of neocolonialism in the U.S.-Japan relationship, with Americans beginning to feel themselves the colonial subjects. These sentiments don't show up in the sterile statistics proffered by learned economists eager to demonstrate the many benefits of foreign investment. But when Americans begin to feel jealous of others in their own land, xenophobia is sure to follow. A violent political backlash even becomes a possibility.

- The supercomputer industry offers yet another example of America's poor performance in the global marketplace. As recently as 1989, two American companies, Cray and Control Data, were supposed to be far ahead of the Japanese competition in this key future sector. But in April of that year, Control Data dropped out of the supercomputer business. The company said it could no longer afford the $100 million-a-year losses it was sustaining, and foresaw only intensified Japanese competition and even greater losses down the road. *"We have greatly reduced the U.S.' long-term capabilities of competing with the Japanese. But that's not my problem anymore,"* declared Control Data's chairman, Robert Price.[2]

  The Japanese were shocked to hear this news—more shocked than anyone in Washington. A spokesman for one Japanese company asked an American reporter, "Does your country have any idea what it is doing? There are certain technologies absolutely essential to your future . . . and your industry walks away from them." Hitachi wondered out loud how Americans could drop out of the race over measly sums like $100 million—didn't they realize that supercomputers are "the flagship of all computing technology" and the key to future profits?[3] Next, Cray decided to split in half and restructure itself in order to keep its appeal on Wall Street, where it had been losing favor. Shortly thereafter, several new Japanese computers were announced that surpassed the processing speed of Cray's top models, which had previously served as industry benchmarks.

- Read the 221-page report, issued in June 1990 by the Republican-led U.S. Commerce Department, on the state of the American electronics industry, which is portrayed as being in crisis. Only a few years ago, electronics was touted as a bastion of American competitiveness. Then, the low end of the industry was ceded to foreign competition, while experts rushed to explain that the U.S. would make its stand at the high end. Now, however, just as with supercomputers, the high end of a wide range of products is under siege as well, from Japanese and, in some cases, European competition. According to the Commerce Department report, "the situation is even bleak for some of the newest technologies: X-ray lithography, optical storage devices and flat panel displays. . . . In contrast to foreign governments, the U.S. government has not had a coordinated set of policies towards this sector. In general, the U.S. has followed an ad hoc approach, the effect of which has been to place the U.S. electronics sector at a competitive disadvantage vis-à-vis some of its foreign competitors."[4]

Even so, a number of influential analysts in the United States deny that any of the above problems matter much. New American economic theorists have taken the lead in disputing the importance of national economic power. Many of them insist that Americans should not care whether the United States has its own indigenous semiconductor manufacturing industry, or its own national HDTV project. In a borderless world, there's nothing wrong with depending on Japan to supply the products America needs if the Japanese can do so more efficiently. The talk of "trade wars" and "techno-nationalism" is overblown rhetoric, this school of thought contends. The interests of all nations today are so diverse and interdependent that it would be counterproductive for them to use their financial and trade surpluses, control of valuable technology, or market access as "weapons." And what's so bad about America becoming number two or number three anyway? If the marketplace deems Japanese and German businesses to be more efficient, why should that be a cause for alarm?

These views are implicitly endorsed by the Bush administration's three top economic officials: White House Chief of Staff John Sununu, Budget Director Richard Darman, and Chairman of the Council of Economic Advisors Michael Boskin. They have made it a point of principle to oppose all efforts to win government support for domestic technology ventures. President Bush embraces this approach as well, declaring: "I remain strongly opposed to any shift of industrial policy in which the government, not the market, would pick winners and losers. Second guessing the market is the way to raise government spending and taxes, not living standards."[5]

In a global marketplace that is allegedly converging, there is precious little international unity in support of the Bush-Sununu-Darman-Boskin line of reasoning. The other governments within the Triad are continuing to hone the art of picking their winners. Indeed, the argument that national (or regional) economic power no longer matters seems to be made almost exclusively by *American* experts.

In Japan, as in the EC, few serious thinkers wonder whether they can do without a semiconductor manufacturing industry. Japanese business and political leaders continue to take extraordinary measures to maintain their country's global leadership in this field. The EC, meanwhile, is fighting tooth and nail for a place in the semiconductor race, as evidenced by its $5 billion JESSI program, designed to produce next-generation chips and the equipment to manufacture them.

Europeans need not ask themselves how well they might fare in a world where they had little global influence: That has been their experience for most of the last forty years. Now, they want to change the situation. As Jacques Delors explains it, "We must think in terms of power. I want for Europe the possibility to play a world role. This is my ultimate goal."

And the Japanese don't question whether nations in economic competition will intentionally use economic weapons. They have already felt themselves victimized by unilateral American and European restrictions. On several occasions, they have also demonstrated their ability to respond in kind, adopting retaliatory measures. The most popular book in Tokyo recently has been *The Japan That Can Say No,* in which Shintaro Ishihara, a former government minister and possible future prime minister, argued that Japan should make more strategic use of its ability to boycott American Treasury bond auctions and to sell military technology to Moscow. Exploiting these options, Ishihara said, could offer Japan greater leverage in negotiations with the U.S. over how best to shape the global economy and the U.S.-Japan trade relationship. "If Japan told Washington it would no longer sell computer chips to the United States, the Pentagon would be totally helpless," Ishihara declared. "Furthermore, the global military balance could be completely upset if Japan decided to sell its computer chips to the Soviet Union instead of the Unided States."[6]

"War," the great German military historian Karl von Clausewitz wrote in the nineteenth century, "is the continuation of politics by other means." The twenty-first century may give rise to a further dictum: *Economic competition is the continuation of war by other means.*

THE MYTH OF THE STATELESS CORPORATION

"Who is Us?" asks Harvard political economist Robert Reich, one of the most prominent figures in the American debate about competitiveness and industrial policy. "Across the United States, you can hear calls for us to revitalize our national competitiveness. But wait—who is 'us'? Is it IBM, Motorola, Whirlpool, and General Motors? Or is it Sony, Thomson, Philips, and Honda?"[7] Reich's point is that in the new era, the country in which a company is incorporated or the nationality of its stockholders has ceased to matter. What matters is where that company does its manufacturing, especially where it locates its high-skilled jobs. By Reich's standard, Philips, although it is based in the Dutch town of Eindhoven, is a better "American" company than Zenith, which is headquartered in Chicago. Philips employs more American workers than Zenith and is more likely to train them in advanced production techniques.

There is some truth in Reich's observation, although he greatly overstates the case. There is also endless irony in the fact that the Japanese and European investors who have chosen to buy or build companies in the United States are often more committed to the American market and more willing to make long-term investments in state-of-the-art equipment and worker training than many so-called American companies. Chrysler sources more and more of its parts in Japan; Honda builds more and more of its cars in the United States. Firestone ran its tire plants into the ground; Bridgestone, a Japanese company, bought Firestone and plowed a billion dollars into upgrading the facilities and making the company competitive again.

All of this is evidence that the world is moving toward a borderless economy. But we aren't there yet. These examples are just early anomalies that have arisen as corporations with global interests have begun to take advantage of new cross-border opportunities. To infer too much from these initial cases would be to overlook the difficult struggle that lies ahead as the world seeks to forge a new global economic order. In some ways, what these anomalies actually tell us is that the *nation-state is still enormously influential*. While some clever global companies have *chosen* to locate major production facilities in foreign markets for strategic business reasons, many have been *compelled* to do so by the power of the host country. Political forces within nation-states have written laws and established an overall climate that effectively says, "If you want to profit from selling your goods in our market, you'd better create jobs here."

The EC has developed the most explicit array of policy tools to encourage companies to locate in Europe. The Japanese way is more subtle and sometimes hard to pin down, but perhaps even more purposeful: The lesson of virtually every foreign "success story" in Japan is that outsiders desiring to do business there *must* make an extraordinary commitment of time, energy, and money to the local market. The most successful foreign companies tend to be those that have most "Japanized" their operations, often including selecting indigenous nationals as senior executives— something Japanese companies don't typically do when *they* go abroad.

Although state governors are actively involved in seeking foreign investment, there is no great federal campaign to encourage foreign companies to locate their production in the United States. Although this *is* a big trend, usually the initiative comes not from U.S. policy-making circles, but from foreigners themselves. This is particularly true of the Japanese, who have discovered that locating manufacturing facilities in the U.S. can be an expedient palliative to the poison politics of the trade deficit—and a long-term strategic business advantage at the same time. The fact that the United States is running a persistent $50 billion annual trade imbalance with Japan, however, suggests that relying on Japanese initiative is not the most efficient way to solve the problem.

The borderless economy is not shaping up as a single free-flowing marketplace in which "stateless" corporations make or sell goods and services wherever they find maximum efficiency, opportunity, and profit. As it turns out, the borderless economy is open chiefly to those corporations whose home market fulfills two essential, obvious, and typical functions of the nation-state:

First, the home nation (or again, in the EC's case, the region) must promote the maximum level of competitiveness in the domestic environment, creating the basic nexus of product and service excellence, education, training, management, and financial resources which the corporation can then draw upon as it builds its market share abroad.

Second, the home nation must protect with some vigilance the interests of its own companies, both domestically and abroad, in writing the rules of the road for the global interchange among companies of many nations.

In these areas, the Japanese and Europeans seem remarkably clearheaded about how to answer the question "Who is Us?" Once again, it is principally Americans who are at a loss. Even many conservatives in the front ranks of American business and political leadership have grown concerned about Washington's confusion on this score. Despite their flag-waving American patriotism, those who have been in power in Washington since 1981 have displayed a shocking inability and unwillingness to defend American economic interests.

"You've asked me to identify U.S. industries that are in competitive decline. My response is that we are experiencing a competitive decline across the board," said former Defense Secretary Frank Carlucci in hearings on business and financial competitiveness held by the U.S. Senate Banking Committee. In the same hearings, Admiral Bobby Inman, former deputy director of the CIA, noted, "Unless we begin to deal with our ability to compete, we're going to see our standard of living continue to erode." John Reed, chairman of Citicorp, maintained that "some place on this path we are going to lose our will and ability to be a leader in the world." And Robert Galvin, chairman of Motorola, specifically acknowledged "heresy" to his own conservative beliefs. He declared bluntly, "The American industrial system can no longer cope with the Japanese industrial system."[8]

The myth of the "stateless corporation" is often invoked to suggest the world is becoming denationalized much faster than it really is. AT&T's Robert Allen is keenly aware of this problem. Effectively barred from international business involvement by regulation until the court-ordered breakup of the Bell system in the 1980s, AT&T is now trying to sell its excellent products and services abroad. AT&T is a good case study because it brings only its competitive technology to the global market, not a history of prior investment and ownership abroad built up in the "old days" before the advent of the borderless new order.

Describing himself as a free trader, Robert Allen notes that it is considerably easier for Siemens, Alcatel, NTT, NEC, and other foreign competitors to do business in the U.S. than it is for AT&T to do business overseas. "These companies are able to subsidize their entry into the U.S. market with the profits from their protected market at home. I'm not against the openness of the U.S. market, but I believe we are being foolish if Washington doesn't pursue a course designed to open up foreign markets as well." In Japan as well as Germany, he says, "a government-business consortium exists which gives their people a competitive edge and a long-term view. Both countries have a national agenda that we don't have."

IBM offers a case study from the opposite end of the spectrum. Unlike AT&T, it has long been involved in the global marketplace. No company anywhere in the world can lay greater practical claim to "statelessness," because no company sells as much as IBM does outside its home market. In 1989, revenues from outside the U.S. amounted to $31 billion. "Big Blue" is the leader in every major computer market of the world, with the exception of Japan (where IBM was once number one but is now third, behind Fujitsu and Hitachi).

Why is IBM president Jack D. Kuehler so worried about U.S. competitiveness? Why does he say it would be "irresponsible" *not* to be involved in efforts to "strengthen the competitiveness of American industry?"[9] Why is IBM supporting the Sematech consortium of American companies in semiconductor R&D? Why did IBM launch the efforts to create the U.S. Memories manufacturing consortium—offering to give other American companies access to some of its best technology for free? Why, when the Japanese company Nikon appeared ready to take over the semiconductor equipment division of Perkin-Elmer, did IBM step in and help create an American investor group to buy it instead?

Kuehler's IBM is not acting out of charity or patriotism. The long-term future of a company even as vast and powerful as IBM is threatened by new global competitors. IBM's senior management—cool, rational, non-paranoid, and non-Japan-bashing—is simply too smart to fall for the myth of statelessness. If they allow their Japanese competitors to gain a monopoly over the supply of the chips from which computers are built or the equipment from which chips are made, they will suffer. Japanese computer makers (who are often also the chip makers) will get first look at new designs, first access to new chips, and preferential pricing, delivery schedules, and allotments during shortages. A company cannot remain a global leader in the computer business when faced with such competitive disadvantages.

Nationality, in short, still matters.

FREE TRADE, MANAGED TRADE, TOUGH TRADE

The Bush administration says it wants a twenty-first century of free trade—free of nationality and national political considerations. The Japanese and Europeans, while claiming to desire free trade, don't have to be pressed too far to admit they prefer strategies which amount to politically managed forms of trade, in which the pursuit of national (or regional) interests is an accepted fact. Both Tokyo and Brussels are succeeding at drawing even the most adamant free traders in Washington into negotiations that amount to managed-trade deals.

A naive eighteenth-century misconception has prevailed in Washington and London during the Reagan-Bush-Thatcher years as the result of an overly literal reading of Adam Smith. According to this view, the marketplace is a pure zone of commerce, devoid of nationality, politics, and power struggles. In fact, however, all of these elements are *central* to the marketplace, right along with labor costs, productivity, and innovation. If Adam Smith were alive today, he would likely recognize the market-managing strategies of Europe, Japan, and the Asian NIEs as essential elements of their growing comparative advantage. Just as he called for government, not the market, to play the leadership role in constructing the physical infrastructure needed by business (such as roads and bridges) and in ensuring national security, Mr. Smith himself might recognize as new responsibilities of government the need to ensure the competitiveness of the business infrastructure and the economic security of the nation.

What lies ahead is neither blanket free trade nor blanket protectionism. Instead, the world will see what might be best characterized as an era of *tough trade*. Corporations, nations, and regions will push and shove. Sometimes they will handle their disputes through the niceties of GATT and international trade law. At other times, they will rely ruthlessly on the law of the jungle. For some products and services, relatively free trade will prevail. For others, protectionist policies will be put up, until they are challenged by those with enough incentive to sustain the fight to tear them down. Countries and regions will make attempts at managed-trade agreements. Some of these will work—that is, at least, until they fail. The more open the global marketplace becomes, the more those with the best set of comparative advantages will be tempted to try to monopolize it. After all, it is not the joy of competition that propels capitalists forward. It is the joy of *winning* the competition.

A vivid glimpse of the future was showcased at the end of 1990 when George Bush visited Europe. Here was the American president along with his European and Soviet colleagues, formally declaring the Cold War over. Here was the American and European leadership expressing unanimity about the need to stand up collectively to Saddam Hussein. Yet, at the very moment all this political, military, and strategic solidarity was being professed, the GATT talks were breaking up over the fundamental philosophical differences between American and European capitalism, and the sharpening conflict between transatlantic economies.

At some point along this road, perhaps after enough damage has been inflicted on American business interests, it will occur to those in Washington that, with the most powerful government in the world at their disposal, they ought to begin to use it to promote American economic interests, in much the way Europeans and Japanese use their governments.

THE NEW REALITIES AND THE TWO REALITIES

"Pessimism is the new cottage industry in America," writes Charles Morris, who has made a bullish case for America's future in a recent book, *The Coming Global Boom*. Morris probably would not like the above discussion much. "Almost every day," he notes, "someone identifies a new impending catastrophe—the budget deficit, America's 'international debt,' the junk bond overhang, the savings and loan crisis, the loss of American competitiveness. . . . Despite all the predictions of catastrophe, the world and the United States are on the threshold of a long-run economic boom. The boom will last well into the next century and will be marked by rising manufacturing output and productivity, steadily falling interest rates, and a broad distribution of economic benefits."[10]

In *Microcosm*, George Gilder claims that Americans should not worry about their loss of global dominance in hardware manufacturing, because they remain the leaders in software and design: "To say that foreign conglomerates will dominate the world information industry because they have the most efficient chip factories or the purest silicon is like saying the Canadians will dominate world literature because they have the tallest trees."[11] Gilder even welcomes the idea that the U.S. semiconductor industry might disappear. The faster Americans leave the business of making such hardware to the Japanese, Koreans, and Europeans, the better. Software is "what the contest is all about," Gilder maintains, and software is what Americans are good at.

In any full discussion of the future of American high technology, opponents of government involvement will invariably mention T. J. Rodgers, CEO of the hard-driving, highly competitive Silicon Valley company Cypress Semiconductor. Rodgers is obviously better informed about what goes on inside a computer chip than most of the political scientists and economists who usually debate the question of the government's role in the industry. Yet he is dead set against American initiatives to emulate Japanese-style consortia. "Big enterprises, dominated by big companies, subsidized by big grants from Washington," he says, might turn out to be a remedy "worse than the disease."[12]

Meanwhile, Joseph Nye, a prominent Harvard professor and former undersecretary of state, has taken up a crusade to combat the exponents of the American decline thesis. What America has to fear, he asserts, is not decline as such, but Americans *coming to believe* in U.S. decline. In his 1990 book, *Bound to Lead,* he stresses that the United States remains the "largest and richest power with the greatest capacity to shape the future." It will still be the leading force in the twenty-first century, provided Americans don't become so obsessed with decline that it develops into a self-fulfilling prophecy.[13]

Morris, Gilder, Rodgers, Nye—they represent just a small sampling of the thinkers who are expressing a fundamentally optimistic view of the United States as the nation braces for the challenges of the twenty-first century. They have studied the data and considered the arguments of those who are so concerned about a crisis in American competitiveness. They have simply drawn vastly different conclusions.

The phrase "the new realities" is often invoked these days to describe the conditions of global economic competition that now prevail. Perhaps the most important of these new realities—the key to understanding the rest—is that *two realities* are now at work in the world as never before and two opposing sets of data are used in forming judgments about major issues. Although we are bombarded with more information than ever, the conclusions we are able to draw are becoming less and less clear:

- If the U.S. trade deficit and budget deficit are really such gigantic problems, why has nothing negative yet happened that can be directly attributed to them?
- Is the U.S. really a debtor nation at all? If you valued American foreign assets bought long ago at today's market prices, wouldn't the U.S. be a creditor nation? And if you factor in all the production of U.S.-owned companies overseas, isn't the trade deficit really a myth?
- If American living standards are supposed to be eroding under the pressure of competition with foreign economies, why were so many new billionaires created in the 1980s, and why did yuppies seem so ubiquitous?
- If foreign investment in the U.S. is so dangerous, would Americans prefer the alternative of foreign *disinvestment?*
- Is Japan still ascending as a power in the world, or is the sun about to set as a hail of negative circumstances finally catches up with the Japanese miracle?
- Is the European Community's march toward a unified marketplace really good for its economy? Or does it simply conjure up an old

Industrial Age desire to create larger, more monolithic companies and institutions, which in fact will never be able to keep pace with the decentralized risks and challenges of the Information Age?

• If the world is really becoming more peaceful, why have the two biggest American military expeditions since the end of the Vietnam War taken place in the last two years (Panama '89, Mideast '90)?

And so on down a long list of similar issues where a good debater, armed with selected facts and figures, can make an impressive case for either side.

Of course, there have always been those who choose to see a glass as half empty when others describe the same glass as half full. However, the ambiguities of the present global economic situation stem from more than a simple difference in attitude between optimists and pessimists.

The essence of the problem is that impulses and messages from a new age are arriving while the prior age is still in force. There will be new trends; new laws of economics, politics, and history; and new truths of all kinds which we cannot yet fully apprehend. No one knows how fast this new age will institutionalize itself, how revolutionary it will be, or how much of our past knowledge will still be valid. We must carefully survey today's trends in order to formulate an educated guess as to how they will develop. All the conflicting impulses and messages of the old society and the new must be examined in the attempt to judge which will predominate and for how long.

The United States, as the preeminent industrial society of the twentieth century and the birthplace of most of the technologies and social forms which are likely to drive the twenty-first-century Information Age, is a society riddled with conflict. In fact, at least two radically different Americas could be said to exist today. Whether the nation's outlook for the 1990s is good or bad depends largely on which aspect of the American reality is being considered.

One America is to be found in the labs of schools such as MIT and Cal Tech. No other society in the world can match these. The most competitive Japanese and European companies send their best and brightest young people here for advanced training. But an altogether different America is found in the typical big-city elementary school. There, literacy rates are falling, and average test scores in areas such as science would be unacceptable even by the standards of many developing countries.

There is the America of the top one-third of wage earners—the software writers, advanced RISC-chip designers, aerospace engineers, bioengineers, TV producers, ice-cream entrepreneurs, restaurant designers, heart-transplant surgeons, M&A deal-makers, journalists, talk-show hosts, rock stars, commodities traders, and shopping-mall developers. While such people face competition from abroad, no competitive *threat* actually looms over them. They are the world leaders at what they do, and they are comfortably ensconced in growth markets. This is good news. But then there is the America of the bottom two-thirds to think about—the ordinary and not especially well educated factory and service workers, as well as the growing underclass. Even during the boom of the 1980s, real wages at the broad bottom of the American pyramid fell 1 percent a year, precisely because this population lacks the skills to compete effectively with foreign work forces.

The American CEO, the best paid in the world, on average receives five times the income of his Japanese counterpart and twice that of a European. His annual salary and bonus package has grown in inverse proportion to American industry's declining share of world markets. Failure to act in the face of competitive challenges will not affect his reality much. For his employees, however, and for their children, America's declining competitiveness will be evident in the reality of their declining living standards.

These two realities help explain why competitiveness is so often discussed and yet so rarely acted upon. For the most influential Americans, competitiveness is still an intellectual concern, not a pocketbook issue. They remain the beneficiaries of Ronald Reagan's tax cuts. They are still encouraging the country to consume more than it can afford—indeed, they are leading the way in their own life-styles. They *own* the properties that can be sold to foreigners at premium prices. The underclass, the working poor, and the average factory worker suffered in the 1980s. But the *majority* of that *minority* of Americans who actually vote still enjoys unprecedented material prosperity.

Emotionally and morally, of course, many well-to-do Americans fear the reckoning that may lie ahead and worry about the homeless the society is leaving behind. But these concerns are not yet great enough to inspire meaningful action. And the complacency of the electorate discourages even the most committed congressional champions of change from enacting measures that carry any suggestion of even short-term sacrifice.

The growing crisis of the bottom two-thirds of America's population will increasingly affect the affluence of the top third. It already does: Signs of the troubles to come can be found now in the junkie who breaks into the executive's car, doing $1,500 damage to steal a tape deck that will sell on the street for a $25 crack fix; in the hours added to commuting time because of clogged traffic and collapsing infrastructure; or in the two-income professional couple who, despite their high-paying jobs, face a squeeze to pay for the private child care and private schools that have been made necessary by the failure of the public education system.

The top third of American society is more dependent on the bottom two-thirds than it likes to think. Because of the appreciation of the yen and the D-mark, the United States in the late 1980s enjoyed one of the lowest average labor costs in the Triad. But America's newly inexpensive labor hasn't provided the nation with the competitive advantage it should have, because of the poor education and training of the domestic work force. American companies that depend on highly complex, high-quality or low-error-rate production still prefer to pay more to manufacture abroad than to bring those manufacturing jobs back to the United States.

Gather a cross section of a leading American company's most talented managers in a room and talk to them. They are likely to be more intelligent, more sophisticated, more resourceful, more creative, and more well-rounded as human beings than a similar group from a competitor company in Japan. This may not continue to be the case forever, but at least as of today, it is generally a fair characterization.

But the Japanese—and now the Europeans as well—are winning the competition. Why? The first part of the answer is that their systems are generating better-educated, better-trained, and more loyal, disciplined, and ambitious work forces at the lower echelons and throughout a given company's ranks. Secondly, their societies make it easier for managers to do their job—by keeping low-cost capital available to them, by defending their home market, and by a hundred other means.

REBUILD AMERICA

When I discuss these issues in public forums, I am invariably asked, "What is the most important thing Americans can do to reverse the current situation?" My version of the number-one priority is one that requires neither legislation nor funding. It entails no negotiations with the Japanese or the Europeans, nor is it likely to produce any adverse reaction among our trading partners.

America's *number-one priority* as a nation—as a social-economic-financial-technological-political system—should be to bring an end to our self-defeating focus on short-term interests, short-term rewards, and short-term solutions. We must shift our energies instead to thinking, leading, planning, building, creating—and, when necessary, sacrificing—for the long-term well-being of ourselves and our children. We must rise above partisanship and dispense with the narrow-focus, knee-jerk, special-interest, now-now politics that have generally prevented America from responding to the great international challenges posed to its competitiveness. We must think deeply, broadly, and more globally about how we will deal with such challenges in the future.

When you begin to think long-term, you understand that America must raise its private savings rate, lower the federal budget deficit, and discourage excessive high-interest-rate corporate borrowing. These measures are essential in order to ensure the supply of domestic capital necessary so that long-term investments in future industries, badly needed infrastructural improvements, and other important capital expenditures can be made.

Japanese and German business gained a massive advantage in the 1980s due to the low cost of capital in those countries. Go out and look at what kind of home you can afford with an 11 percent mortgage—and then compare it with what you could buy if your interest rate were going to be only 4 percent. At 11 percent, you probably have to settle for inadequate space and amenities; at 4 percent, you get your dream house. The Japanese and Germans are building their industries with the equivalent of 4 percent mortgages, while American executives are struggling to develop theirs with an interest rate of 11 percent. Most of America's great economic successes in the twentieth century were achieved when the cost of capital was low—much as it was in Japan and Germany during the 1980s. It is very hard to invest and build for the future when you have to worry about making the next junk-bond interest payment.

Reducing the budget deficit and raising the savings rate is not the arduous undertaking many believe it to be. Dozens of economists have suggested any number of ways to accomplish these goals. We Americans like to complain about taxes, but the fact is, we are taxed less than anybody else in the Triad. We pay only 40 percent of what the heavily taxed Europeans and Japanese pay for gasoline. As much as half the federal budget deficit could be wiped out overnight through aggressive taxes on gas, cigarettes, and alcohol. Yet the political will to impose even simple measures such as these is absent.

The peace dividend is at hand, yet government lacks the courage to make substantial cuts in the defense budget. What's more, it seems no one is able to envision how those funds should be redeployed to spur civilian economic restructuring. Thus, whatever small savings are reaped may well end up being frittered away.

When you think long-term, you begin to realize that however many instant billionaires are created by speculative stock markets, managerial emphasis on quarter-to-quarter profits, highly leveraged corporate take-overs, and rapid-fire mergers-and-acquisitions, what you are witnessing is not the competitive restructuring of American business but a suicidal dismemberment of the very companies, sectors, and industries in which America now has global competitive strengths. Again, one needn't be an economic genius to recognize that more patient capital is desperately needed. Tax incentives for long-term capital gains—especially in areas of designated productive value to the economy—could play a role here, as could taxes on short-term trades to minimize stock market volatility.

When you think long-term, you must wonder if it is healthy for the U.S. financial-services industry to become so thoroughly penetrated by foreign banks and brokerage houses. Japanese institutions are now often the dominant forces in the U.S. government bond market, and are expected to control 25 percent of American bank lending in the 1990s. One need not "bash" Japan or launch a financial war simply to encourage Japanese financial institutions to slow down their rapacious growth in the U.S. or to enter the market through joint ventures with American partners.

When you think long-term, you begin to question whether it is advisable for the "free market" alone to determine such important elements of a nation's economic life as currency and interest rates—especially when the "free market" turns out to resemble a casino, with heavy participation by foreign governments whose interests are not necessarily similar to our own. The devaluation of the dollar has been one of the greatest blows to American competitiveness. A conscientious fiscal policy is badly needed to strengthen it, but more than that, we need to rethink our commitment to floating exchange rates.

When you think long-term, you begin to notice how much the shape of global economic life has changed since the period immediately after World War II, when the U.S. adopted its basic worldview on international economic matters that it still largely adheres to even now. That was a time when the greatest economic competition in the world was taking place *within* the United States, among domestic American companies. As you start to orient your thinking toward the future, you run up hard against deeply entrenched American assumptions about such issues as antitrust law, the government's role in determining the private sector's agenda, the adversarial nature of government-business-labor relations, tax neutrality, and a whole series of other matters, all of which need to be reconsidered.

When you think long-term, you realize that America's inconsistent, incoherent, and frequently contradictory approach to global trade continues to deliver us poor results in negotiations with our partners. It is obvious that the United States needs a high-powered, high-level Department of Trade and Industry to develop a postindustrial policy for the country's economy; to find creative ways to stimulate competitiveness at home; to encourage investment in capital equipment, R&D, and training; to promote an export mentality among American businesses; and to bolster all these efforts with consistent, strategic trade policies abroad.

Instituting a postindustrial policy need not require huge federal expenditures, but it will demand careful thinking. B-1 bombers cost a billion dollars apiece and now appear useless. The savings-and-loan bailout may cost $500 billion. But launching a major new industry of the future can take as little as a few hundred million dollars of government money. Will the government be able to pick "winners," though? Actually, the U.S. government's track record is not so bad: Its legendary successes have included rural electrification, the Manhattan Project, and putting a man on the moon, to name but a few. Certainly, government must find a way to involve the private sector, the innovators, the risk-takers, and the venture capitalists in this process. But if we are willing to be creative about our institutions, that shouldn't be too hard.

And perhaps most of all, when you think long-term, it becomes obvious that as a nation, we have been allowing ourselves to squander precious political energy on emotional and highly personal issues such as flag burning, abortion, obscenity in art, and the private lives of our political leaders. At the same time, we have been systematically ignoring the profound economic challenges we face in the world and avoiding the badly needed political debate over how we should address them.

The Japanese and the Germans both have their share of problems. But the most important thing to understand is that their social, economic, financial, technological, and political systems are structured to emphasize long-term planning, long-term efforts, long-term goals, and ultimately, long-term rewards. Conversely, in America today, despite our enormous national assets, our vast resources, and our wondrous virtues as a people, we have allowed our system to become skewed in such a way as to encourage us to act for short-term gains, even when doing so may threaten our future well-being.

Having a long-term focus is not some sort of inherently Japanese or Germanic characteristic. It is as American as apple pie. The long-term vision has been central to much of American history. It can be seen in the way the Founding Fathers went about creating the American democracy itself in the eighteenth century. It continued through the exploration of the West and the building of the railroads in the nineteenth century. The big long-term vision is synonymous with the heyday of American industrial innovation in the early twentieth century and the thinking of pioneers such as the Wright brothers and Henry Ford. From FDR's New Deal to the safe, stable, prosperous global order forged by Truman and Eisenhower, Washington's policies were long-term in their orientation. Even as recently as the 1960s—when John F. Kennedy spoke with visionary zeal of the New Frontier, and the Reverend Martin Luther King, Jr. delivered his impassioned account of his dream of racial equality—the United States was still a nation that fervently espoused long-term goals and believed in working long and hard to achieve them.

Over the last generation, however, and particularly in the 1980s, we ceased to be that nation. Vision, creativity, the spirit of innovation and of problem-solving—the very qualities we like to think define the American character—are nowhere to be seen as we stand before today's dilemmas. Fortunately, we still possess these basic virtues; we simply are not using them wisely.

But don't be fooled. It is not just hardware manufacture or chip making which is swiftly moving across the oceans on either side of our continent. It is vision, creativity, and leadership as well. If Americans don't respond now to the global economic challenge, we will awaken in the twenty-first century to discover that even these quintessential American characteristics have slipped from our grasp. Then it will be too late to rebuild.

10

100 Predictions for the Year 2000

> What we anticipate seldom occurs; what we least expect generally happens.
>
> BENJAMIN DISRAELI

THE ONE-ARMED ECONOMIST

It is said that Harry Truman grew weary of his cautious economic advisers, who would invariably temper their forecasts by saying, "On the one hand this, but on the other hand that." Finally, utterly frustrated after listening to yet another of these gutless forecasts, he blurted out, "Would someone please send a one-armed economist!"

What follows is a "one-armed" analysis of how some of the issues addressed in this book may develop over the course of the 1990s. Presented here are 100 specific predictions about events, trends, and in a few cases, individual personalities.

Making such predictions is a dangerous business. It is far easier to be wrong than to be right. The rapid pace of events wreaks havoc with forecasting. Even being right may be irrelevant. A prediction that seems today like a daring idea for the year 2000 might be fulfilled just a few weeks later, while we are still in the early days of the 1990s.

No attempt has been made in this list to cover all the countries and regions affected or to comment on every issue of concern. For those who have made it all the way through the book, some of this material may seem like a recap of ideas discussed along the way. Indeed, it is a summary of sorts. For those reading only this list, it is worth noting that many other thoughts about the future are discussed in the preceding chapters.

In assessing the issue most crucial for Americans—how the United States will fare in facing the twin challenge of economic competition with Europe and Japan—I certainly hope I am wrong. Nevertheless, I have performed this evaluation not with my heart but with my head. This particular vision of the future represents my one-armed forecast. It is not what I would like to see happen, but what I believe is most likely to happen.

Perhaps, if thinking Americans contemplate this list, they will conclude that this is not, after all, the world they would choose to live in. Maybe they will even be moved to try to prevent some of these developments from coming to pass. That, of course, would be the very best purpose I could hope for this book to serve.

Forecast: Europe

1. The European Community's 1992 program will be a substantial economic success. Most of its ambitious agenda *will* be accomplished by December 31, 1992, although a number of important matters won't be resolved. Completely free movement of people throughout the EC, for example—one of the 1992 program's main goals—will not be achieved by that date. There will be a crisis or two as the deadline draws closer. But the problems will be a overshadowed and ultimately solved as the 1992 program continues to generate impressive results. The "home market" for European companies *will* be enlarged, corporation rationalization and restructuring *will* take place on a grand scale, and productivity *will* be stimulated. New world-class corporate competitors will come out of Europe to join the global race in every industry.

2. Economic growth rates in the EC as a whole, and particularly in France and Germany, will average more than 3.5 percent and will

exceed U.S. norms for the entire decade of the 1990s. Even though many sectors will remain protected and the "supply-side shock" of full-throttle competition will *not* be as radical as originally envisioned, the pan-European cost savings and the pump-priming impact of 1992 will be *even greater* than the optimists had forecast.

3. The EC will surpass the United States and emerge as the largest single market in the world by the end of 1993. In raw population numbers, it already has the distinction of being the world's largest market. Measured by GNP, however, today's EC is still about 10 percent smaller than the United States. It will surpass the United States toward the end of 1993 due to continued high growth and the admission of several new members: Austria, Norway, and possibly Sweden and other EFTA countries.

4. The ECU will become the common currency of the European Community by 1997. It will be backed by a "EuroFed" central banking system linking the various central banks of participating countries. The preponderant force in managing this system will be Germany's Bundesbank, which will aim to maintain an ECU zone characterized by low inflation, low interest rates, stable prices, and strong exchange values. Not all of Europe will adopt the ECU at first. Various national currencies will remain in use into the twenty-first century and Britain will be the last to dispense with its national currency. But the ECU will also draw into its orbit countries that are not now part of the EC. Switzerland may link its franc to the ECU prior to actually joining the Community, in order to remain an important banking center. Hungary, Czechoslovakia, and Poland will strive for ECU linkages to solve their currency-convertibility problems.

5. The EC dialogue on political union will start out vague, but Europe will evolve steadily into a supranational, federal entity, whose institutions will be in place by the year 2000. It will be a complex structure not quite like anything ever seen before—what Jacques Delors calls "an unidentified flying political object." It will be a "United States of Europe" in which Brussels is much weaker on most matters than Washington ever was and the "states" are more powerful than those in America have historically been, even at the height of the "states' rights" movement. In making economic and trade policy, however,

Brussels, along with the EuroFed and various other incipient Euro-institutions, will be quite strong—stronger than Washington has traditionally been.

6. At least half of all significant European legislation on economic and other matters will be determined by the EC, rather than national parliaments, by the year 2000. Jacques Delors may be disappointed that it won't be the 80 percent he foresaw in 1988, but the Community will still represent the greatest supranational political experiment in the world and the most advanced case of an economy without national borders.

7. The first-ever election for the "president of Europe" will be held in the year 2000. This directly elected leader will serve as the chief executive of a revamped European Commission. Handicapping a campaign for an office that doesn't yet exist in an election that hasn't yet been called is virtually impossible. But a likely candidate would be Felipe González, the charismatic Spanish prime minister, who has demonstrated a track record of combining socialist ideals with pragmatic economic policies. Another possibility is German Foreign Minister **Hans-Dietrich Genscher.** Genscher is probably second only to Gorbachev in the ranks of individuals responsible for ending the Cold War, and he was doubtless *the* most important figure in bringing about German reunification.

8. The Europe Parliament will finally settle on Brussels as its operational headquarters and will become a true legislature. Other institutional changes likely to occur will include the formation of a Senate-style "upper house," made up of the ministers of European governments, to work in tandem with the lower-house parliament. An expanded portion of European VAT will be earmarked for Brussels's growing budget. Although EC officials swear they are against it, **a corporate income tax** may be imposed on all European companies in the late 1990s to fund the huge programs for infrastructure, collaborative high technology, and redevelopment of Eastern Europe.

9. Europe will face a brief downturn in 1991–92 as the U.S. economy experiences difficulties (see *Forecast: Americas,* pages 332-338) **and as the EC undergoes a consolidation phase after today's rapid growth.** The actual extent of this contraction will be small—but it will loom large in the minds of European business and political leaders grappling with some of the 1992 program's most delicate issues, such as the establishment of a common currency. **The threat of recession** will be used to justify postponing tough decisions and maintaining various forms of protectionism for longer transition periods. In fact, however, the EC will come out of its downturn and begin growing again in 1992, while the U.S. will continue to be paralyzed by recession.

10. German reunification will prove to be one of the great economic success stories of modern times. Over the next few years, West Germany will get all the economic benefits it anticipates out of the drive to rebuild the East—and then some. **East German living standards will rise to meet today's West German levels by the year 2000.** Nevertheless, not everything in the process of reunification will proceed perfectly smoothly. The social residue of forty years of communist rule in the East will prove difficult to eradicate. A small but forceful cadre of remaining East German communists will cause political trouble. Workers accustomed to the "you pretend to pay us and we pretend to work" tradition of communism will turn out to be less disciplined and entrepreneurial than is now hoped. As a result, **the costs of reunification will be higher and the inflationary impact greater than Bonn now expects**—although not as severe as foreign pessimists predict they will be. Thus, Germany will need to deploy much of its surplus capital internally from 1991 through 1994. This will be **one of the factors causing Europe to seek and encourage more investment from Japan.**

11. German influence will grow increasingly powerful in Europe. German companies will lead the drive to invest in Eastern Europe. German bankers will be the architects of Europe's financial policies. The German government will have the greatest say-so in the development of European-Soviet relations. German political leadership will be more visible in the daily operations of the European Community. The Germans will be much admired—but also much criticized. **The high-handed doings of the "ugly German" will become the subject of much complaint throughout Europe.** New right-wing groups will spring up, especially in East Germany, giving Europe cause for fright. On the whole, however, **there will be little danger of a fascist revival.**

12. The biggest Western European beneficiary of German leadership will be France. German investment in France will be strong. The industrialized areas along the Franco-German border will become one of the most seamless regions in the post-1992 "Europe without frontiers." The financial and monetary links between the two countries will help France keep inflation at bay, interest rates low, and the franc strong. Although Germany will assert greater political leadership within the EC than it has in the past, it will continue to support French candidates for many of the leading posts in the emerging Euro-institutions. **The Germans will also encourage French visions of EC political union,** allowing Paris the principal public role as architect of the New Europe.

13. Germany will reacquire some of its old territories, but not through military force. Poland will limp along through several more hard years. German-speaking Poles will grow more vociferous in their appeals for reunification with Germany. Polish workers will flood into East Germany to take the jobs East Germans no longer want. With Warsaw's blessings, **Germany will establish a "special economic zone" on its former territory in Poland** in return for large financial benefits to the Polish government.

14. Berlin will emerge as the most important city in Europe. Beginning in 1992, and continuing through the course of the '90s, an increasing number of German government functions will be transferred to Berlin. **The city will be proclaimed the formal capital of Germany in the year 2000**—although some departments and ministries may remain permanently in Bonn. To alleviate a potential crash in the Bonn real estate market and a depression in the surrounding economy, the German government will take measures to expand Bonn's role as a regional commercial and administrative center, not just for Germany but also for the rapidly growing trade and investment between Germany and Belgium, the Netherlands, Luxembourg, and France. **The Bundesbank will move its headquarters back to Berlin**—as called for by its charter—in the early part of the '90s. The big private-sector banks will follow suit, causing Berlin to eclipse Frankfurt as a financial center. As with Bonn, plans will be made to keep Frankfurt a thriving regional center. Several of the new Euro-institutions now being discussed will be sited in Berlin, including the Secretariat of the Conference on Security and Cooperation in Europe (CSCE). Avant-garde art will flourish, energized by the meld-ing of East and West. Berlin will be the center of the post-postwar cultural world.

15. German workers will win the thirty-two-hour workweek by 1999. The metalworkers' union is already scheduled to scale down to a thirty-five-hour week by 1996, and the labor movement as a whole is pushing for further reductions in working time. Those demands will obtain new relevance as the still-swollen ranks of Germany's unemployed are augmented by millions of East Germans laid off due to the restructuring of formerly state-owned enterprises. Reducing the workweek to thirty-two hours will help the social market absorb this sudden surfeit of labor and still keep the peace.

16. *Mitteleuropa* — a German cultural zone running through the heart of Europe—will come back in vogue. Austria and Switzerland, already closely connected to Germany, will develop an even tighter affiliation with it. Czechoslovakia and Hungary will emphasize German-language training in their schools and will be the recipients of substantial German investment. The re-Germanization of Alsace will gather momentum. In the English-speaking world, it will be fashionable to regard Poland, Hungary, and Czechoslovakia the same way the Germans do—as part of Central, not Eastern Europe.

17. There will be no fortress Europe. Although many areas of EC trade policy will still have a protectionist bent after 1992, the general trend will be toward openness. American investment in Europe will grow significantly. U.S.-EC trade disputes will continue, but on the whole, the European market will be more hospitable to U.S. companies than it is today.

18. An economic alliance will evolve between Europe and Japan. Japanese investment in Europe will surpass current annual levels of Japanese direct investment in the United States. Japanese capital, technology, and industrial management techniques will turn out to be the "missing link" that will enable Europeans to fulfill their grandest aspirations.

19. The Mitsubishi/Daimler-Benz alliance will prove to be the deal of the decade. This partnership will help Japan emerge as a leader in the global aviation industry, expand the predominance of Mercedes-Benz autos as the luxury vehicle of choice in Asia, revolutionize the mass production of middle-market automobiles in Europe, and set a precedent for joint Japanese-European exploitation of the Soviet market.

20. Peugeot and Fiat, the two companies most forcefully resisting the Japanese onslaught in Europe, will form joint ventures with Japanese companies by 1995. Other large-scale Japanese-European corporate alliances will follow, further strengthening the strategic partnership between Japan and Europe.

21. Continental European equities will be among the best investments of the 1990s. The net effect of liberalizing and integrating the whole financial system will be to make trading in European stocks more aggressive. Most important, the growth prospects for long-stagnant companies are sustainable over the long term, especially in light of the development of the Eastern European market. **The strongest sectors will be: telecommunications, electronics, financial services, media, travel and tourism, real estate, retailing, construction, engineering, and leisure time.**

22. German stocks are currently undervalued and will treble in price over the course of the 1990s. Extremely conservative accounting principles, a historic lack of liquidity, and a general preference for bank debt over equity capital have kept German stocks on a tight leash. With P/E ratios in the low teens, many German companies are undervalued by world standards. As financial regulators loosen up—just a bit—to adapt to the capital needs of rebuilding East Germany, as German companies expand their pan-European networks, and as the domestic economy continues to grow, Germany equity markets in the first half of the 1990s could experience the kind of boom seen in Japan in 1985–90.

23. The Paris Bourse will also perform excellently. Growth in France already mirrors that in Germany, since the economies of the two nations are now so closely connected. French companies have been the most active builders of pan-European operations in the last few years. Prices of some big French stocks remain undervalued because of the companies' years as nationalized entities.

24. British stocks, on the other hand, are quite fully valued owing to the openness and international activity of the London exchange in the second half of the 1980s. With the M&A boom in the U.K. slowing and the manufacturing economy facing major challenges in remaining competitive with continental Europe, British equities will not be standout performers.

25. A single Euro-stock market will be created to handle trading in the shares of the largest European companies. It will be in place on a rudimentary basis by 1994. Although it will utilize a computer-intensive networking system in which trades will take place simultaneously all over Europe and the world, the organizational and administrative functions of this exchange will be headquartered in London. The creation of such an exchange will vastly increase the liquidity and ultimately the market value of many European companies.

26. The EFTA countries will merge with the EC by mid-decade. Austria, Norway, and Sweden are likely to seek individual membership when Brussels begins considering new applications again after 1992. Other EFTA countries will follow soon thereafter. Alternatively, they may join through a collective merger with the EC, or structure an EFTA-EC agreement that makes them EC members in all but name.

27. Hungary and Czechoslovakia will be admitted as EC members in 1997, after achieving substantial economic success. These two economies will be the best performers in what was once the Soviet bloc. **The surprise will be that Hungary will do even better than Czechoslovakia,** despite the latter's higher level of industrialization. The intellectual charm and charisma of Václav Havel notwithstanding, Czechoslovakia will spend too much time trying to invent new forms of social democracy. Unfortunately, this will be a fetter on its competitiveness. Hungary, meanwhile, will zoom ahead, driven chiefly by the engine of foreign investment.

28. Poland will not be admitted into the EC until the year 2000 —and even then, over the opposition of many in Brussels. Despite current "shock therapy" for its economy, Poland will remain mired in internal chaos, lacking both the basic industrial infrastructure as well as the interest of foreign investors to make the difference. Shock therapy will eventually be denounced as the *wrong* way to reform communist economies. **A damaging split will occur within Solidarity** between those who supported and opposed the "shock." Reluctantly, the EC will take Poland in as a member in the year 2000, and will embark on a concerted plan for Polish revival.

29. Europe's regions will become more visible. As the EC's supranationalism increasingly prevails over sovereign national politics, local and regional powers will grow more important, providing the decentralization necessary to balance the mounting centralism of Brussels. Certain highly industrialized areas of Europe are already beginning to function in this way—Baden-Württemberg, Catalonia, Wales, Alpes-Maritimes, etc.

30. "Second cities" of Europe will also gain new prominence. The growing integration of Europe, coupled with the suffocating centralization, traffic, and high costs of cities such as London and Paris, will give a boost to Europe's more "livable" and "workable" cities. Lyon, Nice, Strasbourg, Karlsruhe, Munich, Stuttgart, Edinburgh, and Århus, for example, all have excellent prospects for growth. In Spain and Italy, European unification will finally settle age-old rivalries between city pairs: Milan will be much more important than Rome, and Barcelona will overshadow Madrid.

31. Investment from outside the EC will increasingly shift away from Britain toward Germany and France. Because of the ease of doing business in the U.K., as well as its open investment policies, American and Japanese companies will continue to locate there. In the 1990s, however, non-Europeans will begin to shift more of their new investment to continental Europe, reflecting the need to be closer to the market and to the heart of the boom. The Japanese will begin to show a preference for Germany as their next-favorite investment site after the U.K., while the Americans will favor France. Spain and the Netherlands will also be attractive for manufacturing companies; Belgium for the service-oriented companies that wish to be close to the policy-making circles in Brussels.

32. Spain will continue to be the "hot" country of 1992. Although the Spanish will no doubt be disappointed at lower-than-anticipated levels of German investment, capital flows from elsewhere in the EC and from Japan will be strong. The new ease of buying and selling Spanish companies will attract investor attention, as will the cultural dynamism reflected in Spain's new trend-setting contributions to European food, fashion, and design.

33. The 1992 Summer Olympic Games in Barcelona will focus global attention on Europe in general and on Spain in particular, in much the way the 1964 Tokyo Olympics dramatized Japan's ascendancy. **The united German team will win the most medals of any nation.**

34. The opening of the tunnel under the English Channel in 1993 will be a historic turning point symbolizing the closer links between Britain and Europe. The Chunnel will promote the flow of goods and people as never before. It will be a huge infrastructural and financial success.

35. Europe's high-speed rail system will be in place by the early years of the next century, greatly enhancing business links and the free flow of citizens. Paris-Amsterdam travel time, for example, will be halved from the present five hours. Such trains, effectively faster than air travel because they go from downtown to downtown, will be the envy of much of the rest of the global business world, where dehumanizing airports and airplanes will still be a necessity.

36. EC environmentalism, rather than being a fetter on European competitiveness, will turn out to be good for business. While environmental policies will raise the cost of doing business in Europe in the short term, they will also stimulate the development of new technologies and industries which will become world leaders in the global cleanup of the twenty-first century. Europe's commitment to dealing with global warming, for example, will foster the development of less atmospherically harmful products which will become global standards in due course.

37. "Green" activists trying to stop biotechnological research in Europe will ultimately lose their battle, as bioengineering is increasingly seen not only as a means to boost European competitiveness but also as a way to help protect rather than destroy the environment. The center of the world biotechnology revolution will move from California and Massachusetts to laboratories in Switzerland and Germany.

38. European science and technology will experience a renaissance. Pan-European scientific collaborations, such as the CERN supercollider and the space program, along with applied-technology programs in semiconductor manufacture, HDTV, and ultrasonic transport, will manage to reverse the long-standing "brain drain" to the United States. While Europe will not catch up to the U.S. in all areas of science, it will surpass America on several fronts in the '90s. The EC will be willing to fund "big science" projects that the budget deficit will prevent the United States from undertaking.

39. British Prime Minister John Major will surprise his mentor, Margaret Thatcher, by emerging not only as a kinder, gentler Tory but also as an enthusiastic European. After pursuing a neo-Thatcherian hostility toward EC initiatives in 1991, Major will reverse course as he prepares for the 1992 parliamentary elections. He will take away the Labour Party's "Europe card" by presiding over Britain's enthusiastic entry into European economic, monetary, and political unions. For the same reasons Americans were not ready to consider a Democrat after Ronald Reagan, the British will not yet be ready for a return to a Labour government. Major will thus continue as prime minister well into the decade.

Forecast: Americas

40. The rise of Europe will be a short-term plus for the American economy in the years 1990–2. Western European prosperity and Eastern European reforms will help drive U.S. exports to record levels. American companies with strong positions in the European market will benefit directly. Many U.S.-based multinationals will be earning 20–50 percent of their profits in Europe, compensating for weak domestic markets.

41. U.S. companies with successful European operations will be good stock market plays. The easiest way for individual American investors to tap European opportunities may simply be to invest in companies such as IBM, Ford, Coca-Cola, Disney, and American Express, which are well positioned in Europe and already earn a substantial portion of profits there.

42. The U.S. dollar will enjoy a period of modest strength in the early '90s. The international desire to hold dollar-denominated assets as a hedge against uncertainty in Germany, Eastern Europe, the Middle

East, and elsewhere will be a powerful psychological force balancing the continued negative outlook on U.S. economic fundamentals. Unless Washington takes serious action on its budget deficit, however, the dollar will move precipitously lower in 1992–93, as the U.S. economy moves further away from European and Japanese fiscal norms.

43. American excellence in service industries will be highly exportable and a special bright spot for the U.S. economy in the '90s. In sectors such as telecommunications, software, media, entertainment, leisure time, data-base development, fast food, and travel, American companies will continue to hold leadership positions. They will benefit from the new European prosperity and the opening up of the market—even as the domestic U.S. economy heads into steep and more visible decline.

44. The key to restoring the competitive vigor of the U.S. economy will be to take advantage of these short-term favorable conditions to launch a wide-ranging program for American renewal. Unfortunately, positive developments such as higher corporate profits in Europe, a stable-to-strengthening dollar, and a declining military budget are likely to have a lulling effect. With no imminent crisis confronting Americans save for sluggish domestic economic growth, it will be difficult to rally the political consensus necessary to address deep-seated problems. These will come to a head around 1992–93, if preventive action is not taken sooner.

45. The conflicting fortunes of the advanced service sector and the manufacturing sector of the U.S. economy will create a major new division in American politics. With services doing well against foreign competition but manufacturing losing market share, a new political balance will be created on issues of foreign investment, industrial policy, and trade policy. High-tech manufacturing companies, once champions of free trade, will emerge as corporate standard-bearers for managed-trade and industrial policy solutions.

46. American public attention will increasingly focus on the success of the German social market and other European social systems that emphasize government responsibility for quality-of-life issues. U.S. trade unions will ask why German workers are winning the thirty-two-hour week while Americans are still working forty hours or more. Similar questions will be posed about the whole set of benefits European workers enjoy in areas such as child care, vacation time, job security, and parental leave. With health care already devouring over 11 percent of U.S. GNP, the socialized European medical programs, which cost about half as much, will figure prominently in public policy discussions.

47. On the heels of a modest recession in 1991, the United States will slide into a severe, prolonged recession that will last until 1997. However, due to the complexities of the new global economy, it will not be an across-the-board recession. Sectors such as entertainment and software may continue to thrive because of their world leadership and market. Companies with strong European and Asian operations will weather the storm best; those which are weak internationally will face especially trying times. The overall impact will be most formidable in autos and other consumer durables, electronics, computer hardware, and real estate. Highly leveraged companies still carrying substantial junk-bond debt from the 1980s will be extremely vulnerable. Many will collapse. Some may end up being sold to European and Japanese buyers at depressed prices.

48. Chrysler will again teeter on the brink of bankruptcy. It will be saved this time not by the U.S. government, but by a deal to restructure itself as a joint venture with Honda or Mitsubishi.

49. The cost of capital in the U.S. will undergo an alarming increase as this recession compounds the budget deficit. Having failed to reduce the deficit substantially, the Bush administration will have made optimistic forecasts about 1992 revenues, which will then be contravened by lower-than-expected corporate earnings as the recession begins. The costs of **the savings-and-loan bailout will escalate to almost a trillion dollars. In addition to the S&Ls, banks will be extremely hard hit by real estate and junk-bond losses.** As a result of these difficulties, **U.S. prime lending rates will rise to a range of 12–15 percent**, while typical European and Japanese business lending rates will remain less than half that. High capital costs will force American executives to shy away from making the critical new investments necessary to keep the U.S. competitive with Europe and Japan.

50. George Bush will be reelected president in 1992, despite the deepening recession. The Democrats, led by an eloquent Mario Cuomo, will attempt to focus public attention on the competitive threats from

Japan and Europe and the growing domestic crisis. But they will not be able to find the way to get voters excited in a positive way about these themes. Nor will they be able to prevent their proposals from sounding like a return to the mistrusted Democratic Party liberalism of the past. As in 1988, the 1992 campaign will become bogged down in narrow, emotional issues such as abortion, flag burning, crime, the death penalty, and taxes.

51. The U.S. will be locked in recession and decline in the mid-1990s, while Europe and Japan will continue to grow, creating the first such sustained disjuncture in postwar economic history. During these years, it will finally be recognized that the ''crisis of competitiveness'' is wreaking havoc with the American economy—not in the future, but in the here and now—and this will emerge as the major social and political issue in American life. The Reaganomic chickens will come home to roost, and the inaction and neglect of the Bush administration will become evident.

52. Key future-oriented industries in which the U.S. still dominates will face their most severe tests during this recession. Unable to match Japanese reinvestment and R&D levels, the U.S. may end up relinquishing its lead in supercomputers, desktop computers, fiber optics, and biotechnology.

53. The economic pain of the mid-'90s will trigger intense antiforeigner sentiment in U.S. political life. This will be aimed mostly at the Japanese, but the Germans will also be regarded with some hostility. The public will increasingly turn to the theme of the Axis powers refighting World War II economically—and winning. Even the free-trading Bush administration will be forced to take visible protectionist actions and make some nationalistic, anti-Japanese gestures to maintain public support. Such measures may have useful political effects. But they will have negative economic consequences, dampening (although not curbing) the flow of Japanese capital into the U.S. just when it will be needed most.

54. The U.S. social crisis will take a heavier and more visible toll on American business and its international competitiveness. Homelessness, drug addiction, and illiteracy will be recognized as more than simply the scourge of the poor; society will finally understand that they are sapping the resources of the whole nation and impairing its ability to function as a cohesive unit. **Visionary corporate leaders will develop the agenda for solving these problems**, even as politicians refuse to face up to them.

55. Hope for a U.S. revival will have to wait at least until the 1996 elections, when an inspired new leadership team will be elected with a broad mandate to overhaul the economic system. The seriousness of the nation's problems will lead to changes in the traditional Democrat-Republican rivalry, and partisanship will be minimized. The central political question will become whether or not leaders support an activist, Washington-led, business-community-supported plan for rebuilding America. Many prominent Republicans, such as **Bob Dole** and **Newt Gingrich**, will be in the forefront of this movement. The election itself will be won by a Democrat—**Al Gore**—although only on the basis of a broad, bipartisan coalition that may even include a Republican vice president.

56. The nature of the American political system, however, will work against quick solutions, even with a change of administrations and a strategic shift in Washington's thinking. Addressing the competitiveness crisis will take years. U.S. efforts in the 1997–2000 period may look somewhat like today's Eastern European reforms, although they will not entail such severe chaos. Stops, starts, experiments, and costly failures will all be part of the game; intense public and special-interest criticism will inevitably accompany every attempt—and especially every failure.

57. After flirting with xenophobia in the first half of the '90s, the American public will become more positive about foreign investment by decade's end. The debate will grow especially intense in 1997–2000, with the Gore administration ultimately resolving to utilize and encourage foreign investment. Washington, however, will insist on managing this investment flow to some extent, favoring partnerships and joint ventures rather than outright acquisitions by foreigners, and encouraging investment in certain industries and regions while discouraging it in others. Tokyo, Brussels, Taipei, and Seoul will ultimately agree to this plan.

58. Asian and European investors will thus continue their acquisitive drive in the '90s. By 1999, foreign investors will have raised their stake in the U.S. economy from 10 to 25 percent. Ironically, although foreign economic competition will be responsible for much of America's swift decline in the 1990s, foreign investment will be part of the solution.

59. The *majority* of Fortune 500 firms will embrace a strategic partner in Europe and/or Japan by the mid-'90s. Yet enthusiasm in the U.S. business community for such alliances will run hot and cold. Some of these partnerships will turn out to be inefficient tools for exploring market opportunities. Others will be hobbled by corporate cultural clashes, which may become especially apparent during the recession of the mid-'90s. But U.S.-based companies that stick with the approach and pursue it intelligently will be rewarded later in the decade.

60. The U.S.-Canada free-trade agreement, although a low-visibility issue in the United States, will be put to good use in the '90s. Faced with a myriad of global challenges, American companies will increasingly explore the most accessible of all cross-border markets— Canada. Canadian investment in the U.S. will also be among the friendliest and most beneficial. From its current reputation as America's "boring" neighbor to the north, Canada will come to be seen as a key element in business and political strategy.

61. The United States and Mexico will forge a free-trade pact by 1993. Both countries will recognize the need to promote more strenuous efforts toward regional economic integration as a response to events in Europe. Some U.S. businesses will take advantage of the opportunities opened up in Mexico as a result.

62. Abandoned by the Soviet Union, Fidel Castro will begin to lose control in Cuba. Inspired by the Eastern European events of 1989, **a popular revolt will overthrow him by 1992.** A massive economic resurgence, led by Cuban expatriates now in the United States, will follow.

63. While there will be bright spots in Latin America such as Mexico and Cuba, U.S. business as a whole will remain shortsighted about the region's potential. With industrial companies disinterested in the possibilities there, and banks still reeling from the fallout of the Latin debt crisis, the United States will not be prepared to make the long-term investments necessary to restore economic health to its Latin American backyard. Washington, moreover, will spend the first half of the 1990s preoccupied with the legacy of the Reagan era's Latin American policy, and will be forced to continue focusing on countries such as El Salvador, Nicaragua, and Panama, which are among the *least important* in the region's economy.

64. The Japanese, on the other hand, will be able to concentrate on the two most important Latin economies, Mexico and Brazil. Manufacturing companies will invest especially heavily in Mexico, using it as a route into the North American economy under the U.S.-Mexico free-trade pact. With Japanese banks financing Brazil's highway through the Amazon to the Pacific, trade between those two countries will flourish. Tokyo will also cultivate close ties with Peru, whose president, Alberto Fujimori, is descended from Japanese immigrants.

Forecast: Japan and Pacific Asia

65. The specter of inflation, stock market instability, declining real estate values, and a weaker yen will hover over Japan for the next few years, as Tokyo struggles to respond to changed global circumstances. Even so, **Japan's growth rate will continue to be among the highest in the world**. There will be at least one period of economic slowdown, but on the whole, the real economy in Japan will remain extraordinarily vibrant.

66. Japan's trade surpluses will continue to be high throughout the entire decade of the 1990s. The efforts to minimize these surpluses—undertaken largely as a result of U.S. pressure—are already coming to an end. With the great opportunities of globalization lying ahead, and with people in every corner of the world beseeching the Japanese to come to their aid, Tokyo will now argue that it needs its surpluses in order to do all the beneficent things expected of it. **Japanese officials will also complain that the U.S. has not lived up to its side of the bilateral bargain**—cutting the budget deficit, increasing domestic savings, rebuilding the domestic industrial base, etc. **The early '90s will also usher in a whole new generation of supercompetitive Japanese products**, from luxury automobiles to advanced-function fax machines, revolutionary laptop computers, personal portable telephones, high-definition video equipment, mega-memory chips, and more. Riding this stream of new products, Japanese global trade surpluses are likely to widen in 1991–93, after having narrowed steadily over the previous years. Japan's surplus with Europe should see a sharp increase, as Japanese companies ship the capital equipment and factory systems necessary to ramp up manufacturing inside the EC.

67. Even more important than Japan's trade surplus, its current account surplus will grow consistently, as Japanese investors repatriate their huge income from global assets acquired in the 1980s. With Germany concentrating on Europe, and Europe as a whole focusing on its own pressing needs, Japan will gain still greater stature as it increasingly serves as banker to the world.

68. Following Mikhail Gorbachev's historic 1991 Tokyo visit, a new era in Soviet-Japanese relations will slowly unfold. Eventually, Boris Yeltsin will propose a complex deal for the return of Japan's four northern islands. This will include provisos to keep military forces out of the islands and to steer billions of dollars' worth of aid to the Soviet economy. By 2000, Japanese auto plants will dot the Soviet Union, new port cities will be under construction on the USSR's eastern coast, Siberian timber and other resources will be flowing out to Japan, and massive joint projects will supply Soviet oil and gas to Japanese industry.

69. In response to European integration, Pacific Rim countries will seek to create their own regional alliance. Several such initiatives are already under way, including one launched by Australian Prime Minister Bob Hawke. That one, however, will flounder. During the first half of the 1990s, Japan will play a role similar to that played by West Germany in the recent history of the EC—quietly welding its region together through economic muscle, while staying out of the political limelight. Eventually, **Japan will take the lead in organizing this Asian economic alliance**, which will serve to stimulate growth within the Pacific Rim. **Australia** will be an active member, reflecting its decision to build an indentity for itself as part of a thriving Asia. **China**, which will be struggling to liberalize its society in the post–Deng Xiaoping era, will be included in the partnership. The organizational secretariat will be sited in **Hong Kong**—the ''Brussels'' of Asia—as a sign of Asian confidence in China's post-1997 policy. A debate on American participation will take place. In the end, the U.S. will be offered only observer status.

70. The Pacific Rim will be doing two-thirds of its trade within its own region by 1992. Japanese companies will dominate a robust Chinese market. Most **Americans will have abandoned China**, although a number of European firms will stay on, if only to give the Japanese a run for their money. Heavy Japanese investment in Hong Kong will make Tokyo the effective guarantor of that territory's future. In **Singapore**, local entrepreneurship coupled with Japanese business relationships will help to fulfill former Prime Minister Lee Kuan Yew's dream of transforming this poor third world nation into a bastion of high growth, high living standards, and high technology. **Taiwan** and **Korea** will be major global economic powers, with important investments not only in Asia but in North America and Europe as well. **Thailand** will undergo rapid industrialization, largely as a result of massive Japanese investment. As the growth boom fades in Europe toward the end of the 1990s, the **Pacific Rim will once again capture the world's attention as the land of greatest opportunity.**

71. Taking a cue from Germany, North and South Korea will reunite by 2000, creating a powerful new economic force in East Asia. Though Korean reunification will initially be interpreted as a competitive threat to Japan, it will ultimately prove to be a boon. The specter of Koreans breathing down Japan's back will be conjured by the leaders in Tokyo to prod the Japanese into working even harder. Meanwhile, the capital costs of rebuilding the North will force South Koreans to overcome their remaining suspicions of the Japanese, who will thus be able to enter the Korean economy more fully.

Forecast: Soviet Union and the Balkans

72. Mikhail Gorbachev will fail in his efforts to hold the Soviet Union together through years of gradual economic reform. He will finally be ousted from power by the more strident and enthusiastic liberalizers and democrats, typified by **Boris Yeltsin**.

73. Yeltsin and/or his cohorts, however, will prove no more capable than Gorbachev of finding solutions to the Soviet Union's underlying economic and structural problems. In fact, their rule will be even more chaotic than their predecessor's. They in turn may end up being overthrown by Ligachev-style hard-liners or extreme nationalists.

74. In the chaos, the Baltic republics will break away. At first, they will form their own economic and monetary union. They will benefit from heavy Scandinavian and German investment and will develop favorable trade agreements with the European Community. By the early twenty-first century, they may be ready to join the Community itself.

75. The Soviet Union will become a loose confederation of republics. Besides the Baltic states, a few more republics will opt for independence, but most will stay and adopt a high degree of autonomy. The chaos will continue for years and will include frequent outbreaks of ethnic violence, anarchy, and anti-Semitism.

76. At least one nuclear incident of Chernobyl-style proportions will take place as liberation fronts in the southern Soviet republics attack nuclear installations, and the Red Army and the KGB try to stop them. The world is not going to get out of the nuclear era as easily as most people expect.

77. Despite the turmoil, the Russian Republic itself will remain relatively stable and nonviolent. Even as their empire disintegrates around them, Gorbachev, Yeltsin, and all likely successors—even hardliners—will continue to need and encourage foreign investment and trade in the Russian Republic. The newly independent republics will need outside investment even more. Thus, even though the Soviet Union will undergo wrenching, destabilizing change, the West's worst fears will not be realized. There will be no turning back on attempts to open the economy—although foreign investors will obviously have to be brave. And while military force may be used within the Soviet Union, the violence will not spill over into the West.

78. Ultimately, a new strongman will emerge—perhaps even Gorbachev himself in a comeback role— to lead the Soviet Union through an authoritarian transition to a market economy and a new political configuration. *Stability will return by 1996.* But a real *capitalist market economy will not be operating until at least 2010.*

79. While the Soviets will not attack the West militarily, they *will* use their military power as a bargaining chip to create a new European security order favorable to their interests and to extract a hefty economic tribute from Germany. If a strong and workable EC defense union is not established after NATO's collapse, Europe may even find itself effectively Finlandized, hostage to the strategy of a capitalist Soviet Union, in the twenty-first century. The ultimate irony of the demilitarized post-postwar world may be that the Soviets will use the archaic threat of military force to reposition themselves as major players in the new economic order.

80. The Balkans will live up to their reputation as a powder keg. Romania and Bulgaria will continue to suffer political chaos and internal strife because of their geographic and historic proximity to the Soviet Union. **Yugoslavia** will come apart politically and will have to be restructured into a new confederation with real autonomy for the republics. **Albania** will experience violent internal convulsions as it ends its long self-imposed isolation from the world. The turmoil in the Balkans will not stop the Germans, French, and others in Europe from making small investments in the region and beginning to lay the groundwork for rebuilding these economies and dominating their markets. **By 1998, a reasonable degree of stability will have been achieved in most Balkan countries.**

Forecast: Middle East

81. Instability in the Middle East will threaten to destroy the peace and prosperity of the new world economic order. The geopolitics of oil will make the twenty-first century resemble the nineteenth in certain unfortunate ways. The world will continue to be marred by constantly shifting regional alliances, the vitriol of nationalism, and the need for great powers to be able to project military power in order to control vital economic interests. A U.S.-led global coalition may defeat Iraq's Saddam Hussein in his ambition to dominate the Mideast and set the price of oil, but the possibility that Iraq—or other countries, **such as Iran in its postfundamentalist phase**—will try to pursue the same strategy again will not disappear.

82. Tension in the Middle East—and the skillful exploitation of it by American oil companies and commodity traders—will keep the

price of oil 50–100 percent higher in the first half of the 1990s than it was in the latter half of the 1980s. This will be one of the factors exacerbating the U.S. recession. Rising oil prices will hurt Japan less than in the past, owing to its strong yen, diversification into alternative energy sources, and acquisition of equity in oil fields all over the world. In Europe, higher oil prices will be offset by high growth. **Much of the potential "peace dividend" from the end of the Cold War will be lost** as U.S. defense contractors and their congressional supporters exploit fears about the Mideast to keep the military budget intact—even though the most cost-intensive elements are those designed to counter the Soviet threat, not to handle the types of regional conflicts that are now most likely to require military involvement.

83. Saudi Arabia, concerned that it has made too great a concession by providing bases for American troops in the conflict with Iraq, will ask Americans to leave and will encourage a new round of oil-price hikes in 1992. The Saudis will also arrange a preferential pricing system for Europe as they begin to switch their international political allegiance from the United States to their less threatening and more logical partner, the EC.

84. Due to the new Saudi-European relationship and the declining value of the dollar, most Mideast oil producers will shift to ECU-based pricing in the mid-'90s. Other raw-material producers in other parts of the world may follow suit, although in the Pacific Rim, the switch will be made to **yen-based pricing**. Nondollar pricing of major world commodities will produce an inflationary jolt in the U.S., weaken the dollar further, drive interest rates higher, and play a critical role in the overall financial crisis Americans will experience in the mid-'90s.

85. Israel will be forced to relinquish the occupied territories and accept a Palestinian state on the West Bank. The U.S., under the new economic pressures of the '90s, will cut back aid to Israel. Europeans, eager to court Saudi Arabia and conscious of their own ties to the Islamic world, will become even more active in supporting the cause of a Palestinian state.

Forecast: The New Global Order

86. NATO will be formally disbanded by the year 2000. The Atlantic alliance has already begun the process of withering away. For political reasons, Washington will fight to maintain it. For some lingering security reasons, many in Europe will also want to keep it alive. But it will become increasingly difficult to make the necessary appropriations and keep the necessary political commitments on both sides of the Atlantic, especially after the **Warsaw Pact is formally disbanded around 1992.** Constant Soviet pressure will further encourage Europeans to give up NATO and create a broader security order. This will make sense to those in the West who share the economic and political dream of a greater Europe stretching from the Atlantic to the Urals. The ostensible reason for NATO's demise will be the European desire to establish a new security order in which the Soviets can participate. American leaders will even support this goal, principally in order to prevent the so-called Versailles syndrome from setting in—whereby a decimated Soviet empire would lash out in anger at the West. But the real reason for NATO's collapse will be internal: An ascendant Europe led by a strong Germany in a peaceful world will see little reason to cling to an anachronistic U.S.-led military alliance.

87. The Conference on Security and Cooperation in Europe (CSCE) will be formalized as an institution by 1992. It will replace "superpower summitry" as the main vehicle through which the East-West relationship evolves.

88. The creation of an EC defense union will be adopted as a formal project of the Community in 1993. This will be a powerful issue which will help keep the momentum of unity rolling. With NATO crumbling, Washington will have little choice but to go along with an EC defense union. It will be seen as the alternative of choice, preferable to placing European security entirely in the hands of the CSCE, where the Soviet influence will be strong and the willingness to appease it even stronger. In Moscow, the demise of NATO, coupled with institutionalization of the CSCE, will make an EC defense union tolerable. The lack of forward positioning by the defense union will make it possible for neutral countries such as Sweden and Austria to join the EC, remain outside the defense union, and not be caught in any significant policy contradiction by doing so.

89. A neutral corridor will be fashioned along Europe's old dividing line. Switzerland, Austria, and Yugoslavia will remain untied to any outside military commitments. On the collapse of the Warsaw Pact, **Hungary and Czechoslovakia will opt for neutrality** as well. Germany and the EC defense union will agree not to station troops in the former East Germany. Thus, the neutral corridor will run through the whole of Europe from north to south.

90. Military power will continue to fade in importance, but not without reminders that it is still a crucial part of the global power nexus. The Soviets will use the military card as an effective bargaining tool. Outside the Triad, rogue states such as Panama under Noriega, Libya under Khadafy, and Iraq under Saddam Hussein will arise more frequently as the globe-encompassing discipline of the bipolar order breaks down. Such security dangers will encourage both Europe and Japan to expand their military capabilities, especially their mobile strike forces. Distrusting the United States, and pressured by its military-industrial complex to develop independent capabilities, **Japan will carry out a high-tech weapons systems buildup that will include development of a nuclear deterrent. By 2005, Japan will rank among the world's leading military powers.**

91. Germany, while accepting integration of the Bundeswehr into the European defense union, will also seek its own nuclear deterrent to counter constant pressure from Russia. The EC defense union, equally afraid of "creeping Finlandization," will relent and allow Germany its own nuclear force around the year 2000. This will set in motion one of the biggest geopolitical balancing problems of the early twenty-first century.

92. The disparity between the world's haves and have-nots will grow more intense, creating new security dangers. The new Berlin Wall is the invisible one that divides north and south, Triad and non-Triad, the high-tech world and the left-behind world. On one side of this invisible wall, the nation-state will be in long-term decline. On the other side, nationalism will be resurgent in the '90s, along with religious extremism, politically inspired terrorism, and narco-terrorism. The inability of the world's economic leaders to alter the material circumstances of the planet's impoverished majority is a ticking time bomb. The countdown is being hastened by the loss of U.S. and Soviet interest in the fates of most countries in West Asia, Indochina, Africa, and Latin America. In Europe, the new, Francophonic sense of moral responsibility to do something for sub-Saharan Africa will grow stronger. So too will the pragmatic belief that failure to aid North Africa will lead to an ever more unmanageable stream of legal and illegal emigration out of the Maghreb into the streets of Marseille, Paris, Naples, Rome, and Brussels. But Europe will not be able to do enough to prevent divisive and at times violent conflict from arising as a result of the growing economic gap.

93. Those who write communism off will be surprised by its staying power in the '90s. Related to the contradiction between haves and have-nots will be communism's continuing appeal in some parts of the world. It may even reassert itself in places where it now appears completely discredited. The leaders of the world's two largest countries still consider themselves dedicated communists, after all.

94. The economic boom in Europe and Japan will strengthen the soft left, not the center-right political coalitions responsible for creating most of the new prosperity. The richer both regions grow in the '90s, the more popular the soft left will become. **The second chancellor of a united Germany will be a Socialist**. Left-leaning forces will be on the rise in Japan for much of the '90s, and a Democrat will be elected in the U.S. in 1996. Although the definitions of "left" and "right" will undergo constant change as a new politics evolves, the Triad, by decade's end, will be dominated by political leaders associated with movements that used to be thought of as belonging to the left.

95. A new global currency agreement will be hammered out between 1995 and 1997. Precipitated by the rise of the ECU and the shift to nondollar pricing of raw materials, a global monetary realignment will also be influenced by a variety of factors such as the likely success of the EuroFed in achieving its monetary management aims, the continued strength of the yen, the accumulation of financial surpluses in Japan, protracted weakness of the dollar, and ongoing deficits in the United States. This agreement will be the "new Bretton Woods" that many American economists already favor. It may even be the precursor of a single globe-spanning currency for the Triad as a whole. But under the circumstances of the mid-1990s, it is likely to be German and Japanese bankers, rather than Americans, who will hold the key decision-making power. **The new exchange rates will reflect the economic strength achieved by Europe and Japan, and the erosion of competitiveness in the United States.** Although the system itself will be intricate, the bottom line will be a massive devaluation of American assets roughly analogous to fixing today's exchange rates at **¥ =105 = $1.00 and DM1.2 = $1.00.**

96. The U.S. will appear to be the most protectionist of the Triad economies in terms of new policy measures. But tentative, partial efforts by American political leaders to protect some sectors of the domestic economy will be criticized by a new coalition of Europeans and Japanese, who will allege that even as they open up, the U.S. is closing down. The strong European and Japanese lobbies in the United States will render many of these attempts at protectionism futile anyway.

97. The English language will increasingly predominate in the world, despite economic problems in the English-speaking nations. Japanese will become more popular, especially in Asia. German will also experience an upswing. But the near-official role of English will be consummated by its wide use in most of the new Euro-institutions and in the cross-border business relationships of the world's leading companies.

98. Espionage will become focused on economic and technological issues. The CIA and the rest of the U.S. intelligence community will slowly make this shift in the '90s. Japan will allocate more resources to its low-visibility network of economic spies. The European Community will create a pleasant-sounding ''Office of Competitive Economic Data-Gathering,'' which will play the same role.

99. A new Global Trade Organization will be formed by 1994 to attempt to bring an end to rising trade friction resulting from ''tough trade'' practices all over the world, especially between the U.S. and its two major partners. The GATT will be unsuccessful at dealing with many of the major issues on its agenda. The Global Trade Organization will include only the countries of the Triad, and may even be structured along a qualified majority-vote line, like the EC. At first, the U.S. will be a reluctant partner and the organization will be ineffective. By the late

1990s, however, the Gore administration in Washington will have figured out how to use this multilateral institution to gain the support of America's trading partners for an effort to rebuild America.

100. As for the relationship among the U.S., Europe, and Japan, the world of the year 2000 will look like this: Japan will represent the world's greatest concentration of wealth and technological power. The Asia-Pacific region around it will once again be the fastest-growing part of the world. The German-led Europe will have accomplished a vast economic and geographical expansion in the 1990s and will be enjoying a huge and widely shared prosperity as a result. The Soviet market will finally be ripe for sustaining large-scale successful business ventures. Because of Europe's relationships with the U.S., the former Soviet Union, and Japan, it will have become the most politically influential force in the new global order and will be generating many of the new ideas about the world system. The United States will have become the least economically dynamic of the three regions, and North America the smallest of the Triad's three major regional markets. Nevertheless, the U.S. will still be a wealthy and powerful nation, despite its fall from grace. A process of American rebirth will be just beginning.

Notes

INTRODUCTION

1. Steven Greenhouse, "German Union Instills Vision of a Great Continent Reborn," *New York Times*, April 3, 1990.
2. Floyd Norris, "Time Inc. and Warner to Merge, Creating Largest Media Company," *New York Times*, March 5, 1989.
3. "Translink's European Deal Review," press release, February 6, 1990.
4. "IBM Unit Predicts Strong Market Growth in East German Area," *Wall Street Journal*, April 27, 1990.
5. Alan Cane et al., "IBM's Worldwide Lessons from Europe," *Financial Times*, May 2, 1990.
6. John Markoff, "IBM Joins Siemens in Developing Chips," *New York Times*, January 25, 1990.
7. Stefan Wagstyl et al. "A Door to the West," *Financial Times*, March 7, 1990.
8. *International Management*, October 1988.
9. Earl C. Gottschalk, Jr., "Japanese Investment in U.S. Real Estate Slips," *Wall Street Journal*, March 13, 1990.

CHAPTER 1

1. Mikhail Gorbachev used this passage from Victor Hugo in his stirring 1989 speech before the Council of Europe in Strasbourg, in which he proclaimed

his personal "Europeanism" and his desire for a "common European home." Hugo's writings on Europe are marvelously appropriate to later history and to today's discussion of the borderless world. He appears to have been among the first to use the phrase "United States of Europe," writing toward the end of the nineteenth century, "I represent a party which does not yet exist: the party of revolution, civilization. This party will make the twentieth century. There will issue from it first *the United States of Europe, then the United States of the World.*"

2. Scott Sullivan, "The Czar of Brussels," *Newsweek*, February 6, 1989; "Mr. Europe Leads the Way," *Time*, September 18, 1989.

3. "Thousand-Day Countdown Begins for 1992," *European Community News*, April 6, 1990.

4. Carlo De Benedetti, "The Transformation of European Industry," speech to the Trilateral Commission in New York, March 13, 1989.

5. Karl Kaiser et al., *The European Community: Progress or Decline?* (London: Royal Institute for International Affairs, 1983).

6. Michael Calingaert, *The 1992 Challenge from Europe: Development of the European Community's Internal Market* (Washington, D.C.: National Planning Association, 1989).

7. Peter Drucker, "U.S.-Japan Trade Needs a Reality Check," *Wall Street Journal*, January 10, 1989.

8. James M. Markham, "Europe Looks to '92 as Year Dreams of Union Come True," *New York Times*, July 16, 1988.

9. These figures come from background data on cross-border M&A prepared jointly by the Blackstone Group of New York and Hambro Magan of London as part of a press announcement of their transatlantic investment-banking alliance, April 23, 1990.

10. David Lascelles, "1992 Credited with Sharp Rise in European Interbank Business," *Financial Times*, May 10, 1990.

11. John Wyles, "Exceptional Events, Exceptional Answers," interview with Gianni De Michelis, *Financial Times*, December 4, 1989.

CHAPTER 2

1. Timothy Garton Ash, "The German Revolution," *New York Review of Books*, December 21, 1989.

2. Flora Lewis, "Look Up from the Trenches," *New York Times*, April 23, 1989.

3. Among the many ironies and oddities of the political storms in Eastern Europe during 1989, one of the most curious is that Czechoslovakia, not the United States or Britain, produced the first rock-and-roll-loving head of state. On Havel's first official visit to the United States, he toured downtown

clubs in New York that no American president has ever seen or is likely soon to visit.

4. George F. Will, "Europe's Second Reformation," *Newsweek*, November 20, 1989.

5. George J. Church, "Freedom!" *Time*, November 20, 1989.

6. Josef Joffe, "Deutsche Mark Über Alles," *New York Times*, March 20, 1990.

7. The figure of $10 trillion is derived by computing U.S. defense budgets since 1945 and converting them into 1990 dollars.

8. General Sir John Hackett et al., *The Third World War* (London: Sidgwick & Jackson, 1978).

9. Peter Schneider, "Concrete and Irony: What the Germans Found When the Wall Came Down," *Harper's*, April 1990.

10. James O. Jackson and Frederick Ungeheuer, "He Stopped the Shooting," *Time*, December 11, 1989.

11. "At Home in Suburbia with the Vanquished," *Financial Times*, March 19, 1990.

12. "The Great Moral Stake of the Moment," *Newsweek*, January 15, 1990.

13. Michael Oreskes, "The Realignments on the Home Front," *New York Times*, December 3, 1989.

14. Charles William Maynes, "America Without the Cold War," *Foreign Policy*, Spring 1990.

15. John J. Mearsheimer, "Why We Will Soon Miss the Cold War," *The Atlantic*, August 1990.

16. John Templeman, "Krenz Is Cast from Honecker's Mold," *Business Week*, October 30, 1989.

17. Carl Bernstein, "Voice of East Berlin," *Time*, January 22, 1990.

18. The *New York Times* accounts cited include: Alan Riding, "In Romania, the Old Order Won't Budge," *New York Times*, November 25, 1989; John Kifner, "New Bucharest Leaders Promise Fair Trial for Captive Ceauşescu," *New York Times*, December 25, 1989; and John Kifner, "Army Executes Ceauşescu and Wife for 'Genocide Role,' Bucharest Says," *New York Times*, December 26, 1989.

19. "Today's Leaders Look to Tomorrow," *Fortune*, March 26, 1990.

20. "Looming Germany," *Economist*, March 10, 1990.

21. Bruce W. Nelan, "Anything to Fear?" *Time*, March 26, 1990.

22. Ibid.

23. Charles Krauthammer, "The Real German Danger," *New Republic*, March 26, 1990.

24. "Rush to Unity May Put Brakes on 1992 Process," *Financial Times*, March 19, 1990.

25. Brooks Tigner, "Delors' Superstate," *International Management*, March 1990.
26. Bill Javetski and John Templeman, "One Germany," *Business Week*, April 2, 1990.
27. Walter S. Mossberg and Robert S. Greenberger, "Upheaval in Europe Tests Bush's Capacity for Leadership of West," *Wall Street Journal*, November 14, 1989.
28. Jeane J. Kirkpatrick, "Beyond the Cold War," *Foreign Affairs*, Winter 1989–90.
29. Thomas L. Friedman, "Changes in East Call for a U.S. Balancing Act," *New York Times*, December 7, 1989.
30. Ibid.
31. "Excerpts from the News Conference Held by Bush and Kohl," *New York Times*, February 26, 1990.

CHAPTER 3

1. Joel Kurtzman, "A Brand New Deficit," *New York Times*, September 17, 1989.
2. In 1990, merger talks were begun between two of the biggest banks in the Netherlands, AMRO and ABN, which, if successful, will lead to the creation of another of the world's largest banks that is not American.
3. David Wessel and Constance Mitchell, "Fed Has Lost Much of Its Power to Sway U.S. Interest Rates," *Wall Street Journal*, March 12, 1990.
4. Clyde H. Farnsworth, "U.S. Warns Allies on Aid to Soviets," *New York Times*, March 15, 1990.
5. Brenton R. Schlender, "At Next, Everyone Knows Who Earns How Much," *Fortune*, March 26, 1990.
6. Louise Kehoe, "Silicon Valley Tires of the Old American Way," *Financial Times*, December 12, 1989.
7. Andrew Pollack, "Studies Ask Electronics Aid by U.S.," *New York Times*, November 21, 1989.
8. Vladimir Kvint, "Russia Should Quit the Soviet Union," *Forbes*, February 19, 1990.
9. Alvin and Heidi Toffler, "Grand Designs," *World Monitor*, October 1988.
10. In 1989, new capital investment by Japanese industry was running at a per-capita rate about twice that of new capital investment by American business in the U.S. Economist Kenneth Courtis forecasts that the Japanese lead in this area—a key barometer of future economic strength—might rise to three-to-one after 1990.
11. "EMU's Threat to London," *Financial Times*, December 9, 1989.
12. Alex Keto, "German Unity Expected to Aid Dutch Economy," *Wall Street Journal*, February 26, 1990.

13. Russell Watson et al., "A United Germany: The New Superpower," *Newsweek*, February 26, 1990.

14. Ibid.

15. James Sterngold, "Japan Builds East Asia Links Gaining Labor and Markets," *New York Times*, May 8, 1990.

16. Watson, "United Germany."

17. "Helmut the Stripper," *Economist*, February 24, 1990.

18. "Germany Benign?" *Economist*, January 27, 1990.

19. George F. Will, "Policy by Polls," *Washington Post*, April 1, 1990.

20. Soviet economists allege that even the CIA's highest estimates of Kremlin military spending—usually doubted by all but the coldest Cold Warriors—were actually *too low*, while its lowest estimates of Soviet GNP were too *high*.

21. Although Japan's defense spending has been nominally capped by the Japanese Diet at 1 percent of GNP, real outlays amount to almost 2 percent when U.S. military budget-accounting methods are used.

22. Robert Marjolin, *Architect of European Unity: Memoirs 1911–86* (London: Weidenfeld & Nicolson, 1989).

23. Ibid.

24. R. W. Apple, Jr., "Bush Is Reported Willing to Accept Big Military Cuts," *New York Times*, March 18, 1990.

25. Toward the end of 1989 and at the beginning of 1990, a spate of what seemed to be intentionally leaked rumors appeared suggesting that the administration sought to cut many of the Pentagon programs that indirectly supported high-tech competitiveness. Some $30 million in Defense Advanced Research Projects Agency (DARPA) funding for experimental work on HDTV, paltry though it was, was reportedly about to be cut down to $10 million; of the $20 million difference, $4 million was to go toward a study of Department of Defense procurement methods, and the rest was to be used for rebuilding the Nicaraguan and Panamanian economies, which U.S. military intervention had shattered. It was a policy, one might say, designed to make sure Central America would be a safe haven for the Japanese- and European-made HDTVs of the future. In 1990, DARPA's visionary director, Dr. Craig Fields, was forced out; his departure provided still further proof of the Bush administration's desire to undercut this agency, which Richard Darman, Michael Boskin, and other top Bush advisers apparently regarded as a bastion of the dreaded "industrial policy."

26. "Is Government Dead?" *Time*, October 23, 1989.

27. "Congress: It Doesn't Work. Let's Fix It." *Business Week*, April 16, 1990.

28. Paul Craig Roberts, "It's Time to Scrap America's Postwar Game Plan," *Business Week*, April 9, 1990.

CHAPTER 4

1. Abridged from Paolo Cecchini et al., "Summary and Conclusions," *The European Challenge 1992: The Benefits of a Single Market* (Aldershot, England: Gower Publishing, 1989).
2. Paul Johnson, *Modern Times: The World from the Twenties to the Eighties* (New York: Harper & Row, 1985).
3. Margaret Thatcher, speech delivered at the opening ceremony of the College of Europe in Bruges, Belgium, September 20, 1988.
4. "Beyond the Cecchini Report," *International Management*, November 1989.
5. Giovanni Agnelli, "The Europe of 1992," *Foreign Affairs*, Fall 1989.
6. *European Community News*, December 18, 1989.
7. William Dawkins and Kevin Done, "A Final Lap for Driving Ambition," *Financial Times*, May 21, 1990.
8. Alain Minc, *La Grande Illusion* (Paris: Bernard Grasset, 1989).
9. "Political Europe," *Wall Street Journal*, April 27, 1990.
10. Martin du Bois and Richard L. Hudson, "EC Sues U.K. for Failure to Meet Water Standards," *European Wall Street Journal*, September 21, 1989.
11. "The Greek Dilemma," *Financial Times*, April 12, 1990.
12. Outsiders are often confused about the relationship between the pound sterling and the ECU, owing to the fuss surrounding Mrs. Thatcher's refusal to support a common European currency. The British pound *is* part of the ECU basket. Until October 1990, however, the U.K. resisted full entry into the Exchange Rate Mechanism (ERM), which sets a relatively narrow band (usually plus or minus 2.25 percent) within which national currencies may fluctuate from their assigned value.
13. "Support for the ECU," *Wall Street Journal*, May 17, 1990.
14. *Report on Economic and Monetary Union in the European Community* (Luxembourg: Office for Official Publications of the European Communities, 1989).
15. Tyler Marshall, "The Odd Couple of Europe," *Los Angeles Times*, October 22, 1989.
16. David Usborne, "EC Agrees on Steps to Union," *Independent*, June 28, 1989.
17. Philip Stephens, "Thatcher Pledges to Defend the Pound," *Financial Times*, October 31, 1990.
18. Craig Forman, "Not Surprising When They Won't Even Call Their Chips French Fries," *Wall Street Journal*, November 2, 1990.
19. "If Sterling Stays Parochial," *Economist*, May 21, 1988.
20. "Britain's World View: Mrs. Thatcher's Visceral Foreign Policy Is Leaving Britain Marooned," *Economist*, February 17, 1990.

21. "Britain's Delay Costly," *New York Times*, November 21, 1989.
22. Michael Heseltine, *The Challenge of Europe: Can Britain Win?* (London: Weidenfeld & Nicolson, 1989).
23. David Buchan and John Wyles, "EC Moves Towards Fuller Union Without U.K. Support," *Financial Times*, October 29, 1990.
24. Robert Harris, "The Price of Euro-Phobia," *Sunday Times* (London), June 25, 1989.

CHAPTER 5

1. Alan Riding, "West Europeans Near a Consensus on East-Bloc Ties," *New York Times*, April 2, 1990.
2. "Ein Deutschland?" *Economist*, June 17, 1989.
3. Reginald Dale, "EC Leaders Endorse Step on Monetary Union but Split on Pace and Goals," *International Herald Tribune*, June 28, 1989.
4. David Usborne, "EC Agrees on Steps to Union," *Independent*, June 28, 1989.
5. Tim Carrington and Mark M. Nelson, "Thatcher Is Likely to Seek EC Flexibility on Monetary Issues at Summit in Madrid," *European Wall Street Journal*, June 26, 1989.
6. "Thatcher Fails to Halt Moves Towards EC Economic Union," *Financial Times*, June 27, 1989.
7. "Be Nice to the Germans," *New York Times*, July 20, 1990.
8. Sheila Rule, "A British Official, Stirring Outcry, Says Germans Are Taking Over," *New York Times*, July 13, 1990.
9. Tim Carrington, "Delors, Thatcher Set Aside Differences in Show of Unity Ahead of EC Summit," *Wall Street Journal*, December 4, 1989.
10. Karen Elliott House and E. S. Browning, "Mitterrand Sees Europe at the Crossroads," *Wall Street Journal*, November 22, 1989.
11. Alan Riding, "Mitterrand to Press Community Ties," *New York Times*, December 8, 1989.
12. David Buchan et al., "EC Heads Isolate Thatcher," *Financial Times*, December 9, 1989.
13. Ibid.
14. Steven Greenhouse, "European Talks Called a Success," *New York Times*, December 11, 1989.
15. Riding, "Community Ties."
16. Craig R. Whitney, "Europe Giving Thatcher Bad Press on Germany," *New York Times*, March 10, 1990.
17. Craig R. Whitney, "Kohl Emerging as Europe's Top Leader," *New York Times*, March 31, 1990.
18. Serge Schmemann, "Two Germanys Adopt Pact and Back Polish Borders," *New York Times*, June 22, 1990.

19. Alan Riding, "Hesitation Now Greets Europe's Unity Plans," *New York Times*, October 1, 1990.
20. Ibid.
21. Peter Norman, "Pöhl Rejects U.K.'s Hard ECU Plan," *Financial Times*, November 10–11, 1990.
22. For an interesting etymo-political history of "the German question," see William Safire's "On Language" column in *The New York Times Magazine*, April 1, 1990.

CHAPTER 6

1. Tom Peters, "The German Economic Miracle Nobody Knows," *Across the Board*, April 1990.
2. Robert J. McCartney, "Superpower Status for Bonn?" *International Herald Tribune*, November 21, 1989; "A United Germany: The New Superpower," *Newsweek*, February 26, 1990.
3. "Germany Benign?" *Economist*, January 27, 1990.
4. Robert H. Hayes and William J. Abernathy, "Managing Our Way to Economic Decline," *Harvard Business Review*, July–August 1980.
5. Craig R. Whitney, "German Momentum," *New York Times*, December 19, 1989.
6. Serge Schmemann, "German Economic Union Gains as Kohl Leads and Modrow Follows," *New York Times*, February 14, 1990.
7. Serge Schmemann, "Billions in Help for East Germany Approved by Bonn," *New York Times*, February 15, 1990.
8. Craig R. Whitney, "Bonn Leader Softens His Plan for German Unity," *New York Times*, December 12, 1989.
9. David Marsh, "Car Maker Spreads Its Wings," *Financial Times*, April 23, 1990.
10. Unlike Japanese automakers, which were pressured politically by the U.S. and other countries into moving some manufacturing out of Japan to the various national markets, Mercedes insists on doing all its manufacturing in Germany. This is a sound policy from the point of view of maintaining quality and production standards. But, as the Japanese have found, manufacturing locally can be the best way to gain marketplace dominance.
11. Peters, "German Economic Miracle."
12. Reinhard Mohn, *Success Through Partnership: An Entrepreneurial Strategy* (New York: Doubleday, 1986).
13. "U.K.'s Push, Europe's Pull," *Financial Times*, April 11, 1990.
14. Norman Macrae, "Wanted: Blue Bloods for American Boards," *Business Month*, April 1990.
15. Lothar Spaeth, the governor of Germany's most dynamic state, Baden-

Württemberg, is so enthused about regionalism that he has set up a network including like-minded states and provinces throughout Europe to collaborate on issues such as technology policy.

16. Joel Kotkin, "Reports of America's Death Are Greatly Exaggerated," *Washington Post Weekly*, May 28, 1990.

17. Serge Schmemann, "East Germans Await Capitalism, Uneasily," *New York Times*, February 2, 1990.

18. That 1 percent figure could be significantly higher if the usually prudent think tank IW is right in its forecast. IW sees East German productivity doubling during the course of the 1990s.

19. Steven Greenhouse, "German Union Instills Vision of a Great Continent Reborn," *New York Times*, April 3, 1990.

20. "VW Deal for Venture in East Bloc," *New York Times*, March 13, 1990.

21. Walter S. Mossberg, "Whispers of a Soviet-German Concord Are Heard Under Kremlin's Grumbling," *Wall Street Journal*, May 14, 1990.

22. Greenhouse, "German Union."

23. Dan Rather, Copyright CBS Inc., 1990. All rights reserved. Originally broadcast on May 30, 1990, over the CBS Radio Network.

24. "The Final Summit," *Wall Street Journal*, May 30, 1990.

25. David Marsh, "Bonn and Berlin to Negotiate Monetary Union," *Financial Times*, February 14, 1990.

26. Recently, the ratio of capital flows to merchandise trade has been around 40:1.

27. Blanca Reimer and Jonathan Kapstein, "The West German Mark May Soon Rule the East," *Business Week*, November 27, 1989.

28. Blanca Reimer and William Glasgall, "As the Wall Falls, the Mark Rises," *Business Week*, January 15, 1990.

29. Michael R. Sesit, "Capital Floods into Germany at Frantic Pace," *Wall Street Journal*, January 8, 1990.

30. Reimer and Kapstein, "West German Mark."

31. "Will Fundamentals Prevail in the German Bond Market?" Bayerische Landesbank Bulletin, March 1990.

32. Andrew Fisher and David Lascelles, "Herrhausen Swallows a Bank Before Lunch," *Financial Times*, November 28, 1989.

33. Steven Greenhouse, "Deutsche Bank's Bigger Reach," *New York Times*, July 30, 1989.

34. David D. Hale, "Economic and Political Consequences of German Unification," Kemper Financial Services, July 2, 1990.

35. Peter Schjeldahl, "German Art After the Wall," *Elle*, June 1990.

36. Robert S. Boynton, "Boss Is the Name, Boss Is the Game," *Manhattan inc.*, March 1990.

37. "A United Germany: The New Superpower," *Newsweek*, February 26, 1990.

38. Brian D. Johnson, "Hollywood Meets the New Europe," *Maclean's*, February 26, 1990.
39. "After-lunch Delights," *Financial Times*, March 1, 1990.
40. "Global Warming in Davos," *Economist*, February 10, 1990.
41. David Marsh and David Goodhart, "West Germans Take to the Language Trail," *Financial Times*, April 14, 1990.
42. Charles Krauthammer, "The German Revival," *New Republic*, March 26, 1990.
43. Marsh and Goodhart, "Language Trail."
44. Henry Ashby Turner, "Baseless Fears of a Unified Germany," *New York Times*, February 11, 1990.
45. Robert D. Kaplan, "The Character Issue," *Atlantic Monthly*, May 1990.
46. Francis X. Clines, "World Vote Urged by Shevardnadze on German Unity," *New York Times*, February 3, 1990.
47. Bruce W. Nelan, "Anything to Fear?" *Time*, March 26, 1990.
48. A. M. Rosenthal, "Germany: Hidden Words," *New York Times*, February 4, 1990.
49. Arthur Miller, "Uneasy About the Germans," *New York Times Magazine*, May 6, 1990.
50. David Binder, "As Usual, Germans Can't Agree on What Is German," *New York Times*, December 10, 1989.
51. Günter Grass, "Don't Reunify Germany," *New York Times*, January 7, 1990.
52. William Pfaff, "Germany Can Fortify Democracy's Family," *International Herald Tribune*, May 10, 1990.
53. "German Questions," *Economist*, January 27, 1990.
54. "A Soviet Hobble for Germany," *Economist*, May 12, 1990.
55. "*Lebensraum* All Over Again," *Newsweek*, July 24, 1989.
56. Marc Fisher, "Not East or West—Just Germany," *Washington Post National Weekly*, April 9, 1990.
57. Robert Pear, "Kohl Writing to Rabbi, Says Fear of Fascist Germany Is Unjustified," *New York Times*, March 2, 1990.
58. David Marsh, "Take German Unity Seriously, Allies Warned," *Financial Times*, February 2, 1990.
59. Especially noteworthy is the fact that the Bundesbank's independence, though much admired in Europe, has recently been greatly compromised. When the two biggest questions in the Bundesbank's history came up— German monetary union and European monetary union—the political leaders in Bonn took over and dictated terms to the supposedly independent central bankers in Frankfurt. Because the reunification process is so political, the chance for instability is greater than if the Bundesbank was really managing its own show.

CHAPTER 7

1. David Lawday, "The Widening Atlantic," *U.S. News & World Report*, May 14, 1990.
2. Even the staggering sum of $180 billion for American investments in Europe is deceptively low, because it includes some investments made as far back as the 1950s and '60s but still valued for reporting purposes only at original costs.
3. Paul-Henri Spaak, "Rapport des chefs de délégation aux ministres des affaires étrangères," presented in Brussels, April 21, 1956.
4. Jean-Jacques Servan-Schreiber, *The American Challenge*, trans. Ronald Steel (New York: Atheneum, 1968).
5. William Safire, "Whither Europe?" *New York Times*, May 1, 1989.
6. Michael Meyer, "Storming Fortress Europe," *Newsweek*, November 7, 1988.
7. Walter S. Mossberg, "Europe Could Become the New Trade Villain," *Wall Street Journal*, August 1, 1988.
8. Steven Greenhouse, "The Growing Fear of Fortress Europe," *New York Times*, October 23, 1988.
9. Paul Erdman, "A Call for Iacocca," *Manhattan inc.*, February 1989.
10. Meyer, "Fortress Europe."
11. Clyde H. Farnsworth, "Bentsen Warns Europe Not to Set Trade Curbs in '92," *New York Times*, April 6, 1989.
12. Lester C. Thurow, address to the World Economic Forum, Davos, Switzerland, 1988.
13. Edwin A. Finn, Jr., "Sons of Smoot-Hawley," *Forbes*, February 6, 1989.
14. From AT&T's European headquarters in Brussels, its own commercial telephone calls—as well as all those of the European Commission, and of everyone else in town, for that matter—must pass through a 1940s-vintage central switching system operated by the Belgian national telephone monopoly. This antique system produces an extraordinarily high error rate, which a thorough overhaul would certainly reduce. The chief problem is that the companies with the necessary technology are foreign, and Belgium, like many other European countries, would apparently prefer to suffer poor communications rather than award such a big contract to foreigners.
15. Kenjiro Ishikawa, *Japan and the Challenge of Europe 1992* (London: Royal Institute of International Affiars, 1990).
16. John G. Heimann, "U.S. Perspectives on 1992," address to the Euromoney International Financial Markets Conference, Frankfurt, October 20, 1988.
17. Michael Calingaert, *The 1992 Challenge from Europe: Development of the European Community's Internal Market* (Washington, D.C.: National Planning Association, 1988).

18. Stephen Brooks, "U.S. Fears Being Locked Out of Unified European Market," *Insight*, September 19, 1988.

19. Willy de Clercq, foreword to *The Second Wave: Japan's Global Assault on Financial Services*, by Richard W. Wright and Gunter A. Pauli (London: Waterlow, 1987).

20. Keith M. Rockwell, "On the Way Up," *Europe*, April 1990.

21. *Wall Street Journal*, August 11, 1989.

22. Thane Peterson, "The Power Behind Compaq's European Powerhouse," *Business Week*, June 26, 1989.

23. Steven Prokesch, "Getting It Right at GM Europe," *New York Times*, February 4, 1990.

24. Richard D. Hylton, "Developers Rushing into Europe," *New York Times*, October 10, 1989.

25. Calvin Simms, "The Baby Bells Scramble for Europe," *New York Times*, December 10, 1989.

26. Joann S. Lublin and Craig Forman, "Europe's Merger Boom Triggers an Invasion by U.S. Deal Makers," *Wall Street Journal*, August 23, 1989.

27. David J. Jefferson, "Chevron, Soviets Sign Study Pact for Oil Venture," *Wall Street Journal*, June 4, 1990.

28. John Holusha, "Business Taps the East Bloc's Intellectual Reserves," *New York Times*, February 20, 1990.

29. Ibid.

30. Patrice Duggan, "These Countries Are Up for Sale," *Forbes*, December 25, 1989.

31. Celestine Bohlen, "U.S. Envoy in Hungary Quits to Handle Investment in the East," *New York Times*, January 26, 1990.

32. Ferdinand Protzman, "U.S. Avoids Germany's Ground Floor," *New York Times*, June 11, 1990.

33. Ibid.

34. Jeffrey E. Garten, "Japan and Germany: American Concerns," *Foreign Affairs*, Winter 1989–90.

35. Richard A. Gephardt, address to the International Marketplace Forum, Norwich, Conn., October 13, 1989.

36. James P. Sterba, "Yanks Stay Home from Seville World's Fair in 1992," *Wall Street Journal*, May 8, 1990.

37. Craig Forman, "Europe's Banks Grapple with Sea Change," *Wall Street Journal*, May 17, 1990.

38. Philip Revzin, "Gulf Crisis Shakes European Optimism, and the Effects May Be Long Lasting," *Wall Street Journal*, September 28, 1990.

39. David White, "Former NATO Chief Calls on EC to Assume Defense Role," *Financial Times*, June 7, 1990.

CHAPTER 8

1. Bill Powell, "Goodbye Pacific Century?" *Newsweek*, February 26, 1990.
2. "Japan Prepares to Staunch Euromarket's Lifeblood," *Financial Times*, December 11, 1989.
3. Robert Neff et al., "Japan: Can It Cope?" *Business Week*, April 23, 1990.
4. Bill Emmott, *The Sun Also Sets: The Limits to Japan's Economic Power* (New York: Times Books, 1989).
5. Michael R. Sesit and Marcus W. Brauchli, "Nikkei's Surprise Rebound Brings Back Tokyo Bulls," *Wall Street Journal*, June 15, 1990.
6. Paul H. Aron, "Japanese P/E Multiples in an Era of Uncertainty," Report no. 38, Daiwa Securities America, May 1, 1990.
7. Stephen H. Axilrod, "The Economic Outlook for Japan," speech delivered at Princeton University, April 21, 1990.
8. Richard I. Kirkland, Jr., "The Big Japanese Push into Europe," *Fortune*, July 2, 1990.
9. Thomas Kamm and Mark M. Nelson, "Europe Underrates Tokyo's Juggernaut," *Wall Street Journal*, April 17, 1989.
10. Bill Powell, "Japan and Europe: Battle of 1992," *Newsweek*, October 2, 1989.
11. Despite a pretense of scientific accuracy, determining the "local content" of any of today's complex finished products is actually a highly subjective process. Various standards for measuring local content proposed in Brussels have included the percentage of the *number* of parts used in a finished product, the percentage of the *value* of the parts used, and the percentage of the *highest-value-added* parts and production processes. Although it is generally assumed that production today is largely "standardized," few automobiles are, in fact, made of exactly the same parts from month to month. Even for the same year's make and model, suppliers change and technical problems arise that lead to retooling and the use of new parts. The fact that an auto manufacturer sources some carburetors locally doesn't mean that all of them will be of local manufacture. Thus, Fiat engineers claim that when they took apart a Nissan Bluebird, they discovered that its EC content was actually less than 50 percent, not 70 percent, as Nissan had maintained. Monitoring compliance in automobile manufacturing appears to be just as complicated as monitoring compliance on arms-control treaties.
12. Steven Greenhouse, "Europe's Agonizing Over Japan," *New York Times*, April 30, 1989.
13. In the modern world, "dumping"—like "local content"— is increasingly difficult to define objectively. Fluctuating exchange rates, differing accounting systems, and different levels of horizontal and vertical integration within

corporations make it almost impossible to prove that a company is intentionally "dumping" its products—that is, selling them for less than reasonable market prices. As one of the leading U.S. lawyers specializing in antidumping inquiries points out, "At any exchange rate below ¥ =150 = $1.00, I can argue convincingly that every single Japanese product imported into our market is being dumped." As a result, dumping cases, with all the time and expense they entail, usually serve less to resolve abstract legal matters than to test a nation's ability to manage trade policy successfully.

14. Kevin Done, "Nissan Chief Attacks EC Car Import Restrictions," *Financial Times*, March 7, 1990.
15. Sumito Takahashi, "Firms Find Entry into Europe a Rocky Road," *Japan Economic Journal*, June 10, 1989.
16. Powell, "Battle of 1992."
17. Kamm and Nelson, "Tokyo's Juggernaut."
18. "Iacocca Talks on What Ails Detroit," *Fortune*, February 12, 1990.
19. Jacques Attali, "Lines on the Horizon: A New Order in the Making," *New Perspectives Quarterly*, Spring 1990.
20. Kirkland, "Japanese Push."
21. "Free Frankfurt," *Economist*, November 12, 1988.
22. "Tokyo Set for Investing Shift," *Asset International*, June 4, 1990.
23. Zan Dubin, "Teraoka's Exhibition Takes on AIDS," *Los Angeles Times*, March 19, 1989.
24. Patrick L. Smith, "Tokyo's Money Will Reshape Europe," *International Herald Tribune*, May 29, 1990.

CHAPTER 9

1. Francis Fukuyama, "The End of History?" *The National Interest*, Summer 1989.
2. David Sanger, "Supercomputers Worry U.S. . . . As Japan Challenges American Dominance," *New York Times*, May 1, 1989.
3. Ibid.
4. Peter Ridell, "Japan Set to Take Lead in Electronics, Says U.S. Study," *Financial Times*, June 13, 1990.
5. Peter Ridell, "Contesting the Cost of Rebuilding America," *Financial Times*, June 14, 1990.
6. Shintaro Ishihara, *The Japan That Can Say No* (New York: Simon & Schuster, 1991)
7. Robert B. Reich, "Who Is Us?" *Harvard Business Review*, January–February 1990.
8. U.S. Senate, Committee on Banking, Housing, and Urban Affairs, *Oversight Hearings on the Condition of U.S. Financial and Industrial Base*, July–November 1989.

9. Jack D. Kuehler, "Who 'Us' Is," letter to *Harvard Business Review*, March–April 1990.

10. Charles Morris, *The Coming Global Boom: How to Benefit from Tomorrow's Dynamic World Economy* (New York: Bantam, 1990).

11. George Gilder, *Microcosm: The Quantum Revolution in Economics and Technology* (New York: Simon & Schuster, 1989).

12. T. J. Rodgers, "Landmark Messages from the Microcosm," *Harvard Business Review*, January–February 1990.

13. Joseph P. Nye, *Bound to Lead: The Changing Nature of American Power* (New York: Basic Books, 1990).

Acknowledgments

The research for this book could not have been completed without the aid of a stellar group of political and business personalities all over the world. A great many leaders of the New Europe generously contributed their time and their ideas to this project. I would especially like to thank Jacques Delors, president of the European Commission. He is one of the most interesting, capable, and intellectually impressive figures on the current global scene. I would also like to thank Andreas van Agt, former prime minister of the Netherlands and current EC ambassador to Washington; Enrique Baron, president of the European Parliament; Edith Cresson, French minister of European affairs; Willy de Clercq, member of the European Parliament; Sir Roy Denman, former EC ambassador to Washington; Jean François-Poncet, former French foreign minister and current member of the French senate; Sir Geoffrey Howe, former British foreign secretary; Werner Hoyer, member of the Bundestag; Uwe Jens, member of the Bundestag; John Kerr of the U.K. Foreign Office; Philippe Lagayette, deputy governor of the Bank of France; Ruud Lubbers, prime minister of the Netherlands; Marianne Neville-Rolfe of the U.K. Department of Trade and Industry; and Simone Weil, former president and current member of the European Parliament.

Several key figures in the European business world not only provided me with excellent interviews, but also helped open doors and introduced me to their peers and colleagues. I would particularly like to thank Wisse Dekker of Philips, Etienne Davignon of Société Générale de Belgique, Alastair Morton of Eurotunnel, Mark Wössner of Bertelsmann, John Forsyth of Morgan Grenfell, Yves Sabouret of Hachette, and P. Bögels of the Eureka HDTV project. The late Alfred Herrhausen of Deutsche Bank offered great clarity of perspective at a time when everything was in flux. With his death, I felt I lost my best teacher on the subject of Europe's new realities.

CEOs and senior executives of a number of important American companies proved to be as eager as I was to learn about the New Europe and to think with me about its implications. I would like to thank James Robinson III of American Express, R. L. Crandall of American Airlines, Robert Allen of AT&T and Arthur Davie of AT&T Europe, John Magee of Arthur D. Little, Andrew Napier of Ford of Europe, Robert Dilenschneider of Hill & Knowlton, Eric Friberg of McKinsey & Co., John Heimann of Merrill Lynch Europe, and Richard Mahoney of Monsanto.

Peter G. Peterson, former U.S. Secretary of Commerce and currently chairman of the Blackstone Group, has been a mentor in my effort to understand the thinking of senior American business leaders. His ideas have also had an important impact on my analysis of several key geopolitical and macroeconomic trends.

I benefited greatly from the viewpoints and input of many other global thinkers: Naohiro Amaya of the Dentsu Institute for Human Studies; Nicholas Colchester of *The Economist;* Kenneth Courtis of Deutsche Bank Capital Markets; David Hale of Kemper Financial Services; Daniel Hamilton of the Carnegie Endowment for International Peace; Robert Hormats of Goldman, Sachs; Gary Hufbauer of Georgetown University; Kenichi Ito of the Japan Forum on International Relations; Serge July of *Libération;* Koichi Kimura of the Daiwa Research Institute; Makoto Kuroda, former vice-minister of MITI; Richard Lamm, former governor of Colorado; Peter Ludlow of the Center for European Policy Studies; Kenichi Ohmae of McKinsey & Co.; Hirohiko Okumura of the Nomura Research Institute; Jean-Jacques Servan-Schreiber; Anthony Solomon of S.G. Warburg; David Stockman of the Blackstone Group; Kenichi Takemura; Lester Thurow of MIT; Alvin and Heidi Toffler; Angelika Volle of the German Society for Foreign Policy; and William Wallace of the Royal Institute for International Affairs.

Although this book is critical of the lack of leadership in today's Washington, there are a few brave souls in Congress who are trying to instigate change. I would particularly like to thank those among them who have recently helped me to develop a better firsthand understanding of the politics of the competitiveness debate: Senator Max Baucus, Representative Anthony C. Beilenson, Senator Bill Bradley, Senator Robert Dole, Representative Richard Gephardt, Representative Newt Gingrich, Senator Albert Gore, Jr., Representative Marcy Kaptur, Senator George Mitchell, Senator Sam Nunn, Senator Donald Riegle, Jr., Representative Don Ritter, Senator Ted Stevens, Senator Tim Wirth and Representative Frank Wolf.

Quite a few diplomats in Europe shared important perspectives with me. I would especially like to thank Thomas Niles, U.S. ambassador to the EC, and William H. Taft IV, U.S. ambassador to NATO. I would also like to express my appreciation to the many directors, staff members, cabinet members, diplomats, and experts involved with the European Community and its history, who tirelessly answered my questions and pointed me in the right direction. Among them are: Brian Bender, Reinhard Büscher, Ambassador John Campbell, Bruno Dethomas, Joly Dixon, Martin Donnelly, Yiannis Drymoussis, Geoffrey Fitchew, Damián Hernandez, Max Kohnstamm, François Lamoureux, Pascal Lamy, Hugo Paeman, Riccardo Perissich, Claus Haugaard Sorenson, Stergios Stagos, Peter Sutherland, Edmund Wellenstein, Ambassador Carlos Westendorp, and Cees Wittebrood. The EC's press and information corps was helpful to me throughout the writing of this book. I would like to take special note of the assistance provided by Bob Cox, Margaret Frankhom, Sheila Kinsella, and Ella Krucoff.

Tom Peters was most kind in allowing me to make extensive use of his seminal article on Germany, "The German Economic Miracle Nobody Knows," from *Across the Board*. My thanks also to Dan Rather and CBS News for allowing me to quote from the *Dan Rather Reporting* CBS radio broadcast.

The research for this book took three years and spanned a quarter million miles through all three zones of the Triad. Hundreds of people provided help along the way. Although I cannot list every one of them here, I would be remiss if I didn't offer a public thank-you to the following:

C. Michael Aho, Council on Foreign Relations; Wayne Atwell, Goldman, Sachs; Janet Bacon, British Information Service; Dénes Baracs,

MTI Hungarian News Agency; Robert Boone, Jr., AT&T Communications Europe; Charles Bradford, UBS; Piet Brouwers, Philips Press Office; Michael Calingaert, Pharmaceutical Manufacturers Association; Jean-Michel Charpin, Centre d'études prospectives et d'informations internationales; Robert Cottrell, *The Independent;* Guy de Jonquières, *Financial Times;* Mark Dixon and the *1992 M&A Monthly;* Peggi Drum, American Express; Craig Dunkerly, USNATO; Gareth Dyas, INSEAD Martin Edelston, *Boardroom Reports*; European Business Publications and *The German Brief*; Barry Fulton, USNATO; Justus Fürstenau, VDMA; Inge Godenschweger and the staff of the German Information Center, New York; Steven Greenhouse, *The New York Times;* Hellmut Hartmann, Deutsche Bank; Bernd Heinzemann, BDA; Philippe Herzog, PCF; Jochen Hippler, Green Party; Jobst Holborn, Ministry of Finance of the Federal Republic of Germany; Kenjiro Ishikawa, author of *Japan and the Challenge of Europe 1992;* Michael Johnson, *International Management;* Werner Kaufmann-Bühler, Tokyo embassy of the Federal Republic of Germany; Maryann Keller, Furman Selz; Manfred Körber, Bundesbank; Reinhard Kudis, BDI; Nancy LeaMond, Congressional Leadership Institute; Mark Linton, USNATO; Sarah Ludford, American Express Europe; Jackie Markham, Bertelsmann; Marge McKean, AT&T; Gérard Moatti, *L'Expansion;* Minoru Mori, Daiwa Europe; Damien Nevin, INSEAD; Richard O'Brien and the *Amex Bank Review;* Julian Oliver, American Express Europe; Manfred Osten, Tokyo embassy of the Federal Republic of Germany; Joseph Philippi and Rosemarie Walsh, Shearson Lehman; Christopher Plummer, the WEFA Group; Paul Provost, AT&T Europe; Jean-Claude Renaud, NATO Economics; Helmuth Runde, Bertelsmann; Hans Gunther Schmitt, West German Ministry of Finance; Joachim Schnurr, West German Ministry of Economics; Jeffrey Schott, Institute for International Economics; Peter Schulze, Frankfurt Stock Exchange; L. E. Simons, Inter Nationes, Bonn; Barbara Sollner, Inter Nationes, Frankfurt; Andrew Somogyi, Arthur D. Little; Joan Spero, American Express; Veit Steinle, CDU staff; Iain Stitt, Arthur Andersen; Teizo Taya, Daiwa Research Institute; Bill Taylor, USNATO; Rüdiger Thiele, chancellery of the Federal Republic of Germany; Siegried Utzig, BDI; Michael Wessel, staff of Representative Richard Gephardt; David Michael Wilson, U.S. mission to the EC; and Peter Yeo, staff of Representative Sam Gejdenson.

It is hard to believe now, but when I first conceived the idea for this book in 1988, it was not easy to get Americans interested in what was happening in Europe. A notable exception was Fred Hills, my editor at Simon & Schuster. Well before the historic events of 1989, Fred understood the potential of the New Europe to emerge as a powerful issue on the American agenda of the 1990s. He encouraged and believed in this book from beginning to end. I deeply appreciate his enthusiasm at the conceptual level, as well as his tireless attention to critical details that often make the difference between success and failure in publishing. Throughout the course of the two books I have now done with Simon & Schuster, I received outstanding assistance from a legion of people at all levels. I am especially grateful for the consistent support of Jack McKeown, the publisher, and Charles Hayward, president of Trade Publishing.

Perry Knowlton, my literary agent, did his usual superb job of shepherding this book through the publishing world. So too did Dave Barbor, who handled the international rights.

As I have ventured personally into global markets with this book as my "product," it has meant a great deal to me to have the support of agents, editors, translators, and publishers around the world. I am especially indebted to Yoshihiro Mita, one of Japan's most visionary industrialists, whose Mita Press is publishing this book in Japanese, and Akio Etori, my editor at Mita Press. I would also like to thank Kiyoshi Asano, my agent in Japan, Chikara Suzuki, my translator, as well as all the people who have worked on this book at First Inc. in France, at Wilhelm Heyne Verlag in Germany, at Leonardo Editore in Italy, and at the other publishing houses which are bringing this book to readers in other countries.

In the course of the extensive travel required for research—as well as during a few beautiful days of rest and relaxation between trips—my family and I enjoyed the gracious hospitality of a number of outstanding hotels. I would like to thank the management and staff of the Akasaka Prince, Tokyo; the Hyde Park Hotel, London; the Hôtel du Cap, Cap d'Antibes; the Royal Windsor, Brussels; and the Westin Maui, Kaanapali Beach. Special thanks also to Carol Poister and Leading Hotels of the World.

Friends, colleagues, and family members provided me with an invaluable support network. Arne J. de Keijzer was my soul mate in brainstorming through the constantly changing world conditions. He also contributed the best research assistance imaginable. Craig Buck lent moral support as well as software support. Leon Burstein, master of negotiating life's difficulties, could always be counted on for words of wisdom in arduous moments. Joan O'Connor baby-sat across seven thousand kilometers of family travels in Europe, clipped articles, and helped out in many other ways.

My son, David Daniel Burstein, was a constant inspiration to think about America's future. As for my wife, Julie O'Connor—well, without her, there would be no love, no life, and certainly no book.

Index

About the Author

Daniel Burstein is an expert on global economic and financial issues. His 1988 book, *YEN! Japan's New Financial Empire and Its Threat to America,* was a best-seller in the United States, Japan, Australia, and fourteen other countries. An award-winning journalist, Burstein has written articles that have appeared in *The New York Times,* the *Los Angeles Times, New York* magazine, and more than 200 other publications in the United States, Europe, Latin America, and Asia. He has also served as a consultant to some of the world's leading businesses in the fields of high technology, financial services, and investment banking.